Institutions, Innovation and Growth

The Saint-Gobain Centre for Economic Studies Series

Series Editor: Robert Solow, *Emeritus Professor of Economics, Massachusetts Institute of Technology; President of The Saint-Gobain Centre for Economic Studies.*

Conference Editor: Jean-Philippe Touffut, *Director of The Saint-Gobain Centre for Economic Studies.*

This innovative new series – edited by Nobel Laureate Robert Solow – is an important forum for debating major issues in European economic policy. Drawing on the latest theoretical and empirical research, it will make an authoritative contribution to economic debates.

Showcasing cutting-edge research by world-renowned economists, the books in this series will be essential reading for both scholars and policymakers concerned with the economic challenges facing Europe in the twenty-first century.

Institutions, Innovation and Growth

Selected Economic Papers

Edited by

Jean-Philippe Touffut

Director of The Saint-Gobain Centre for Economic Studies, Paris, France

THE SAINT-GOBAIN CENTRE FOR ECONOMIC STUDIES SERIES

Edward Elgar

Cheltenham, UK • Northampton, MA, USA

Published by
Edward Elgar Publishing Limited
Glensanda House
Montpellier Parade
Cheltenham
Glos GL50 1UA
UK

Edward Elgar Publishing, Inc.
136 West Street
Suite 202
Northampton
Massachusetts 01060
USA

A catalogue record for this book
is available from the British Library

Library of Congress Cataloguing in Publication Data

Institutions, innovation and growth : selected economic papers / edited by Jean-Philippe Touffut.
    p. cm.
Translated from the French.
Texts selected from two conferences of the Saint-Gobain Centre for Economic Studies, Paris, held in November 2000 and June 2001—Preface.
Includes index.
1. Technological innovations—Economic aspects—Congresses. 2. Technological innovations—Social aspects—Congresses. 3. Industrial management—European Union countries—Congresses. 4. Labor market—European Union countries—Congresses. I. Touffut, Jean-Philippe. II. Centre Saint-Gobain pour la recherche en économie.

HC79.T4I56695 2004
338.94—dc22

2003056460

ISBN 1 84376 527 6 (cased)
ISBN 1 84376 528 4 (paperback)

Typeset by Cambrian Typesetters, Frimley, Surrey
Printed and bound in Great Britain by MPG Books Ltd, Bodmin, Cornwall

Contents

Preface

This volume is one of a series arising from the conferences organized by The Saint-Gobain Centre for Economic Studies, Paris. These conferences explore current issues, with particular focus on Europe. Speakers, along with other participants and members of the audience, are drawn from backgrounds in academia, business, finance, labour unions, the media and national or multinational governmental and non-governmental agencies.

The specific texts presented here have been selected to permit the reader an overview of the first two conferences. The first one took as its theme 'Institutions and Growth' (9–10 November 2000). The second focused on 'The Sources of Technical Change' (7–8 June 2001).

J.-P. TOUFFUT

Acknowledgements

Special thanks go to Alan Sitkin for translations and to Derek Edgell for his accuracy in editing this text, which only an historian could provide.

Contributors

Philippe Aghion is Professor of Economics at Harvard University and University College, London. His research interests include economic theory, development, industrial organization, economic growth and contract theory.

Bruno Amable is Professor of Economics at the University of Paris X-Nanterre MODEM as well as a researcher at CEPREMAP (Centre d'études prospectives d'économie mathématique appliquées) and director of its doctoral school. His current research centres on social systems of innovation, institutions and the diversity of modern capitalism.

Timothy Bresnahan is Professor of Economics at Stanford University and Senior Fellow at SIEPR (Stanford Institute of Economic Policy Research). His main research interests include industrial organization, applied econometrics and the economics of technology.

Paul David is Professor of Economics at All Souls College, Oxford, and Senior Fellow at SIEPR (Stanford Institute for Economic Policy Research). His current research interests include reputation and competence in publicly funded science and standards, trade, and emerging global information infra-structures.

David Marsden is Professor of Economics at the London School of Economics. His main research interests lie in areas of industrial relations, employment relationships in Western Europe and the links between pay and performance.

Pascal Petit is a researcher in economics at CEPREMAP (Centre d'études prospectives d'économie mathématique appliquées), Paris.

AnnaLee Saxenian is Professor of City and Regional Planning at the University of California, Berkeley. Her research interests include regional economic development, technology regions such as Silicon Valley and the contributions made by skilled immigrants to Silicon Valley and to home regions in Asia.

Günther Schmid is Professor of Political Economics at the Free University of Berlin and director of the research unit on labour market policy at the Social Science Research Centre, Berlin (Wissenschaftszentrum Berlin für Sozialforschung). His main research is on equity and efficiency in labour markets.

Robert Solow is Emeritus Professor of Economics at the Massachusetts Institute of Technology. He has been a major figure in the neo-Keynesian synthesis of macroeconomics. He was awarded the Nobel Prize in 1987 for his contribution to the theory of economic growth. He is President of The Saint-Gobain Centre for Economic Studies.

Wolfgang Streeck is Director of the Max Planck Institute for Social Science Research in Cologne. His research interests include national systems of interest association under the impact of Europeanization and globalization, and the effects of the internationalized economy on the organization of business interests. He is a member of the scientific advisory committee of The Saint-Gobain Centre for Economic Studies, Paris.

About the Saint-Gobain Series

Professor Robert Solow

The Saint-Gobain Centre for Economic Studies is not a think-tank or a research bureau. It is intended to be a catalyst. My old student dictionary (dated 1936) says that catalysis is the 'acceleration of a reaction produced by a substance, called the *catalyst*, which may be recovered practically unchanged at the end of the reaction'. The reaction we have in mind results from bringing together (a) an issue of economic policy that is currently being discussed and debated in Europe and (b) the relevant theoretical and empirical findings of serious economic research in universities, think-tanks and research bureaux. Acceleration is desirable because it is better that reaction occurs before minds are made up and decisions taken, not after. We hope that The Saint-Gobain Centre can be recovered practically unchanged and used again and again.

Notice that 'policy debate' is not exactly what we are trying to promote. To have a policy debate, you need not only knowledge and understanding, but also preferences, desires, values and goals. The trouble is that, in practice, the debaters often have only those things, and they invent or adopt only those 'findings' that are convenient. The Centre hopes to inject the findings of serious research at an early stage.

It is important to realize that this is not easy or straightforward. The analytical issues that underlie economic policy choices are usually complex. Economics is not an experimental science. The available data are scarce and may not be exactly the relevant ones. Interpretations are therefore uncertain. Different studies, by uncommitted economists, may give different results. When those controversies exist, it is our hope that The Centre's conferences will discuss them. Live debate at that fundamental level is exactly what we are after.

There is also a problem of timing. Conferences have to be planned well in advance, so that authors can prepare careful and up-to-date texts. Then a publication lag is inevitable. The implication is that The Centre's conferences cannot take up very short-term issues of policy. Instead a balancing act is required: we need issues that are short-term enough for them to be directly concerned with current policy, but long-term enough for them to remain directly relevant for a few years.

I used the words 'serious research' a moment ago. That sort of phrase is sometimes used to exclude unwelcome ideas, especially unfashionable ones. The Saint-Gobain Centre does not intend to impose narrow requirements of orthodoxy; but it does hope to impose high standards of attention to logic and respect for facts. It is because those standards are not always observed in debates about policy that an institution like The Centre has a role to play.

Introduction

Robert M. Solow

It is not certain that faster, stabler economic growth is the key to all the other preoccupations of economic policy. But nearly everyone thinks it is; and we can agree that strong economic growth cannot be a disadvantage. Even issues having to do with the inequality of income and wealth, though not automatically solved by economic growth, are thought to be easier to deal with when 'a rising tide is lifting all the boats'.

It is also universally believed, probably rightly, that innovation – both technological and organizational – is the key to faster growth for modern industrial economies. So it is natural that the first two conferences of The Saint-Gobain Centre should have been devoted to the conditions of European growth, and the institutional prerequisites for fast and successful innovation. This volume includes a number of the papers presented at these conferences.

I have already, in these two harmless paragraphs, exemplified what seems to me to be a bad habit. Economists and the broader community interested in these questions tend to speak vaguely of 'faster growth' when they mean, or ought to mean, something different. The theory of economic growth teaches the importance of distinguishing between the long-term sustainable rate of growth (the 'steady-state' growth rate of output or output per person) and the *level* of the growth path itself. It is much harder and more problematic to achieve a faster long-term growth rate than to *raise the level* of output all along the long-term growth path. Two economies may have the same long-term rate of growth of output per person, while one of them is consistently 10 per cent more productive than the other, just as two children may be growing in height by the same number of millimetres per year while one of them remains taller than the other.

Suppose the less productive economy can close the productivity gap with the more productive economy. It must temporarily increase its growth rate, but, once it catches up with the other, it may revert to the old common growth rate. That achievement should be described as an improvement in, say, 'growth prospects', but not as an increase in 'the growth rate'.

That is how I propose to interpret the ideas in these essays. Everyone will agree that a better educated, better trained, more skilled workforce will be more productive than it was before. But it is not at all clear that the better-educated economy will grow faster. To achieve faster growth might require a faster rate of improvement of the educational level, and that can probably not go on for very long. This is not a cause for frustration; it may be the way nature works. More pointedly, an improvement in the efficiency of the financial system may allow an economy to achieve higher output forever, by permitting a better allocation of capital to available investment opportunities. But the rate of growth will probably increase only temporarily, while the economy adjusts to its new advantage, but not permanently.

The most difficult and interesting case is that an economy may devote more resources, say a larger fraction of GDP, to research and development. It seems likely that more resources will generate more new technology. But will it lead to a *permanently* faster rate of improvement of technology? We do not know, nor do I think there is any special presumption that it will. That does not mean that an increase in R&D spending has somehow become insignificant. A proportional increase in the level of national output, maintained forever, is a major achievement: hundreds of billions of euros per year, every year. (It is not impossible that some feasible institutional developments or policy changes will indeed lead to a higher steady-state growth rate. But it is not a claim that should be made casually. The evident convergence among advanced industrial economies is reason for caution.)

The different chapters in this volume direct attention to institutional changes that may well improve what I called the *growth prospects* of modern economies. They are at least routes to improved economic efficiency. Wolfgang Streeck considers possible changes in corporate organization and governance, an important question that was once rather neglected, but has now come into unhappy prominence. He is not always optimistic about the effects of likely changes. (By the way, one of Enron's many problems was that it was trying to grow too fast, or at least to give the appearance of very rapid growth.) The chapters by David Marsden and Günther Schmid turn to the labour market, an institution that has not lacked for attention in Europe recently. Changes in technology and the composition of demand have altered the nature of the employment relation and the characteristics of a career. Pretty clearly labour-market institutions have to adapt to safeguard both the ability of economies to benefit from innovation and the lifetime welfare of wage and salary workers. It is not certain whether failure to adapt will result in lower efficiency or slower growth, but neither one is desirable.

The remaining chapters, by AnnaLee Saxenian, Timothy Bresnahan, Philippe Aghion, Paul David and Bruno Amable take up different aspects of the system that produces innovations and then translates them into increased productivity. Aghion studies the extremely important question of the relation between the degree of competition in product markets and the incentive for firms to innovate. The question was asked by Joseph Schumpeter long ago, but not analytically answered. At one extreme, a complete monopoly can weaken the incentive to innovate: John Hicks suggested that 'The best of all monopoly profits is a quiet life.' At the other extreme it is possible, but not certain, that competition can be too intense: Schumpeter thought that *some* prospect of monopoly profit would be necessary to induce entrepreneurs to invest valuable resources in research and development. Patent rights are one way to deal with this problem, but the whole character of competition policy may be of even broader importance with respect both to innovation and to general productive efficiency. This is obviously an immediately relevant issue for Europe.

Bresnahan considers another economy-wide question. The surge of productivity growth in the USA between 1995 and 2000 has raised difficult analytical questions about the role of information technology in that episode. (Episode? We do not yet know if that acceleration will last; the recession and stagnation in 2001 and 2002 have muddied the waters, though superficially at least productivity has done better than it usually does in such periods.) We know that the sectors that *produce* computers and related products contributed a lot to the productivity surge. The extent to which computer *use* has contributed is less clear, and expert opinions differ. Bresnahan tries to understand the mechanisms that must underlie the productivity effects of information technology.

The chapters by Saxenian, David and Amable reflect on a different and very difficult matter: the internal working of the institutions that create technological and organizational innovations. Saxenian talks of 'technical communities', David of 'research networks' and 'epistemic communities', and Amable of 'social systems of innovation and production'. These locutions suggest that, while it will be necessary to consider incentives, resources and constraints in the usual way, the situation may be more complex. Out of such considerations may eventually come insights into the question mentioned earlier: what is required to convert an increased level of productivity into a faster rate of growth of productivity? And what can we do about it?

This book ends with an overview by Jean-Philippe Touffut of the role of institutions in growth and innovation, outlining in the process the growth possibilities for Europe.

1. The transformation of corporate organization in Europe: an overview

Wolfgang Streeck

INTRODUCTION

The rising significance of small and medium-sized enterprises notwithstanding, very large firms still account for most of the employment and wealth creation in Europe and will continue to do so for the foreseeable future.[1] They also, to a large extent, determine the political institutions that regulate the relationship between economy and society, in particular the status of workers and the way in which the public interest is brought to bear on the economy. The overview presented here of the current transformation of corporate organization in Europe begins by asking whether there is in fact a European model of the large firm, despite the considerable differences which exist between European countries. It also asks whether, or to what extent, European integration is likely to bring about convergence towards a more uniform pattern. Next, it reviews those changes in the organization of large European firms and in corporate governance in Europe which took place during the 1990s in response to the evolution of two of the major 'task environments' of firms, namely product markets and financial markets. Thirdly, the chapter discusses the consequences of corporate transformation for the social embeddedness of large European firms, especially the challenges posed by current changes in corporate organization to European systems of industrial citizenship and to the capacity of European states and governments to hold large firms socially accountable. In conclusion, the chapter emphasizes the growing autonomy of large firms as strategic actors, and it comments on the problems of corporate adjustment under high and endemic uncertainty.

1 A EUROPEAN MODEL OF CORPORATE ORGANIZATION?

Corporate Organization in Europe

The standard literature on corporate governance analyses the relationship between shareholders and management (Shleifer and Vishny, 1996). More specifically, it is about institutional arrangements within corporations by which shareholder 'principals' can best control their managerial 'agents' in order to prevent the latter from diverting resources entrusted to them to purposes other than the maximization of shareholder returns (Fama, 1980). The underlying assumption is that company efficiency is inversely related to the extent to which the interests of owners are diluted by the interests of management. In other words, corporate governance as a concern of mainstream institutional economics is about the efficient use of resources as well as about reassurance for investors against interference by management or other interests with their property rights (the main subject being 'how investors get their money back').

Standard theories of corporate governance reflect a situation of separation of ownership and control, in which share ownership is widely dispersed and management, facing a myriad of small shareholders, is potentially in a position to run a company in line with its own preferences ('managerial capitalism'; see Berle and Means, 1999). This is a situation which has historically prevailed in liberal capitalist societies, especially the United States and Great Britain. Indeed corporate governance, as normally defined, is strictly speaking an Anglo-American concept. On the European continent, where ownership was, and still is, much less dispersed than in the Anglo-American bloc (Becht and Roel, 1999; La Porta *et al.*, 1998), the relationship between investors and management has traditionally been quite different. Moreover, the continental European view of the corporation recognizes a public interest in the management of large firms (Donnelly *et al.*, 2000), and provides for legally based, or collectively negotiated, systems of industrial citizenship of workers to be balanced and reconciled with the interests of investors and of the public (Jackson, 2001b).

Several factors need to be taken into consideration in this regard:

- Historically, ownership in continental European firms was more concentrated than in the USA and the UK, which made for closer relations between owners and managers (Beyer, 1999). Management power was derived from the support of large shareholders (van Apeldorn, 2000), whilst managerial independence was sometimes rooted in corporate law passed by governments to promote better, more professional, management, itself a way of fostering high national economic performance. It also arose from the needs of managers to balance the interests of shareholders, interventionist governments and other organized groups such as labour. Bank ownership of stock, together with cross-shareholding between companies and public ownership of shares, protected holders of large blocks of capital from being taken unawares by anonymous market forces. Financial systems helped make corporations and their managers independent of capital markets as companies financed their operations primarily from bank credit and retained earnings, instead of selling equity. Above all, a market for corporate control was missing as there was strong protection, of various sorts, against hostile takeovers. With capital more patient and less interested in short-term returns, management in continental European firms came to see themselves as mediators between different interest groups inside and outside companies, rather than as agents of owners or, alternatively, as a self-seeking interest group in their own right. While this situation is changing today, as will be pointed out below, differences between continental Europe and the Anglo-American world in terms of corporate ownership and finance are still strong.

- 'Industrial citizenship of workers' refers to the rights of workforces to be involved on a continuous basis in the management of firms. Such rights – for example to information, consultation, or co-decision making ('co-determination') – may have originated in employer paternalism, social-ist trade unionism or a mix of the two. Industrial citizenship may be based in labour law, company law, or both. The way industrial citizen-ship is institutionalized differs considerably between European coun-tries. For example, arrangements as they have historically evolved may or may not include unions and collective bargaining; and workforce rights may be weak, as in France, or strong, as in Germany. Still the legal order of most continental European countries recognizes the stake work-ers have in their firms and the right of workforces to have some voice in management. This differs from the Anglo-American model where labour is not recognized as having a permanent interest in the firm and is, as a consequence, mostly reduced to 'exiting' the external labour market as a principal way of expressing discontent with company management.

- While continental European legal systems protect the rights of share-holders, they often recognize a public interest in good and orderly management and high economic performance that is not necessarily identical with shareholder interests. In most continental European coun-tries, corporations are considered to be not just private associations of shareholders with the public interest limited to protection of the latter against fraud or misrepresentation of facts; rather they are treated as 'constitutional associations' whose internal structures of decision making are a matter of public concern (Donnelly *et al.*, 2000). Good corporate governance in the continental European sense is one that ensures an equitable, and socially beneficial, balance between the inter-ests of the various stakeholders in the corporation, thereby protecting social peace and enabling the firm to function in harmony with its social environment. Put otherwise, corporations are seen as having obligations, not just to their shareholders, but also to society at large (for example in skill formation, equal treatment of women/minorities and environmental protection) in ways that go beyond Anglo-American notions of voluntarily accepted 'corporate responsibility'. As a consequence, governments assume a right to intervene in the internal structures and governance arrangements of corporations in order to institutionalize the public obligations of firms within their internal bargaining, or decision-making, arrangements.

Does a European model of corporate organization exist? Given the close similarities between the UK and the USA, it is clear that, if a 'European model' exists, it can only be a continental European one (cf. Mayer, 2000). Even within continental Europe, corporate organization is embedded in distinctive national institutions and traditions, making for considerable diversity between legal regimes as well as between firms of different national origins. Still Anglo-American theories of corporate governance, focusing exclusively on the shareholder–management nexus in disregard of the interests of the public and the workforce, neglect important aspects of corporate organization that most continental European countries have in common. Continental models of the large firm – German law uses the felicitous concept of an 'enterprise constitution' or *Unternehmensverfassung* – tend to envisage a stakeholder enterprise in which not only owners but also workers and the public at large have legitimate interests that need to be reflected in corporate organization and behaviour. The prominence of issues relating to business governance, conventionally defined, in continental European debate today reflects pressures from capital markets and elsewhere to abandon a model of the firm that includes a plurality of stakeholders in favour of a monistic model in which only shareholder interests are considered legitimate. Such pressures also propagate a concept of economic efficiency which excludes all interests other than those of shareholders from having a direct influence upon, or internal representation in, company management.

The Europeanization of Corporate Governance in Europe?

For some time, well into the 1980s, progress in European integration was expected to eliminate the differences between national systems of company law and industrial citizenship by absorbing them into a unified European system. But attempts at institutional harmonization consistently failed as national differences, even excluding those pertaining to the UK, proved too wide to be reconciled. Today harmonization is no longer being seriously pursued. Whereas European legislative proposals now focus on the coordination of national regimes and the standardization of the interfaces between them, what used to be regarded as inefficient legal fragmentation is increasingly seen as an opportunity for healthy regime competition and innovative institutional and organizational experimentation in a period of economic and technological uncertainty. Indeed, while remaining firmly rooted in divergent national systems of corporate law and workforce participation, multinational European companies have increasingly acquired a capacity to operate comfortably within a plurality of national regimes, moving between them for regime arbitrage or creating their own individual patchworks of national institutional environments in order to exploit different comparative advantages.

In the area of company law, efforts to enact a statute for a European Company (*Societas Europea,* SE) date back to the early 1970s. At the time, governments and large firms were convinced that an integrated European economy could not exist without a unified legal framework for corporate governance. However successive proposals remained elusive, largely because it proved ultimately impossible to accommodate the postwar German system of co-determination at the enterprise level. The first drafts of a 'Fifth Directive' on company law aimed at extending the German co-determination regime to the rest of Europe. This was resisted by business, including German business, as well as by many governments and most trade unions. Subsequently weaker proposals included, in an effort to to secure German support, safeguards preventing German firms from exiting from co-determination arrangements by incorporating them into European law. This turned out to be technically too difficult. Still later drafts referred to multinational firms only, and offered menus of supposedly functionally equivalent systems of workforce representation on company boards, from which governments could select a regime close to their national tradition which would then be made obligatory for firms based in their countries. In the second half of the 1990s, the Davignon Committee reduced still further the scope of the proposed legislation on mergers and joint ventures, leaving it to the firms involved to negotiate with their workforces the extent of board representation above a fallback minimum level, and with ample provisions protecting existing national practice. The Davignon proposal failed at the Cologne meeting of the European Council in 1999. By that time, however, an unprecedented wave of cross-national mergers and acquisitions had been under way for a number of years, apparently unimpeded by the lack of a European company statute.

Still efforts to create a European company statute continue. But whatever will result – if anything – will stop far short of legal harmonization, and in this respect will be in line with the general thrust of European integration during the 1990s. Like Davignon, the proposal that was provisionally adopted at the Nice summit is restricted to mergers and joint ventures. Rather than undertaking to regulate worker participation as such, it merely seeks to reconcile different national systems of participation if firms from two or more European countries create common business. This will facilitate transactions across borders between divergent national regimes that otherwise remain unchanged. In particular, and in order to protect German co-determination – the sticking point of all past initiatives – the Nice compromise stipulates that, unless workers and managements agree differently, a merged company, or a joint venture incorporated in European law, must adopt the highest level of participation existing in the countries involved. It will need to be seen what the protests of German firms will achieve should they choose to complain that the Nice solution will disadvantage them in the market for inter-firm cooperation across European borders.

In any case, indications are that, over the years, pressures for harmonization of company law at the European level have abated considerably, and not only because firms have, somewhat surprisingly, learned to live with different national regimes and even benefit from them. Rather, two other, perhaps related, factors seem of importance. First, national states, competing with each other and acting on their own, changed their rules on matters such as financial regulation in order to enable firms based in their territories to adjust to new market pressures and to take advantage of new economic opportunities. More often than not, parallel national reforms in response to the internationalization of financial markets seem to have pre-empted supranational legislation, or made it less essential for the conduct of business. Second, during the 1990s many national regimes turned out to be much more flexible and less restrictive with respect to individual firm behaviour than was conventionally assumed. Under pressure from product and capital markets, many firms apparently learned to 'stretch' the boundaries of national regimes in order to meet their individual needs; consequently, as shown below, corporate structures and strategies became possible that might otherwise have been thought to require major changes in legal rules. As parallel national reforms, made in response to new international economic conditions, allow firms to act in ways determined less by different legal systems and more by the identical demands of common international markets, they may give rise to the same responses regardless of national systems. In such a way they could contribute to cross-national convergence. At the same time, national systems granting firms more strategic freedom allow for more varied behaviour within systems, thereby increasing the overall diversity of responses. This theme of convergence and divergence will return as our discussion proceeds.

Europe-level developments with respect to workforce participation in labour law resemble those in company law. From the early 1970s various attempts were made to make different versions of the German system of work council representation obligatory for all European firms, or at least for all multinational firms. It was only in 1995 that a European Works Council Directive was passed. It applies to multinational firms only and leaves most of the procedural and substantive details to negotiations at company level. National systems of worker representation, at both headquarters and subsidiary locations, remain intact as the Directive merely combines them into an additional channel of representation for companies' overall European work-forces. Typically, the legal and contractual rights of European works councils are weak in comparison with their national counterparts. Moreover the way European works councils are structured and operate is largely determined by national practice in companies' countries of origin. Basically, European works councils are no more than a loose coupling of national systems of representation inside multinational companies, offering workforce representatives and management a border-crossing communication network which revolves around company headquarters and home countries.[2]

Summing up, instead of supranational harmonization, European integration has increasingly developed and encouraged sometimes quite sophisticated arrangements of coordination between a variety of essentially unchanged national institutional settings. Within the emerging and quite unexpected pluralism of regimes inside an integrated economy, firms have become important strategic actors as they gain the capacity to create idiosyncratic regime patchworks shaped to their own needs. Moreover it seems that the deep restructuring of the European economy in the 1990s was able to progress regardless of persistent differences in national company law and national industrial citizenship regimes. An important factor in this seems to have been the growing ability of multinational firms to construct their own, company-specific, regimes of cross-border corporate governance and industrial relations through freely negotiated contractual arrangements. This happened at Europipe, Airbus and Aventis (where German unions and German co-determination were included in the organization of companies partly or fully chartered in French law). Rather than legal harmonization, the Europeanization of corporate governance and corporate organization seems above all to imply the hybridization of national institutional legacies at the level of large firms, in experimental bottom-up fashion.

Also, and at the same time, Europeanization obviously offers firms ample opportunity for regime shopping and regime arbitrage. Here, too, large companies are the main driving actors. A recent ruling of the European Court of Justice (*Centros*, 9 March 1999, C.21/297) seems to imply that firms can incorporate inside the European Union wherever they find local corporate law that suits their interests, regardless of where they actually do their business. If this is indeed the view of the court, the 'Delawarization' of European company law might become a reality, as firms could easily switch between legal bases, for example to a country such as the United Kingdom where very few obligations and responsibilities exist for private companies. (Of course political considerations and the economic value of social peace with a company's home-country workforce might be mitigating factors, and countries might try to reassert their legal autonomy by amending the European treaty so as to make 'regime shopping' more difficult.) Similarly, in the area of labour law, multinational European firms increasingly require plants in different countries to compete with each other for investment and production, with workforce representatives in effect becoming business agents of local workforces, looking to convince central management that their plant is more efficient than competing plants owned by the same company. In internal competition of this sort, cooperative labour relations at the local level clearly are an asset which local management and local workforce representatives are keen to cultivate.[3]

2   CORPORATE ADJUSTMENT TO CHANGING PRODUCT AND FINANCIAL MARKETS

Within a nationally fragmented institutional environment, European multinational firms have, by and large, successfully defended their positions in a period of unprecedented economic change. Beginning in the 1980s, growing internationalization of product markets, together with a new technological dynamism, gave rise to intensified competition, which has forced fundamental changes in corporate organization. The simultaneous internationalization of financial systems has laid firms open to new pressures from capital markets which are serving to drive further corporate restructuring (Amelung, 1999; Zugehör, 2000). In response to the global integration of formerly nation-based financial systems, countries have reformed their financial market and corporate governance regimes, facilitating access by domestic firms to international finance as well as increasing the pressure for structural adjustment.

Product Markets: Internationalization, Technological Change and Intensified Competition

International integration of product markets was in part a result of political decisions, such as the adoption by the European Union of its 1992 Internal Market programme. More open markets were, however, also sought by firms which needed sufficient scale to take advantage of the opportunities for growth associated with new technological advances, especially in the area of information technology. By abolishing what had remained of the protected home markets of the oligopolistic postwar era, international market integration not only enabled, but in effect obliged, large European firms to expand internationally. By the end of the 1980s at the latest, the leading European corporations, organized within the European Business Roundtable, had come to the conclusion that even an integrated west European market was not large enough for the challenges ahead, and that a 'Fortress Europe' with a European 'industrial policy' supporting 'European champions' was an inadequate response to the demands of the time. Nevertheless, in spite of the eventual accession of the European Union to the Uruguay Round agreement, and regardless of their increasingly global outlook, the majority of large European companies remain rooted in Europe, and indeed in their home countries, where they continue to do by far the largest part of their business.

Growing competition, even in home markets, forced firms to seek larger scale and to reduce costs, the latter leading to increased procurement of supplies from abroad or relocation of production to other parts of Europe or beyond. Movement of production to other countries was also motivated by the need to get closer to increasingly important product foreign markets with their different structures of demand. It was facilitated by new information technologies capable of controlling and coordinating not just long-distance trade, but also far-flung international production systems. Internationalization of production made it possible for firms to shop for comparative advantage in cost and also in infrastructure, skills and social institutions. A recent study of the 100 largest German firms found that businesses which sell a large share of their production abroad also tend to employ a large, and increasing, share of their total workforces in countries other than their country of origin.[4]

In particular, corporate reorganization during the 1990s involved a continuing process of mergers and acquisitions, the privatization of what used to be large parts of countries' national infrastructures, and profound changes in firms' operational structures, both between companies and within them.

- Even before 1992, large European firms embarked on an unprecedented wave of mergers and acquisitions which continued into the 1990s and reached a peak in 1999.[5] As firms try to grow as fast as possible into their expanded international markets, they rely on foreign acquisitions because internal growth may otherwise be too slow. Moreover, in order to finance investment in new technologies, firms may need a minimum size which is best achieved by merging with others. Mergers and acquisitions also serve to reshuffle a firm's technological portfolio in response to accelerating innovation and shorter product cycles, with technological advantage becoming a function, in part, of a creative corporate strategy of buying and selling subdivisions possessing different technological potentials. Finally, international mergers and acquisitions may increase a firm's market share in a global economy where concentration in nearly all sectors is far lower than in most national economies.
- Privatization of national infrastructures, such as the telecommunica-

tions industry, took place partly in response to American pressure for the opening up of domestic markets. But it also reflected new technological possibilities which old regimes were unable to exploit, as well as new consumer demands on increasingly cost-conscious corporations that state authorities were incapable of undertaking themselves. Moreover adjustment to technological change often required investment on a scale which public authorities were unable, or unwilling, to find.[6] In most European countries, the European Union and its directives proved instrumental in breaking domestic resistance, especially by public sector unions, to the wave of privatizations that occurred throughout the 1990s.

- While pursuing new international opportunities, many European firms underwent a process of vertical disintegration. To cut overheads and spread risks, firms increasingly preferred buying, rather than making, non-essential components, relying on close cooperation with subcontractors and system suppliers. Extended production networks involving large communities of small and medium-sized firms were built, or reactivated, as alternatives to both hierarchies and markets. This was partly in imitation of Japanese just-in-time systems and partly a rediscovery of older European traditions of regional cooperation found in 'industrial districts' which stressed shared resources and mutual trust.

- Throughout Europe, firms also restructured their internal organization in order to decentralize decision making. Operational decentralization is a response to needs associated with intensified domestic and international competition aimed at cutting managerial overheads. But it is also made necessary by international production systems which, notwithstanding the capacity for centralized control offered by new information technologies, must leave enough discretion to local decision makers to enable them to serve differentiated local demand. 'Lean management' was the catchword of the 1990s. Its pursuit was accompanied by a new emphasis on the social integration of the firm on the one hand and the incorporation of market elements in corporate hierarchies on the other, the two being closely related. The former, operating under headings such as 'corporate culture' and 'corporate identity', emphasized a newly discovered need for values and identities shared across hierarchical levels and territorial borders in order to ensure that autonomous decision makers in various locations acted on roughly the same general premises. The latter, in the form of increasingly frequent transformation of decision-making units into profit centres or spin-offs of subdivisions on the stock market, replaced hierarchical discipline with material self-interest in order to make close operational supervision redundant.

Financial Markets: Internationalization and Pressures for 'Shareholder Value'

In recent years large European firms have come under pressure to extend similar attention to shareholders, especially minority shareholders, to that found in Anglo-American firms; this is reflected in the debate on 'shareholder value' (Rappaport, 1986; Prowse, 1994) as well as in current changes in European regimes of corporate governance. Anglo-American 'arm's-length' financial relations, mediated through a developed capital market, are increasingly beginning to invade and replace traditional European systems of national insider finance. In the process, the behaviour of continental European companies is changing as they find themselves forced to address many of the issues emphasized in standard corporate governance literature: for example, how to ensure that minority shareholders are given reliable information; how to prevent 'insider trading' at the expense of outsiders; and how to hold management accountable to the interests of minority investors.

The new significance of the stock market and the growing shareholder value orientation of continental European corporations are apparently not explained by changes in corporate finance (Achleitner and Bassen, 2000, p.12). During the 1990s, large firms were able to raise the capital they needed for international expansion internally and there seems to be no significant increase in equity finance, international or national, during this period.[7] Indeed, amongst German firms, internationalization of product markets and production systems between the mid-1980s and mid-1990s was only weakly related to the internationalization of credit and ownership.

Moreover, whilst cross-shareholding amongst national firms declined,[8] holders of large blocks of shares held on to their position and certainly remained far more significant on the European continent than in the USA and the UK. Consequently, although ownership did become more international, the amount of capital held by dispersed owners did not rise dramatically. The obvious exceptions are the formerly public – now privatized – sectors, such as telecommunications. In many countries, the privatization of what used to be parts of the national infrastructure served as a strategic opportunity for governments to strengthen national capital markets, in part to increase their own return and in part because an internationally attractive capital market came to be perceived in the 1990s as a national asset essential for good economic performance. Privatization thus often went hand in hand with changes in regulatory regimes designed to make them more compatible with mass ownership of shares, and offering middle-class households incentives to shift their savings to investments in the stock market.

The most important development outside the newly privatized sectors, which soon affected these, nonetheless, was that dispersed shares were

increasingly bought up by institutional investors such as investment or
pension funds, many of which were internationally based (OECD, 1997;
Jackson, 2003).[9] In large German firms, more than half of the dispersed shares
are now estimated to be in the hands of institutional owners; for example, at
E.ON, the former VEBA, institutional owners hold about 75 per cent of total
capital; at Bayer, 68 per cent, and at Lufthansa, 59 per cent. There is, as yet,
little research on the preferences and the behaviour of institutional investors,
although most agree that, in order to get them to buy shares, firms must pay
good dividends and, in particular, grow faster in value than other companies.
Failure to do so means institutional investors, with little attachment to particular firms, are more likely than traditional investors to sell their stock and
make themselves heard through the market, unlike the large block holders
which dominated European capital markets in the past.

By comparison, it seems to be the limited patience of the emerging new
institutional investors and the arm's-length distance they maintain from
management (their preference being to remain outsiders to the firms they
invest in) which explain why the themes of Anglo-American corporate governance have become so prominent even in the core countries of Albert's 'Rhine
model' of capitalism (Albert, 1991). Firms trying to persuade new investors to
buy their stock, or alternatively not to sell it, must offer assurances against
being taken advantage of by insiders. Given that share price is the single most
important piece of information for outside investors, firms which compete for
their favour must do what they can to augment it and to keep it as high as
possible. As firms begin to cater to market-oriented outsiders, traditional insiders are bound to lose influence and, with their capacity to play strategic insider
games diminishing, not least because of changing stock market regulations,
they too are likely to behave more like outsiders: that is to say, comparing the
value of their present investment with the potential yield of alternative investments, and getting ready to 'jump ship' should the 'shareholder value' of a
given firm remain unsatisfactory over a long period.

In the 1990s, pressures from shareholders and the need to attract footloose
investors (or alternatively to keep formerly patient investors from becoming
footloose) seem to have become sufficiently important to make large European
firms adopt practices in relation to their stock owners which, while not necessarily required by law, amounted to a significant emulation of Anglo-
American practices of corporate governance. Among these are the following:

- The voluntary adoption of American accounting standards, sometimes in
  conjunction with the listing of a firm's share on the New York Stock
  Exchange, in order to increase transparency for investors.
- The introduction of stock options for management in order to align the
  economic interests of managers with the interests of investors in a high

stock price. Often this means a significant increase in managerial income, close to American or British levels.

- The elimination of differential voting rights or voting restrictions, and generally a guarantee of equal rights for minority shareholders in the shareholder assembly.

- The creation of 'Investor Relations' departments and the introduction of regular meetings with investors, especially institutional investors and analysts, in order to provide detailed information about firms and their business prospects.

Also, in order to become attractive to more market-minded investors, many European firms introduced numerical profitability targets, either for the entire company or for subdivisions. Such targets are publicly stated, implying that if they are not met the respective divisions will be restructured or sold off. They are also used internally to support managerial efforts to improve efficiency and competitiveness. For similar purposes, firms may take individual subdivisions public,[10] replacing the hierarchical authority of corporate management with the discipline of the stock market.[11]

Moreover, as highly diversified firms (whose performance is difficult for outside investors to assess) find their share price reduced by what analysts call a 'conglomerate discount', they are increasingly selling off parts of their business and concentrating on a limited number of core activities (Amelung, 1999; Lang and Stulz, 1994; Zugehör, 2000). German conglomerates which are exposed to the capital market are de-diversifying, whereas conglomerates that are not traded on the stock market tend to retain their traditional structure (Zugehör, 2000).[12] Capital market pressure for 'shareholder value' thus seems to drive further restructuring, adding to the effect of more competitive product markets. De-diversification implies a fundamental reversal in corporate organization away from the prevailing philosophy of the 1980s, with its emphasis on a balanced internal distribution of profits and losses. In effect, it transfers decisions about the structure of investment portfolios from corporate management to individual shareholders or to their agents in the 'financial services industry'.

The trend towards market finance was reinforced by independent developments on the supply side of the capital market. Even faster than in industry, internationalization proceeded in the financial sector. European banks which looked to establish themselves in the emerging international financial sector soon found that the profitability of American-style investment banking exceeded that of European-style credit allocation under traditional 'house-bank' systems. To achieve growth and profit rates comparable to those of their international competitors, European banks, such as Deutsche, gradually withdrew from their traditional role as house-banks for national firms and became unwilling to function as infrastructures of national economies and national industrial policies. Instead they increasingly behaved like conventional businesses, maximizing their profit in an integrated international financial services industry in which they competed with American and British investment banks.

The ultimate way for outside investors to secure the attention of corporate management is, of course, the threat of a hostile takeover. Where such takeovers are legally or factually impossible, outsiders may feel less certain of being treated fairly, and may therefore be unwilling to invest their capital. Responding to this, a market for corporate control is slowly developing in Europe, even in countries where the legal framework of corporate governance has so far remained unchanged. The trend towards more frequent hostile takeovers[13] is reinforced by the changing business strategies of large banks which seek to make the same profits from investment banking in their domestic markets as do Anglo-American competitors in theirs. Banks have also been foremost amongst the forces which have lobbied national governments to remove political, institutional or legal obstacles to hostile takeovers and thereby open up new business opportunities for the financial industry.

The three major German takeover cases of the 1990s follow a telling trajectory. While the attempt by Pirelli to take over Continental, which lasted from 1990 to 1993, was prevented by a coalition of government and cross-shareholding German firms (the so-called 'Deutschland-AG'), the attempted takeover of Thyssen by Krupp in 1997 was renegotiated into a merger after union protests; and the Vodafone bid for Mannesmann in 1999–2000 was handled by all involved, including the union, more or less as business-as-usual, with careful avoidance of ideological rhetoric. Impending legislation on tax reform in Germany will vastly reduce, if not eliminate, capital gains taxes for banks and corporations selling their stock holdings. This is likely to be the beginning of the end of the German pattern of bank ownership of stock and of cross-shareholding, which was difficult to penetrate from the outside and represented a major obstacle to hostile takeovers (Höpner, 2000b; 2000c).

As hostile takeovers become more possible, firms are forced to pay more attention to their increasingly disloyal shareholders – new ones as well as old ones – who may react to declining share prices by 'exiting' through more liquid capital markets. Because low share prices may in turn attract hostile takeovers, large firms have very strong incentives to do what they can to raise the value of their stock. They may do so, amongst other ways, by de-diversifying operations in anticipation of what new management might do following a successful takeover. High stock prices, as generated by a management policy of 'shareholder value', may also be essential for fast international expansion because they allow firms to use their own shares as currency for mergers and acquisitions (Bühner, 1997; Rappaport and Sirower, 2000).[14]

National States: Changes in Corporate Governance and Financial Regimes

A number of European countries have in recent years changed their company laws and capital market regulations, both to improve the access of national firms to outside capital, especially foreign capital, and to strengthen the competitive position of the national financial sector in the emerging global market for financial services. With respect to corporate governance, recent national legislation, among other things, raised the disclosure requirements for firms, extended the rights of minority shareholders, liberalized the use of stock options, made it possible for firms to apply international accounting standards or to buy back their shares, and removed obstacles to hostile takeovers.[15] Also measures were taken to prevent insider trading in stock exchanges and generally make dealings in financial markets more transparent.

Responding to international market pressures that were felt by all continental European countries alike, national reforms of corporate governance and financial regulation tended to move in the same direction, even without explicit international coordination or a binding mandate from the European Union. The resulting cross-national convergence was probably the most important reason why a unified European company law seems to have become less urgent in the 1990s. (European Union influence was more important in the reform of financial markets, similar to the situation in the 1980s when the Union had mandated its member states to open up large segments of their public infrastructures to international competition and privatization.) Parallel national reforms had the advantage of remaining limited to corporate governance in a narrow sense, thereby avoiding the issue of co-determination that had so effectively blocked the progress of European company law. National industrial citizenship regimes thus remained largely unchanged during the 1990s. As a result, with company law beginning to converge on a more market-driven pattern, industrial citizenship became the main source of diversity in corporate organization, both within Europe and between continental European countries and the Anglo-American world.

National reforms of European corporate governance regimes were frequently preceded by changes in the practice of leading companies, and to this extent they only ratified and generalized what was already under way. In adjusting to new capital market pressures, such as the furnishing of improved information to minority shareholders, firms in different countries adopted similar practices, regardless of differences between their national regimes ('functional convergence', see Gilson, 2000). At the same time, company practices within national regimes seem to have become more variable over a period of time. German responses to hostile takeovers, from Continental to Mannesmann, changed fundamentally in spite of a basically unchanged legal environment.[16] Both identical behaviour in different systems and different behaviour in identical systems indicate a declining capacity on the part of national regimes in an internationalized economy to control domestic firms. They also signify the emergence of large firms as independent strategic actors with a growing capacity, in a more competitive and uncertain environment, to respond autonomously to challenges in ways that best suit their individual circumstances.

3   CHALLENGES TO INDUSTRIAL CITIZENSHIP AND PUBLIC ACCOUNTABILITY

European 'stakeholder' firms, as has been pointed out, are embedded in national regimes of industrial citizenship and public accountability, more so than Anglo-American companies which are regarded by legal systems in their home countries as the private affair of shareholders. The present section will explore how the pressures for corporate restructuring arising out of changed international product and financial markets, and the responses to these on the part of large firms, are affecting the social institutions designed to hold large European firms accountable to their workers and to the public interest. Most European firms seem up to now to have been able to respond successfully to the new economic challenges in spite of institutions such as co-determination and the welfare state. They have managed to do so, indeed, without rejecting these institutions. Sometimes firms have managed to make a virtue out of necessity by turning their institutionalized social responsibilities into sources of comparative advantage. At the same time, national institutions which sustain the stakeholder model of the firm have also changed, if only because firms seem to have gained greater freedom with respect to choices over structure and strategy. Even where legal rules have remained the same, this amounts in important respects to deregulation. The central question seems to be whether the social institutions which support stakeholder capitalism, to the extent that they are not pushed aside or made irrelevant by the pressures of product and financial markets, will allow European firms to develop an economically sustainable answer to new economic conditions. Such things might be achieved by developing specific productive strengths and comparative advantages matched to the demands of particular categories of customers and capital givers.

Industrial Citizenship under Market Pressure

Unlike corporate governance, there has been no major national legislation on workforce participation since the 1970s. In most continental European countries, firms continue to live with strong unions and more or less well-institutional-ized systems of workforce information, consultation and even co-decision making. While initial attempts at unifying such systems at the European level have failed, so have hopes that Europeanization would make them disappear. Indeed in most countries ideological conflicts about 'industrial democracy' have abated. This is so even in Germany, where workforce participation rights are comparatively strong. Once passed, the European Works Council Directive was implemented without much debate, even in countries not used to formal institutions of workplace representation.

Rather than lobbying national governments for retrenchment of traditional regimes of workforce participation, large European firms seem to prefer making a virtue out of necessity. They do so by using extant institutions of workforce participation as infrastructures of labour–management cooperation in pursuit of consensual adjustments to new competitive conditions. Indeed, where obligatory national participation regimes are missing, firms sometimes voluntarily set up institutional arrangements for joint information and consul-tation, often prompted by their experience with the new European works councils. Moreover, some firms try to capitalize on the institutional legacy of industrial citizenship and seek comparative advantage over Anglo-American competition. They do so by means of economic strategies which emphasize human resources and human capital and which depend for their success on the good will of the workforce and the social integration of the firm as a compet-itive community. In support of such strategies, efforts are made to turn the institutions of industrial citizenship, which originally reflected antagonism between capital and labour, into a substructure of social partnership and 'co-management'.

Workforce participation in management has been modelled differently, in theory at least. From the vantage point of theories of property rights, work-force participation results in an inefficient allocation of decision rights to actors whose income from the enterprise is fixed contractually, as opposed to being a residual whose size depends on the efficiency of the firm. Also co-determination is seen as making it unduly difficult for owners, or 'principals', to prevent their managerial 'agents' from catering to interests other than those of the owners; it may thus exacerbate the principal–agent problem of large corporations. Similarly, in a price-theoretic view, co-determination is likely to cause a distortion of relative factor prices, thereby forcing firms to use more capital than would be economically efficient.

Theories that try to model the economic effects of cooperation, by compar-ison, emphasize that firms depend on investment, not just from capital owners but also from workers. This extends the concept of a firm's installed capital to include the workplace-specific skills of workers and the general willingness of the latter to cooperate with management (this being the issue of 'good will').

By strengthening the trust of workers in management, participation in enterprise decision making may increase worker willingness to invest in current employment relationships, thereby expanding the 'capital' available to the firm. As a consequence, the productivity of the enterprise may rise, creating the conditions for joint realization of cooperation rents.

Similarly, theories of participation emphasize the economic benefits of a stable workforce with low turnover and correspondingly high social integration. Granting employees a right to 'voice' their concerns enables them to stay in, rather than 'exit', a firm. This lowers a firm's search and transaction costs in the labour market and gives it confidence that its investment in the generation of firm-specific skills will be redeemed. Rights to participation also give workers reason to expect fair treatment from management, which in turn encourages them to supply information that might be crucial for improving the efficiency of firms. Such rights are therefore conducive to 'information-intensive' management and work organization. Mutual confidence, rooted in claims to representation, further supports a more flexible organization of work by making a priori the specification of joint rights and responsibilities less necessary; it thus lowers transaction costs, not just in the external labour market, but also between hierarchical levels.

Which of the different economic effects of participation will take precedence in a given case may be impossible to specify a priori. Indications are, nonetheless, that the European institutional heritage of industrial citizenship, up to now, has not significantly obstructed adjustment of European firms to new economic conditions. Indeed it may sometimes have been an economic asset:

- Recent evidence from Germany suggests, at the very least, that even strongly institutionalized rights of industrial citizenship need not stand in the way of high competitive performance, even in a period of rapid economic internationalization (see pages 23 to 25).
- While conflicts between management and labour over industrial adjustment, especially to more demanding capital markets, cannot be ruled out, initial research indicates that firms are able to devise structures and strategies that are acceptable to both sides (see pages 25 to 27).
- Product and capital markets seem to offer firms which are constrained, as well as supported, by regimes of industrial citizenship, strategic niches that allow them to satisfy the demands of their stakeholders without experiencing competitive disadvantages (see pages 27 to 29).
- Although legal changes in workforce participation regimes were rare in recent years, in practice firms and workforce representatives have often informally modified existing arrangements to fit the specific economic, technological and organizational circumstances of individual companies.

Customized solutions of this sort increase variety within national systems, while sometimes giving rise to similarities across national borders (see pages 29 to 31).

- While today's regimes of industrial citizenship, with some modifications, have not prevented, and indeed have sometimes helped, firms adjust to new market pressures, it remains to be seen whether they will allow fundamental changes in the organization of the employment relationship, even if these were required for higher productivity and more rapid innovation (see pages 31 to 32).

The report of the German co-determination commission

In 1998, after two years of work, a semi-official, high-level commission set up by two major foundations and composed of representatives from unions, business, the government, the judiciary and academia, delivered a report on the condition and the economic effects of the German co-determination system some 20 years after the last major piece of legislation on the subject (Kommission Mitbestimmung, 1998).[17] In its economic part, the report emphasized the high prosperity of postwar Germany, and especially the lasting success of its industrial sector in world markets, which it attributed to high productivity compensating for high wages. The report noted that it is in the exposed sectors of the German economy, whose export surplus reached a new record in 2000, that co-determination through works councils and company supervisory boards is especially firmly established. It further pointed out that, owing to the high international competitiveness of German industry, the de-industrialization of the economy has proceeded more slowly than in comparable countries; that industrial employment is, as a consequence, higher than in all other large countries; and that the employment deficit of the German economy is located not in its exposed sectors but in its sheltered ones, especially in low-productivity services where co-determination hardly exists.

Slow de-industrialization, according to the report, does not indicate technological backwardness or lack of structural dynamism. Investment rates are higher in Germany than in the USA and the UK, and capital stock is larger (see also de Jong, 1997). Successful restructuring is reflected in strong growth in production-related services; the dominant international position of sectors which use advanced technology, such as industrial engineering; rapid organizational change during the 1990s; and the accelerated internationalization of German companies. The report mentions an increasing use of foreign supplies by German manufacturers and draws attention to the fact that Daimler–Benz, Volkswagen and Siemens employed more than 60 per cent of their total workforces outside Germany. Had it appeared a few weeks later, the report could also have commented on the Daimler–Chrysler merger and on the new company's decision to remain incorporated in German law and to continue with co-determination arrangements. Had it perceived such things to be economically burdensome, the new corporation could easily have moved its seat to the USA in order to escape the German system's way of operating.

The report did not seek to establish a direct causal connection between co-determination and the prosperity of the German economy. It pointed out, however, that the strong rights of workforces to information, consultation and co-decision making had obviously not interfered with international competitiveness. It also suggested that co-determination might have contributed to the evolution of a specific mode of production in Germany which emphasizes the cultivation of human resources and of dedicated, long-term, employed workforces. The report furthermore described in detail the experience of the 1990s, when most firms responded to the dual challenge of globalization and German unification with a policy of 'cooperative modernization' negotiated with workforce representatives and jointly implemented in spite of considerable pain to employees.

Competitiveness and shareholder value: strains on industrial citizenship and labour management cooperation?
While struggling to adjust to more competitive product markets and to an increasingly marketized capital nexus, large European firms strive to protect traditionally cooperative relations with their workforces in order to maintain social peace. This is something that itself serves as an important competitive benefit. Although balancing the demands of customers and investors on the one hand with those of workforces on the other does not come without its difficulties, it is not impossible either. Even so, one of the central questions for corporate organization in Europe is whether the disappearance of more or less protected national product markets, and the growing role of anonymous market mechanisms in corporate relations with capital, will result in a more market-driven, less negotiated, less regulated, and therefore, more conflictual relationship with labour; or whether traditional systems of industrial citizenship, originally matched to protected markets and negotiated finance, can be used, or rebuilt, to satisfy new capital and product market requirements without undermining cooperative efforts between management and labour.

Industrial citizenship and competitiveness A number of trends associated with organizational restructuring as a means of restoring competitiveness in product markets has become evident in recent years. These include the following:

- relocating production abroad. This has been accepted, more than might have been anticipated, by home country workforces and their representatives, just so long as it was shown to contribute to the competitiveness of companies as a whole, and thereby to the long-term protection of domestic core employment;[18]

- the movement of production to other countries, or the 'outsourcing' of parts. This has been avoided where productivity-enhancing concessions have been accepted by domestic workforces.[19] German works councils joined management during the 1990s in search of organizational, and other, improvements which would allow firms to continue production in-house and in Germany. In the report of the co-determination commission of 1998, this development was referred to as 'co-management';

- competitive benchmarking between plants of the same company and across national borders: such benchmarking is not necessarily resisted by workforces. Workforce representatives sometimes act as 'business agents' for their constituents and seek to put forward competitive pack-ages to central management when decisions about the allocation of production or new investment are pending. Alliances between plant-based, worker representatives and local management teams lobbying headquarters on behalf of a particular production site seem to be frequent. Where labour forces are well-organized, as for example at Volkswagen, workers stand a very good chance of devising convincing business plans involving internal competition for work and investment, as well as competition with suppliers or potential suppliers;[20]

- the negotiation with workforces of comprehensive restructuring pack-ages designed to enhance the competitiveness either of companies as a whole, or of individual plants: in Germany, about half of the 100 largest companies have negotiated at least one such 'location agreement' *(Standortvereinbarung)* with their works councils (Rehder, 2000). One third of the agreements entail an understanding of the amount of invest-ment firms will make in a given location in exchange for workforce concessions on productivity and the lowering of production costs. Agreements of this sort activate organizational productivity reserves and make it possible for management to give assurances on future levels of investment and employment. The vast majority of such understandings in large firms are not in breach of sectoral industrial agreements with trade unions. Often, indeed, the unions concerned take part in the nego-tiations. Even where this is not the case they are usually indirectly involved, the reason being that most works councils are not willing to sign an agreement that has not been at least tacitly approved by the union. In fact some industrial agreements now explicitly contain 'open-ing clauses' that offer firms and workplace representatives flexibility for location agreements within a framework defined by industry-wide collective bargaining (Bispinck, 1997);

- cuts in employment following restructuring. Where these take place, as frequently occurred during the first half of the 1990s, management seeks agreement with worker representatives and tries to avoid forced and involuntary redundancies. Here, as elsewhere, extensive access by worker representatives to information is essential. Where internal redeployment or natural attrition are not sufficient to bring about a necessary employment reduction, companies and workforces often protect their cooperative relations by jointly calling upon welfare states to take care of those people whose jobs have to go. Early retirement is a major instrument in many continental European countries, enabling management and employee representatives to preserve social peace at the workplace while rebuilding workforces and raising productivity. In this way, some of the costs of restructuring are externalized to the public. Also employers and unions have jointly lobbied governments to subsidize working time cuts and to devise public retraining programmes for redundant workers in such a way that net wages are replaced by unemployment insurance or other public monies;

- corporate measures to make labour – ideally with workforce consent – more contingent upon product demand, and thereby foster what in Germany is called 'breathing enterprises'. Where flexible working time arrangements have not sufficed, firms have found ways, again often in negotiations with workforce representatives, to discriminate between a safely employed core workforce and a marginal workforce to be expanded, and reduced, in response to changing demand. While European unions normally oppose a dual employment regime, at the enterprise level they are often willing to safeguard the interests of the unionized core workforce by allowing firms to rely on the external labour market for temporary adjustments to employee input. In effect, this tends to exclude parts of the workforce from full rights of industrial citizenship. Among the more inventive methods devised in this context is an increasing use of temporary workers employed by work agencies that are themselves unionized.

Industrial citizenship and shareholder value   The growing attention by firms to 'shareholder value' is often thought to undermine cooperative labour relations and to jeopardize European notions of industrial citizenship by replacing negotiated labour relations with market-driven ones. Also the continuing evolution of a 'market for control' for firms seems likely to have adverse distributional consequences for labour. This is because takeovers, including defensive measures adopted against them, are bound to increase share prices compared to the value of capital involved, forcing companies to devote a larger share of their value-added to dividend payments at the expense of shares to labour and to retained earnings.[21]

Other elements of shareholder value, however, seem to be quite compatible with worker interests and cooperative labour relations, or at the very least can be made compatible with them.

- To the extent that outsider capital and new capital market and corporate governance regulations force companies to publish more detailed and accurate information on their economic condition, this also benefits worker representatives. In fact, even in Germany, where the obligations on firms to share information with their workforces are comparatively strict, unions and worker-directors on supervisory boards have welcomed firms using US reporting standards, and have supported legislation raising transparency requirements for joint stock companies.
- It is interesting to note that, in the current debate on a new German takeover code, unions refrain from pressing for extended possibilities for target firms to defend against takeover bids (see Köstler, 2000). This indicates that unions and works councils expect to be able to defend their position even under new 'rules of the game' in capital markets.[22]
- Although the introduction of management stock options in continental European corporate governance regimes will very likely increase the income differential between workers and managers (which could cause discontent in a country such as Germany where management pay has traditionally been low compared to that of the USA or Britain) it has, in a number of cases, been made acceptable to workforces by simultaneous introduction of employee stock-ownership plans.[23] Depending on how these are designed, they may lay to rest some of the distributional concerns regarding the relative size of each side's share in a firm's value-added, doing so by ensuring that part of the relative increase in the share of capital owners is allocated to employees.
- Measures taken by management to raise the share price to insure against hostile takeovers often meet with the support of workforce representatives. These even extend to de-diversifications, where parts of companies that are unrelated to core businesses are sold off. In Germany, there are cases in which works councils and worker directors were among the first to urge the managements of firms to restructure in order to increase stock market value. Significant stock ownership by employees may make joint labour–management efforts in pursuit of higher stock prices even more likely. Especially when share ownership is widely dispersed, employee schemes involving 1 to 3 per cent of outstanding stock may in themselves provide insurance against takeovers.[24]
- Research on large German firms suggests that de-diversification may be supported even by workers whose divisions are sold off in the course of strategic concentration on core businesses. Within diversified companies,

some divisions may be used as 'cash cows' to generate funds for invest-ment in other divisions. In the case of Mannesmann, it seemed that workers and worker representatives in the automotive and other sections were content to be sold off as they had for years been starved of invest-ment in favour of the fast-growing telecommunications division. In fact union and works councils made it one of their central demands during the takeover negotiations that the automotive section should be taken public in order to allow it to raise its own capital. (This in the end was not done, as the division was sold to Bosch; see Höpner and Jackson, 2000).

- The Mannesmann case is instructive also inasmuch as, after some hesi-tation, union and works councils accepted the takeover procedure as legitimate, and limited themselves to bargaining with old and new management representatives in order to secure reassurances about their roles, as well as the company's future policies. In the end the union, whose national president sat on the Mannesmann supervisory board as an outside worker representative, expressed satisfaction with the under-standings that were reached. Also the works council saw no reason to refuse the new management the sort of cooperation that it had offered the old one. Contrary to what might have been expected, the Mannesmann case is not seen by the unions as a threat to their position or to the German system of 'social partnership'. No steps have been taken by the unions or by the social-democratic government to rule out similar takeovers in the future.[25]

Product and capital market niches for stakeholder firms?
Institutionalized workforce participation has been found to reduce price-competitive economic strategies by firms while encouraging quality-competi-tive ones (Streeck, 1991). Different regimes of corporate governance appear to be associated with different productive strengths and strategic predispositions, making firms that are subject to a given regime likely to be more successful in some market segments than in others.[26] Because strong workforce representa-tives can force firms to provide for long-term employment and pay high wages, they in effect oblige them to invest in skill upgrading. Also legally guaranteed rights to information and co-decision making, while imposing costs on firms, tend to generate the trust of workers in managements' actions. This, in turn, gives rise to worker identification with firms and produces high motivation in the workplace. Both skills and motivation support worker attention to quality and productivity, which create an incentive for firms to devise competitive strategies that look to these factors for comparative advantage. Trust also makes it possible for workers to tolerate high profits as credible assurance can be given that a large share is invested in research and development in pursuit of a

high-skill, high-wage business strategy. Managements of stakeholder firms, confronting strong workforce representatives who insist on steady employment, high wages and skilled work, thus face constraints, as well as opportunities, when seeking international market niches for quality-competitive customized goods which make the most of workers' skills and trust.

The attention paid to shareholder value by managements, as required of them by new capital markets, is sometimes thought to encourage businesses to adopt a short-term perspective that makes it impossible to invest in the productive capacities required for diversified quality production. Shareholder value thus turns social partnership from a potential strategic asset into an expensive liability which firms need to cut. However, while capital market pressures have been found to make German conglomerates de-diversify, they have not seemed to interfere with long-term investment in research and development, or in human resources. Initial statistical analyses of the investment behaviour of the largest German firms show that capital market pressure and shareholder value orientation by management have no negative influence on investments of a long-term nature that workforce representatives particularly welcome (Zugehör, 2000). To the extent that workforces take an interest in firms developing long-term business perspectives, such interest does not seem to be in conflict with the interests of stock owners, even if these are now mediated by an anonymous stock market and interpreted in terms of 'shareholder value'. While worker representatives may have to accept de-diversification in order to protect firms from being punished by a 'conglomerate discount' in the stock market, there is still space for them to influence business investment strategies in line with the interests of their constituents and without fear of retribution from stockholders.

Other evidence that there is no 'co-determination discount' in stock markets comes from interviews with stock market analysts and other officials of large German companies. In meetings with executives, analysts never seem to ask questions about the role and strength of co-determination bodies; instead they are exclusively concerned with the present performance of firms and their long-term prospects. Investment in technology and human resources, of the kind that German works councils typically demand, does not seem to be held against companies by 'the markets', even under standards of strict shareholder value, so long as they are seen to benefit shareholders in the future.[27]

Moreover the demands of stockholders with respect to the performance of firms in which they invest need not be assumed to be homogeneous. This allows corporations a strategic capacity not only in choosing the type of product market in which they want to compete, but also in selecting investors whose preferences match firm-specific performance profiles. Businesses which, on account of internal structures such as the stakeholder type of corporate governance regime, are predisposed to excel in activities that require long-term investment perspectives and skilled and motivated core workforces, may attract investors looking for a long-term stable return. Pronounced differences in preference seem to exist between institutional investors. Indications are that European firms actively seek out investment funds whose strategies are compatible with their own. This insures them against excessive volatility in capital markets and means they acquire sufficient time for their projects to mature. In effect, this amounts to the creation of a niche in international capital markets for firms which perform best when pursuing long-term business perspectives. Such a situation parallels the market niche for diversified quality production that socially embedded firms, with demanding industrial relations regimes, have found and developed in international product markets.

From legal prescription to voluntary negotiation: increasing variety within national regimes

Because workforce representation regimes remained largely unchanged during the 1980s and 1990s, national diversity between multinational firms today resides mainly in different arrangements of industrial citizenship, rather than in matters of corporate law. At the same time, with management of the employment nexus being rediscovered as an important strategic parameter for firms, national workplace participation regimes underwent numerous adjustments at the firm level within, and on top of, extant legal rules, all of them driven by a desire to build, or defend, competitive advantage. In continental European firms such adjustments, which substituted for legislative reforms, were made mostly through negotiations between management and workforce representatives. In the process, traditional systems of industrial citizenship and industrial relations were reoriented from passive entitlements on the part of workers to the joint pursuit of cooperation rents. As firms developed new forms of institutionalized labour–management cooperation, adding to and modifying legally prescribed arrangements, differences between firms within national systems increased, whilst practices of firms from different countries sometimes converged, irrespective of the different legal regimes in their home countries.

The new relationship between legal and voluntary arrangements for workforce participation, and the growing attention paid by large firms to internal institution building, became particularly visible in the implementation of the European Works Council Directive. The Directive allows firms, together with their workforces, wide discretion with regard to the implementation of its provisions. It is true that the obligatory requirements of the Directive are not demanding and remain far behind German or Dutch standards. But it is also true that many large firms, including some British ones which, owing to the British 'opt-out' were originally not covered by the Directive, used the creation of a European works council as an opportunity to initiate a direct channel of communication to the workforces of their plants in other European countries. That is to say, they used the Directive as a device to advance social integration in a multinational organizational setting. Research indicates that only in rare cases did firms agree to formal workforce participation rights exceeding the low minimum standard prescribed by the Directive. It indicates, nonetheless, that a surprising number of firms take the meetings of their European works councils seriously, that they send high-level managers to meet with workforce representatives and that they generally express satisfaction with the European works council as an instrument of internal communication and social integration across national boundaries.

Similar tendencies were observed by the German Co-Determination Commission. On the basis of evidence provided by works councillors and management from a number of large firms, the Commission concluded that, in terms of co-determination, firms often inform and consult their works councils above and beyond legal requirements, even though these are already high in Germany. The Commission also found a wide variety of arrangements that had consensually come into being to adapt co-determination to the specific circumstances of individual companies and workplaces undergoing rapid change. In a number of cases, legally prescribed procedures had entirely fallen into disuse and had been replaced by improvised structures more suited to changed circumstances. Nevertheless, the Commission emphasized that the legal basis of co-determination, although having lost prescriptive power with respect to everyday details, continued to be important because it took major dimensions of the relationship between management and labour out of direct contention. In this way, it provided each side with an assurance against possible opportunism on the part of the other, offering a last resort in cases where one side abused the other's trust under voluntary procedures. According to the Commission, the growth of voluntary cooperation did not make the legal framework of industrial citizenship redundant. Without the underlying, legally enforceable obligation to cooperate in good faith, the informal elaborations and amendments that had been developed as a result of pressure from increasingly demanding markets would very likely have been less effective.

Also interesting to note is that evasion of national systems of workforce participation, in particular by moving the seat of companies to countries with weaker industrial citizenship rights, has not yet occurred. The example of Daimler–Chrysler has already been noted. So has that of Aventis, a merged Franco-German company which, although incorporated in French law, made provisions in its charter for workforce participation that satisfied unions and works councils at its German component, the former Hoechst AG. Generally the practice of writing participation rights into the charters of new multinational firms in the absence of supranational law and where national legal systems do not fit, seems to be becoming more common. Contractualization of participation regimes, as in the case of European works councils, coincides with tendencies towards customization of labour–management cooperation at the company or workplace level. Obviously the fact that no major case of evasion of strong workforce participation systems has yet occurred does not mean that none will take place in the future. Also more research would be required to determine what concessions national unions and works councils had to make for their institutional influence to be protected in newly-created multinational European companies. Nevertheless most large European firms do not at present find it worthwhile to risk a deterioration in labour relations by attempting to eliminate workforce rights to information and consultation. Instead firms actively try to use traditional national participation regimes as a foundation on which to build stable cooperative relations between management and labour at the company level.

Industrial citizenship as a limiting condition for organizational modernization?

European regimes of industrial citizenship originated in the world of large bureaucratic firms. They were, and continue to be, based on long-term internal labour markets. They foster identification on the part of workers with employing bodies, cultivating a preference for 'a say' in organizational matters rather than for 'an exit' from firms whenever discontent arises. They presuppose an employment relationship that distinguishes sharply between employer and employee, the latter being given security of employment and income in return for broad acceptance of the former's 'right to manage'. Modern work organization has in part debureaucratized the role of employees, assigning them more responsibility for the quality and profitability of their work and expecting them to internalize a range of managerial tasks and to identify with the 'corporate culture' and objectives of a firm. In Europe this has mostly been supported by workforce representatives under existing participation regimes. It has been helped by more contingent pay, stock ownership by workers, increasing contributions by employees to the costs of their training and the general inclusion of more entrepreneurial elements in the work roles of operators, for example through the introduction of profit centres and internal competition between plants for employment and investment.

Although on the whole going along with the modernization of the employment relationship, unions and workforce representatives have always insisted that new elements of work organization be incorporated into the basic framework of dependent long-term employment. Where they have conceded a more dualistic employment regime which distinguishes between a safely employed core and a contingent marginal workforce period. This has been done, not to abandon, but rather to defend, their fundamental preference for a bureaucratic employment model. Modern unions and works councils, having attached themselves to the structure of large corporations and interest-homogenizing bureaucratic employment relationships, find it difficult to organize and integrate the heterogeneous interests of workers wherever subcontracting, casual employment and self-employment regimes exist. If it is true that, in present conditions, high economic performance and leading-edge innovation ideally require more fluid employment, a fast turnover of specialists, 'outsourcing' on a large scale and a wide variety of employment and subcontracting regimes – in other words, a breaking up of the long-term employment relationship and of the bureaucratic organization of firms – then European industrial citizenship may turn into a limiting condition for organizational modernization.

There is always more than one way 'to skin a cat'. It is an open question whether modernization of work organization and innovation regimes can be accommodated (assuming unions and works councils agree) in a revised, debureaucratized, more heterogeneous employment relationship; and, similarly, whether long-term employment with the same employer can still be put to economic advantage. Certainly continental European firms, unlike Anglo-American ones, will explore the economic and organizational potential of the waged employment relationship to the last. They probably have no other choice, given the institutional framework under which they operate. The outcome will very much determine the economic future of the European model of corporate organization, and indeed of the European 'social model'. Indications are that, at least at the level of top management, long-term employment has been losing some of its economic advantages even in European firms. Research on the chief executive officers of 40 large German firms shows the following: unprecedented turnover during the 1990s; a significant decline in length of tenure as well as general association with a particular firm; and a growing 'professionalization' indicated by a reduction in the number of CEOs possessing careers stretching from the shopfloor to the top (usually in the same company).[28] It remains to be seen whether tendencies which break with traditional practice are responses to general economic pressures which will also trickle down to the lower ranks of the hierarchy, in particular to the non-managerial workforce represented by unions and works councils.

Corporate Accountability in an International Economy

Traditional European conceptions of the corporation include the notion of a legitimate public interest in a firm existing alongside and in some cases superseding the interests of shareholders.[29] What those interests may be, now that inside ownership and owner management have ended, and how firms might be held accountable to such interests in an international economy, are fundamental issues behind current discussions on the 'stakeholder firm'. Such discussions currently lack clarity and precision in terms of both questions and answers.

In terms of empirical evidence, we observe a growing variety of business structures and strategies designed to satisfy the (potentially conflicting) demands on firms of capital markets and industrial relations institutions. Such developments reflect increased corporate autonomy in relation to national financial and industrial citizenship regimes, even on the European continent. Increased differences between firms subject to the same national regime indicate that national public policy is losing its grip on corporate organization and behaviour. International private markets are increasingly taking the place of public legislation as the main mechanism shaping corporate discipline and accountability. One consequence seems to be that 'industrial citizenship' (as it used to be called) is changing from a publicly guaranteed right of workers, created to hold firms accountable not just to their employees but to 'the public interest', into an economically expedient internal arrangement strategically chosen by firms in pursuit of improved productivity and competitiveness.

As large firms learn to treat internal social integration as an important parameter of their competitive structure and strategy – as they turn into 'institutional firms' (Crouch and Streeck, 1997) – new lines of division are emerging between their workforces and other workers which may be difficult to reconcile with continental European notions of equal industrial citizenship rights for all, regardless of place of employment. Equally critical from a public policy perspective are dualistic tendencies inside corporate employment systems in which safely employed core workforces, increasingly of the co-manager and co-owner type, are separated by a growing gap from a marginal workforce on which corporations rely for flexibility, but whose advancement to the core is difficult. Paradoxically, consensual closure of corporate internal labour markets may utilize traditional European institutions of industrial citizenship in ways which transform them from universal rights into particularistic privileges, thereby effectively privatizing what was intended to be a public good.

Closed institutional firms are difficult to govern from the outside. They also tend to be quite adept at externalizing some of the costs of their internal integration to society at large. An important example is the use of old age pension systems in numerous continental European countries to slim down workforces by placing older workers on early retirement. Not only does this increase a firm's economic competitiveness; it also safeguards internal social peace at the workplace during difficult restructuring periods. This is because workforce representatives are usually prepared to agree to employment cuts if those affected are allowed to retire on generous terms. Indeed unions and works councils typically join managements in lobbying governments to provide for extensive opportunities for early retirement of workers made redundant by their employers. As the experience of several countries shows, the costs to the public purse of private consensus building of this sort, as well as consequential increases in non-wage labour costs to levels of employment and economic activity, can be significant.

The externalization to society of the costs of corporate social integration through early retirement schemes is one of several factors contributing to a growing gap between the increasing demands which autonomous large firms make on public policy and the declining contributions they make to it. Large multinational firms can easily shift their taxable profits from one country to another, enabling them to choose where they contribute to the maintenance of infrastructure and social cohesion outside their corporate domains. Amongst other things, this results in strong pressures on national governments to lower corporation taxes, or even to rely exclusively on income and consumption taxes for financing public goods. All of this threatens social peace, if not at the workplace, then in the polity at large.

The issue is considerably complicated by the increasingly international character of large firms. More and more firms press governments for liberalization of national capital markets and industrial relations regimes, with the inevitable consequence of cross-national convergence. Such liberalization, however, gives rise to greater inter-firm diversity as businesses identify their own responses to new economic and technological conditions. Because firms have acquired the power to exit from non-accommodating national regimes, they are likely to be heard by governments, although more on capital–market regulation issues than on industrial relations ones. At the same time, multinational firms often appreciate national differences in production regimes and associated productive capacities precisely because they can benefit from comparative advantages and put together portfolios of plants in different countries based upon different specializations. Sometimes, however, developing local or national advantages requires firms to accept obligations, the discharge of which may be expensive for them. But while the failure of national governments to invest in infrastructural provision may cause firms to go to other jurisdictions,[30] so may high taxes. Thus governments find themselves facing growing demands for public investment from increasingly less taxable firms. This in effect encourages them to pursue specialization in infrastructural endowment and competitive cost cutting at the same time.

From a public policy perspective, economic success and social peace in European countries depend on large firms cooperating with society in crucial ways: to create employment; to open up internal labour markets to outsiders; to establish appropriate gender and generational balances amongst the employed; to help integrate immigrants at the workplace and in society; to make work and family commitments compatible; and to provide good quality training so that workers remain employable in external labour markets whenever firms are no longer able to retain them. Firms do some of these things on their own, especially when labour markets are tight and bottlenecks in the labour supply need to be overcome. But this is unlikely to be sufficient. As national regimes lose their hold on large firms, which themselves emerge as effective institution builders and major foci of social integration and identification, new means of public intervention in private markets and hierarchies need to be devised in order to make public and private purposes compatible; new means are also needed in order to safeguard the social sustainability of competitive economies. Here close cooperation, and a new division of labour between firms and public authorities of a sort hitherto unknown, are required.

4 CONVERGENCE, COMPARATIVE ADVANTAGE AND STRATEGIC CHOICE: CORPORATE CHANGE UNDER UNCERTAINTY

In trying to sum up what we seem to know about the dynamics of change in corporate organization in Europe today, it is fruitful to distinguish between the level of the firm and that of national regimes, if only because it is where the two interact that the most important developments are tending to take place. Ten points come to mind by which the present overview may be tentatively concluded.

1.   Large firms appear to be less willing than in the past to let their structures and strategies be determined by prescriptive national regimes with respect to relations with shareholders or, to a lesser extent, with workforces. In the more turbulent, politically less protected, economic environment of today, 'strategic choice', as first discovered by the US industrial relations literature of the late 1980s, has become a key category in accounting for the structure and behaviour of large companies. As firms strive to meet their individual competitive requirements, corporate organization becomes more diverse within countries. Firms develop their own variants of national systems of industrial citizenship, while at the same time learning to meet the behavioural requirements of a more marketized and arm's-length capital nexus. Continental European countries may, as a consequence, appear to be becoming more similar to each other and to the Anglo-American world, losing some of their previous capacity to impose particular corporate governance and labour arrangements on national firms. Instead they concede de facto or de jure freedom to firms to follow their own relevant market signals. To this extent it seems justified to speak of a movement towards cross-national convergence at the regime level.

2.   Growing diversity between firms *within national regimes* may amount to declining diversity between firms *across national borders* as a result of

adaptation of corporate strategies and structures to jointly experienced international market pressures. Indeed, at the same time as firms gain in securing freedom from national regulation, we seem to observe a narrowing of their range of strategic alternatives. For example, firms increasingly give up export-oriented strategies of internationalization in favour of locating production in foreign countries. Also, as firms come under intensified competitive pressure, they apply more stringent methods to assessing the profitability of their operations, frequently in the form of shareholder value-oriented management. Introduction of the latter is, of course, also caused by the need to satisfy more demanding investors, principally institutional ones. Pressures of this sort for cross-national convergence between firms originate both in capital markets and within sectors in product markets.

3. At the same time, there is still considerable diversity between firms in terms of both strategy and structure. For example, no single 'best practice' seems to be emerging with respect to the management of internationalizing, or multinational, operations. In particular, expectations that multinational firms will all develop a territorial–divisional matrix form of organization seem not to have materialized. The apparent absence of a universally preferred model which corresponds to the increased autonomy of firms and the observed variety in the management structures of multinational firms may reflect nothing more than a prolonged period of uncertainty and experimentation. It may also mean, however, that the optimal solution to the problems of managing internationalization is indeterminate; either that or it is conditional upon particular firms' histories – including country of origin – the result being that functionally equivalent, but otherwise different, responses develop.

4. Another source of diversity between firms appears to be the resilience of national industrial relations and industrial citizenship arrangements. Comparatively *sticky* national labour regimes force firms to invent new ways of reconciling traditional relationships with worker-stakeholders, all the while accommodating the demands of new stockholders who favour 'shareholder value'. To the extent that national labour regimes constrain company strategies and structures more than those of national capital markets, adjustment to shareholder value is bound to take place in national colours, even though, as has been pointed out, labour regimes are themselves being idiosyncratically redefined at the firm level and thereby internally diversified. As firms subject to relatively 'rigid' labour regimes adjust to new capital markets, they might try to discover capital market niches in which certain types of financial performance best suit their industrial citizenship regimes. This would enable them to survive without having to adopt a convergent, standard response to shareholders

which might jeopardize the stability of their labour relations. In this respect, convergence would occur only in the sense of all firms trying to develop individualized responses to new challenges which best fitted their national legacies and productive capabilities.

5. More generally, even the most multinational companies, a few exceptions apart, remain clearly identifiable in terms of their country of origin regarding, for example, preferred management practices at headquarters, or differential prospects of internal advancement for managerial staff from different countries. National differences may further contribute to variations between multinational firms through the latter's strategic choices with respect to operational locations in national settings which make up their international environments. A multinational company can be seen as a collection of national subsidiaries held together by a nationally identifiable centre and organized not merely as a way of enabling the firm to be present in key markets, but also in ways which allow it to take advantage of the specific productive capabilities associated with different national locations and different national institutional arrangements. Multinational companies, in other words, may be regarded as portfolios of various productive capacities and opportunities offered by different countries. In this sense they comprise distinctive combinations of national economic, organizational and cultural characteristics.

6. Because state regimes can no longer protect national firms from international competition, businesses demand greater freedom in adapting to new and changing product, capital and labour markets. In this sense firms press for convergence of regimes in the form of universal liberalization as a precondition for themselves diverging with respect to their structural and strategic responses to new competitive conditions. However, apart from the fact that in continental European countries this serves to raise issues about accountability to public interests and about political stability in relation to industrial relations, it may also affect the different productive capacities and proclivities supported by different national institutions. While clearly it is a long step from supervisory board co-determination to 'diversified quality production', or from insider finance to excellence in incremental innovation, indications are that certain capital and labour market regimes are conducive to certain kinds of economic performance and endow firms with specific comparative advantages. To the extent that the distinctiveness of national regimes may be rooted in institutionalized obligations for market participants that would be lost in the course of convergent liberalization, they erode not only the regimes themselves, but also the comparative advantages which firms derive from them. At this point, the interest of firms, even those operating in international markets, in liberal convergence of national regimes would become ambiguous.

7. Pressure by firms on national regimes for liberalization is less painful if
    companies operating under given rules and institutions have adjusted
    their operations over time to make the best of those rules and even, in
    ideal cases, turned seeming constraints into opportunities. For example,
    firms subject to co-determination which offer workforces stable employ-
    ment may have acquired the habit of investing heavily in workforce
    training in order to specialize in high-quality products for market niches
    in which price competition is modest. Investment in specialization of this
    sort amounts to sunk costs that militate against short-term strategic reori-
    entation and may make firms discount the benefits of liberalization. (Of
    course firms can hope to gain the same benefits derived from collective
    regulation by individual efforts or by the market, but the extent to which
    this is realistic is uncertain.) In addition, firms may be afraid of the disor-
    der potentially associated with rapid institutional change, the economic
    costs of which would further detract from the potential benefits of
    convergence towards a more liberal system.
8. Pressures for regime-liberalization should be further alleviated by the
    possibility of global – or globalizing – firms shopping around interna-
    tionally for the best regimes and institutional infrastructures for specific
    functions or tasks. As firms become customized configurations of differ-
    ent national or regional competitive advantages, they can selectively buy
    themselves into those national institutional arrangements that best suit
    their needs. This makes it less urgent to have domestic institutions
    changed to fit their competitive requirements, provided, that is, there is
    sufficient 'requisite variety' in their institutional environment. In the
    process, firms may not just lose interest in cross-national convergence;
    they may begin positively to appreciate the advantages of cross-national
    diversity.
9. As far as national regimes themselves are concerned, public policy faces
    difficult alternatives between convergent liberalization on Anglo-
    American lines (in all probability) and cultivation of distinctive compar-
    ative advantages based on the industrial citizenship and public interest
    obligations of firms specializing in selected market niches or modes of
    production. Neither approach is without risks. Convergence may not be
    achieved without significant domestic conflict. Its economic results may
    be uncertain in any case, given the existence of many competitors pursu-
    ing the same strategy. Specialization, by way of contrast, may locate a
    national regime in a market niche too small for an entire economy, or
    else in one that may soon disappear. In the latter case, the institutions
    which supported specialization may lose their usefulness. Between
    convergence and differentiation, a 'third way' may consist of regime
    pluralism, with countries offering different regimes for, say, long-term

and short-term oriented finance. Internal diversity of this sort would be the equivalent at the regime level of the mixed regime portfolios assembled by large multinational firms. As such it would avoid a potentially vulnerable institutional monoculture. The question is whether, and to what extent, different regimes in capital or labour markets can coexist in the same country without undermining each other: in other words, whether non-liberal regimes require something like monopoly status in order to produce their specific benefits.

10. Internal differentiation of national regimes which allows those regimes to support different structures and strategies of economic organization, is often – increasingly so indeed – accomplished by means of regional decentralization of public policy and collective labour relations. As regions concentrate on particular sectors and comparative advantages, decentralization and increased competition between regional units result, not in convergence, but in specialization. Regional autonomy and specialization seem to interact in as yet unexplored ways, with the growing autonomy of firms from national regimes as well as corporate resolve to locate different functions in areas where they are optimally supported by local conditions and institutions.

Convergence, between firms as well as national regimes, seems far off, with no 'one best way' to international competitiveness in sight. Corporate organization, as with technology, is today going through a period of dynamic experimentation and serendipitous discovery in which no ready recipes are on offer and with theory needing to catch up with reality. Internationalization proceeds apace even as the country of origin of multinational firms remains clearly recognizable. At the same time, there is extensive eclectic hybridization of practices and structures across national borders. Both firms and national regimes seem to be poised between pressures for convergence on the one hand and the promises of specialization on the other; between meeting competition head-on and, alternatively, building up distinctive capabilities which others will find hard to emulate. The transformation of corporate organization in Europe will, for some time to come, offer a rich field for empirical research and theory generation.

NOTES

1. For empirical detail the chapter draws to a large extent on research by Bastiaan van Apeldoorn, Jürgen Beyer, Anke Hassel, Martin Höpner, Gregory Jackson, Britta Rehder and Rainer Zugehör at the Max Planck Institute for the Study of Societies in Cologne. I am particularly indebted to Martin Höpner for invaluable help in reading the literature and organizing the quantitative information on the German case.

2. Attempts by the Commission to enact a Directive on minimal standards for workforce participation in national firms have yet to get off the ground. If they ever result in legislation, the standard set will almost certainly be lower than in all member countries except, perhaps, the United Kingdom.

3. How international competition for employment between plants of the same company may affect the functioning of European Works Councils is an interesting question about which we know little. Initial evidence suggests that discussion of specific investment projects are rare, owing to unbridgeable conflicts of interest; and solidarity is limited to the exchange of information on current decisions and 'bidding procedures'. This seems to vary only if managements try to play off plants against one another by using biased or false information, or if pressures for higher productivity are selectively applied to only a subset of plants.

4. In 1986, the correlation between foreign turnover and foreign employment in terms of percentage of a firm's total turnover and employment, was 0.668 for the 100 largest German firms. Ten years later, it had risen to 0.725 (Hassel *et al.*, 2000).

5. As reported by *The Economist* (29 April 2000, p.10), the value of European mergers and acquisitions increased from roughly $200 billion in 1994 to $1.5 trillion in 1999, with 'almost as many cross-border deals as domestic deals'.

6. Privatization thus both coincided with, and gave rise to, a public interest in liquid stock markets and the changes in financial regulation necessary to create these.

7. Deutsche Bundesbank (1999, p.139). It is, however, conceivable that shareholder value orientation was sometimes promoted by a desire to raise capital for overseas investment from local capital markets, especially the USA.

8. *The Economist* estimates that cross-shareholding in Europe outside Britain declined between 1994 and 1999 from 19 to 10 per cent of total stock market value (29 April 2000, p.14). On Germany see Höpner (2000c).

9. Van Apeldoorn (2000) also observes a slow decline in the share held by traditional owners and a transformation of industrial capitalists into 'money' capitalists.

10. These, in turn, are likely to fetch a higher price if the firm is credibly committed to high shareholder value.

11. Among the 100 largest German firms, shareholder value orientation is strongly related to the internationalization of product markets, indicating that it may be a response, in part, to strong competitive pressures (Höpner, 2000b).

12. Also conglomerates tend to be more shareholder value-oriented than other firms, especially if they have significant foreign ownership, something which is likely because of the need to make themselves attractive to 'the markets' (Zugehör, 2000).

13. In 1999, according to *The Economist* (29 April 2000, p.10), the value of hostile takeovers in Europe, at $400 billion, was four times the combined total for the years 1990–98. Over half of the hostile takeover bids were successful.

14. The story of the progress of shareholder value policies among large firms is a complex one. According to a survey undertaken among German firms, managements shifted to shareholder value not just because of pressure from shareholders – which, however, seems to have been the most important factor – but also to improve performance and managerial control (Achleitner and Bassen, 2000). This might explain why there is a correlation between the internationalization of product markets and shareholder value orientation. Moreover, shareholder value may have become 'fashionable', as indicated by a very high correlation (at r=0.69) between a company's shareholder value orientation and its reputation among German managers (Höpner, 2000d, p.29).

15. For example, the German law on Control and Transparency in Enterprises (KonTraG), which was passed in mid-2000, made it illegal for firms to restrict the voting rights of particular categories of shares. In other countries too, voting restrictions and voting caps seem to be losing favour. Overall, German legal rules concerning corporate governance, especially with respect to the situation of minority shareholders, have changed in a UK direction between 1996 and 1999, although they still have a long way to go (Donnelly *at al.*, 2000).

16. Apart, perhaps, from the fact that Mannesmann used to have voting caps which, by the time of the takeover, had become illegal.

17. The Commission included, among others, the founder of Bertelsmann, Reinhard Mohn; the

CEO of BASF, Jürgen Strube; the Presidents of the German Trade Union Confederation, Dieter Schulte, and of the Federal Labour Court, Thomas Dieterich; and the Secretary of State in the Federal Ministry of Labour, Werner Tegtmeier.

18. In 1986, sales by large German firms in foreign markets as a proportion of total sales was on average more than twice as high as the ratio of employees abroad. In 1996, the relationship had declined to 1.3, indicating a rapid and significant shift of production abroad and a change in strategy away from the export of home-country products (Beyer, 2000).

19. In about 40 of the 100 largest German firms, there was at least one formal agreement of this sort during the 1990s.

20. There were also several cases of employee buy-outs in the 1990s, under which plants or divisions of large firms looking to be sold off were taken over by employees. The new firms remained, at least for a while, within the production network of the former mother companies, which provided them with the bulk of their work, or even with financial support.

21. De Jong (1997) explains the relatively low share of value-added that continental European firms have traditionally paid out to their shareholders, and the correspondingly high share that went to labour, by the presence in national regimes of strong protection of corporate governance against hostile takeovers. Amongst the largest German firms, the share of capital in value-added increased slightly during the 1990s, and most strongly in firms with dispersed share ownership.

22. Union demands with respect to the new German takeover code focus on improved access by workforce representatives to information, especially on the intentions and business plans of the bidder; and on an obligation for management to include the views of the workforce in the official statements of the company.

23. Workforce influence may also have caused management stock option plans in European firms to be somewhat less exorbitant and inviting of opportunism than is characteristic of the USA.

24. At least one firm expanded employee stock ownership after an unfriendly takeover bid failed at the last minute. In a number of companies, employee stock owners are beginning to think about organizing themselves collectively in order to make their voices heard in the shareholder assembly. In some cases, employee stock owners are represented by works councils, whereas in others they are independently organized. The potential problems that may result for management if workers take an active role as stock owners – in addition to the benefits for firms in terms of better protection from hostile takeovers – are yet to be discussed; they are likely to be an important subject of future debates on the transformation of industrial citizenship.

25. On Mannesmann, and especially the reactions by the union, see Höpner and Jackson (2000) and Jürgens *et al.* (2000).

26. The same seems to be true for regimes of corporate finance. See Mayer (2000) who shows that different capital market regulations are associated with different types of economic performance and competitiveness. Indeed industrial citizenship and financial market regimes may complement each other by supporting certain types of performance, for example in diversified quality production (Jackson, 2003; Soskice, 1999).

27. To what extent social peace, worker goodwill and a company's social integration are positively valued by the stock market is not known. It would constitute an interesting subject for future research (Jackson, 2001a).

28. More specifically, the percentage of CEOs without an academic degree declined from the early to the late 1980s from 14 to 0; the average length of tenure fell between the early 1980s and the late 1990s from about 13 to 6.5 years; and the percentage of CEOs who had been recruited into their current positions from outside the firm more than doubled, from 17 to 36 (Höpner, 2000d).

29. The strongest expression of this sort of interest was when governments nationalized firms or entire sectors to ensure that their operation was in harmony with the interest of the community. In the twentieth century this was a frequent practice in Europe, even in the United Kingdom. Today the movement is in the opposite direction as formerly public sectors have been, and continue to be, privatized on a large scale. Very appropriately, a major issue in current privatization debates is how to ensure that privatized utilities continue to provide a minimum of 'public service', even where this is not necessarily profitable.

30.   During the 1990s, one out of ten large industrial firms in Germany signed agreements with their works councils on employment and investment, the government offering subsidies, land or infrastructural investment in order to help the two sides reach an agreement.

BIBLIOGRAPHY

Achleitner, Ann-Kristin and Alexander Bassen (2000), 'Entwicklungsstand des Shareholder-Value-Ansatzes in Deutschland: Empirische Befunde', EBS Finance Group Working Paper Series 00–02, Oestrich-Winkel, EBS Finance Group.

Albert, Michel (1991), *Capitalisme contre capitalisme,* Paris: Le Seuil.

Amelung, Torsten (1999), 'Globalisierung, Conglomerate Discount und Auswirkungen auf die Unternehmensstrukturen', *Journal für Betriebswirtschaft,* 27–38.

Apeldoorn, Bastiaan van (2000), 'The Rise of Shareholder Capitalism in Continental Europe?', paper prepared for the XVIIIth World Congress of the International Political Science Association, Quebec City, 1–5 August.

Becht, Marco and Ailsa Roel (1999), 'Blockholding in Europe: An International Comparison', *European Economic Review,* **43**, 1049–56.

Berle, Adolf A. and Gardiner C. Means (1999), *The Modern Corporation and Private Property,* New Brunswick and London: Transaction Publishers.

Beyer, Jürgen (1999), 'Unternehmensverflechtungen und Managerherrschaft in Deutschland', *Leviathan,* **27**, 518–36.

— — (2000), ' "One Best Way" oder Varietät? Strategischer und organisatorischer Wandel von Großunternehmen im Prozess der Internationalisierung', unpublished manuscript.

Bispinck, Reinhard (1997), 'Das Märchen vom starren Flächentarifvertrag: Eine Analyse von tariflichen Öffnungsklauseln aus über 100 Tarifbereichen', DGB-Tarifarchiv, Düsseldorf.

Bühner, Rolf (1997), 'Increasing Shareholder Value Through Human Asset Management', *Long Range Planning,* **30**, 710–11.

Crouch, Colin and Wolfgang Streeck (1997), 'Introduction: The Future of Capitalist Diversity', in Colin Crouch and Wolfgang Streeck (eds), *Political Economy of Modern Capitalism: Mapping Convergence and Diversity,* London: Sage, 1–18.

de Jong, Henk Wouter (1997), 'The Governance Structure and Performance of Large European Corporations', *The Journal of Management and Governance,* **1**(5), 27.

Deutsche Bundesbank (1999), 'Jahresabschlüsse westdeutscher Unternehmen 1971 bis 1996', *Statistische Sonderveröffentlichung,* **5**, Frankfurt am Main: Deutsche Bundesbank.

Donnelly, Shawn, Andrew Gamble, Gregory Jackson and John Parkinson (2000), 'The Public Interest and the Company in Britain and Germany', London: Anglo-German Society for the Study of Industrial Society.

Fama, Eugene (1980), 'Agency Problems and the Theory of the Firm', *Journal of Political Economy,* **88**, 288–307.

Gilson, Ronald J. (2000), 'The Globalization of Corporate Governance: Convergence of Form or Function', Columbia Law School, Center for Law and Economic Studies, working paper no. 192.

Guillén, Mauro F. (2000), 'Corporate Governance and Globalization: Is There Convergence Across Countries?', *Advances in International Comparative Management,* **13**, 175–204.

Hassel, Anke, Martin Höpner, Antje Kurdelbusch, Britta Rehder and Rainer Zugehör

(2000), 'Zwei Dimensionen der Internationalisierung: Eine empirische Analyse deutscher Großunternehmen', *Kölner Zeitschrift für Soziologie und Sozialpsychologie*, 500–519.

Höpner, Martin (2000a), 'Kapitalmarktorientierte Unternehmensführung: Messung, Bestimmungsgründe und Konsequenzen', Beitrag zu einer Konferenz des Research Network on Corporate Governance, Wissenschaftszentrum Berlin, 22–3 June.

—— (2000b), 'Ende der Deutschland AG?', *Die Mitbestimmung,* **46**(11), 12–16.

—— (2000c), 'Unternehmensverflechtung im Zwielicht: Hans Eichels Plan zur Auflösung der Deutschland AG', *WSI-Mitteilungen*, **53**, 655–63.

—— (2000d), 'Professionalisierung, Internationalisierung, Vermarktlichung: Die soziale Welt deutscher Topmanager in den 1990er Jahren', Max-Planck-Institut für Gesellschaftsforschung, Cologne, unpublished manuscript.

Höpner, Martin and Gregory Jackson (2000), 'The Political Economy of Takeovers in Germany: Institutional Change and the Case of Mannesmann', paper presented at the 14th International Conference of the Society for the Advancement of Socio-Economics (SASE), London, July.

Jackson, Gregory (2001a), 'Comparative Corporate Governance: Sociological Perspectives', in Andrew Gamble, Gavin Kelly and J. Parkinson (eds), *The Political Economy of the Company*, Oxford: Hart Publishers.

—— (2001b), 'The Origins of Non-Liberal Corporate Governance in Germany and Japan', in Wolfgang Streeck and Kozo Yamamura (eds), *The Origins of Non-Liberal Capitalism: Germany and Japan*, Ithaca, NY: Cornell University Press.

—— (2003) 'Corporate Governance in Germany and Japan: Liberalization Pressures and Responses', in Kozo Yamamura and Wolfgang Streeck (eds), *The End of Diversity: Prospects for Germany and Japanese Capitalism*, Ithaca, NY: Cornell University Press.

Jürgens, Ulrich, Joachim Rupp and Katrin Vitols (2000), 'Corporate Governance and Shareholder Value in Deutschland', WZB discussion paper FS II 00–202, Wissenschaftszentrum, Berlin.

Kommission Mitbestimmung (1998), 'Mitbestimmung und neue Unternehmenskulturen: Bilanz und Perspektiven', *Bericht der Kommission Mitbestimmung, Bertelsmann Stiftung und Hans-Böckler-Stiftung*, Gütersloh: Verlag Bertelsmann Stiftung.

Köstler, Roland (2000), 'Anforderungen der Arbeitnehmer an eine effektive Unternehmensüberwachung', Beitrag zu einem Workshop über 'Institutioneller Wandel in den industriellen Beziehungen' am Max-Planck-Institut für Gesellschaftsforschung, Cologne, December.

Lang, Larry and René Stulz (1994), 'Tobin's q, Corporate Diversification and Firm Performance', *Journal of Political Economy*, **102**, 1248–80.

La Porta, Rafael, Florencio Lopez-de-Silanes and Andrei Shleifer (1998), *Corporate Ownership Around the World*, Cambridge, MA: National Bureau of Economic Research.

Mayer, Colin (2000), 'Institutions in the New Europe: The Transformation of Corporate Organization', unpublished manuscript.

OECD (1997), 'The Impact of Institutional Investors on OECD Financial Markets', *Financial Market Trends*, **68**, 15–55.

Prowse, Stephen (1994), 'Corporate Governance in an International Perspective: A Survey of Control Mechanisms Among Large Firm', Bank for International Settlements, Basle.

Rappaport, Alfred (1986), *Creating Shareholder Value: The New Standard for Business Performance*, New York: The Free Press.

Rappaport, Alfred and Mark Sirower (2000), 'Unternehmenskauf – mit Aktien oder in bar bezahlen', *Harvard Businessmanager*, 32–46.

Rehder, Britta (2000), *Abweichung als Regel? Die Mitbestimmung*, 12–16.

Shleifer, Andrei and Robert W. Vishny (1996), 'A Survey of Corporate Governance', NBER Working Paper Series, Working Paper no. 5554, Cambridge, MA: National Bureau of Economic Research.

Soskice, David (1999), 'Divergent Production Regimes: Coordinated and Uncoordinated Market Economies in the 1980s and 1990s', in Herbert Kitschelt, P. Lange, G. Marks and D. Stephens (eds), *Continuity and Change in Contemporary Capitalism*, Cambridge: Cambridge University Press, 101–34.

Streeck, Wolfgang (1991), 'On the Institutional Conditions of Diversified Quality Production', in Egon Matzner and Wolfgang Streeck (eds), *Beyond Keynesianism: The Socio-Economics of Production and Employment*, Aldershot, UK and Brookfield, USA: Edward Elgar, 21–61.

Zugehör, Rainer (2000), 'Die neue Macht des Kapitalmarktes: Der Einfluss des Kapitalmarktes auf das Investitionsverhalten deutscher Großunternehmen', unpublished manuscript.

2. Adapting European labour institutions to global economic and technical change

David Marsden

INTRODUCTION

Although most of the labour institutions that characterize the labour markets of European countries have a long history, their present form has been profoundly shaped by the postwar 'historic compromise' and the subsequent years of economic prosperity. That period consolidated the pre-eminence of the open-ended employment relationship as the leading contractual form adopted by firms and workers, and it became the guiding assumption for labour protection and social insurance. It became the norm not just in the statistical sense, but also in the sense that it was the desirable state of affairs.

The open-ended, indefinite duration, employment relationship has come under pressure in recent years, not least because of the rise of the 'new economy'. As a result of new communications' technologies, firms are able to adopt radically different methods of internal management and coordination between businesses. The management literature is now full of articles about networked organizations with flatter structures and more permeable boundaries (for example, Arthur and Rousseau, 1996). The globalization of businesses and of markets, as a result of both technical change and political decisions such as the Single European Market, have increased competition and the speed with which firms are challenged in established activities. As a result, they find that they need to be more flexible, not just with respect to the size of their workforces, but also regarding the mix of activities in which they engage. Should they 'make' or 'buy'? Should they search more aggressively for new partners and new markets and, because a number of such ventures inevitably fail, should they be ready to close down or sell off operations they cannot manage effectively? Whereas Peters and Waterman (1982) urged firms to 'stick to the knitting' and concentrate on what they are good at, in many sectors the pace of change is such that the 'core competencies' which led firms to market success a few years previously are now less relevant.

Some of these changes are also reflected in institutional responses. The recent international comparative study by Katz and Darbishire (2000) shows clearly how far there has been a shift away from neocorporatist national and sectoral level industrial relations at the workplace level. Their study covered the USA, Japan, Australia and several European countries. One of the driving forces behind this shift of focus has been the demand from employers for institutions that enable them to negotiate new technology and new organizational patterns. Likewise, unions have responded to a demand from their members for representation on these issues. The growth of non-union employee relations can be seen in a similar light. It is not that employers have become more hostile to unions per se. Rather they believe it is harder to implement rapid change if everything has to be negotiated, especially when those negotiations involve other employers whose needs may differ from their own. In Germany, it seems that the growth of non-union relations has taken the form of a flight by firms from employer organizations because many find they do not have enough in common to warrant a sectoral agreement on wages or job classifications.

In many countries firms have sought to increase their use of contingent labour and to contract out activities for which they wish to avoid long-term commitments. The most famous study of employer practices and intentions in this area, by Atkinson and Meager (1986), gave rise to the much-cited 'Atkinson model' of the flexible firm. This too can be understood as part of a response to a perceived increase in the volatility of markets, and consequent reluctance by firms to invest too heavily in human resources which they may not require in the future. Even the public sector has not escaped such pressures. In Britain, universities, once thought to be the ultimate 'protected sector', turn out to have very high levels of temporary employment: two-thirds of academic staff at Cambridge and Oxford universities and just over half at the London School of Economics (LSE) fall into this category, figures that correlate quite strongly with university research ratings.[1] The intensity of increasingly international competition for research funds and for lucrative overseas student markets is part of the explanation for this development.

The European Commission's Supiot Report, written by a group of leading labour lawyers and economists, concluded that the changes which were taking place were sufficiently important to require a rethink on the assumptions which had underpinned labour law for the past 40 years.

WHAT DO THE PRESSURES FOR CHANGE SIGNIFY?

There is a paradox in the evidence. Despite the various changes, aggregate statistics on the use of atypical forms of employment and on job tenures paint a picture of stability that belies case study evidence. An international survey by the OECD showed that roughly 90 per cent of workers across OECD countries continue to be engaged in open-ended, indefinite duration employment relationships (1992, ch. 4). Moreover, apart from one or two dramatic cases, self-employment has not grown very much, and the number of countries in which it has grown is roughly similar to the number in which it has declined or stagnated. Even Britain, which showed a sharp increase in the 1980s, did not continue this trend during the 1990s. In Spain, where a large percentage of workers are on fixed-term contracts, it turns out that many such contracts serve as a staging post to permanent employment with a firm.[2] The OECD survey of job tenures (1993, ch. 4) leads to a similar conclusion as, on average, job tenures have changed remarkably little. Indeed, in some countries, such as France and Germany, they have increased, and among shorter job tenure countries, such as Britain, some reduction in men's job tenures has been offset by an increase in those for women, so the net result is little changed.

It is of course possible that either the enterprise case studies are not representative or that the aggregate statistics are not measuring the right things. However there has been a marked increase in the *perceived* instability of employment, a point also highlighted by the OECD (1997, ch. 5). This suggests that many workers no longer believe that they have a permanent job just by working reasonably hard. As a result they feel less committed to their current employers.

There is a need to take all sides of the evidence seriously. The pressures on firms to become flexible are real, and these lie behind part of the perceived decline in employment stability. Nevertheless the lack of movement in the aggregate statistics indicates that there may be an institutional blockage in our labour markets. I shall argue that, while the established open-ended employment relationship has been a truly remarkable social institution, enabling flexible cooperation between partners who do not trust each other very much, it may be reaching its limits. Consequently, we need to consider ways in which it can be reformed.

THE MISTAKEN ASYMMETRY OF THE 'FLEXIBILITY' DEBATE

One of the fundamental mistakes of the flexibility debate has been to look at it from only one side. The public debate has been dominated by Atkinson and Meager's model of the 'flexible firm'. On the basis of interviews with managers in Britain, they highlighted the desire on the part of firms to hire and fire, and to redeploy labour more easily: in short, the need to increase numerical and functional flexibility. The fact that this became known in continental

European debates as the 'Atkinson model' is testimony to the widespread echo of its themes outside the UK (for example, the special issue of the International Labour Organization (ILO's) journal *Labour and Society*, **12**(1), 1987). Much of the subsequent policy debate took the needs of firms as the starting point, and when the needs of workers were considered, it was very much in moral terms. The underlying theme in the critique by Pollert (1991) and her co-authors was that the open-ended, indefinite duration contract was better for workers, and if alternative forms were spreading it was because high unemployment meant that it was being imposed on workers against their will. To some extent, the same point of view was taken by the then Conservative government, namely that trade union power and labour legislation should be weakened so that firms could adopt more flexible forms of employment.

Although legal structures, collective bargaining arrangements and social security systems have all played important parts in developing the employment relationship in modern economies (as Supiot, 1994, and Deakin, 1998, demonstrate), what is striking about such a relationship is the near universality of its key features, especially its open-ended nature and its (commonly) indefinite duration. This is so despite the current diversity of labour law, collective bargaining arrangements and social insurance systems. The prominence of such factors in policy analysis has arisen because they are perceived to be the key levers by which governments and social partners can act upon labour markets. However they leave the most important actors in the shade: namely, individual firms and individual workers. Writing about French industrial relations, Sellier (1961) once remarked that legislation was like currency: the state cannot make it circulate if people reject it.[3] In other words, social institutions in labour markets require acceptance, not just by formally organized social actors, but also by the thousands of firms and millions of individual workers who use them. If they are to be adopted, they have to be perceived as serving the needs of all parties more than the alternatives do.

It is often supposed that individual workers wield little power compared with the organizations employing them. Industrial Relations writers on labour law often critically contrast the formal equality of employer and employee in law with the real-life subordination of the latter within the employment relationship. It is also common within the discipline of Industrial Relations to suppose that the great majority of workers have power, and hence choice, only if and when they combine. If this were so, one might expect the wage differential between equivalent workers covered by collective agreements and those not covered to be far greater than most empirical estimates show it to be.[4] Indeed, it is worth remembering that several of the early studies of output restriction, such as those conducted by Weber (1909) and by Roethlisberger and Dickson (1939), were carried out in non-union workplaces. For this reason, Hugh Clegg (1972) devoted the opening chapter of his famous textbook on industrial relations to the work group rather than to the union. For him, collective action was needed in order to institutionalize and to regulate pre-existing power relations.

The problem, I would argue, with the flexibility debate has been that it has considered the employment relationship as the fruit of legislative or trade union action, that is to say of collective action. It has ignored the role of decentralized choices by firms and workers. When we consider the employment relationship from this point of view, it becomes clear why there is currently a blockage between the perceived need of firms for greater employment flexibility and the apparent lack of movement shown by aggregate statistics. Essential to finding a more flexible solution is recognition of the way in which the employment relationship functions in reality, and understanding how it might be adapted to better meet the interests of both workers and firms. More flexible solutions have to protect the interests of both parties if they are to be widely adopted.

WHY IS THE OPEN-ENDED EMPLOYMENT RELATIONSHIP STILL SO WIDELY USED?

One of the most remarkable features of the employment relationship is that it solves a very difficult economic question, namely how to enable open-ended cooperation between parties who are basically self-interested and in conditions that are ripe for opportunistic behaviour. Future demand is uncertain; each party knows more than the other about important aspects of their joint work; they have only 'bounded rationality', and each knows that the gains from cooperation also imply costs of separation. Even if one side does not wish to behave opportunistically itself, it may fear that the other side will. For much of the nineteenth century, subcontracting had worked well when outcomes could be easily defined and monitored.[5] But it reached its limits as technical change and increasing complexity of production meant firms wanted more direct control over the work process and a closer tailoring of work tasks to their organizational needs. This meant being able to redefine workers' assignments without renegotiation or with greatly reduced negotiation. To do this, they needed a new contractual form: the open-ended employment relationship.

For workers who distrusted the intentions of potential employers, an open-ended contract seemed a recipe for exploitation, and so it became acceptable only as various protections were included. Coase, in 1937, captured its essence: it gave employers the authority to define workers' tasks ex post 'within certain limits' (Coase, 1937). These limits cannot be set by exhaustive job descriptions and complex contingency clauses (Williamson, 1975). Apart from the cost of writing such contracts, they would not work because their very detail would create endless scope for job-level bargaining. The solution which gradually emerged was to use certain kinds of transaction, or work, rules to identify the limits of managerial authority and of employees' obligations. To be effective, such rules need to be simple and sufficiently robust to be applied by ordinary workers and line managers working at a distance from personnel departments and legal advice. The earliest such rules tended to identify certain kinds of work tasks. They did this either by their complementarity, as in the case of the 'work post' rule common in French and US forms of *taylorism*, or by the tools and materials associated with certain tasks, as was common under British and US craft demarcation rules ('job territory' rules). Although 'taylorism' was originally a management invention, as field studies by Crozier (1963) and Slichter *et al.* (1960) show, the work posts were very quickly transformed into a defensive mechanism for workers.[6] Defining jobs served to delimit workers' obligations.

In more recent years, work rules have developed which focus on functions rather than individual tasks. Although more flexible, they also require higher levels of trust and more complex relationships between work groups and management. Well-known examples can be found in the flexible work organization of large Japanese firms, where, as will be explained in more detail later on, the 'competence ranking' rule often guides the distribution of tasks within work groups (Koike, 1997, Yamanouchu and Okazaki-Ward, 1997). Similarly, in Germany, the 'qualification' rule commonly assigns work according to skill requirements (Sengenberger, 1987). Both of the latter rules establish a much looser relationship between tasks and workers' jobs, improving task flexibility, and focusing on functions related either to production needs or to workers' skills. Labour law and collective agreements have helped reinforce these work rules.[7]

If we look more closely at the research on the pressures for change, and on the 'crisis' in the employment relationship, it becomes clear that one type in particular is under pressure. Indeed, Supiot and his colleagues refer explicitly to the 'Fordist' model being in crisis, although they take this to be the general model of the open-ended employment relationship. What company case studies show to be in crisis is the traditional model of employment in large industrial and service firms possessing well-developed internal labour markets. The American 'Organization Man', and maybe also the Japanese 'salaryman', are in crisis as firms find it hard to offer long-term employment to large numbers of workers as they did in the past; and with that goes the motivational model that exchanged organizational commitment for long-term employment. In trouble too is the model of skill formation that went with long-term employment, namely heavy reliance upon informal on-the-job training of the kind brought to widespread attention by Doeringer and Piore (1971). These developments also challenge the method of job regulation that focuses on individual work posts or stations.

A CLOSER LOOK AT THE NATURE OF THE EMPLOYMENT RELATIONSHIP

The reason why these developments challenge only one model of the employment relationship becomes clear if we look more closely at the different principles that can be applied to limit management's authority.

To understand why workers and firms should voluntarily choose the employment relationship as the framework for cooperation, one needs to know the alternatives. The most practical and economically significant one is that of self-employment, where the worker operates in effect as a one-person firm. Across the OECD countries, about one person in ten is self-employed, and this covers a range of sectors and occupations (OECD, 1992). From the growth of self-employment in certain activities, and from mobility studies reviewed by the OECD, we can see that people do indeed move between employment and self-employment, and that firms also decide whether to hire people as employees or, say, as consultants. Historically we know that, in the nineteenth century, various forms of contracting predominated over employee status (Mottez, 1966). We know too that tax arrangements also serve to affect the choices firms make, which presumably indicates that net economic advantages weigh heavily in their decisions.

The key to the relative economic advantages of one or other form of contract lies in the need for ex ante specification of work outcomes or tasks in the case of self-employment, and the scope for ex post definition of workers' duties within the employment relationship. There is also a grey area in which some ex post specifications of tasks occurs for the self-employed. However, it can be shown that such cases often depend upon the existence of the same kinds of work rules as those found in the employment relationship, notably where there are strongly developed occupational skills (Marsden, 1999, ch. 8). Enforcing open-market contracts, such as self-employment, is made relatively easy because the terms of contract are agreed in advance, and the parties have an interest in ensuring that the degree of ambiguity is small. Because the agreement is ex ante there are few sunk costs to cloud negotiations. The situation is quite different with the open-ended employment relationship which is more an agreement to work together under the employer's direction than a market exchange. Sunk costs can be considerable on both sides: at a minimum, job search and recruitment are expensive, and the sunk costs rise if there is significant investment in firm-specific skills. There are great potential gains, particularly for employers, from the open-ended nature of the relationship. The costs and rigidities of defining tasks or outputs ex ante are avoided, and firms do not need to know the precise timing for certain kinds of work. Coase and Simon develop different aspects of these benefits with great elegance in their two famous articles. Slichter *et al.* (1960) and Williamson (1975), all in different ways, show the costs of trying to work with tightly defined tasks and work assignments; and Crozier (1963), also with great elegance, shows the perverse effects of defining work tasks in too much detail. No doubt this helps explain why, even though there is real choice, nine out of ten workers are engaged as employees in advanced industrial economies.

Coase puts his finger on the central problem of the employment relationship by saying that it gives the employer the authority to assign work 'within certain limits'. Unlimited employer power would be slavery, and in a liberal economy possessing a free labour market there would be few takers. What he does not explore, however, is how these limits are set. Indeed almost no one does. It is often assumed that there is a set of tasks about which employees are indifferent, and that they agree to employer discretion within this set. It is assumed that employers might pay a supplement for tasks outside that set. However, as is shown in *A Theory of Employment Systems* (1999), this opens the door to opportunistic bargaining. A similar point is made by Teulings and Hartog (1998), who see the attraction of the employment relationship to employers as being its insulation of work assignments from further bargaining, thereby avoiding the opportunistic renegotiation associated with the 'hold-up' problem. Willman (1986) shows just how damaging continuous bargaining over assignments was for productivity in the British car, dock and printing industries during past decades.

Limits to managerial authority are essential, and they can only be provided by some kind of rule. We need therefore to consider the sufficient and necessary attributes of a rule that enables a viable employment relationship to flourish and which ensures that this relationship is freely chosen over its main alternative. Taken together, these attributes are represented by the efficiency and the enforceability constraints.

A *sufficient* condition for workers and firms choosing to cooperate in an employment relationship is that it should be mutually beneficial compared to the alternatives. The arguments of Coase (1937) and Simon (1951) take us part of the way by showing the overall gains that can arise compared with the main alternative, some kind of sales contract. However, it is not sufficient, because it is possible that one party will try to appropriate all the gains. Given the sunk costs each has in the relationship, the losing party may be worse off if this happens. A *necessary* condition, therefore, is the existence of a rule which ensures that both parties gain, clarifying the extent of employees' obligations to employers in ways that can be enforced. Unless this can be done, one or the other party will refuse to engage in the relationship. However, enforceability is not enough on its own. Work assignments could be determined by the colour of an employee's eyes or some other criteria. There has to be a reason for them. Enforceable rules must be productively efficient and define obligations in such a way that employees' competencies match employers' job demands.

By aligning the two, the rule boosts the 'added value' of the employment relationship by organizing training processes and job classifications.

Satisfying the enforceability and efficiency constraints is both necessary and sufficient to ensure a viable employment relationship. As a result, one can regard the two constraints on employment rules as the basis for an exhaustive classification of employment rules given the basic assumptions of the Coase–Simon approach. Broadly speaking, employment rules may satisfy each constraint in one of two ways, thus creating the typology of rules shown in Figure 2.1.

There are two broad approaches by which employment rules establish the *enforceability* of work assignments. They may focus either directly on attributes of individual work tasks or on functions within production or service processes. A famous example of the first, widely found in craft work environments, is to identify the tasks belonging to particular 'job territories' by reference to the tools or materials used, these being 'the tools of the trade'. Such simple rules provide a very robust way of delimiting the boundaries of the jobs of one group of workers and determining where those of another group begin. Within professional work, where distinctive tools figure less prominently, boundaries are often drawn by identifying key operations that must be undertaken only by those holding a particular qualification. Another famous rule, common in both blue- and white-collar environments, is that of the 'work post' under which tasks are grouped according to complementarities in

		Efficiency constraint	
		Job demands identified by:	
Enforceability constraint		Production approach	Training approach
The focus of enforcement criteria	Task-centred	'work post' rule	'job territory'/ 'tools of trade' rule
	Function/ procedure-centred	'competence rank' rule	'qualification' rule

Figure 2.1   The contractual constraints and common employment rules

production, and assigned exclusively to individual work stations for which particular workers are responsible. Usually neither of these rules is enforced rigidly, but the important thing is that everyone knows they might be invoked should work relations deteriorate. Likewise management tends to enforce work rules strictly only in periodic 'crackdowns', when effort seems to be drifting in the wrong direction. 'Working to rule' is a pressure tactic and not usually the normal method of working.

The other approach to enforceability is to assign work tasks on the basis of functions. Mostly these transcend the jobs of individual workers and so place a heavy reliance on stable dynamics within work groups. It can be shown that a seniority, or competence-based, ranking rule can enable a flexible allocation of tasks within a work group (Marsden, 1999, ch. 2). Similarly, recognized qualifications can be used to assign types of work which pose similar technical demands. With function-centred rules, enforcement is trickier than with task-centred ones and depends on a higher degree of cooperation between workers and management. This is vulnerable to a breakdown in trust, there being no safety net of minimal compliance as under task-related rules. Such vulnerability is a strong incentive for employers to behave cooperatively.

To satisfy the *efficiency* constraint, work assignments can be organized according to complementarities either in *production* or in *training*. These are the production and training approaches. They diverge mainly because of the different cost structures of informal on-the-job training (OJT) and formal off-the-job instruction (OJI). The first has low set-up costs, but these rise steeply as the share of trainees increases. The second has high set-up costs because of the investment in special training facilities, but falling average costs per trainee. Organizing work according to production complementarities leads to what Williamson calls 'idiosyncratic' jobs, whereas seeking to maximize the utilization of expensive training causes firms to group tasks according to their training requirements. Intermediate forms, in between the production and training approaches, tend to be unstable, gravitating to one type or other over time (Marsden, 1999).

Seen in this context, the crisis of the employment relationship is above all one of employment rules associated with the 'production approach', and especially those involving task-oriented enforcement criteria. This was the classic solution of taylorism. But such is not the guiding principle of rules within the 'training approach' and especially those combining this method with the function-centred approach to enforcement.

The following sections of this chapter outline how some forms of transaction rules serve to regulate management authority, doing so using the training approach. The key to their potential contribution to modernizing employment lies in the way they combine a means of regulating management authority within open-ended contractual relationships, all the while providing a basis for movement between firms.

SOME LESSONS FROM NINETEENTH-CENTURY CRAFT LABOUR MARKETS

Organizing work according to skills has a long pedigree, and has been characteristic of many craft labour markets. The great ease with which it can be adapted to the more flexible organizational structures sought by many firms can be seen if we consider nineteenth-century British shipbuilding. For the present argument, this case is of greater interest than the more familiar German apprenticeship system which has coexisted with high levels of employment stability. In contrast, when British shipbuilding was at its peak, it was organized on what in modern parlance is called a 'project basis', with workers hired specifically for each new ship. This was possible because of a system of craft labour markets that regulated training, work organization and standards of job performance.

One reason why classical occupational labour markets were so successful was that they provided a stable framework within which shipbuilding firms could organize highly-skilled labour on a transient basis. Craft norms gave a clear guide to the division of labour and mechanisms for resolving demarcation disputes between different occupations and the unions representing them. The Webbs (1920) provide a fascinating account of how such norms functioned and were adapted to new materials and new technologies. In one example analysed by them, the arrival of new sanitation facilities on ships brought a conflict between plumbers and established shipbuilding trades. It was eventually resolved by distinguishing between different types of pipework – sanitation as compared with other types – and assigning each to its respective trade. Beyond assisting the organization of work, these norms also enabled workers to know at once what kind of work they were expected to do, and what performance standards were expected of them. In addition to regulating work organization and standards, these norms gave structure to the training process, which was important because the transient nature of employment meant that few firms were willing to invest heavily. Apprenticeship, funded by long years of work on low apprentice rates of pay, went a long way towards covering employers' costs (Elbaum, 1991).

Turning to more recent years, it is significant that those areas where self-employment has grown in Britain have tended to be either for casual labour or for work where professional or craft skills are involved. This has echoes of the craft system of nineteenth-century Britain. The difficulties of reviving apprenticeship in Britain, and of cultivating German-style apprenticeships outside Germany and some of its neighbours, are well-known. Rather than follow that line of inquiry, we will consider how far some of the recent flexible markets of the USA's 'New Paradigm' economy contain important elements of occupational markets. Bear in mind that these have to resolve the Coase–Simon problem in one way or another, which they appear to do, partly by means of structured social networks, and partly by the development of special types of reward systems. We will also consider the 'counter example' where franchising has been substituted for employee status, as in the case of milk delivery in Britain.

SOME LESSONS FROM MODERN OCCUPATIONAL COMMUNITIES

The labour markets of Hollywood and Silicon Valley merit close examination because of the way they seemingly handle the problem of highly skilled and creative work which requires cooperation, yet is also exposed to the risk of opportunism by the various parties. On the surface, work in such labour markets seems to be shorn of the protections of both enterprise and occupationally based employment systems. Is it not often suggested that knowledge moves too fast in high technology activities to be codified into institutionalized occupations or professions? And might not the same also apply to the media industries? Of course, there are many mundane and low-skilled jobs in both sectors (Jacoby, 1999), we will focus on the higher-level skills for the moment.

The return towards greater market mediation in highly-skilled employment has been analysed very perceptively by Tolbert (1996) and by Jones and Walsh (1997), taking respectively Silicon Valley and Hollywood as examples. For a viable employment relationship in such an environment, labour mobility requires the training approach to work organization and some form of occupational market, as well as a means of avoiding the restrictions of the task-centred regulations associated with the craft markets mentioned earlier. The fluidity of relations implied by the project basis of many ventures increases the scope for opportunism, and such pressures must be contained if cooperation is to be successful. Workers can lie about their past work experience and their abilities, and firms can lie about the work involved; and each side can seek to exploit the sunk costs of the other in the relationship once the project has started. In the absence of guarantees offered by German-style apprenticeship systems and occupational markets, what substitutes are there? In both Hollywood and Silicon Valley, the authors stress the role of the 'occupational' or the 'industrial' community based on personal networks that are structured by occupational or industrial affiliation.

Information networks are essential to the control of opportunism. It is sometimes urged that 'reputation' can be an effective enforcement mechanism for cooperation: workers and entrepreneurs who prove unreliable gain a reputation for such things, and it becomes harder for them to find future collaborators. Alternatively, a higher price has to be paid for the collaboration, a higher risk premium in effect. However reputation is an effective sanction only if other people get to learn about it. In a world of atomistic markets and imperfect information, reputation will not travel very far. In any case, if the atmosphere is such that an individual is able to damage competitors by casting aspersions upon their reliability, reputation ceases to convey much information. Thus one needs some way of verifying reports about the reputation of potential collaborators. Social networks can play a very important part in this because they provide information about informants, and about possible motives for saying what is said. Because of networks, people's reliability or unreliability become known to others. Granovetter (1974) has described networks as 'weak ties' which are most effective when linking university alumni or people within occupational groups. Arguably they provide an essential constraint against opportunism in the absence of more strongly institutionalized occupational norms.

The other element of great interest is that of income from transient employment. The classical employment relationship solved this problem for employees by tying stable rates of pay to jobs of indefinite duration. This mechanism breaks down, however, in the two cases considered here. Of especial interest is the role played by 'residual payments' in Hollywood, and by share options and various forms of employee or collaborator share ownership in Silicon Valley. Both provide a mechanism by which workers can claim a continuing income from creative work to which they have contributed, but with which they may no longer be associated.

The workings of a project-based form of organization and their substitution for large employing organizations are better documented in the case of Hollywood than in the case of Silicon Valley. Hollywood illustrates many of the problems facing such organization: creative work by artists is commercially very important, is very competitive and takes place within a fast-moving product market. Whatever role talent plays, much work performance is based upon solid training and experience. The project method of job organization superseded the old studios following their dissolution in the 1950s and 1960s; but a solution still had to be found to the problem of opportunism referred to earlier (Paul and Kleingartner, 1994). Creative work generates income that goes beyond simple box-office receipts, notably income accruing from residual obligations – analogous to copyright – deriving from further use made of work. One example is use of a film's name in advertisements for other products. Such income is often considerable. For Screen Actors Guild members in 1988, about 45 per cent of total income came from residuals, compared with 55 per cent from initial compensation. There is often a conflict of interest between creative artists anxious to avoid overexposure of work that would tire the public, and companies keen to earn additional residual income. Other potential conflicts arise between artists and producers, as the former are concerned about how their work is adapted, and how this might affect their reputation and, hence, future work prospects. Scope for opportunism is considerable on both sides.

Essential to the Hollywood case is the functional equivalent of an occupational market. This example is underpinned by a strong union organization which administers the all-important 'residual obligations' distributed on the basis of film credits. This puts the union at the centre of all information networks; it *has to know* current addresses in order to distribute residual incomes. Being independent of the producers, the union is better trusted by artists to keep track of payments, and also to follow new sources of residual income as they are identified by film companies. In the absence of formal qualifications, the information network is a very important vehicle for establishing reputation. Although individual actors may be seen on the screen, the separate contributions of many other creative workers are not so easily identified, and networks provide a channel along which information about good – and poor – quality work or performance is transmitted.

With regard to Silicon Valley, Saxenian (1996) and other writers stress the critical importance of networks among professionals working in small, hi-tech firms or on projects. But as Tolbert (1996) points out, such networks depend upon the existence of identifiable occupational groups, a point which echoes Granovetter's (1974) finding that the most effective personal networks for getting jobs depend upon contacts with people in the same occupation. Thus, as Tolbert argues, occupations play a special role in structuring the information flows within 'boundary-less' careers. Although knowledge in hi-tech activities often progresses much faster than the formal codification of skills associated with established professions, one should not overlook the often important role played by major research universities in underpinning labour market networks. Not only are they a source of graduates, but also consultancy activities by professors keep them in contact with the wider occupational community of the commercial world (Zucker, 1991). The reputation of universities also provides a form of quality control, at least in terms of workers' capabilities, if not their output. Thus systems of boundary-less careers contain mechanisms analogous to those of occupational markets in many respects. Although less codified than those of blue-collar crafts and established white-collar professions, they are dependent upon institutional structures to cope with the many problems of opportunism that would otherwise beset them.

Finally, in all cases, there have developed innovative alternatives to the steady flows of wages and salaries associated with indefinite duration employment. With project-based employment, workers do not get continuous employment, and there is a problem of ensuring that they receive a continuous flow of income. In the case of Hollywood, the flow of income from residuals provides a measure of income continuity between 'projects'. In the case of Silicon Valley, it seems natural to conclude that share options and other forms of employee share ownership play a special role. Far from being clever tax dodges, as they have often been interpreted in Europe, they provide one solution to motivating employees or partners, and thereby ensuring that they give of their best in a relationship they know will be transient. Thus, if employees contribute to a really good product, the chances are that this will be reflected in their share of the firm's value and may provide a source of future income for them. Thinking back to the previous example, it is notable that, in Britain at least, the craft unions were pioneers in early forms of 'mutual insurance', setting up funds to tide their members over periods of temporary unemployment.

FRANCHISING: AN EXAMPLE OF THE BREAKDOWN OF AN EMPLOYMENT RELATIONSHIP

Not all types of market-mediated employment have been as successful in their operation. In particular, where firms have tried to use market-mediated forms as a substitute for an employment relationship that was slipping out of their control, problems of opportunism remained unresolved and may even have been aggravated. A common form of self-employment which has been expanding in the service sector in Britain, and which has often followed this logic, has been that of 'franchising' (Felstead, 1991). Franchisees usually appropriate the profits of their trade, but only after paying a fee or a royalty to the franchiser. Although they operate without close supervision, they are required to follow certain procedures in order to ensure quality.

One particularly revealing study has been the introduction of franchise contracts for doorstep milk delivery staff in Britain who previously had worked under employment contracts (O'Connell, 1994). Milk delivery had always fitted uneasily with the employment relation owing to the high degree of trust needed and the rather limited skills involved. Trust is needed because of the amounts of money handled, the importance of dairies' reputations with customers on such matters as reliability of delivery and accurate billing, and the increasing need to make delivery more profitable by selling other goods as well. Absenteeism was also a problem, owing to unsocial hours and unpleasant weather. Simple incentive contracts had proved difficult to operate effectively. Rewarding the number of milk sales in a round implied faster deliveries, whereas collecting money and selling additional services was time-consuming. Because many milk deliverers held second jobs later in the day, they often wanted to finish quickly, and the income from the second job outweighed any bonus the dairy could offer for developing customer bases and building customer relations. With increased competition from supermarket sales, the established dairies found it increasingly difficult to manage the employment relationship profitably.

Introducing a self-employed franchise system enabled the dairies to shift the monitoring costs onto the franchisee, especially with regard to sales, billing and work hours. Under the new system, franchisees bore the cost of book-keeping and debt collection from customers, and they lost income during absences from work. In return, the franchisee delivered milk and other goods for a fixed margin on sales. According to O'Connell's study, several problems remained. The dairies were unable to prevent the franchisees from obtaining their own goods for sale from the local cash-and-carry instead of selling those provided by the dairy. They also found it difficult to get franchisees to expand customer bases. Because the franchisees carried the financial risk, they were often reluctant to take on potentially uncreditworthy customers. The dairies still faced a problem if their franchisees allowed customer debt to build up too much. Overall, those dairies which shifted to self-employed franchising did so because the employment relationship was not working as intended, and in a low-trust environment mechanisms of bureaucratic control were expensive to operate and not very effective. But, in changing, they also discovered – or rediscovered – similar problems of opportunism within the franchise relationship as those that had existed within the outworking system (for the latter, see Craig *et al.*, 1980; 1982).

Unlike the Hollywood and Silicon Valley examples, the franchising case lacked a developed occupational community capable of enforcing employment norms and obligations in a reciprocal manner. In many respects, dairies were seeking to reconstruct bureaucratic employment controls without the benefits of an open-ended, long-term employment relationship. Firms were relying upon manipulating financial incentives in order to steer behaviour in contexts in which those incentives were weighed against the strength of alternative rewards for outside work.

PROBLEMS OF OPPORTUNISM IN 'TRANSITIONAL MARKETS'

In recent years, there has been a growing development of what Schmid (1998) has called 'transitional' labour markets, especially in areas between full-time education and employment, and between unemployment and employment. As Europe's unemployment problems and government employment promotion initiatives have grown in recent decades, so has the share of the labour force working under special state-sponsored arrangements. These have been criticized by Supiot on the grounds that they compromise the clarity of employment norms, thus making them harder to enforce, yet without doing much to boost employment. One of the problems such special schemes often encounter is that of opposition from incumbent workers who fear that state-offered subsidies mostly encourage employers to substitute jobs 'on schemes' for regular jobs.

There are some interesting case studies of transitional markets which have evolved out of the interaction between firms and workers. It is worth considering how these have dealt with the problems of potential substitution. One of the most notable cases has involved apprenticeship training for blue-collar skills in Germany, the UK, the USA and other countries. A common fear of skilled workers is that, as apprenticeship periods come to an end, young trainees are able to undertake numerous tasks of a skilled kind. Indeed, in earlier centuries, when apprenticeships often lasted for seven years, trainees during their final years were paying back the master craftsmen for the cost of training. Elbaum (1991) provides an interesting historical study of how the inability of employers to enforce long apprenticeships in the USA led to the eventual demise of the system.

A common solution, in the absence of government action, has been to pay apprentices a special trainee wage set below the value of their output. In Becker's theory, this would be such as to compensate the employer for the full costs of training. In fact most empirical work indicates that employers commonly bear a substantial share of the net costs. Nevertheless, the wage discount for apprentices plays an important part in alleviating employers' costs, and so affects their incentives to provide training places.

Ryan has argued that this wage discount is problematic because if it is very low employers have an incentive to substitute apprentices for fully-trained skilled workers. He shows that this was a common complaint among British skilled engineering unions during the depression years of the 1930s, and argues that it was one of the reasons why they sought to raise apprentice pay during the postwar era (Ryan, 1986). The problem was that they could control substitution only by raising the relative price of apprentice labour. Ryan (1995) shows that similar fears of substitution by cheap labour were encountered on the British government's Youth Training Scheme which subsidized on-the-job training places during the 1980s. In contrast, during the postwar years, German unions and works councils have been much better at controlling substitution by regulating the quality of apprenticeship and by insisting that it is first and foremost a training position, and not a job with training thrown in. Thus, when Jones (1985) compared apprentice training costs in Britain and Germany in the 1970s, he found that, for a roughly equivalent price, pay represented about two-thirds of the total in Britain, with about one-third going on training. The reverse ratios applied in Germany.

What has distinguished the apprenticeship training system in Germany from that in Britain and in many other non-German-speaking countries, has been the level of workplace regulation. This has helped contain substitution pressures, and so made the low rates of pay for German apprentices far more acceptable to skilled adults than is the case in other countries. Indeed, in many countries where the main route by which young people enter the workforce is through firms' internal labour markets (as for example in France), there is practically no youth trainee discount outside of special government programmes, and the minimum wage takes effect at age 18, with a uniform rate for all. Marsden and Ryan (1991) argue that this is because trainee status is not at all clear within firms' internal labour markets, and so it is much harder for adult workers to control; for this reason a youth trainee discount is seen as a threat.

There are some other factors which also help to make the system of trainee discounts attractive in Germany. Because apprenticeship qualifications are well-established and respected by employers, young people are more confident in the investments they make. Also, because of a strong pattern of institutional regulation, employers are retained within the system and discouraged from opting out despite the net costs they have to bear.

EXPANDING THE MIDDLE GROUND OF MARKET-MEDIATED EMPLOYMENT

All of these examples underline the importance of institutional regulation of flexible employment systems if they are to prosper. Employees' fears of employer opportunism are real, and are likely to stand in the way of adapting to more fluid business conditions. It is perhaps ironic that the type of employment rule best able to function under conditions of low trust is that of the 'work post', which combines task-centred and production approaches. Dividing work obligations between a system of work posts is relatively easy to enforce, and no doubt was part of the reason for its working so well in Henry Ford's early twentieth-century factories. However, the flexibility and learning opportunities for workers provided by a functional approach to work organization, and the need for workers to be able to ply their skills more easily across firms, represent a serious challenge to that model. The difficulty many firms have experienced in trying to break away from taylorism is that the work post system offers protection for workers. Fearful of arbitrary action and favouritism by management, employees have come to see the work post as a limit to what management can demand of them. Because work posts are usually integrated into job classification systems, workers can also compare their own jobs to those of others in the same workplace in order to judge what constitutes fair performance standards. A telling comment by British workers placed under new functional systems of work organization was that they wanted clearly defined responsibilities in order to determine the circumstances in which management could punish them (Clark, 1993). Dugué (1994) and Baraldi *et al.* (1995) have observed similar reactions among French workers and their representatives. Workers' fears of employer opportunism may not lead to submissiveness then; sometimes they can lead to a defensive attitude and a resistance to change that blocks attempts by firms to respond to shifting markets.

Absent from much of the literature on the flexible firm is the employees' worry about employer opportunism and its likely consequences. If workers are to sign up for 'project-based' or other new ways of organizing jobs, then one needs to find substitutes for the protections contained within the established employment relationship. Otherwise they will have little appeal, and will be adopted only where employers have sufficient market power to impose them. In the absence of such power, employees will cling to protective, but also to rigid, forms of employment.

The solutions developed in Hollywood and Silicon Valley may not be universally applicable, but their interest lies in the fact that they have emerged out of the decentralized decisions taken by employers and workers, and both parties have found a way of developing effective sanctions against those who behave opportunistically. In fact the underlying difference between these labour markets and the highly institutionalized occupational markets in Germany may be less than at first appears. One important feature of the German apprenticeship system has been the way in which the reputation firms gain for training helps maintain both the quantity and quality of training places. The peer pressures of chambers of industry and commerce may well function because they provide strong social networks amongst employers. Along these networks reputation for good or bad behaviour passes, sources of information being known and trusted all round. The role of social networks in labour markets as mechanisms of quality control is not a new discovery, of course. The famous studies of recruitment practices and labour market structures of the 1950s and 1960s all stressed the heavy use made of them by employers (see, for example, Rees, 1966).

These solutions also share a key feature with more institutionalized occupational labour markets. In effect they make workers, rather than jobs, the 'bearers' of skills. How far the Silicon Valley experience can develop without further institutionalization is unclear. Its rapid growth has probably meant that many workers there have not had to worry too much about risk sharing and about codifying skills in order to widen their currency. Rapid growth and good incomes may also cause people to attach less importance than is wise to labour law and social insurance, simply because of the human tendency to believe that the 'good times' will go on forever.

Thus expanding the middle ground – those areas of economic activity which fall somewhere between traditional employment and self-employment – to a larger group of workers no doubt means also adapting and broadening the protections of labour law and social insurance, as indeed the Supiot Report advocates. Nevertheless we should not lose sight of the way in which these new forms of occupational markets tackle the moral hazard problems that can undermine cooperation. The potential gains are illustrated by those associated with the invention of the open-ended employment relationship which helped release the great industrial potential of the past century. They did so by facilitating a pattern of cooperation between workers and firms that had previously been problematical.

NOTES

1. These figures were extracted from the university performance league tables for 2000, published by *The Times Higher Education Supplement* in its issue of 14 April 2000. The median percentage of non-permanent staff across Britain's 97 universities was about 40 per cent. Overall, there is a correlation of 0.77 between university research ratings in the national Research Assessment Exercise and the percentage of non-permanent staff. The RAE is one measure of success in the competition for research funds, and it also serves as a quality index in the search to attract overseas students.
2. The treatment of part-time workers muddies the debate. Often they are treated as 'atypical', and, because part-time employment has grown in several countries, it has appeared that atypical employment has expanded. However, evidence from both the USA and Britain highlights the fact that the majority of part-time workers are engaged in employment of indefinite duration. Most part-timers in Britain are married women struggling to balance domestic and market work.
3. 'La législation est comme la monnaie. L'Etat ne peut la mettre efficacement en circulation si la société la refuse' (Sellier, 1961, p.15).
4. The estimates of the union/non-union wage differential are mostly averages, and there is a dispersion around these. This indicates that unions can do more to help weaker groups in the labour market; that is, those with less than average individual bargaining power. No doubt too they help to even out fluctuations in workers' individual bargaining power over the business cycle and over their working lives. See Blanchflower and Freeman (1992).
5. There were of course other moral hazard problems, notably the tendency to flog the entrepreneur's capital equipment, to skimp on quality and frequent disputes over the use of raw materials. On the employers' side there was a frequent reluctance to provide training (Slichter, *et al.* 1919).
6. See Crozier (1963) and Slichter *et al.* (1960).
7. Although the argument is presented here in terms of limitations on the task content of jobs, in *A Theory of Employment Systems* (1999) I endeavour to show the same also applies to performance standards.

BIBLIOGRAPHY

Arthur, M.B. and Rousseau, D.M. (eds) (1996), *The Boundaryless Career: A New Principle for a New Organizational Era*, New York: Oxford University Press.
Atkinson, J. and Meager, N. (1986), *Changing Working Practices: How Companies*

Achieve Flexibility to Meet New Needs, London: National Economic Development Office.

Baraldi, L., Dumasy, J-P. and Troussier, J-F. (1995), 'Accords Salariaux Innovants et Théorie du Salaire', Économie Appliquée, **48**(4), 105–37.

Becker, G.S. (1975), *Human Capital: A Theoretical and Empirical Analysis*, Chicago: University of Chicago Press.

Blanchflower, D. and Freeman, R. (1992), 'Unionism in the US and Other Advanced OECD Countries', in M. Bognanno and M. Kleiner (eds), *Labor Market Institutions and the Future Role of Unions*, Oxford: Blackwell.

Clark, J. (1993), 'Full-Flexibility and Self-Supervision in an Automated Factory', in J. Clark (ed.), *Human Resource Management and Technical Change*, London: Sage.

Clegg, H. (1972), *The System of Industrial Relations in Great Britain*, Oxford: Blackwell.

Coase, R.H. (1937), 'The Nature of the Firm', *Economica*, 386–405.

Craig, C., Rubery J., Tarling, R. and Wilkinson, F. (1980), 'Abolition and After: The Cutlery Wages Council', Department of Employment Research Paper no. 18, Department of Employment, London.

— — (1982), *Labour Market Structure, Industrial Organization and Low Pay*, Cambridge: Cambridge University Press.

Crozier, M. (1963), *Le phénomène bureaucratique*, Paris: Seuil.

Deakin, S. (1998), 'The Evolution of the Contract of Employment, 1900–1950: The Influence of the Welfare State', in N. Whiteside and R. Salais (eds), *Governance, Industry and Labour Markets in Britain and France: The Modernising State in the Mid-Twentieth Century*, London: Routledge.

Doeringer, P.B. and Piore, M.J. (1971), *Internal Labor Markets and Manpower Analysis*, Lexington, MA: DC Heath.

Dugué, E. (1994), 'La gestion des compétences: les savoirs dévalués, le pouvoir occulté', *Sociologie du Travail*, **3**, 273–292.

Elbaum, B. (1991), 'The Persistence of Apprenticeship in Britain, and its Decline in the United States', in H. Gospel (ed.), *Industrial Training and Technological Innovation: A Comparative and Historical Study*, London: Routledge.

Felstead, A. (1991), 'The Social Organization of the Franchise: A Case Study of "Controlled Self-Employment",' *Work, Employment and Society*, **5**(1), 37–57.

Ferner, A. (1997), 'Country of Origin Effects and HRM in Multinational Companies', *Human Resource Management Journal*, **7**(1), 19–37.

Granovetter, M. (1974), *Getting a Job: A Study of Contacts and Careers*, Cambridge, MA: Harvard University Press.

Jacoby, S. (1999), 'Are Career Jobs Headed for Extinction?', *California Management Review*, **42**(1), 123–45.

Jones, C, and Walsh, K. (1997), 'Boundaryless Careers in the US Film Industry', *Industrielle Beziehungen*, **4**(1), 58–73.

Jones, I. (1985), 'The Costs of Apprenticeship Training in British Manufacturing Establishments: The Results of a Pilot Survey and Comparisons with Germany', Discussion Paper 58, National Institute for Economic and Social Research, London.

Katz H, and Darbishire, O. (2000), *Converging Divergencies: Worldwide Changes in Employment Systems*, Ithaca: ILR Press/Cornell University Press.

Koike, K. (1997), 'Human Resource Development', Japanese Economy and Labor Series, no. 2, Japan Institute of Labour, Tokyo.

Marsden, D.W. (1999), *A Theory of Employment Systems: Micro-Foundations of Societal Diversity*, Oxford: Oxford University Press.

Marsden, D.W. and Ryan, P. (1991), 'The Structuring of Youth Pay and Employment in Six European Economies', in P. Ryan., P. Garonna and R. Edwards (eds), *The Problem of Youth: The Regulation of Youth Employment and Training in Advanced Economies*, London: Macmillan.

Mottez, B. (1966), 'Systèmes de salaire et politiques patronales: essai sur l'évolution des pratiques et des idéologies patronales', Centre National de la Recherche Scientifique, Paris.

O'Connell, J. (1994), 'What Do Franchisors Do? Control and Commercialization in Milk Distribution', *Work, Employment and Society*, **8**(1), 23–44

OECD (1992), 'Employment Outlook, 1992', OECD, Paris.

— — (1993), 'Employment Outlook, 1993', OECD, Paris.

— — (1997), 'Employment Outlook, 1997', OECD, Paris.

Paul, A. and Kleingartner, A. (1994), 'Flexible Production and the Transformation of Industrial Relations in the Motion Picture and Television Industry', *Industrial and Labor Relations Review*, **47**(4), 663–78.

Peters, T.J. and Waterman, R.H. (1982), *In Search of Excellence: Lessons from America's Best-Run Companies*, New York: Harper and Row.

Pollert, A. (ed.) (1991), *Farewell to Flexibility*, Oxford: Blackwell.

Rees, A. (1966), 'Information Networks in Labor Markets', *American Economic Review*, 559–66.

Roethlisberger, F.J. and Dickson, W.J. (1939), *Management and the Worker*, Cambridge, MA: Harvard University Press.

Ryan, P. (1986), 'Apprentices, Employment and Industrial Disputes in Engineering in the 1920s', paper presented to The Workshop on Child Labour and Apprenticeship, University of Essex, May.

— — (1995), 'Trade Union Policies Towards the Youth Training Scheme: Patterns and Causes', *British Journal of Industrial Relations*, **33**(1), 1–34.

Saxenian, A. (1996), 'Beyond Boundaries: Open Labor Markets and Learning in Silicon Valley', in M. Arthur and D. Rousseau (eds), *The Boundaryless Career: A New Employment Principle for a New Organizational Era*, Oxford and New York: Oxford University Press, 23–39.

Schmid, G. (1998), 'Transitional Labour Markets: A New European Employment Strategy', WZB Discussion Paper 98–206, Wissenschaftszentrum Berlin für Sozialforschung, Berlin.

Sellier, F. (1961), *Stratégie de la lutte sociale: France 1936–1960*, Paris: Les Editions Ouvrières.

Sengenberger, W. (1987), *Struktur und Funktionsweise von Arbeitsmärkten: die Bundesrepublik Deutschland im Internationalen Vergleich*, Frankfurt: Campus Verlag.

Simon, H.A. (1951), 'A Formal Theory of the Employment Relationship', *Econometrica*, **19**(3), 293–305.

Slichter, S., Healy, J. and Livernash E. (1960), *The Impact of Collective Bargaining on Management*, Washington, DC: Brookings Institution.

Supiot, A. (1994), *Critique du droit du travail*, Paris: Presses Universitaires de France.

— — (chairperson) (1999), *Au-delà de l'emploi: rapport pour la Commission européenne*, Paris: Flammarion.

Teulings, C. and Hartog, J. (1998), *Corporatism or Competition? Labour Contracts, Institutions and Wage Structures in International Comparison*, Cambridge: Cambridge University Press.

Tolbert, P. (1996), 'Occupations, Organizations, and Boundaryless Careers', in M.

Arthur and D. Rousseau (eds), *The Boundaryless Career: A New Employment Principle for a New Organizational Era*, Oxford and New York: Oxford University Press, 331–49.

Webb, S. and Webb, B. (1920), *Industrial Democracy*, London: Longman.

Weber, M. (1909), *Zur Psychophysik der industriellen Arbeit*, Max Weber Gesamtausgabe, vol. 11, *Schriften und Reden 1908–1912*, reprinted Tübingen: J.C.B. Mohr (Paul Siebeck), 1995.

Williamson, O.E. (1975), *Markets and Hierarchies: Analysis and Antitrust Implications*, New York: Free Press.

Willman, P. (1986), *Technological Change, Collective Bargaining and Industrial Efficiency*, Oxford: Oxford University Press.

Yamanouchu, T. and Okazaki-Ward, L. (1997), 'Key Issues in HRM in Japan', in S. Tyson (ed.), *The Practice of Human Resource Strategy*, London: Pitman.

Zucker, L. (1991), 'Markets for Bureaucratic Authority and Control: Information Quality in Professions and Services', *Research in the Sociology of Organizations*, **8**, 157–90.

3. Activating labour market policy: 'flexicurity' through transitional labour markets

Günther Schmid

INTRODUCTION

In continental Europe, 'activating labour-market policy' (ALMP) has become a fashionable slogan to counter the neoliberal 'workfare' philosophy. This approach, however, has produced little more than wishful thinking. It only vaguely suggests a 'third way' between 'left' and 'right', between 'modernists' and 'traditionalists', or between an unfettered new capitalist economy and an old-fashioned (Bismarckian) capitalist welfare state as represented by hard-headed trade unionists, conservative Social Democrats and centrist Christian Democrats. Even the catchier term, 'flexicurity', invented by the pragmatic Dutch, remains unclear. The purpose of this chapter is to design a possible institutional framework which gives both 'activating' and 'flexicurity' a clearer meaning.

Our main arguments are as follows. First, many of the results of evaluation studies of ALMP are disappointing because they have not examined implementation failures. Systematic consideration of such failures gives us a better understanding of the meaning of 'activating', thereby allowing us to formulate suggestions for improving conventional labour market policy. Second, the lack of directed labour market policy is a further reason for the poor outcomes of many labour market programmes. Analysing such things will suggest ways of directing labour market policy towards transitional labour markets. If we accept the fact that people may wish to move during the course of the life cycle between various kinds of productive activities of which gainful work in the labour market is only one possibility, then labour market policy in Europe has to address a broader spectrum of possible activities. For their part, firms also have an interest in promoting greater flexibility on the part of the workforce. In addition to 'making work pay', a modern labour market policy could include the objective of 'making transitions pay'. It would give 'activation' an operational meaning, and it would provide a clear basis for combining 'flexibility' with 'security'.

The chapter begins with some facts about what we know from evaluations of labour market policies. It goes on to look at their impact on full employment and selected target groups, and especially to consider their effectiveness in containing long-term unemployment. Since little emphasis has been placed on the reasons why the impact of so-called ALMP has often been disappointing, the third section considers systematically the critical points at which policies can fail and suggest ways of overcoming these problems. The next two sections demonstrate the potential of 'transitional labour markets' as a regulative idea for 'activating' labour market policy in two critical situations of transitions: specifically the transitions between education, training and work, and, in the sixth section, between various working time regimes or employment statuses. The chapter concludes by seeking to revitalize the idea of a European Social Model.

1 LABOUR MARKET POLICIES

In 1997, the typical OECD country spent about 2.3 per cent of its GDP on active and passive labour market policy. However, there is a wide variation between countries, ranging from a low of less than 0.5 per cent GDP in the USA to a high of almost 6 per cent in Denmark. If we consider only active measures of labour market policies, meaning those expenditures which are directly devoted to bringing people back to work or to maintaining their employability, the average public expenditure in the OECD is 0.8 per cent and ranges from a low of 0.1 per cent of GDP in Japan to a high of 2 per cent in Sweden. The distribution is skewed, with a few high spenders, especially the Scandinavian countries, and many low spenders (Figure 3.1).

At this high level of abstraction, there are three interesting points to note. First, there is a high correlation ($r = 0.82$) between active and passive expenditures on labour market policy. Second, high-spending countries (such as Denmark and the Netherlands), as well as low-spending countries (such as the UK and the USA), belong to the small group of countries that succeeded in reducing unemployment during the 1990s to a level which mainstream economists like to call the 'natural rate of unemployment'. The third point is often neglected in this context. The most successful countries did not, at least in recent years, reduce labour supply through early retirement or through the containment of women's labour force participation. Indeed the opposite is true. There is a high negative correlation ($r = -0.65$) between labour force participation and unemployment among OECD countries, and the dynamics of change between these two performance indicators appear to validate this negative relationship.[1] In theory, this fact can only be explained by two alternative arguments: either wage dispersion increased or there was some effective work

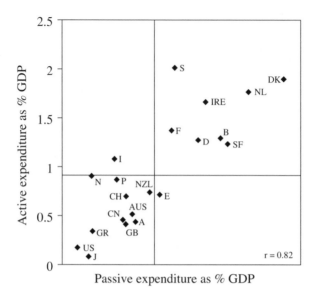

Active expenditure as % GDP

Passive expenditure as % GDP

Notes: Key for Fig 3.1
S = Sweden; IRE = Ireland; DK = Denmark; NL = Netherlands; F = France; D = Germany; B = Belgium; SF = Finland; I = Italy; N = Norway; P = Portugal; NZL = New Zealand; CH = Switzerland; E = Spain; AUS = Australia; CN = Canada; AUT = Austria; GB = Great Britain; GR = Greece; US = USA; J = Japan.

Figure 3.1   Expenditure on active and passive labour-market policy in OECD countries, 1997/8

sharing combined with some income sharing or income redistribution (Figure 3.2).

This leads us to the first hypothesis. Countries which succeeded in reducing unemployment without increasing wage dispersion (the second alternative) could only do so through an ALMP which enhanced labour force participation in terms of skills and competencies (employability), and/or working time flexibility, and/or spatial mobility. The low-spending Anglo-American countries have opted for the first alternative, whereas the high-spending countries, such as Denmark and the Netherlands, have implemented the second.[2]

Apart from the higher social costs with which low-spending countries are probably burdened (such as higher crime rates), and notwithstanding the excellent work done by the OECD in making figures comparable, there remain good reasons for questioning the differentiation of 'high' and 'low' spenders. Especially in the 'welfare-to-work' countries such as the USA and the UK,

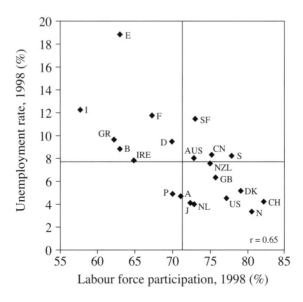

Notes: Key for Fig 3.2
S = Sweden; IRE = Ireland; DK = Denmark; NL = Netherlands; F = France; D = Germany; B = Belgium; SF = Finland; I = Italy; N = Norway; P = Portugal; NZL = New Zealand; CH = Switzerland; E = Spain; AUS = Australia; CN = Canada; AUT = Austria; GB = Great Britain; GR = Greece; US = USA; J = Japan.

Figure 3.2 Labour force participation rates and unemployment in OECD countries, 1997

expenditure on in-work benefits (so far not included in the figures presented by the OECD) could be added to either the 'active' or the 'passive' part of labour market policy. Additionally, Earned Income Tax Credits in the USA, amounting to 30.5 billion dollars for fiscal year 1999, make up about 0.3 per cent of GDP. In the UK, another 'low-spending' country, the Working Families Tax Credit represents an expenditure of 6 billion GBP as part of the 2001/2002 budget, compared to only 900 million GBP for the New Deal, the largest labour market programme. This led the British economist Peter Robinson to make the following observation: 'A strategy appears to be emerging . . . of trying to use job-search-focused programmes to move people into regular employment in a relatively cost-effective way and then to subsidize households, especially [those] with children, so that their net incomes can come above the poverty line. Most of this expenditure could be classified as good, old-fashioned fiscal redistribution to the poor' (Robinson, 2000, p.25).

2   CONSEQUENCES OF LABOUR MARKET POLICIES

Now what do we know, specifically, about the effectiveness of labour market policy? What worked, especially with the so-called 'active' measures? The evidence from *macro studies* is scarce, and the results cannot yet be considered conclusive as these studies lack adequate data and proper methodology. The problem of endogeneity, which means the policy reaction to unemployment, has not yet been convincingly solved. Altogether, a picture emerges.[3]

First, ALMP tends to support wage moderation. The wage pressure from labour market measures, which provides an alternative to accepting employment below the reservation wage, is counterbalanced by maintaining and increasing the employable labour supply through training or retraining programmes. A larger employable labour supply increases competition, reduces the bargaining power of insiders and possibly reduces mismatches.[4]

Second, with respect to the *matching process* as a dependent variable, recent macro studies are more ambiguous. They usually come up with no significant effects, or small positive effects relating to men. With regard to women, several studies even found a negative effect. However the plausible explanation for this result is the impact of labour market policy on higher participation rates for women which, from an equal opportunity point of view, can be considered a desirable effect.

Third, with respect to the objective of containing long-term unemployment, most studies have positive things to say about ALMP. It must be acknowledged, however, that a few surveys come to the opposite conclusion. Of the different types of labour market measures, the most promising instruments are training policies, especially short duration ones which are specifically aimed and market-oriented. There is widespread consensus that wage subsidies, and especially temporary public jobs, often produce high displacement, substitution, deadweight or 'revolving door' effects. However some studies show positive outcomes if these measures are specifically aimed at the very long-term unemployed. It should be mentioned that, in really depressed regions, such as those found in East Germany during the recent transformation process, the danger of displacement and substitution of such measures was relatively small, and unmeasured social effects possibly high. Finally it should be noted that, despite the excellent reputation of job search assistance, almost nothing is known about its effectiveness at the macro level. The few studies available, at least those pertaining to Europe, are not encouraging (de Koning and Mosley, 2001).

If we consider the evidence provided by micro studies, we can rely on several summary reports, especially those from the OECD (Fay, 1996; Martin, 2000).[5] John Martin, for instance, comes to the following conclusion: 'It seems that a mix of carrot-and-stick elements . . . combining use of active labour-market policies and benefits sanctions in case of non-compliance, may well contribute to better labour-market outcomes for benefit recipients' (Martin, 2000, p.104). With respect to the lessons to be drawn from empirical evidence, most summaries come up with a clear hierarchy of measures: first, job search assistance through placement services and intensive counselling; second, training or retraining; third, selective wage-cost subsidies or in-work benefits; and fourth, temporary public employment.

However it is probably not unfair to say that such lessons are not far from wishful thinking as they rely on ambivalent and often contradictory evidence. Only for job search assistance is the microeconomic evidence little contested, although only a few sophisticated evaluation studies actually exist. The most impressive results were found for the Work Trials initiative in Britain. This encouraged employers to hire people who had been out of work for more than six months on a trial period of up to three weeks, with participants continuing to receive benefits in addition to work expenses. An evaluation found that typical participants in the scheme increased their employment rate by 34–40 percentage points after six months (White *et al.*, 1997).

Because OECD summaries emphasize the USA and Canada, I add briefly some additional evidence from recent studies in Sweden, Denmark, the Netherlands and Germany.[6] Studies on temporary public job creation usually find negative effects in the short term, but positive effects in the long term. For Germany, especially East Germany, public job creation seems to be more effective than its rather negative reputation suggests. A recent development consists of matching this policy instrument with training and education, while at the same time involving local private enterprises in the implementation of projects by means of competitive bidding.

In the case of further training and retraining, the relationship between evidence and reputation is reversed. Many studies find either small positive effects or no effect at all; and some studies even find negative effects, especially during the first transitional period in East Germany. All in all, it is fair to say that the evidence from empirical studies is disappointing compared to the generally positive reputation that training and education enjoy. The few serious evaluation studies that are available in Denmark and Sweden report that job rotation and selective recruitment subsidies bring the best results. There are good reasons, however, for contesting the reported success of job rotation. It consists of off-the-job training for the employed and, if required, on-the-job training for the unemployed who take the place of the employed during their training period. As such, it does little to help the long-term unemployed, nor is it well-suited to the employment problems of small and medium-sized firms. It is expensive to implement and, as shown by a simulation study, only becomes cost-effective when the resulting productivity and earning effects are high and sustainable for some years.

Finally evaluation studies of two new ALMP measures provide encouraging results. First, a careful, quasi-experimental study in Germany assessed the impact of placing the long-term unemployed and the very hard-to-place (for example, old or disabled people as well as former addicts) through commercial or semi-public temporary work agencies instead of the more traditional public employment service. It found that the reintegration success for the experimental group was some 13 percentage points higher (27.4 per cent) than that of the matched control group (14.2 per cent). Second, several European countries offer unemployed people the opportunity to exchange benefit entitlements for subsidies which enable them to become self-employed. Evaluations usually report quite positive results, especially for business projects that are carefully pre-assessed and then implemented.

3 WHAT FAILS TO WORK AND WHY?

What shall we conclude from the present evidence? Before we draw lessons, we should reflect more systematically upon the fact that many evaluation studies are pessimistic about the potential of ALMP. Why should this be so? We will not go into the theoretical debate about the potential role of ALMP. This debate is over, and the general message from it is clear: its part in containing unemployment can only be modest, whether considered from a neoclassical, institutional or Keynesian point of view (albeit, of course, with different respective emphases). However, since the negative evaluations do not correlate with the variation in expenditure levels across countries, there must be something else. This 'something else' is a mixture of implementation failure and failure of conventional econometric evaluations to deal with contextual aspects and to differentiate programme effects among specified target groups. Recent evaluations clearly indicate how important it is to separate the phases before, during and after programme participation (Figure 3.3).

First, the announcement effect associated with such programmes has been neglected. People who expect to use such programmes suspend or reduce their own job searches. This produces the so-called 'Ashenfelter-dip', which refers to a substantial reduction of the probability of re-employment[7] compared to a control group. Evaluation research consistently shows that this negative announcement effect is highest among the most qualified people and lowest amongst the difficult-to-place people.

Second, any job search activity is often further reduced during programme participation in order to enable people to receive a certificate at the end of it. Very often, programme conditions are such that participants who withdraw are punished by cancellation or reduction of benefits, and implementation agencies suffer through the withdrawal of subsidies or loss of the sunk costs of investment.

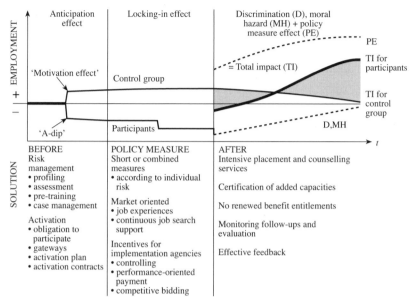

Figure 3.3   Stylized implementation failures in active labour market policy and solutions

Third, we have the well-known stigmatization effect after programme participation as well as various kinds of 'moral hazard' in the form of exaggerated expectations concerning job content, excessively high reservation wages or even renewed entitlements to unemployment benefits. In Germany, some community programmes catering to the long-term unemployed on the social assistance payroll even have the explicit objective of re-establishing unemployment benefit entitlements, thus shifting the burden of the fiscal costs of unemployment from the communities back onto the unemployment insurance system.

From these possible failures one can clearly deduce some important lessons for enhancing the effectiveness and efficiency of ALMP. First, announcement effects in the pre-participation phase can be avoided, or at least contained, by an early identification of the individual risk of long-term unemployment, for example through formal 'profiling' procedures (as in the USA) or through establishing easy-to-handle risk categories (as in the Netherlands). Other ways include systematic assessment of individual capacities, abilities and motivations; case management reviews; compulsory programme participation after six to nine months of being 'on benefit' (as in Switzerland, Denmark and the UK); individual 'activation contracts' or 'activation plans' (as in Denmark and the UK); and finally – albeit little used – competitive bidding for subsidies on publicly financed programmes by private or semi-private enterprises and implementation agencies. (This was the case in a specific wage subsidy programme in East Germany).

Second, failure of active job searching during programme participation can be avoided, or at least reduced, through individual case management. Evaluation suggests that, for the better qualified, short training programmes are in order, and for hard-to-place people long-term programmes are best, combined with other policies tailored to individual circumstances. Other measures include work experiences in firms, continuing placement activities during programme participation, incentives for implementation agencies (such as performance-related subsidies), and transparent monitoring procedures for both public and private placement agencies. Implementation studies (de Koning and Mosley, 2001) as well as actual trends (see de Koning, 2000) indicate that contracting out employment services leads to higher efficiency and larger benefit reductions. These results are obtained only when there is public cofinancing, regulation of quality standards and some performance-related allocation of public funds. It seems also that the supply-oriented approach of employment services, which takes target groups as the starting point for placement, leads to better results than the demand-oriented method, which starts with the inflows of vacancies from employers (de Koning, 2000).

Third, implementation failure after programme participation can be solved, or at least contained, through intensive placement activities, good follow-up advice and monitoring, rigorous follow-up studies and evaluation, and bench learning through the diffusion of best practices. Again contracting out placement services and/or cooperation by public employment services and professional agencies (for example, temporary work agencies or specialized training agencies) promise effective implementation. However privatization is far from being the panacea for solving all difficulties associated with implementation. Numerous studies on its effectiveness have shown that the costs of regulation and associated control following privatization may exceed the gains from competition or specialization, especially in services or products related to infrastructure (Hodge, 2000).

Apart from organizational improvements, attention has to be paid to incentives after programme participation. For instance, the re-establishment of unemployment benefits should be avoided, especially in relation to training measures and temporary public job creation. One way to control the entitlement effect is by making the duration of subsidies to the private sector shorter than the minimum contribution period required for benefit entitlement. This would avoid the so-called 'carousel effect' whereby a considerable number of the long-term unemployed move between spells of benefit receipt and programme participation. The latter recommendation (Martin 2000, p.106), however, may stand in conflict with the need to provide long-term subsidies for disabled or older people with impaired abilities. These people require long-term support to remain in the labour market. For such particular target groups, in-work benefits seem to be a better solution than wage-cost subsidies.

These are the important lessons to be learned from considering sophisticated, albeit rather conventional, evaluation approaches. However, significant problems remain. Conventional programmes and respective evaluations do not yet take proper account of the changing needs of individuals during their life cycles, or of the specific needs of firms with regard to their long-term capacity to employ people. Conventional evaluation is still devoted to the traditional full employment concept, and therefore single-mindedly focuses on 'making work pay'. Lastly conventional evaluation is not yet well suited to assessing the impact of preventative measures, such as those which help people avoid unemployment by enhancing their long-term employability and which help raise the employment capacity of firms. This is the point where the concept of transitional labour markets comes in.

4   TRANSITIONAL LABOUR MARKETS

The concept of transitional labour markets[8] draws attention to the fact that all labour market flows can occur in both directions: outflows from unemployment are linked to inflows into unemployment. A narrowly defined unemployment insurance system, or ALMP, focusing only on flows between unemployment and employment, is likely to overlook other flows. For example, in Germany, the share of inflows into unemployment from the status of employment decreased from a level of about 80 per cent to 44.3 per cent over the last 15 years.[9] Conversely, in 1999, outflows from unemployment into employment made up only 34.7 per cent of all outflows from unemployment compared to a level of 80 per cent 15 years previously.[10] This means that more than half of all labour turnover takes place, not within the core labour market, but between the labour market and other subsystems of social activities. These are dramatic changes which have not yet been clearly recognized in the corresponding selectivity of employment policies (Figure 3.4).

The new ALMP has to take into account the interaction of these various flows. For instance, increasing the outflow from unemployment into employment through deregulating employment protection might just increase the inflow from employment into unemployment because of increased labour turnover. Increasing the outflow from the unemployment of older wage-earners through early retirement might not have the expected effect of increasing the inflow of young people into the labour market if the increased non-wage cost for financing early retirement reduces the overall hiring rate. In other words, activating labour-market policy requires *coordinated and*

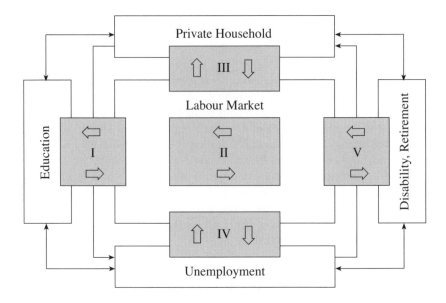

Figure 3.4   The concept of transitional labour markets

complementary institutional responses for five main types of risks which occur during the life cycle (Figure 3.5).

1. Maintaining and enhancing income *capacity* during transitions between education or training and employment.
2. Guaranteeing income *security* during critical transitions between various employment relationships, especially between part-time and full-time work, and between dependent employment and self-employment.
3. Providing income *support* during phases in the life cycle in which market-income capacity is restricted because of social obligations such as (in particular) the care of children.
4. Securing income *maintenance* during transitions between employment and unemployment.
5. Providing income *replacement* in the case of reduced, or even lack of, income capacity, for instance because of disability or during retirement.

We know that these employment risks are changing for at least four reasons: first, the changing aspirations of women and men seeking equal opportunities in the labour market; second, the revolution in skills and competencies attributable to new information technology; third, the ageing of the workforce; and fourth, rising competition resulting from globalization. These

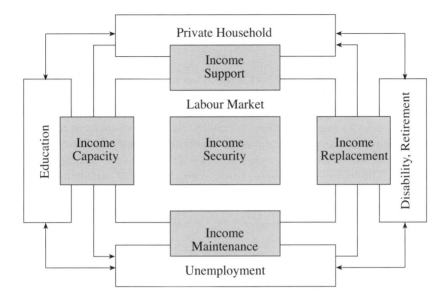

Figure 3.5   Typology of labour market risks

changes call for a differentiation of social protection and employment policies according to the new 'nature of risks'. Such a differentiation corresponds, on the one hand, to the positive principle of 'requisite variety' in systems theory, namely 'only variety in institutions can meet varieties in problems'. On the other hand, such a strategy follows the (normative) principle of 'cybern-ethics' articulated by the philosopher of science, Heinz von Foerster, as follows: 'Act always in a way that the number of possibilities increases'.

The increasing variety of employment risks requires a move from unemployment insurance (UI) centred on income maintenance for jobless people, to a system of employment insurance (EI). Compared to the unique orientation of unemployment insurance, employment insurance would establish interfaces with other systems of social security as a way of increasing the set of possible adjustments to labour market changes. Such an extension of unemployment insurance would enhance the interactive capacity of systems. In return, traditional social security systems would need to be reconsidered and partially restructured in order to become more employment-friendly (Figure 3.6).

The reasons for extending the UI system are straightforward. Classical UI responded only to *external* risks such as cyclical ups and downs, seasonal influences on the product market or technological innovations. An extended EI carries the idea of risk management one step further, namely to *internal* or 'manufactured' risks. Paradoxically, one of the functions of EI is to encourage people to take on risks by providing a simultaneous institutional solution to cover related risks. For instance, EI could provide income support during sabbaticals or parental leaves, enhance employability through lifelong learning arrangements and maintain income during changing working time regimes. The future world of work requires not only 'making work pay', but, more importantly, '*making transitions pay*'.

In short, transitional labour markets are institutions providing a large set of opportunities for negotiated mobility between different employment statuses. The employment relationship during the transitions is usually (but not necessarily) maintained, and the income risks of such transitions are to some extent insured. The impact of activating labour market policy through transitional labour markets can easily be explained by means of the extended matching model in advanced textbooks.[11] The unemployment rate (ur), here, is simply a function of the separation rate (s) and the finding rate (f):

$$ur = s / (s + f). \qquad (3.1)$$

A higher separation rate increases unemployment and a higher finding rate decreases unemployment. Labour market policy, correspondingly, can influence this rate by improving the quality of matches which lead to lower separation rates or, alternatively, by increasing the number of matches by putting pressure, for instance, on the unemployed to take up jobs, perhaps by means

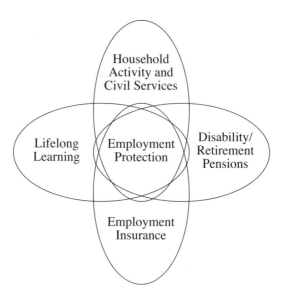

Figure 3.6   Risk management through employment insurance

of lower, or shorter duration, benefits. It is not, therefore, the number of separations or findings that is decisive, but their relationship, as the following simple reformulation of (3.1) shows:

$$ur = 1 / (1 + f/s).$$ (3.2)

There are two options for containing or reducing unemployment, which will be simplified for the sake of clarity:

- maximizing f and also allowing high s; as long as f is larger than s, unemployment will be reduced. This model results in high labour turnover or external mobility and corresponds to the 'US model';
- minimizing s and allowing low f; as long as s is lower than f, unemployment will also become, or remain, low in the steady state of 'frictional' or 'natural' unemployment. This model results in low labour turnover or external mobility and generally corresponds to the continental European model.

During the 1970s and 1980s, the models seemed to perform equally well.[12] Since the early 1990s, something has gone wrong with the continental European model.[13] At the turn of the twenty-first century, however, we see a few successful performers, notably Denmark, the Netherlands and Portugal. Portugal, with a relatively low living standard, had no other option than to maximize f, since coverage by unemployment insurance is one of the lowest in Europe.[14] The Netherlands, to a large extent, applied work sharing, thereby also increasing f and containing s by controlling and lowering benefits for early retirement or labour market disability. Denmark also deviates from the continental European model by combining traditionally low employment protection and high labour mobility with generous benefits (in terms of both amount and duration).

How can this model of high (internal) flexibility and security operate in reality? Transitions are by their nature risky. To promote this model, we need tough criteria to distinguish good transitions from bad. Modern social choice theory[15] and new public management theory[16] suggest four criteria which institutional arrangements have to fulfil in order to support 'good transitions' and prevent 'bad transitions':

1. enhancing *individual freedom or autonomy* by empowering people and establishing not only entitlements to transfers but also entitlements to participation in employment decisions; in exchange, individual employees take on more risks, duties and obligations;
2. promoting *solidarity* through generality and inclusiveness in risk sharing;

the problem of adverse selection implies some ex ante redistribution
through the inclusion of high income groups with usually lower employment risks;

3. improving *effectiveness* through specialization, coordination and cooper-
    ation; this implies, usually, a public–private implementation mix.

4. increasing *efficiency* through risk-management techniques in labour
    market policies, for example controlling, monitoring, evaluating and self-
    regulating by means of decentralization or management by objectives.

We will now examine in greater detail two of the five types of transitional
labour markets: those between education/training on the one hand and
employment on the other; and those between various working time regimes,
including dependent employment and independent (or self-) employment.[17]
The propositions are ordered according to the four criteria for good transitions
set out immediately above, namely freedom, solidarity, effectiveness and efficiency.

5   ACTIVATING TRANSITIONS BETWEEN EDUCATION OR TRAINING AND EMPLOYMENT

The most important change in our perception of risks related to human capital
investment is the generalization of these risks over the life cycle. Thus not
only the transition from school to work entails risks and uncertain returns on
investment, but also the transition between jobs during the life cycle, or the
transition between family work and labour market work. In addition, the risk
of obsolescent skills for adults increases. This can be attributed to several
factors. First, we are faced with a two-speed labour market. Each year, about
10 per cent of jobs are lost, and about 10 per cent of new jobs with new skill
requirements are created. But the natural labour turnover (exchange of gener-
ations) is only between 2 and 3 per cent. Second, new technologies that rapidly
depreciate investments in human capital on the one hand, and promote the
'ageing' of the labour force on the other, both argue in favour of lifelong learning. As a general fact, it has been estimated that 80 per cent of the technology
used between 1995 and 2005 will be less than 10 years old, but 80 per cent of
the workforce will have received their education and training at least 10 years
before.[18] The shortfall of at least one million people competent in information
technologies is already a serious handicap for the competitiveness of Europe's
economies.[19]

Third, competition between (highly) educated people increases because
new information technology provides easy access to price information (labour
costs) and to specialized skills anywhere in the world. Fourth, women have

significantly lower training experience than men owing to less continuous employment, and they take a larger share of part-time work where access rates to training are lower. Thus gender-neutral risk sharing should become a top priority for social protection and employment policies because good education and lifelong learning are increasingly decisive determinants in competitive labour markets. The tremendous differential in unemployment rates based on skill level clearly demonstrates the significance of this risk (Table 3.1).

We can observe three main institutional forms designed to meet the new risks related to income capacity (employability): firstly, the transformation of

Table 3.1   Unemployment rates (per cent) according to skill levels, selected countries, 1997

Country	Academics (1)	Secondary II (2)	Primary I (3)	Ratio (3)/(1)	Total
Germany					
Women	7.0	10.9	15.9	2.3	0.9
Men	5.1	9.2	17.7	3.5	9.1
The Netherlands					
Women	4.0	5.6	10.1	2.5	6.4
Men	2.8	3.0	5.3	1.9	3.6
Austria					
Women	3.4	4.2	7.3	2.1	5.0
Men	2.2	4.3	7.9	3.6	4.7
Denmark					
Women	3.7	5.5	10.2	2.8	5.8
Men	3.2	4.0	6.1	1.9	4.1
United Kingdom					
Women	2.7	5.2	6.0	2.2	4.9
Men	3.4	6.3	9.7	2.9	6.8
France					
Women	7.3	12.3	16.9	2.3	12.8
Men	6.2	8.0	13.9	2.2	9.6
Sweden					
Women	3.3	9.8	12.1	3.7	8.2
Men	5.2	10.5	11.9	2.9	9.6

Source: Eurostat Labour Force Survey 1997; own calculations.

unemployment benefit entitlements into vouchers for training and education; secondly, the internalization of new risks by means of new legal rights within employment relationships, including the right to negotiate for paid, or unpaid, training or educational leave; and thirdly, favourable tax treatment of continuous human capital investment as a way of enhancing positive externalities and of overcoming the sort of Prisoner's Dilemma problem associated with this form of investment. A good case study, detailed below, is the paid leave scheme for education or training, also called job rotation. This has been successfully practised in Sweden since 1991 and in Denmark since 1994. More and more countries within the European Union are following this example and are introducing their own education, or training leave, programmes.

The design of such schemes would have the following 'ideal type' characteristics according to the four criteria for good transitions.

1. It would empower individuals through legal entitlements to paid leave during which the employment relationship was protected and income loss replaced to some extent. However the right to training and education breaks would be contingent upon negotiations with employers. Entitlements to unemployment benefits would be transformed into training subsidies, and a progressive taxation system would subsidize lower wage income in relation to periods of training. In exchange, employees would participate in financing the schemes, for instance by means of wage moderation involving elements of investment wages (wages or working time accounts linked to human resources investment). In some professions, where adjustments to new technologies is crucial for proper performance and damage prevention (medicine, teaching, engineering and management of complex technical facilities), it might even be necessary to require recurrent training through regulation.
2. Solidarity requires that all incomes contribute to the public financing of training and education. The element of solidarity should also be enhanced by giving priority to target groups, such as the low-skilled or older women re-entering the labour market. These groups should receive preferential public support in the form of higher subsidies.
3. Effectiveness would be enhanced through a rich infrastructure of specialized training institutions and local promoters or agencies. Competition between these organizations could be implicitly established by allocating regional budgets and by establishing quality standards which would have to be met when applying for public support.
4. The efficiency of education or training leave schemes would be guaranteed by means of co-financing arrangements between employers and employees. Negotiations between such partners (assuming there is a balanced power structure) would ensure that the cost-containing principle

of fiscal congruity (the equivalent balance of costs and benefits in the long run) was observed. Allocated regional budgets, and to some extent performance-oriented allocations of public funds, would also provide incentives for local actors to use financial resources efficiently.

The Danish leave schemes for training and education meet almost all four criteria for good transitions. Since 1994, they have granted a generous educational leave of up to one year following a period of five years' participation in the labour market. Special public support is provided if trainees are replaced by unemployed individuals, this constituting the aforementioned job rotation programme. However the experiences of the last few years teach us something about the strengths and weaknesses that have to be taken into account when adjusting such a model to a specific country or region. The following are the most interesting observations relating to the experiences of Danish leave schemes.[20]

Firstly, it was important for employers that the replacement of trainees by unemployed persons was not made compulsory. In practice, much flexibility in implementation and corresponding discretion in negotiation with respect to co-financing was built in. Both employers and employees took a very positive view of educational leave.

Secondly, as revealed by the large proportion of leave-takers from the public sector, small and medium-sized enterprises (SME) in the private sector often have great difficulty in implementing such a scheme. This imbalance is also the reason why 75 per cent of those taking training leave are women. To educate the increasingly important SME sector about employment insurance (EI), training leave and job rotation programmes requires more sophisticated regulations, as well as a rich network infrastructure dealing effectively with transaction costs. For example, risks that are demanding for small firms could be managed through job pools run by temporary work agencies.

Thirdly, the long-term unemployed were under-represented amongst the substitutes, which means that the schemes did not affect the recruitment behaviour of firms in relation to 'outsiders'. In fact, it transpired that around 50 per cent of substitutes belonged to the 'extended' internal labour market, that is to say, were formerly employed by the firm or at least well-known by it. Pre-training of the proper target groups within job pools might increase their chances of participating in such measures.

Fourthly, one of the evaluations reported that 49 per cent of the substitutes (persons replacing the trainees) in the private sector and 34 per cent in the public sector continued to be employed by the same employer; 10 per cent (in the private sector) and 4 per cent (in the public sector) remained on the former job of the participant in the training leave scheme. This means, in turn, that employed persons taking training leave probably found a better job either within the firm or outside it. Thus there is some indication of a mobility chain, helped too by the good economic climate in Denmark. The short-term public net costs per participant in a leave scheme were estimated at between 670 and 2670 euros per person. Taking into account the social costs of unemployment and the potential productivity gains in the long term, the cost–benefit relationship for society appears to be positive.[21]

The European ADAPT programme has adopted the Danish idea of job rotation and sponsors various innovative pilot projects for small or medium-sized firms. At the European Union level, the absolute figure for job rotations corresponding to the peak level in Denmark (1994–8) would have amounted to two million people (1.3 per cent of the employed).[22] Other ideas related to EI concern lifelong learning in the form of training vouchers, subsidized saving accounts for education and training and favourable tax treatment for expenditures on continuous human capital investment.

6   ACTIVATING TRANSITIONS BETWEEN VARIOUS WORKING TIME REGIMES OR EMPLOYMENT STATUSES

The new employment insurance should also cover, to some extent, the risks related to the erosion of the standard employment relationship. This phenomenon, often characterized as the 'feminization of the labour market', can be summarized in four points.[23] Firstly, firms organize working time more and more flexibly around the 24-hour day, and part-time and temporary work are expanding. New employment relationships are often fixed-term contracts, and permanent contracts are increasingly arranged as yearly time accounts and, in the near future, may even appear as lifetime accounts. Secondly, working time preferences are shifting and becoming linked to phases of the life cycle dependent upon family situations and educational plans. Thirdly, employment contracts entail more item-specific clauses, for instance results-oriented wages, bonuses and cost sharing of recurrent education and training. Fourthly, employers are more and more outcontracting tasks to the so-called 'new self-employed', thus shifting risks to formerly dependent employees. These new entrepreneurs, or freelancers, enjoy neither employment nor social protection.

Since international comparative figures are scarce or disparate,[24] the erosion of the 'standard employment relationship' is demonstrated by a country-specific example. In 1985, the standard employment relationship made up 54.4 per cent of the total active labour force in Germany, including the unemployed and people participating in labour market measures. By 1999, this percentage had been reduced to 50 per cent (Table 3.2). The difference between men and women is much as one would expect: about 60 per cent of active men in the labour force enjoy 'standard employment', whereas only 40 per cent of women do. This particular difference between men and women is declining. The speed of the process, nonetheless, is slow and much less spectacular than fancy speculations about the 'end of work' suggest. It should also be noted that behind apparently 'standard' employment relationships are arrangements which guarantee flexibility for both parties or, more frequently, for the employer. An example is the collective agreement at DEBIS, one of the largest enterprises in modern business services. Wages here are split into a basic component (the dominant share), a profit-related component and an individual performance-related component. Although the basic component still makes up about 80 to 90 per cent of the total wage, the trend shows an extension of the variable components, especially in the new economy sector, for example through equity shares as a form of wage compensation.

Germany is not an isolated case. The fact that the trend towards de facto, or regulated, flexible employment relations is international and also supply-driven, can be briefly demonstrated by reference to an important survey

Table 3.2   *Change of employment relationships in Germany, 1985 to 1999 (per cent)*

Women and Men	1985	1997	1999	Tendency
1 'Standard relationship'	54.4	51.2	50.0	–
2 Civil servants and soldiers	7.6	4.5	4.3	–
3 Apprenticeships	5.3	3.7	3.9	–/+
4 Fix-term contracts	2.9	3.4	4.8	++
5 Temporary work	0.1	0.5	0.7	++
6 Part-time work (>15h. a week)	8.2	11.3	9.8	+/–
7 Part-time work (<15h. a week)	2.2	4.2	5.6	++
8 Self-employed (full-time)	7.4	7.6	7.9	+
9 Self-employed (part-time)	3.4	0.9	1.5	–/+
10 Participants in LMP[1]	0.4	2.0	1.5	+/–
11 Unemployed	7.9	10.7	10.0	+/–
Broad LF participation rate[2]	68.0	73.0	73.4	+/?

Notes:
1.   LMP = Labour Market Policy
2.   Labour Force
Refers to: the employed, the unemployed and those who are the targets of labour market measures as a percentage of the working age population in the age range 15–65. The latter group excludes those people accounted for in other categories of employment relationships: for instance, employees claiming public benefits while working in private enterprises, or people participating in schemes providing temporary public sector employment.

Source: Microcensus; author's calculations.

recently undertaken by the European Foundation for the Improvement of Living and Working Conditions. This focused on European member states, plus Norway. Studies derived from this survey summarize the main findings in the following typical way:

> there is wide interest in 'new' work forms different from the current standard among those who are employed at present, as well as among those who want to (re-)join the workforce within the next five years. Self-employment, part-time work and work at home are attractive for many more persons than those who practise [them] at present. Preference for these various work forms, however, is closely linked to certain phases of a person's life-cycle. Therefore, it is important not only to provide non-standard work-forms but also to facilitate changeovers between 'new' and standard work forms (e.g. from full-time to part-time and *vice versa*). (Atkinson *et al.*, 1999, p.5)

Social insurance and labour market policy have not yet adjusted to these emerging trends and shifting preferences. What should be the proper policy directions? Transitional labour markets suggest the following features of an ideal-type institutional scenario.

- Enhancing *individual freedom* through new entitlements to choices and bargaining rights on working time issues. In exchange, individuals would have to accept more flexibility in their work contracts, such as the accumulation, or corresponding reduction, of working time according to work requirements (flexible time accounts). The employers' advantage would be the reduction of overtime pay. The insiders' advantage would be increased time sovereignty; the outsiders' advantage would be higher labour intensity.
- The *solidarity* criterion requires the generality of regulation about working time issues and employment statuses. This implies, for instance, the inclusion of the self-employed and civil servants in general social protection schemes as such categories of workers are also affected by new risks. Social protection has to be extended to cover the risks related to discontinuous income streams as well. Collective or individual agreements, including performance-oriented payment systems, can become more widespread if connected to specific insurance schemes. Alternatively, established insurance schemes should include elements of flexibility entitlements accumulated during 'good times' of stable employment.
- The criterion of *effectiveness* requires a rich network of local public–private partnerships in order to implement flexible working time arrangements or transitions between various employment statuses. Small and medium-sized enterprises with limited organizational capacities particularly need such support. Local and regional job pools, jointly

established by temporary work agencies and public employment services, could enhance such a network infrastructure.

- The criterion of *efficiency* requires risk-sharing elements to guarantee *cost containment*. Collective agreements, or individual contracts, have to find ways of explicitly formulating such risk sharing in order to strengthen self-regulation. An example of enhancing individual freedom would be the entitlement to (bargain for) intermediate part-time work (as recently stipulated in the Netherlands), supported perhaps by a general scheme of part-time unemployment benefits which would apply under certain conditions. To this author's knowledge, only Finland has introduced a truly part-time unemployment benefit scheme, something which started in 1994.[25] Sweden provides benefits, at least in the case of involuntary part-time work, when those who are unemployed and looking for full-time employment can only find part-time jobs. These part-timers then enjoy legal priority for full-time status when the labour demand of the firm increases (Tálos, 1999, p.328). On the other hand, minimum standards are required to protect people in weak bargaining positions. Restrictions affecting 'on-call' work were recently established by the Dutch government and involve setting a minimum working time. Another possible adjustment to new types of employment relationships would be legally to formalize multiple (usually part-time) employment relationships as a regular procedure. Germany, for example, has introduced part-time benefits in cases of multiple employment relationships.[26]
- An extended employment insurance could support negotiated work-sharing arrangements through work-sharing benefits.[27] In addition, people temporarily unable to work in the labour market could receive large-scale support through work assessment and training, medical and physical rehabilitation or special work in sheltered workshops.[28] In economic terms this would be cheaper than paying transfers for income support, and in social terms it would prevent exclusion and would enhance social capital, a factor of some importance in promoting reintegration.

An interesting case is 'concession bargaining' which regulates an explicit exchange of wage moderation and employment protection. Collective agreements, especially in East Germany, contain more and more working time and corresponding wage corridors, usually between 32 and 40 hours a week. Another case is represented by lay-off schemes which can be considered as a hybrid (some would argue 'perverse') form of UI. Their function is to maintain relationally specific investments through implicit contracts in which UI takes over the income maintenance function. The objective of this arrangement is not only to maintain income during shortened working hours, but also to maintain (firm-specific) skills and other investments in human capital, including social capital. If we look more closely at the functioning of UI systems in Europe we discover much more of this kind of lay-off than might be expected. In Denmark and in Austria, the practice of employers 'recalling' the unemployed is widely deployed. This means the UI system is already subsidizing or cross-subsidizing such transitions, whether for seasonal reasons, internal restructuring, health problems or even educational leave (Auer, 2000, p.70). A recent Swedish study surprisingly discovered that about 40 per cent of the unemployed return to their original employers. If this observation is correct and augurs a new tendency, then the shift from UI to EI needs to take such a factor into account. Although it will be difficult to maintain the balance between, on the one hand, the gains in flexibility (especially for small firms) in using recall or lay-off options, and on the other the efficiency loss through moral hazard or the distortion of markets, something needs to be done to contain the costs of such (mostly hidden) cross-subsidies, for example through risk-related contributions.

7   CONCLUSION: TOWARDS A NEW EUROPEAN SOCIAL MODEL

The main contributions of this chapter can be summarized in three points.

1. Activating labour market policy means making benefit entitlements for unemployment contingent upon active job searches as well as supporting such searches through individual empowerment. Classical labour market policy covered only the standard income risks of unemployment. Despite some interesting modifications in recent times, it has not yet properly adjusted to the new employment risks which arise from the advent of globalization, the new economy and 'the new family'. These risks change during an individual's life cycle and require a varied set of management techniques. Most important is the risk of loss of income capacity through depreciation of human capital, discontinuity in career paths or jobs which simply disappear.
2. The proper response of labour market policy should be to shift from unemployment insurance to employment insurance. Unlike the former, which focuses on income maintenance, the latter looks to maintain and enhance the income capacity, or employability, of individuals. The aim of an employment insurance system should be to induce flexibility in job-holders, thereby increasing the employment chances of job-seekers. To set this process in motion, transitional labour markets need to be institution-

alized. Such markets internalize flexibility into the contractual employment relationship by providing a set of legal mobility options whose
income risks are to some extent insured. The elements of flexibility are
open to individual, or collective, bargaining.

3. Employment insurance, or new labour market policy, has to be effectively
coordinated with other forms of social protection: specifically, lifelong
learning as a means of maintaining and enhancing income capacity;
income support for family work and unpaid voluntary service; employment protection and income security because of changing working times
or employment statuses; income maintenance during spells of transitional
or involuntary unemployment; and income replacement resulting from
incapacity/disability at work or from retirement. In this respect, transitional labour markets are institutional devices for coordinating and
networking various systems of social security.

Viewed from the perspective of mainstream labour market theory, transitional labour markets suggest a revitalization of internal or functional flexibility, doing so by enlarging the set of possible moves within the employment
relationship. Thus transitional labour markets would allow a minimization of
job separations by increasing internal flexibility. They would contribute to
increasing the job finding rate through, for example, in-work benefits for
involuntary part-time work and part-time work for family reasons or as a result
of job-rotation. In stimulating or supporting these, and other, mobility options,
activated labour market policy would take aim at fresh targets. In particular, it
would explicitly single out gender equality in the labour market by emphasiz-
ing social security for flexible work arrangements linked to family obligations.

In terms of the normative traditions in the European social model, transitional labour markets can be related to the extended model of justice first developed by John Rawls some 30 years ago (1971).[29] From this perspective,
departures from equality are subject to two provisos: first, they must benefit the
least advantaged; and second, they must be attached to offices and positions
which are open to all. The literature on social mobility shows that many sectors,
trades and occupations remain 'closed' and that family background, rather than
'talent', is still one of the most important determinants of people's work, and
life, chances. The literature documents a slight increase in poverty rather than
a decrease, as well as poverty 'immobility' in Europe. Disadvantaged individuals and groups in particular are trapped in low-wage, or dead-end, jobs
because of the perverse institutional design of both labour markets and welfare
systems. Whereas Rawls's notion of justice emphasized equality in terms of
material goods and resources (usually income), the concept of transitional
labour markets focuses on a more dynamic notion of equality centred on capacities and 'empowerment' (Sen, 1993). In a knowledge-based economy, with

increasingly flexible labour markets and fluid social fabrics, the sort of equality which matters centres on those resources which enable people to 'keep pace', and cope, with change. With respect to the labour market, this means resources which effectively and equitably deliver high quality education and training and increase opportunities for mobility. These are matters of particular importance to low-skilled groups and individuals entering, or re-entering, the labour market.

Such things require that job holders accept risks. From a Rawlsian perspective of justice it is morally acceptable to reduce the protection of insiders and allow for more flexibility and greater earnings dispersion if this serves to deliver enhanced opportunities for the worst off. The extension of unemployment insurance to a multifunctional employment insurance would support such an objective. It would stabilize the employment relationship by increasing opportunities for mobility, as well as providing social security during periods of transition. Employability is a necessary, but not sufficient, condition for sustainable employment. People need, and want, real jobs. However employment protection and employment insurance can no longer guarantee specific job security. Security can only be gained in exchange for accepting lifelong learning opportunities, working time flexibility and spatial mobility, meaning commuting, migrating and tele-work. Security could even possibly require changes in employment status, meaning moving between, or combining, dependent employment and independent self-employment. In combination with improvements in the implementation of conventional labour market policy mentioned in the second and third sections of this chapter, labour market policy would become a powerful instrument for coordinating monetary, fiscal and wage policies. The new European social model would be less interventionist on the income transfer front and more interventionist on the mobility front. In implementation, however, it would give more autonomy at the individual, local and regional levels.

NOTES

1. Of course, correlations are no proof at all and are, at best, only indications. However, even on a dynamic basis, countries which reduced labour force participation of older men through aggressive early retirement schemes in the 1980s and 1990s did not perform better in reducing unemployment than countries without such a policy. On the contrary: the correlation between the change of labour force participation for persons aged 55 to 64 in the OECD countries (1983–98) and the change of unemployment (1983–98) is negative ($r = -0.30$). This means that, in countries where labour force participation in this age group increased (or decreased only slowly), the fight against unemployment was more successful than in countries with a dramatic decline of older labour force participation. However an interesting difference in the correlation between men and women has to be noted: the correlation relating to the labour force participation of older men and overall unemployment is virtually zero ($r = -0.02$), and among women significantly negative ($r = -0.42$). A plausible interpretation

is that success in employment or labour market policy is closely related to success in stimulating job growth in services, these being jobs which are usually taken up by women.

2.   I am not commenting about the field of macro-wage policy (or related monetary and fiscal policy) which is beyond the scope of this discussion. However, in the Netherlands, relative unit wage costs changed much more slowly during the 1980s and the first half of the 1990s, thereby giving Dutch exporting firms a competitive edge over their German counterparts.

3.   The most comprehensive studies have been provided by the OECD (1993); Appelbaum and Schettkat, and Bellmann and Jackman, in the *International Handbook of Labour Market Policy and Evaluation* (1996); Nickell and Layard in *The Handbook of Economics* (1999); and a European research network in the 'targeted socioeconomic research programme' (TSER) of the European Commission, collected in the volume by de Koning and Mosley (2001).

4.   It must be acknowledged that this assessment does not go unchallenged: Calmfors and Forslund (1991) come to a contradictory result.

5.   For the state of the art, see Schmid *et al.* (1996) and Schmid (1997).

6.   For a literature review and a summary of evidence from macro and micro studies, see Rabe (2000); for a UK-centred summary, see Robinson (2000).

7.   According to an early finding by Orley Ashenfelter (1978) related to training and education programmes.

8.   For the first formulation of this concept, see Schmid (1995) and Gazier (1998).

9.   Corresponding figures are 63.5 per cent for Denmark and 53.8 per cent for the Netherlands (with slightly lower figures for women).

10.   Only 30 per cent of people over 50 leaving unemployment moved into the state of employment, and one can only assume that this ratio further decreases with age.

11.   For example Mankiw (1998, pp.140–43). I owe the idea of embedding the transitional labour market concept in the framework of mismatched or matching models to Entorf (1998).

12.   It may be worth recalling the fact that the unemployment rate in West Germany was 2.9 per cent in 1980 and still 4.6 per cent in 1992, whereas the corresponding figures in the USA were 7.0 per cent and 7.4 per cent.

13.   I abstract here from the special case of Germany due to the reunification.

14.   Only about 25 per cent of the unemployed are covered by unemployment insurance; see Schmid and Reissert (1996, p.247).

15.   I refer especially to Sen (1995, 1999) and, in relation to the labour market, to Solow (1990). The basic distinction between modern, as opposed to traditional, social choice theory and rational choice or public choice is, first, the acknowledgment of 'social knowledge' (Arrow, 1994); second, the emphasis on social consequences (for instance, inequalities in earning capacities or employability) without neglecting important procedural rules (for example, individual liberties and rights) in the formation of social values or decisions.

16.   For a critical overview, see Grey and Jenkins (1995). New public management theories try to overcome weaknesses of the first wave in public management approaches which, for instance, were often championing results over administrative processes, and imposed or substituted economic values for legal values such as accountability and fairness.

17.   For an extended examination, see Schmid (2001).

18.   Europäische Kommission (1999, pp.6–7).

19.   Europäische Kommission (1998). At the end of February 2000 the German Chancellor, Gerhard Schröder, decided to allow the immigration of about 30 000 IT specialists from Eastern Europe and other non-European countries to fill this gap by means of a 'green card' system, expecting a tenfold employment growth to remove the bottleneck. On a European scale (EU15), the size of this bottleneck for highly skilled IT specialists would amount to 140 000.

20.   Following Madsen (1998) and Kruhoffer (1999). Recently, with the shifting of job-rotation to the private sector, larger firms are affected and the proportion of women has declined.

21.   I am not discussing the macroeconomic side effects in the long run which could affect employment, for instance wage cost pressure due to the reduced labour force, or the incentive for inactive people to enter the labour force.

22.   The 'job rotation' network reports that 13 EU member states practise job rotation in 3000

firms, affecting about 100 000 employees and 25 000 unemployed; this means the average replacement rate is one to four.

23. This summary cannot do justice to fine distinctions such as the fact that, in some countries, notably Scandinavia, part-time work is stagnating or even in decline.

24. See, among others, Felstead and Jewson (1999), Mangan (2000), and Tálos (1999).

25. The public employment service pays an income supplement of 50 per cent of the difference between the former full-time wage and the present part-time wage for a maximum duration of 12 months on the condition that the resulting vacancy is filled partly by unemployed people. Thus the Finnish scheme is a kind of national job-sharing programme. At the beginning, in 1994, 390 people were involved. In 1997, participation reached 6525 people (about 0.3 per cent of the total), most of whom were women, and whose numbers were increasing.

26. Another case is the Italian legal concept of 'para-subordination' where a person works part-time for several employers simultaneously, but is treated as continuously employed for the purposes of employment rights and social protection.

27. A case in Germany is the agreement between trade unions and employers' associations in the metal industry in Lower Saxony, although the government or public employment service does not yet participate.

28. A curious feature of Germany's system is that vocational rehabilitation or retraining of self-employed artists is financed by old age pension insurance.

29. This note is inspired by Ferrera *et al.*, (2000).

BIBLIOGRAPHY

Appelbaum, Eileen and Ronald Schettkat (1996), 'The Importance of Wage-bargaining Institutions for Employment Performance', in G. Schmid, O'Reilly and K. Schömann (eds), *International Handbook of Labour Market Policy and Evaluation*, Cheltenham, UK and Brookfield, USA: Edward Elgar, 791–810.

Arrow, Kenneth J. (1994), 'Methodological Individualism and Social Knowledge', *AEA Papers and Proceedings*, **84** (2), 1–9.

Ashenfelter, Orley (1978), 'Estimating the Effect of Training Programmes on Earnings', *Review of Economics and Statistics*, **6** (1), 47–57.

Atkinson, John, and Harald Bielenski, Giovanni Gasparini, Josef Hartmann and Fred Huijgen (1999), 'Employment Options of the Future: First Analyses of a Representative Survey in all Fifteen EU Member States and Norway on Behalf of the European Foundation for the Improvement of Living and Working Conditions', Infratest Burke, Dublin and Munich: mimeo.

Auer, Peter (2000), 'Employment Revival in Europe: Labour-market Success in Austria, Denmark, Ireland and the Netherlands', International Labour Office, Geneva.

Bellman, Lutz and Richard Jackman (1996), 'The Impact of Labour-market Policy on Wages, Employment and Labour-market Mismatch', in G. Schmid, J. O'Reilly and K. Schömann (eds), *International Handbook of Labour Market Policy and Evaluation*, Cheltenham, UK and Brookfield, USA: Edward Elgar, 725–46.

Calmfors, Lars and Anders Forslund (1991), 'Real Wage Determination and Active Labour-market Policy', *The Economic Journal*, **101**, 1130–48.

Entorf, Horst (1998), *Mismatch Explanations of European Unemployment: A Critical Evaluation*, Berlin/Heidelberg: Springer.

Europäische Kommission (1998), 'Beschäftigungsmöglichkeiten in der Informationsgesellschaft', Amt für amtliche Veröffentlichungen der Europäischen Gemeinschaften, Luxemburg.

– – (1999), 'Die Europäische Beschäftigungsstrategie: Europa geht wieder an die Arbeit', *ESF InfoRevue*, **9**, 1–8.

Fay, Robert G. (1996), 'Enhancing the Effectiveness of Active Labour-Market Policies: Evidence from Programme Evaluations in OECD Countries', *Labour Market and Social Policy*, Occasional Papers, no. 16, Paris.

Felstead, Alan and Nick Jewson (eds) (1999), *Global Trends in Flexible Labour*, Houndmills and London: Macmillan Press Ltd.

Ferrera, Maurizio, Anton Hemerijck and Martin Rhodes (2000), 'The Future of Social Europe: Recasting Work and Welfare in the New Economy', report for the Portuguese Presidency of the European Union.

Gazier, Bernard (1998), 'Ce que sont les marchés transitionnels', in J.-C. Barbier and J. Gautié (eds), *Les politiques de l'emploi en Europe et aux Etats-Unis*, Paris: Presses Universitaires de France, 339–55.

Grey, Andrew and Bill Jenkins (1995), 'From Public Administration to Public Management: Reassessing A Revolution?', *Public Administration*, **73**, 75–99.

Hodge, G.A. (2000), *Privatization. An International Review of Performance*, Boulder, CO.: Westview Press.

de Koning, Jaap (2000), 'How Can We Make Active Policies more Effective? The Role of Organization, Implementation and Optimal Allocation in Active Labour-Market Policy', revised version of a paper presented during the Conference 'Labour-market Policies and the Public Employment Services', Prague, July: Social Economic Research (SEOR), Rotterdam, mimeo.

– – (2001), 'Introduction: Models for Aggregate Impact Analysis of Active Labour-Market Policy', in J. de Koning and H. Mosley (eds), *Active Labour-Market Policy and Unemployment. Impact and Process Evaluations in Selected European Countries*, Cheltenham, UK and Northampton, MA, USA: Edward Elgar.

de Koning, Jaap and Hugh Mosley (eds) (2001), *Active Labour-Market Policy and Unemployment. Impact and Process Evaluations in Selected European Countries*, Cheltenham, UK and Northampton, MA, USA: Edward Elgar.

Kruhoffer, Jens (1999), 'Job Rotation in Denmark. Status and Problems', in G. Schmid and K. Schömann (eds), 'Learning from Denmark', Discussion Paper FS I 99–201, Social Science Research Centre, 17–23.

Madsen, Per K. (1998), 'A Transitional Labour-Market: the Danish Paid-Leave Arrangements', in European Academy of the Urban Environment (ed.), *New Institutional Arrangements in the Labour-Market: Transitional Labour-Markets as a New Full Employment Concept*, Berlin: EA.UE ISSN 0949-5029, 68–73.

Mangan, John (2000), *Workers Without Traditional Employment: An International Study of Non-Standard Work*, Cheltenham, UK and Northampton, MA, USA: Edward Elgar.

Mankiw, N. Gregory (1998), *Makroökonomik*, 3rd edn, Munich and New York: Schäffer-Poeschel (first published as *Macroeconomics*, New York, Worth Publishers, 1997).

Martin, John P. (2000), 'What Works Among Active Labour-Market Policies: Evidence from OECD Countries' Experiences', in OECD Economic Studies, no. 30, 2000/1, 79–113.

Nickell, Stephen and Richard Layard (1999), 'Labour-Market Institutions and Economic Performance', in Orley Ashenfelter and David Card (eds), *Handbook of Economics*, vol. 3, Amsterdam: Elsevier Science, 3029–84.

OECD (1993), 'Active Labour-Market Policies: Assessing Macroeconomic and Microeconomic Effects', *Employment Outlook*, Paris: OECD Publications, 39–80.

Rabe, Birgitta (2000), 'Wirkungen aktiver Arbeitsmarktpolitik. Evaluierungsergebnisse für Deutschland, Schweden, Dänemark und die Niederlande', Discussion Paper FS I 00–208, Wissenschaftszentrum Berlin fur Sozialforschung, Berlin.

Rawls, John (1971), *A Theory of Justice*, Cambridge, MA: Harvard University Press; quoted from Oxford University Press edition, 10th impression, 1990.

Robinson, Peter (2000), 'Active Labour-Market Policies: A Case of Evidence-Based Policy-Making?', *Oxford Review of Economic Policy*, **16** (1), 13–26.

Schmid, Gänther (1995), 'Is full Employment Still Possible? Transitional Labour-Markets as a New Strategy of Labour-Market Policy', *Economic and Industrial Policy*, **11**, 429–456.

— — (1997), 'The Evaluation of Labour-Market Policy: Notes on the State of the Art', *Evaluation*, **3** (4), 409–34.

— — (2002), 'Towards a New Employment Compact: Transitional Labour-Markets and the European Social Model', in Günther Schmid and Bernard Gazier (eds), *The Dynamics of Full Employment. Social Integration Through Transitional Labour Markets*, Cheltenham, UK and Northampton, MA, USA: Edward Elgar.

Schmid, Günther, Jacqueline O'Reilly and Klaus Schömann (eds) (1996), *International Handbook of Labour Market Policy and Evaluation*, Cheltenham, UK and Northampton, MA, USA: Edward Elgar.

Schmid, Günther and Bernd Reissert (1996), 'Unemployment Compensation and Labour Market Transitions', in G. Schmid, J. O'Reilly and K. Schömann (eds), *International Handbook for Labour Market Policy and Evaluation*, Cheltenham, UK and Northampton, MA, USA: Edward Elgar, 235–76.

Sen, Amartya (1993), *Inequality Reexamined*, Cambridge, MA: Harvard University Press.

— — (1995), 'Rationality and Social Choice', *The American Economic Review*, **85** (1), 1–24.

— — (1999), 'The Possibility of Social Choice', *The American Economic Review*, **89** (2), 349–78.

Solow, Robert M. (1990), *The Labour Market as a Social Institution*, Oxford: Basil Blackwell.

Tálos, Emmerich (ed.) (1999), *Atypische Beschäftigung. Internationale Trends und sozialstaatliche Regelungen*, Vienna: Manzsche Verlags- und Universitätsbuchhandlung.

White, Michael, Steve Lissenburgh and Alex Bryson (1997), 'The Impact of Public Job Placing Programmes', report, Policy Studies Institute, London.

4. Transnational technical communities and regional growth in the periphery

AnnaLee Saxenian

Discussions of globalization in the early twenty-first century focus primarily on the liberalization of trade and capital flows. However the integration of world labour markets has historically been one of the most significant drivers of economic change, and promises to be at least as far-reaching during the current era. One indication of these changes is the growing political attention paid to highly skilled immigrants. Regular increases in the number of H1–B (Temporary Professional Class) visas for foreign-born workers in the USA in the 1990s and the spate of 'copycat' policies in Europe and Asia designed to attract foreign technical skill underscore the perception among policy makers of the need to integrate domestic economies into global labour markets.

This chapter examines the labour market behaviour of increasingly mobile and sought-after skilled workers in Silicon Valley – a model for policy makers around the world – where one-third of the technical and professional work-force is foreign-born. It suggests that, whilst highly skilled immigrants have generated substantial wealth and employment in the region, their long-term contributions to the economies of distant regions will be still more significant. Several thousand US-educated immigrant engineers and scientists have returned from Silicon Valley to their home countries, either temporarily or permanently, in the past two decades. The trend shows no sign of slowing.

These transnational entrepreneurs are transforming the 'brain drain' into a more dynamic and reciprocal process of 'brain circulation' and, in so doing, creating unprecedented new economic opportunities for formerly peripheral economies, from Israel and Taiwan to India and China. Like the Greeks who sailed with Jason in search of the Golden Fleece, these 'New Argonauts' are undertaking the risky, but economically rewarding, project of starting compa-nies far from established centres of skill and technology. Today's 'Argonauts' depend upon air travel and electronic connections that give real-time commu-nications around the globe and allow the transfer abroad of skills, technology and business models faster and more flexibly than most large corporations can achieve.

This account suggests that policy which treats foreign-born workers as individuals responding to market signals alone will be of limited success. The labour market behaviour of first-generation immigrants is shaped as much by their ethnic and professional identities as by the lure of higher wages. Like their predecessors in low wage, low productivity ethnic businesses (for example Korean grocers, Indian restaurants and Chinese garment shops), Silicon Valley's well-educated, technologically sophisticated immigrants rely heavily on the mobilization of information, capital, skill and know-how in association with co-ethnics sharing the same language, history, culture, education and work experience.

But unlike the isolated Chinatowns or 'ethnic enclaves' which establish few ties to the outside economy, Silicon Valley's highly-skilled immigrants are building professional and social networks which span national boundaries and allow participation in a global, as well as a local, economy. By transferring Silicon Valley's business model and institutions to new settings, while remaining closely connected to its cutting-edge technology and markets, they help create environments where entrepreneurship can flourish far from established centres of wealth and technology. This process can no more be reproduced by granting visas or other incentives to lure foreign engineers to relocate halfway around the world than Silicon Valley can be replicated through the construction of science parks in regions which lack technical skill.

This chapter summarizes the overall themes of my book, *The New Argonauts: How Transnational Entrepreneurs Link Technology Regions in the Global Economy* (Harvard University Press). Much of the empirical and case material underlying the analysis appears in a series of published articles and working papers which are summarized only briefly here. The first section of the chapter argues that the decentralization of Silicon Valley's industrial system and the changing structure of the information technology (IT) industry have created new entrepreneurial opportunities for US-educated skilled immigrants. By returning home frequently, or permanently, such immigrants and their communities are ideally poised to plant new centres of technical specialization in formerly peripheral regions of the world. The second section outlines the evolution, since the 1980s, of the technically skilled immigrant community in Silicon Valley and its growing role in building economic ties to regions in Taiwan, India and China. The third section presents initial results of a large-scale, web-based survey of Silicon Valley's skilled immigrants as a way of exploring their current labour market behaviour and their future intentions. A concluding section raises some long-term policy issues.

1 THE SILICON VALLEY INDUSTRIAL SYSTEM

The industrial system which evolved in Silicon Valley during the postwar period is characterized by intense competition amongst specialist producers alongside collaborative practices that blur the boundaries between local firms, as well as those between firms and local educational and financial institutions. The openness of firm boundaries is reflected in the market for skilled labour, which is distinguished by pervasive inter-firm mobility and high rates of entre-preneurship, as well as by dense, cross-cutting social and professional networks and pervasive horizontal information exchanges. The region's finan-cial and educational institutions, in turn, are crucial to the reproduction of such a decentralized industrial system. The institutionalization of venture capital provides a means of seeding and nurturing multiple, parallel trials which experiment with new technologies, new products and new applications. At the same time, local educational institutions provide skills at all technical levels as well as generating leading-edge research findings.

The decentralization of Silicon Valley's system appears to be a response to market relations. Yet this is far from being a classic auction market. Local producers collaborate with customers, suppliers and partners to learn about, and respond to, a fast-changing competitive environment. Timely information and industry-specific know-how accumulate in local universities, venture capital networks and professional associations. And the tacit knowledge that once resided within a corporation is transferred primarily through informal communications and frequent inter-firm movements of individuals. As local entrepreneurs innovate in increasingly specialized markets, intense communi-cations support the speedy, often unanticipated, recombination of these specialized components into changing end products.

This decentralized system provides significant advantages over a more integrated model in a volatile environment because of the speed and flexibil-ity, as well as the conceptual advances, associated with the process of special-ization and recombination. These advantages have contributed to the transformation of the information technology sector. The traditional, highly integrated corporate structure (the IBM or 'national champion' model) has given way to vertical fragmentation and increasing firm-based specialization. Producers no longer compete at all stages of production, from design and development through to manufacturing, marketing and distribution. Rather they focus on a narrow piece of the value chain in which they can excel, while relying on other specialists to provide components and final-system integra-tion. The number of actors in the industry has increased dramatically and competition within most horizontal layers has intensified as well.

Today independent enterprises produce all of the components that were once internalized within a single large corporation, from applications software, operating systems and computers to microprocessors and other components. The final systems are in turn marketed and distributed by still other enterprises. Within each of these horizontal segments there is, in turn, increasing specialization of production as entrepreneurs occupy increasingly narrow new niche markets.

This new model of competition, combined with advances in transportation and communications technologies, has created economic opportunities for formerly peripheral regions which did not exist in the era of highly integrated production. The vertical specialization associated with the new system continually generates entrepreneurial opportunities. By exploiting these opportunities in their home countries, entrepreneurs can build independent centres of specialization, while simultaneously maintaining ties to Silicon Valley in order to monitor fast-changing and uncertain markets and technologies. They are also well positioned to establish cross-regional partnerships that facilitate the integration of their specialized components into end products.

The semiconductor industry provides an example. In the past, large corporations performed all of the stages of production internally, and chip production remained the province of the most advanced industrial nations such as the USA and Japan. Today the industry is thoroughly fragmented. Scores of Taiwanese producers have become globally competitive by focusing exclusively on semiconductor manufacturing or design. Israel is home to some of the world's most innovative semiconductor equipment manufacturers. Indian firms are among the latest wave of specialists to provide the extremely sophisticated intellectual property modules used in chip design.

In this new competitive environment, transnational migrants provide a crucial advantage for backward regions. These regions typically have been treated as low-cost production sites for multinationals, but US-educated and trained engineers can help them leapfrog more advanced economies by transferring up-to-date technology and market information, and by jump-starting a localized process of entrepreneurship. Over time, transnational communities can accelerate the technological upgrading of regional economies by providing the base of skill and know-how needed to help local producers shift to higher value-added activities.

Because of their experience and professional networks, US-educated immigrants can quickly identify promising new market opportunities, raise capital, build management teams and establish partnerships with other specialist producers – even those located at considerable geographical distances. The speed of personal communications and decision making within ethnic professional networks accelerates the process of learning about new sources of skill, technology and capital, as well as about potential business collaborators. It also facilitates the timely responses that are essential in the current competitive environment. This decentralized responsiveness is an advantage which few multinational corporations can match.

Successful US-educated entrepreneurs also serve as role models and mentors for local entrepreneurs, providing advice, contacts and capital as well as the confidence to take risks. Their managerial experience helps them create flexible and transparent Silicon Valley-type companies instead of the traditional, hierarchical businesses that dominate most developing countries. Last, but not least, the returnees often become advisers to domestic policy makers, helping to reshape financial and regulatory institutions as well as the physical and technical infrastructure needed to support the entrepreneurial risk taking needed in today's fast-paced economy.

2   SILICON VALLEY'S NEW IMMIGRANT ENTREPRENEURS

The majority of the approximately 125 000 foreign-born engineers working in Silicon Valley today are from Asia, with Indian and Chinese immigrants (both Taiwanese and mainland-born) alone accounting for 40 per cent of the total. Almost all were attracted to the region's booming labour markets after completing graduate science and engineering degrees in the USA. These immigrants, who initially came in response to the ample fellowship aid available for talented foreign students at American universities during the postwar years, began to stay in growing numbers following passage of the Hart-Celler Immigration Act of 1965. This authorized immigration based on the possession of scarce skills and family ties to US citizens or permanent residents.

The Act, which replaced the former national quota system, significantly increased the total number of immigrants permitted to stay in the USA. For example, Taiwan was historically limited to a maximum of 100 immigrant visas per year. As a result, only 65 engineers immigrated to the USA from Taiwan in 1965. Two years later, the number had grown to 1321. These skilled immigrants were drawn to Silicon Valley in huge numbers as the region's labour market boomed during the 1970s and 1980s.

Indian and Chinese immigrants in Silicon Valley quickly gained reputations for technical excellence, not surprisingly, as they represented the 'best and brightest' from their home countries. However many complained about obstacles to moving into managerial positions. The mobilization of ethnic professional networks was a response to this perception of 'glass ceilings', or invisible barriers, to advancement in the region's established firms. The earliest immigrant professional associations, The Chinese Institute of Engineers and The Asian–American Manufacturers Association, were started in 1979 and 1980, respectively, but many such associations proliferated during the 1990s. Today there are more than 20 ethnic professional associations in the region, the largest and most successful ones being organized by Chinese and Indian immigrants. There are smaller associations representing Korean, Iranian, Japanese, Israeli, Singaporean and Vietnamese engineers.

Today associations such as The Indus Entrepreneur, The Silicon Valley Indian Professionals Association, The Silicon Valley Chinese Engineers Association and The Monte Jade Science and Technology Association are among the most vibrant professional associations in Silicon Valley. As with social and professional networks representing the region's native-born engineers, these ethnic associations create shared identities and support career advancement in a fluid labour market. They provide opportunities for informal socializing, serve as recruitment channels and sources of labour market information, provide role models for aspiring entrepreneurs and managers, and sponsor forums for sharing technical and market knowledge as well as the 'nuts and bolts' of entrepreneurship and management for engineers possessing limited business experience. These associations also serve increasingly as important forums for cross-generational 'angel investment' and mentoring.

The members of these organizations initially came together on the basis of shared educational and professional experiences, languages, cultures and histories. Not surprisingly, the different immigrant groups organized independently from one another, as well as from the region's mainstream professional and technical associations. They also distanced themselves from pre-existing traditional ethnic associations in the area (Chinese hometown or kinship associations, for example). And there is virtually no overlap in the membership of the associations organized by Indian and Chinese immigrants. Even the ethnic distinctions within the Chinese technology community are reflected in these associations. For example, Taiwanese immigrants started the Chinese–American Semi-Conductor Professionals Association in 1991. The Mainland Chinese, who arrived in the USA later, organized the North American–Chinese Semi-Conductor Association in 1996.

These networks provide newcomers with access to role models, contacts, advice and sources of funding. They also generate the local knowledge needed to identify and exploit entrepreneurial opportunities quickly. One indicator of the value of these ethnic networks is the explosive growth of immigrant entrepreneurship in Silicon Valley. Indian and Chinese engineers now operate over 3000 companies, or 29 per cent of the technology companies started in the region since 1980. This compares to a figure of only 12 per cent in the early 1980s. These companies include some of the most successful technology businesses in the country, including Exodus Communications, BroadVision and Yahoo! Collectively they have created US$19.5 billion in sales and 73 000 jobs. The entrepreneurial successes of first generation immigrants underscores the openness of the region's decentralized system: individuals with technical skill and experience who succeed economically to a degree unparalleled in older industries and regions.

This is not to suggest that Silicon Valley immigrants create entirely self-contained ethnic businesses or communities. Many Chinese and Indian professionals socialize primarily within ethnic networks, but work routinely with native engineers and native-run businesses. In fact, there is growing recognition within these communities that, although a start-up might be spawned with the support of ethnic networks, it needs to become part of the mainstream if it is to flourish. It appears that the most successful immigrant entrepreneurs in Silicon Valley today are those who have drawn on ethnic resources while simultaneously integrating into mainstream technology and business networks. Indeed the distinctive advantage of these immigrants is their ability to integrate into the professional networks in Silicon Valley and link them to ones in their home countries.

The 'New Argonauts' and the Globalization of Ethnic Networks

Silicon Valley's immigrant engineers began to return home during the 1980s. Motivated primarily by economic opportunities, they sought to exploit their linguistic and cultural advantages (and perhaps even their privileged access to domestic markets and policy makers) by starting companies in their native countries. Few abandoned their US connections; rather they expanded their professional and technical networks to include classmates and colleagues at home. Many continue to travel to Silicon Valley regularly. Some make the trip so frequently that the Chinese refer to them as 'astronauts' who seem always to be in the air.

Take the example of Miin Wu, who immigrated to the USA in the early 1970s in order to pursue graduate training in electrical engineering. As with virtually all of his classmates from the elite National Taiwan University, he took advantage of the ample fellowship aid available in the USA at the time for poor, talented, foreign students. After earning a doctorate from Stanford University in 1976, Wu recognized that there would be few opportunities to use his newly acquired skills in economically backward Taiwan. He consequently chose to remain in the USA. He worked for more than a decade in senior positions at semiconductor companies in Silicon Valley, including Siliconix and Intel. He also gained entrepreneurial experience as one of the founding members of VLSI Technology.

By the late 1980s, economic conditions in Taiwan had improved dramatically and Miin Wu decided to return home. In 1989, he started one of Taiwan's first semiconductor companies, the Macronix Co., in the Hsinchu Science-Based Industrial Park. He initially recruited 30 senior engineers, mainly former classmates and friends from Silicon Valley, to return to Taiwan. This team provided Macronix with the specialized technical skills and experience to develop new products and move into new markets quickly. Wu also transferred characteristics of the Silicon Valley management model to Macronix, including openness, informality and the minimum of hierarchical structures – all significant departures from traditional Taiwanese corporate models.

Macronix went public on the Taiwan stock exchange in 1995 and the following year became the first Taiwanese company to be listed on NASDAQ. The firm is now the sixth largest semiconductor maker in Taiwan, with close to 3000 employees and with revenues of over US$375 million. Most of Macronix's employees and its manufacturing facilities are based in Taiwan, but the firm has an advanced design and engineering centre in Silicon Valley and Wu continues to recruit senior managers from the Valley. Macronix has established a corporate venture capital fund that invests in promising start-ups in both the USA and Asia. They have invested in at least five companies in California as a way of developing technologies related to their core business.

Individuals such as Miin Wu do not act alone. Entrepreneurship is a social process, and immigrant engineers build communities around shared educational and professional experiences, as well as common ethnic backgrounds. These communities increasingly include peers based in their home countries as well as in the USA. Wu maintains close connections with his classmates from Taiwan University and from Stanford, as well as with former colleagues and business associates. His company is one of 150 companies that belong to Silicon Valley's Monte Jade Science and Technology Association, which was established to promote cooperation and the mutually beneficial flow of technology and investment between Silicon Valley and Taiwan.

Reversing the 'brain drain' is not always so straightforward. Aspiring returnees must work within the political and economic environments of their home countries. Miin Wu's experience illustrates how governments can facilitate transnational entrepreneurship. Taiwanese policy makers aggressively encouraged overseas Chinese professionals to return home during the 1980s, including actively facilitating the formation of The Monte Jade Science and Technology Association. By the mid-1990s, thousands of US-educated engineers had followed Miin Wu's path and returned to Taiwan (Figure 4.1). Today the relationship between Silicon Valley and Taiwan consists of a decentralized mix of formal and informal collaborations between individual investors and entrepreneurs, small and medium-sized firms and the divisions of larger companies located on both sides of the Pacific Ocean. In this complex mix, the rich social and professional ties of Taiwanese engineers based in both countries are as important as formal corporate alliances.

Indian policy makers, by contrast, historically discouraged economic ties with outsiders, even those of Indian origin. The Indian market remained closed until 1991. The legacy of this autarchic past is an environment that has been less conducive to transnational entrepreneurship. Whilst Indian engineers were increasingly successful as entrepreneurs in Silicon Valley during the 1990s, only a handful chose to return to India to work or to start new firms. Even as foreign corporations located branches in regions such as Bangalore in order to take advantage of India's relatively low-cost programmers, the challenges of the country's backward physical and technical infrastructure, and its unresponsive and often corrupt bureaucracy, made it difficult for migrants to return home to start companies. As a result, few did so.

However a transnational community is emerging in spite of these obstacles. A new cohort of US-educated engineers and investors is creating opportunities for industrial upgrading in localities that once could only hope to compete on the basis of relatively low wages. Wipro, a leading Indian software house, provides an example of the change. In 1997, A.V. Sridhar resigned after 17 years as a senior executive in order to form a new company. This event sent shock waves through the industry. Sridhar recruited several other engineers 'from the Indian network' for the start-up, including two former Wipro employees and two with substantial experience in the USA. The start-up

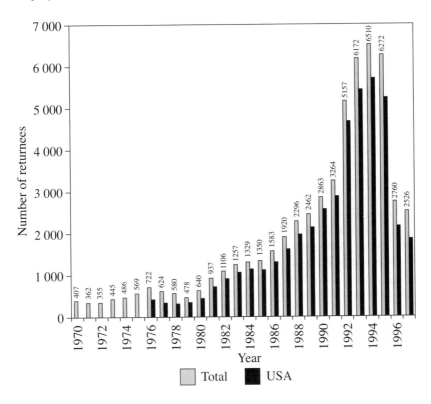

Source: National Youth Commission Taiwan.

Figure 4.1 Returnees to Taiwan from the USA and elsewhere, 1970–97

company, Neta, personalizes software for e-commerce providers. It was based in Silicon Valley because of the need to be close to the US market, but maintains software development in India.

Neta was acquired by a US corporation in 1999, and co-founder Sanjay Anandram returned to India to start a venture fund for early-stage technology businesses. He now draws on his contacts and experiences in Silicon Valley and serves as role model, mentor and financier for Indian entrepreneurs. Anandram is part of a fast-growing community of Indian engineers who share a vision of making money by building up the domestic information technology industry and expanding the traffic linking places such as Bangalore and Bombay to Silicon Valley.

In Taiwan, policy makers consciously invested in the creation of an environment to encourage the growth of technology industries. In India, by contrast, successful Indian entrepreneurs in the USA and India assumed the initiative. In 1999, these Non-resident Indians (NRIs) opened branches of The Indus Entrepreneur in Bangalore, Dehli and Bombay. They are aggressively, and thus far successfully, promoting domestic institutional change, from legislation to encourage the growth of the venture capital industry to deregulation of the telecommunications industry, all of which should improve the environment for entrepreneurs in software services and related sectors. Significantly, a new generation of Indian engineers appears willing to consider returning home rather than settling permanently in the USA as their predecessors did.

Indian and Taiwanese engineers were the earliest and most visible groups to build entrepreneurial networks linking their home countries to Silicon Valley; but they are not the only ones. The approximately 15 000 mainland Chinese engineers working in Silicon Valley, most of whom arrived in the USA after 1990, are poised to contribute to the upgrading of technology regions in China. Chinese policy makers, aware of the sources of Taiwan's success, offer unusually generous incentive packages to Overseas Chinese in order to lure them home to start companies. And successful Overseas Chinese engineers are actively advising these policy makers on the sorts of institutional changes needed to support entrepreneurship: from the reforms needed to promote venture capital to the restructuring of the stock market.

China is still primarily a site for low-cost manufacturing and software development, but this could change very quickly. In addition to a well-developed skill base at home and large numbers of US-educated engineers overseas, China has a solid foundation of basic research in its top universities. The potential for economic upgrading in China is especially promising given the recent influx of personal computer and semiconductor manufacturing capability, know-how and talent from Taiwan. There is much evidence to suggest the emergence of a Silicon Valley–Taiwan–China triangle. Taiwanese entrepreneurs and companies are positioning themselves to play an intermediary role bridging Silicon Valley and mainland China in the technology sectors. Whilst returnees to China face different opportunities and constraints from those in Taiwan or India, they too are contributing to a globally distributed process of entrepreneurial and technological advance.

As the 'New Argonauts' transfer technology and business models from Silicon Valley to their home countries, they create linked centres of entrepreneurship and innovation. Moreover, as these regional economies develop distinctive competencies (Taiwan now excels in IT hardware and manufacturing, India in software services and design), their interactions appear increasingly complementary and mutually beneficial, rather than zero-sum. And as long as the USA remains the largest and most dynamic market for technology products, all will retain strong common ties to Silicon Valley.

Take the example of Ramp Networks, which develops low-cost routers that speed Internet access for small businesses. Mahesh Veerina established the firm in the early 1990s, relying heavily on Silicon Valley's Indian networks. He quickly moved software development to India in order to save money. A few years later a Chinese investor in Silicon Valley introduced him to senior Taiwanese manufacturers, customers and distributors. These relationships accelerated Ramp's shift to high-volume manufacturing, while also cutting costs dramatically. When Ramp went public on NASDAQ in 1999, it was a prime example of the new Argonaut-led globalization: a Silicon Valley-based entrepreneur tapping the skills and capabilities of firms in the specialized technology regions of both India and Taiwan.

The institutions which coordinate Silicon Valley's industrial system locally – venture capital, professional and technical networks – are shaping these global flows as well. Most nations today aspire to develop domestic venture capital; however those with mature transnational communities, such as Israel and Taiwan, are home to the most sophisticated venture capital industries outside the USA. The New Argonauts are transferring the Silicon Valley model of early-stage, high-risk investing to locations which mainstream venture capitalists typically have neither interest in, nor ability to serve.

A new breed of immigrant-run venture capital firms are raising money in both Asia and the USA and are able to create value-added, bridging Silicon Valley's technical and business networks and those located in distant centres of skill and innovation. They understand that native-born professionals can provide the cultural, institutional and linguistic know-how needed to identify promising investment opportunities in their home markets; also that the continued connection to Silicon Valley's markets and technical and managerial knowledge and experience is often critical to the success of these new ventures.

The success of this bottom-up, decentralized process of globalization is in turn transforming established domestic institutions. Multinational corporations are decentralizing their activities as a way of integrating into localized

centres of innovation and entrepreneurship (and actively investing in start-ups
in these regions); meanwhile state policy makers are looking outwards in order
to mobilize distant sources of skill and capital.

3   SURVEY RESULTS

Politico-economic developments in countries such as China and India will
shape the capacity to lure the 'best and brightest' back home, but the actions
and intentions of Silicon Valley's skilled immigrants are equally important.
This section presents the results of a web-based survey of the region's foreign-
born professionals which illuminates the extent and nature of ties between
Silicon Valley and immigrants' home countries, as well as prospects for the
future. The survey was distributed through local ethnic professional associations in May 2001 and generated 1997 responses, equivalent to 20 per cent of
the original sample of 10 659. There may be some bias built into the survey
because this is a self-selecting group. Even so, the sample offers an accurate
mix of the local Indian and Chinese populations, with 46 per cent of the
respondents from India, 33 per cent from China (including Hong Kong) and
10 per cent from Taiwan. (Figures relating to the survey can be found at the
end of the chapter.)

Foreign-born workers in Silicon Valley are more highly educated than their
native-born counterparts: more than 75 per cent hold graduate degrees
(compared to only 50 per cent of native-born engineers); 84 per cent hold technical, scientific or engineering degrees (compared to 41 per cent of the native-
born); and all but 6 per cent obtained their highest degree from a US
university. These groups arrived in the USA in various phases. While
Taiwanese engineers began to settle during the 1970s, by the late 1990s the
flow had slowed considerably: 69 per cent of the Taiwanese settled in the USA
arrived prior to 1990 – only 31 per cent have come since 1990. By contrast, 58
per cent of the highly-skilled Indians and 73 per cent of the Chinese settled in
the USA after 1990.

As the following overview of some of the initial survey results indicates,
Silicon Valley's foreign-born professionals have adopted the region's entrepreneurial culture: 31 per cent of the Chinese, 50 per cent of the Taiwanese and
59 per cent of the Indian immigrants have founded or managed a start-up,
either part-time or full-time. Many also anticipate becoming entrepreneurs
some time in the future. This is especially significant as 52 per cent of the
Chinese, 56 per cent of the Taiwanese and 75 per cent of the Indians in the
sample were contacted during an economic downturn in the region.

The majority of these aspiring and established entrepreneurs (76 per cent of
both Indians and Chinese, and 54 per cent of Taiwanese) report that they

would 'consider locating their business' in their home country. Moreover a significant proportion of the respondents report that they plan to return to their home country in order to work or to start a company in the future: the figures are 45 per cent for Indians, 43 per cent for Chinese and 23 per cent for Taiwanese. This suggests that the scale of brain circulation, particularly between Silicon Valley, India and China, could increase dramatically in years to come.

There is clear evidence as well that these immigrants maintain strong ties to their home countries. Significant proportions of the respondents report having arranged business contracts in their home country (40 per cent of Taiwanese, 47 per cent of Indians and 35 per cent of Chinese). Many also have occasional or frequent contacts with officials from their home countries: 25 per cent of Taiwanese, 28 per cent of Indians and 36 per cent of Chinese. A smaller, but still significant, proportion report having served as advisers to companies in their home countries (34 per cent of Indians, 24 per cent of Taiwanese and 15 per cent of Chinese) or as having invested their own money in start-ups in their home countries (16 per cent of Taiwanese, 22 per cent of Indians and 11 per cent of Chinese respondents).

CONCLUSION

The 'New Argonauts' and their communities are redefining the geography of high-technology production. New centres of entrepreneurship require a base of technology and skill as well as supportive local institutions and continuing connections to the market. The evidence suggests that policy makers need to invest their resources in creating entrepreneurial networks, rather than in top-down efforts to replicate Silicon Valley's structures, or in efforts to lure foreign engineers. The potential gains from upgrading domestic skills and creating the institutions that support transnational, as well as local, entrepreneurship could be substantial in the twenty-first century.

The opportunities created by brain circulation thus far have accrued almost exclusively to developing regions that have made long-term investments in technical education for at least part of their workforce. Other nations, both rich and poor, have been slow to develop the institutions and connections to Silicon Valley needed to support globally competitive, technological entrepreneurship. Many poor countries have not invested sufficiently in their human capital. Advanced nations such as Japan and Germany boast the necessary skills and technology, but appear to be constrained by restrictive corporate, financial and labour structures. Similarly the success of regions such as Singapore and Scotland in luring multinational investment required institutions and policies which encouraged bottom-up experimentation and entrepreneurship. A significant advantage of 'late development' in the twenty-first century may be the ability to benefit from the contributions made by the New Argonauts and their communities.

This diffusion of technology poses potential dangers, however. In particular, it risks creating localized economic nodes (and technical elites) that are connected to major global centres, but poorly integrated into their own domestic economies. This is already apparent in small countries such as Taiwan and Israel. In both India and China, technological entrepreneurship is concentrated in a small number of urban areas. The potential for increased individual, as well as regional, inequalities poses a political, as well as an economic, threat. The ability to develop and serve the domestic, as well as the global, market will be crucial to avoiding this outcome. It could become the all-important area for government action in coming decades.

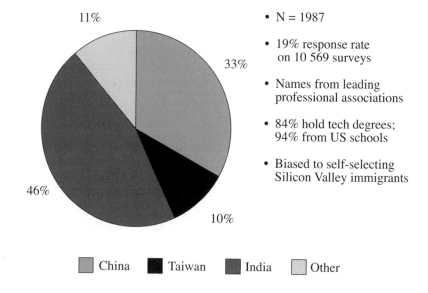

Figure 4.2   Survey overview

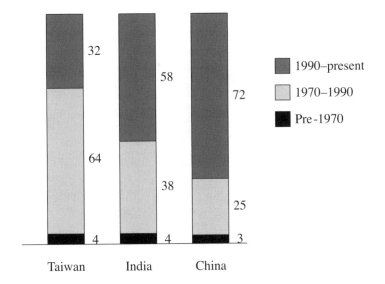

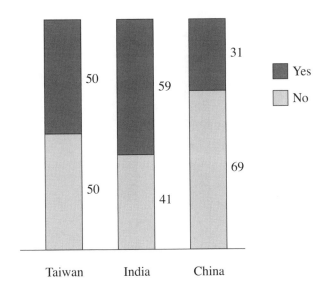

Figure 4.3   Arrivals in the United States (percentages)

Figure 4.4   Start-ups founded or managed (percentages)

Institutions, innovation and growth

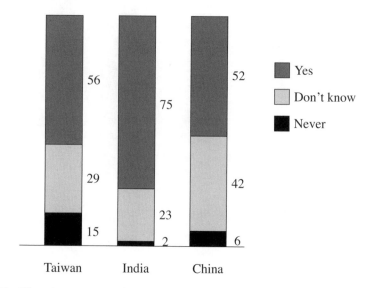

Figure 4.5 Planning to start a business (percentages)

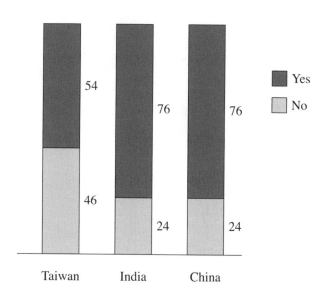

Figure 4.6 Possibility of locating business in home country (percentages)

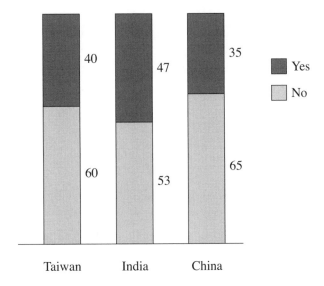

Figure 4.7   Home country business contracts arranged (percentages)

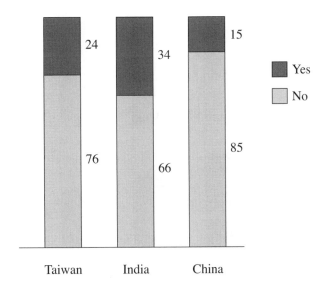

Figure 4.8   Home country companies advised (percentages)

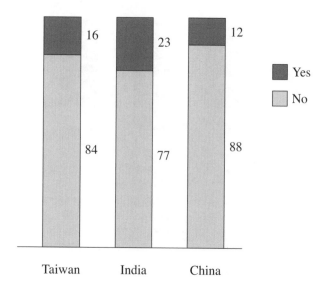

Figure 4.9   Investment in home country start-ups (percentages)

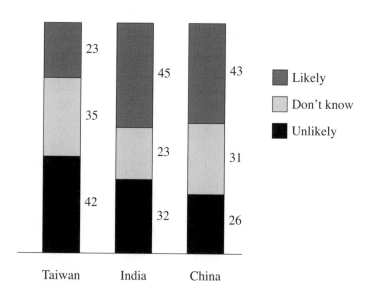

Figure 4.10   Planning to return home to work (percentages)

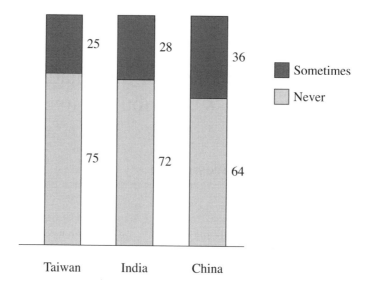

Figure 4.11   Meetings with home country officials (percentages)

BIBLIOGRAPHY

Saxenian, AnnaLee (1994), *Regional Advantage: Culture and Competition in Silicon Valley and Route* **128**, Cambridge, MA: Harvard University Press.
— — (1999a) 'Silicon Valley's New Immigrant Entrepreneurs', Public Policy Institute of California, San Francisco, June.
— — (1999b) 'The Silicon Valley–Hsinchu Connection: Technical Communities and Industrial Upgrading', Discussion Paper 99–10, Stanford Institute of Economic Policy Research, September.
— — (2000a) 'From India to Silicon Valley and Back Again', *The Asian Wall Street Journal*, 24 January.
— — (2000b) 'The Bangalore Boom: From Brain Drain to Brain Circulation?', in Kenneth Kenniston and Deepak Kumar (eds), *Bridging the Digital Divide: Lessons from India*, Bangalore: National Institute of Advanced Study.
— — (2000c) 'Bangalore: Silicon Valley of Asia?', *Proceedings of Conference on Indian Economic Prospects: Advancing Policy Reform*, Center for Research on Economic Development and Policy Reform, Stanford University.
— —(2000d), 'The Silicon Valley–Hsinchu Connection: Technical Communities and Industrial Upgrading', *Industrial and Corporate Change*, Special Issue on Geography of Innovation and Economics of Clustering.
Saxenian, AnnaLee with Jinn-Yuh Hsu (2001), 'The Limits of *Guanxi* Capitalism: Transnational Collaboration Between Taiwan and the US', draft paper.
Saxenian, AnnaLee with Wendy Li (n.d.), 'Bay-to-Bay Strategic Alliances: Network Linkages Between Taiwan and U.S. Venture Capital Industries', draft paper.

5. The mechanisms of information technology's contribution to economic growth

Timothy F. Bresnahan

The mechanisms by which business use of information technology (IT) contributes to growth in living standards are badly understood, leading to a confused debate. This chapter starts from the microeconomic and management literatures that study the use of IT at the individual firm level. IT-using firms, and the IT vendors who support their efforts, are the agents whose incentives, innovations and opportunities matter in the first instance for understanding the mechanisms. Aggregating those agents' incentives towards a nationwide, or worldwide, level leads us towards the issue of growth. Our goal is to explain what existing knowledge about the economics of the IT-using firm and IT markets has to say about the concerns of growth theory, rather than providing evidence for, or against, a particular view.

Modern aggregate growth theory analyses the macroeconomic and microeconomic conditions for sustained economic growth. From the macro perspective, the key idea has to do with accumulating assets of sufficient economy-wide importance to raise aggregate well-being, yet not subject to diminishing returns over an extended period of time. The relevant assets can be a stock of capital – human or physical – or a stock of scientific or engineering knowledge, or a combination of both. What is critical for growth to continue is the existence of a force which raises the return to investment in the accumulating asset over time.[1] Without such a force, diminishing returns set in.

The microeconomic underpinnings of this theory have drawn particular attention to stocks of knowledge. Since knowledge can be reused, it can, with sufficient leverage, have economy-wide implications. Cumulative knowledge, together with a large technical opportunity, can raise the social return to learning for a long time. The microeconomic part of the theory thus draws our attention to increasing returns to scale and to the strength of complementarity between early knowledge accumulation and the same activity later on, that is to say to complementarity over time. The same reasoning leads to gaps between the social and private return to the invention of new knowledge.

Understanding both macroeconomic and microeconomic perspectives is crucial in this analysis, for only then can the incentive effects of economic policy and their growth impacts be understood.

Information technology has important features relating to the key structures of macroeconomic and microeconomic approaches to growth. The first is substantial technological opportunity in the narrowest engineering sense: it is physically possible, with enough resources, to make computers and telecommunications equipment perform better and better. The second is a potential for broad applicability and therefore economy-wide impact. IT is a general purpose technology.[2] Its most widely useful attributes, such as ever cheaper computation, data processing and bandwidth, underlie a wide array of more specific technologies that are in turn used in a number of very different applications. Like all general-purpose technologies (GPTs), IT advances enable, but do not compel, improvements in applications. Applications themselves are the product of complementary co-invention by IT-using firms. Advances in IT *shift the innovation possibility frontier* of the economy rather than directly shifting the production frontier. The third feature is also related to the complementarity between IT invention and co-invention of applications. Inventions in applications increase the size of the market for IT, improving the economic returns to IT invention, which are subject to considerable increasing returns. Typically inventions in applications lag a few years behind IT inventions. This injects a *dynamic feedback loop* whereby advances in IT lead to unpredictable applications invention, which in turn raises the return to improvements in IT whose rate and direction can only be understood after the applications invention is complete.

The related microeconomics follows from the same set of forces. Any GPT is associated with substantial social increasing returns to scale. The externalities among co-inventors are considerable. The externalities between inventors of IT and co-inventors of applications are substantial. The dynamic externalities between inventors of different types of IT are also considerable. Attempts to internalize these externalities have been wildly successful on some occasions and a thorny problem to overcome on others. Contractual, organizational, technological or public policy schemes to internalize these externalities have been partially successful, and remain as difficult as they are important. As a result it is not a straightforward task to appropriate completely the returns to some kinds of invention and to some kinds of co-invention. These contracting difficulties lead to a higher social, rather than private, return to much invention and co-invention, and the possibility that the dynamic positive feedback loop will have weak causation at some junctures. As a result, there is scope for public policy and business policy innovations shaping technical progress (and thus growth) by means of a wide variety of incentive-altering mechanisms.

Understanding the mechanisms by which these forces rise to economy-wide importance, and the means by which they maintain that importance over a long period of time, calls for a broad approach. The chapter takes up five main topics. The first section examines co-invention in narrow IT segments, taking the behaviour of the single IT-using firm *vis-à-vis* a single technical advance as the unit of analysis. The second section examines markets for specific IT capital goods. These two parts complete the microeconomic partial equilibrium portions of the analysis. The third section looks at the widening span of application of IT over time. The fourth section examines the mechanisms by which early IT invention – and co-invention – have come to be complements to, rather than substitutes for, later technical advance. The fifth section considers the forces holding social return to invention above the private return.

1   IT IN USE

We begin with three analytical distinctions. We have already distinguished between invention by the sellers of IT and co-invention by the buyers. We need also to distinguish a stock of knowledge, called information technology (IT) from a stock of capital which embodies that knowledge – computers, software and telecommunications systems – called information technology capital (ITK). Finally, we need to distinguish between different kinds of applications of IT, focusing on two separate sorts of applications: large-scale applications, typically undertaken by an entire organization, which we may call business information systems (BIS), and applications where one person is the user, which are personal applications (PA). Although there are other demand segments, these two capture the extremes of the process of co-invention.

Improvements in IT as a technology expand the scope of what can be invented by IT users. Some IT inventions are well understood as incremental improvements in existing capabilities, as with a microprocessor which can undertake the same functions more cheaply and faster than the previous year's model. Other IT inventions, by their nature, enable new or considerably improved applications. We focus here on the process which begins when either accumulation of incremental progress or substantial breakthroughs make new or improved applications economic. In most years, that happens several times in different parts of IT, marking the beginning, not the end, of a process that shifts out the production function.[3]

The rest of this section briefly sketches the next step of that process, namely co-invention by a single applier.

IT in Use: Co-invention of Business Information Systems

The most valuable IT applications, and those which directly transform the production process of the firm, business information systems (BIS), are associated with substantial co-invention costs. These are costs that a using firm needs to bear 'up front' before getting any value out of the application. The co-invention costs include the costs of programming to make a technology useful in a business information system, the costs of training workers to use it and, importantly, the costs of inventing a business purpose for the system and organizational changes to use it effectively. Co-invention costs are very substantial. Only a small fraction of the costs of inventing and implementing IT-based applications in large firms are costs of ITK.

The reasons for the high costs of business co-invention are well documented in the literature.[4] Co-invention of new BIS often involves linked improvements in white-collar production processes and in difficult-to-value 'soft' output attributes. This co-invention involves the translation of an underlying technical opportunity into business systems which will produce an output using fewer resources (sometimes), or a better output that customers might choose (often). The translation is itself not trivial, nor is the conceptual leap of understanding how customers will value 'soft' output attributes such as timeliness, convenience, flexibility and availability. Improvements in the white-collar production process often call for changes within organizations. Job definitions, division (or firm) boundaries, incentive schemes and other elements of organizational structures and functions will be different in highly-computerized BIS than in set-ups predating such systems. Co-invention takes time and resources, including flashes of inventive brilliance. Inventive brilliance which changes everyone's work is not usually the most common, or cheapest, resource in an organization. Nor is deep understanding of customer valuation of radical changes in 'soft' output attributes.

The underlying features of IT-based production that lead to these substantial adjustment costs lie primarily in the tensions of routinizing and regularizing white-collar work. As databases and business logic have improved and accumulated, bureaucracies have become more accomplished over time in undertaking two very different kinds of functions. First, bureaucracies *know* more about their workers, suppliers and customers. Analytically inclined bureaucracies can thus take advantage of such knowledge to improve service and incentives incrementally. Second, the comparative disadvantage of routinized and regularized processes, inadequately personalized to the circumstances of individual workers, suppliers or customers, declines as IT-based systems are combined with a human face and a human presence.

Once a BIS is installed and working, it creates two other assets that may be of sustained importance. Almost all BIS continue to interact with the rest of a 'human organization', and the system will begin to generate knowledge at the interface. Gripes about the BIS and 'wish lists' (guides to future technical progress) are half of this. The other half depends on the analytical use of BIS.

If there are analytical uses, however, they generate knowledge about the way the organization itself (outside the BIS) functions, knowledge which, once understood and put to use, is valuable in promoting future technical progress. Of course not all BIS produce such knowledge, and not all managers are capable of taking advantage of it even when they do. The creation of such stocks of knowledge in the aggregate, however, has been sufficient to boost substantially the rewards of managers who choose to exploit it.

As a result, co-invention takes time and scarce resources, and is the source of adjustment costs at the individual using firm. IT-using firms designing new business systems are well aware of co-invention costs, which are a central point of discussion in the professional and business literature of IT users. Being risky, co-invention includes costs of experimentation, costs of failed systems and so on. There is some learning from experience and from the experience of other users, so that co-invention costs will sometimes decline over time, as when imitation proves cheaper than original co-invention. Nonetheless much of the cost of inventing new BIS is local, just as many of the problems that are solved are local and specific.

After the period of incremental experimentation with new BIS, any of several outcomes can occur. A system may not be found to be useful, the result being that it is either abandoned or goes unused. Some surveys suggest that this is the most frequent occurrence. Another common outcome is that the system is discovered to be useful, and this results in incremental improvement and refinement. In this case, the demand for the services of the system is likely to put pressure on computer or networking capacity, leading to an increased demand for capacity. Much of the demand for ITK is conditional upon an assessment of its usefulness as a result of this process. The incremental improvement (and capacity pressure) process may well continue for a period of years, with resulting 'upgrades' to the underlying ITK capacity.

This structure of co-invention activities leads to a very particular structure of costs. Look first at narrowly technical activities such as designing computer hardware or writing computer software. When we count up all the software that is written in connection with a single use, we find that more – far more – of this technical invention on a cost basis is done by buyers than by sellers of IT.[5] In the aggregate, buyers of IT do somewhere between half and one whole order of magnitude more technical invention on a cost basis than do sellers. This is so even in the USA.[6]

If we then look beyond the technical costs to the business, and focus on the costs of inventing new uses for IT and new IT-based organizational structures which can achieve those new uses, we find even more investment by buyers. Indeed the costs of co-inventing the non-technical parts of applications appear to be perhaps half an order of magnitude larger than the total costs of technical invention.[7] The total cost of invention in IT in use can be divided into three categories. Most of it is the cost of business co-invention; the second biggest category is technical co-invention; the smallest category is 'technical' invention by the sellers of IT.

The literature on econometrics has found several results that are consistent with this finding.[8] First the usual – and probably correct – interpretation involves a very high measured rate of return to IT investment and use at the firm level.[9] In a number of studies of large firms, Erik Brynjolfsson and others have measured that high return. Such a return is confirmed in the case of firms which use little IT, particularly those that do not have access to co-inventions linked to IT and which have to bear the costs of putting them in place. Perhaps more directly related to the point of this chapter here is the literature on the diffusion of new IT technologies between large firms. Studies such as those undertaken by Saloner and Steinmueller (1995) and Bresnahan and Saloner (1996) find that business co-invention is a major barrier to early adoption. Of course, barriers to adoption at the individual firm level and high measured returns to adoption are consistent in equilibrium if one believes that the adopters have made a large investment in co-invention.

In one econometric study, Shane Greenstein and I looked at the transition to new architectures for BIS during the late 1980s and early 1990s (1997). The transition was quite marked, and strong enough to undercut the rents of the pre-existing dominant vendor, which was IBM. The earliest users to switch, however, were not those which had the most to gain from using the new architectures. Rather they were those which had the smallest adjustment costs at the individual using-firm level, often lower value applications later on. Whilst this 'reverse diffusion' finding may not be general to all cycles of new IT in BIS, the general point is that obviousness, or ease of organizational implementation (meaning low adjustment costs), as well as high value, are important determinants of early adoption.

The above is a longish narrative of what happens at a typical, single firm using IT, beginning with an IT invention and leading on to applications co-invention. That single user firm creates a number of changes. The most immediate is that, assuming the BIS works, the firm demands more ITK and uses it in its own production. That is the simple part; IT having raised the invention possibility frontier of the economy, complementary applications co-invention raises the production function.

Co-invention in the single using firm also leaves behind a number of assets. More of the production process is routinized and regularized, often with databases and the logic to work on them embedded in software. The using firm will often have learned something about its organization and about customers' demands, knowledge that may not only be useful locally, but also be partially portable to other firms. The using firm will have learned, especially in its technical co-invention, what features it desires in purchased ITK and will have communicated these to IT sellers.

Many different using firms build these assets in response to substantial new IT invention. There is enough failure in co-invention and in efforts to learn the broadly applicable lessons of any particular new co-invention, for society to achieve overall benefits from a number of distinct replications. This wide variety of explorations in co-invention increases the likelihood that one or more of them will yield broadly useful new knowledge.

Although we have been considering the response to a particular new invention, exploration and co-invention occur regularly in response to new IT inventions.

IT in Use: Personal Applications

When the user of an application is not a firm or other large organization but an individual, adoption and co-invention have different features. The most important of these is that initial adjustment costs at the individual level are not nearly as important. Many individual adopters buy systems that are ready to run in terms of applications. An individual's PC can run a word-processing programme or a spreadsheet; an engineer's work station can operate a design programme, all without large investments in technical invention at the using firm, and often without large initial investments changing the nature of organizations or the products of firms. The simple solution of 'buy computer and run application' is available.[10] To be sure, not all the value of that application will be available without co-invention. Most of the important applications of spreadsheets had to be invented, and all the organizational changes that came from having presentation-graphics programmes and e-mail had to be invented as well. Yet all of these could be simply undertaken as 'learn-by-using', based on PC systems that could be installed and used without 'up front' business or technical adjustment costs.

The scope of this characterization of demand is limited to personal *applications*, not uses of personal computers; it is a point about demand, not technology. When PCs or PC software are used as one technical element of a BIS, the latter will be subject to the usual adjustment costs.

This is not to say that there are no adjustment costs in personal applications areas, merely that they are not primarily borne by the individual adopter. Instead someone (an application software developer) has to write the applications software that lies behind the ready-to-go systems. Applications software developers learn from their customers' tendency to learn-by-using so that, over time, invention and co-invention together lead to better systems.

Once again, much of the demand for ITK comes either from repeat purchasers conditioning their decision to acquire further capital equipment upon earlier experiences, or else from users who have seen other people adopt the PC. For some kinds of applications, the value of adopting is directly raised when many other users have already adopted. E-mail, for example, is more valuable when friends and colleagues use it. Word processing is more valuable when others can read the file formats. And so on. For almost all applications, however, there is an 'indirect' network effect. Because the costs of writing an application can be spread between all users, the more users there are, the more the economic return to making new applications.

As a result, the structure of IT demand in personal applications is quite different from the BIS we saw in the previous section, pages 118 to 122. Here strong network effects contribute to social increasing returns to scale. The external effects, however, do not arise through individual users' failure to co-invent, but rather through failure to coordinate in creating large markets.

Widespread adoption of particular technologies in personal applications creates human and physical capital. The human capital can be understood simply as 'complex computer use'. Workers know how to use personal computers in order to analyse and communicate. The physical capital is partly the installed base of computers, partly the data and documents stored on them.

We have now looked at the very partial equilibrium of an individual adopter. Let us now move up to the level of markets in particular IT segments.

2   DYNAMIC EXTERNALITY STRUCTURES

In the last section, we looked at the individual user's decision to adopt new IT technology in two kinds of markets differentiated by adoption–adjustment costs of co-invention at the individual user level. Let us now turn to the implications for all users and sellers of ITK. In this section we continue to examine the implications of a single important new IT invention, but now at partial equilibrium, single-market level. We maintain the distinction between BIS-supporting and personal application-supporting markets.

Many of the common implications of the two kinds of markets arise from their general-purpose technology structure. The economic returns to inventors of IT and/or vendors of ITK arise from large markets with many different users. External effects determine usage. The external effects may be direct network externalities, as when users communicate with one another or share files or ideas for applications. Alternatively the external effects may be indirect, as when the total number of users, along with their inventiveness and readiness to pay, determines the quality of ITK on offer *to each*. In either case, the implications are that a new IT invention is associated with social increasing returns to scale because of the GPT structure.

The distinction between high individual-user adoption cost markets and high network effects markets does, however, imply a distinct dynamic for the realization of socially increasing returns.

Socially Increasing Returns under Adjustment Costs

In BIS-supporting markets, substantial co-invention costs at the individual-user level are a bottleneck following new IT invention. If early adopters of new technology are successful in terms of co-invention costs, they typically earn substantial returns. Imitation by laggards follows to take advantage of some of what has been learned from the struggles of early adopters. ITK sales rise as a result of this collective success. IT inventors learn from their customers' experience and improve their offerings in pursuit of what their customers actually want.

This story of co-invention cycles offers the prospect of socially increasing returns to scale arising through two distinct external effects. The first one comes from falling co-investment costs. Early users' experience lowers later users' co-invention costs. This is a one-way externality, spilling out from early to late adopters, and there are few available institutions for internalizing it. The one-way nature of the externality creates an incentive to wait.

The second externality flows from the supply of improved technology. For foresighted technology vendors, the rate of technological improvement in IT will depend on the number of total adopters and their likely adoption dates. The more and earlier the adoption, the greater the incentive for technologists to invest, race or compete for business. The incentive for IT inventors to anticipate co-invention may not always be effective. The anticipation is conceptually quite demanding for important IT inventions as it involves guessing what will be co-invented. Follow-on inventions and incremental improvements are conceptually easier of anticipation, and for these there is considerable opportunity for IT vendors to advance the entire market equilibrium by anticipatory technical investment.

The timing of social returns to important IT inventions is thus often determined by the timing of the co-invention and its spillovers, including IT that follows on from co-invention. This tends to lag awhile behind the period of early adoption of the technology, or the period of the greatest public attention to the technology.[11] There are two lags, the first between invention and initial serious co-invention, and the second between early co-invention and the widespread spillover of co-invented ideas. Historically, for important IT inventions, these lags have been in the region of half a decade to a decade. As a result, there is little reason to look for a contemporary relationship between the introduction of valuable technologies for organizational computing and resulting value creation, and little expectation that there will be a great deal of coordination between co-inventors. The productivity impact will come later and be spread out over time.[12]

The cycle between co-invention and invention in business information systems often leads to standing relationships between using firms and particular vendors or technologies. Users find that their very valuable co-invention and selected vendor's invention are together built into systems. Incremental improvement of these systems using compatible technologies lowers competition but economizes on adjustment costs. Once users begin to chafe under the lock-in, diminishing returns of a different form set in. Existing technologies may be a constraint on the rate of socially increasing returns; but escape from the lock-in may require very difficult-to-coordinate common movement to new technologies, a problematic task if there is considerable co-invention. Such shifts are correspondingly rare and require special circumstances.[13]

Socially Increasing Returns under Network Effects

While personal applications segments are not an area of initial co-invention, they share the same structure of social pay-offs in the long run. Many technologies used by a single person have this structure. Above are suggested the PC, but other technologies, such as word processing, the browser, e-mail or instant messaging have this characteristic as well. Each of these has significant network effects. If there is a substantial body of applications, many users will want PCs; and if there is plenty of online content, many users will want browsers; and those applications and that content will be forthcoming if the technology is widely adopted. As long as there are plenty of other users to communicate with, users will want e-mail or instant messaging. In that case, the network externalities are direct (users want to communicate with one another), whilst in the case of PCs or browsers they are indirect (a large installed base of users will draw rich applications or rich content).

The implications of this particular structure of pay-offs to users are familiar from the literature on network effects which emphasizes change in the nature of equilibrium over time. The first phase is before the invention of the enabling technology. The second is one of waiting for network effects to take effect: for example, one person not adopting the technology because others have not yet done so. The third phase is one of positive feedback once the network effects are taking place. If an important motivation for users of a technology is network effects, one should expect some coordination in the adoption time. That coordination can either start quickly or start more slowly, as the length of the second phase is typically not well determined.

The transition from a regime of not realizing network effects to one of realizing them can add considerable momentum to these markets. Consider the PC market once it was understood that the spreadsheet and word processor would be the dominant 'personal productivity' applications. A series of technical and marketing activities, culminating in the introduction of the IBM PC, put the industry on a high equilibrium in which ordinary business people, not computer hobbyists, knew of the PC and its main uses. Once that was accomplished, there was continuing technical progress that made PCs more powerful, easier to use, cheaper and so on. This technical advance, plus ever-larger network effects, led to a steady increase in the number of users, and constituted a positive spiral effect.

The key to the speed of positive spirals for some personal applications software or support-ITK is their low co-invention costs. These, in turn, tend to follow from the comparatively simple and non-transformable nature of these applications at the time of adoption. Their power comes later on, with the invention of useful systems in which they are embedded.

Whilst the creation of positive network effects in personal applications-supporting IT can be a very powerful force, it can also create and sustain dominant positions for established vendors, especially when the network effects are linked to a proprietary product or standard. This will lead the incumbent dominant firm to seek to maintain control, perhaps by attempting to prevent widespread distribution of alternative new technologies. Users would like competitive experimentation outside, or partially outside, the cluster of existing network effects. As long as they get to choose whether to switch, or whether to switch partially, to a new technology, their interests are preserved. Vendors whose technology embodies a standard will discourage such experimentation and switching.

Implications of Single Market Equilibrium

Knowledge creation generates economic opportunities as well. The beginning of the cycle in the last section was an advance in IT. This new knowledge creates an opportunity for applications. The centre of that section was the invention of those applications and the formulation of the required knowledge. In this section, we see that knowledge, in turn, creates an economic opportunity for sellers of ITK. In the short run, it produces a market for them. In the long run, new knowledge about applications of IT creates an opportunity for IT to change to accommodate those applications.

Many of the benefits of large markets and positive feedback between buyers' and sellers' inventions have been incorporated into IT. The large scale of modern IT markets has created the opportunity to put more and more resources into fundamental hardware improvements. It has also stimulated the emergence of more and more high-quality software of both infrastructural and applications forms. Not all the advantages of large scale have been achieved, however. Experimentation and competition are lacking in some contexts. This is a topic we will return to later.

At this stage what we have seen is complementarity between invention of new IT and co-invention in IT-using sectors on the one hand, and a structure of socially increasing returns to scale and resulting externalities on the other. The limitation so far is that the discussion has been confined to one round of IT invention and related co-invention in a single segment of IT application. We now turn to the question of sustained technical progress over time and, after that, to the degree to which existing market institutions have internalized all the externalities.

3 THE WIDENING SPAN OF APPLICATION OVER TIME

As IT has advanced, and as ITK has grown cheaper, the span of the BIS IT application has broadened in several directions. Three of these are examined in this section. This takes us out of the partial equilibrium framework of the last two sections towards a general equilibrium framework and sustained economy-wide mechanisms.

The first of the three broadenings stems from the reuse of fundamental IT inventions in a number of segments. A PC today is as powerful as a mainframe one was a generation ago and a good deal cheaper. Smaller business units may now take advantage of BIS similar to the sort deployed only in large enterprises 20 or 30 years ago. We take this up below. The second broadening of the application of IT is serving to move the boundary between the specific and the general. What used to be co-invention, localized and hence expensive, becomes invention with the resulting exploitation of scale economies. I take this up later (see pages 132–5). The third broadening, like the first, arises from ever-cheaper IT. In this case, however, both cheaper computing and cheaper communications move towards larger and more complex applications, notably those cutting across the boundaries of firms.

Falling Fixed Costs of Computing

Early IT markets saw investments in fundamental technologies, notably in hardware and systems design. This meant that costs of ITK have been falling, particularly the costs of the smallest capable computing devices. This has led to the emergence of new markets. One way to understand these would be as a movement down a fixed demand curve, suggesting the rapid setting in of diminishing returns. As the smaller-sized categories of computers have, historically, had vastly larger unit sales than the larger-sized ones, the diminishing returns, on this basis, would have been temporarily offset by the shape of the demand curve. Demand must have been elastic over the relevant range to explain the relative size of the PC and mainframe market segments.

Examples of mere diminishing returns do exist. On the data-processing side, we have seen the extension from core applications that undertake the most valuable activities in firms to far more trivial ones, for example keeping track of the football pool in the mailroom. In terms of computers literally 'computing', there has been diffusion of cheaper and cheaper floating-point arithmetic, varying from very critical problems in physics (with urgent military applications) to drawing 'bad guys' on computer screen games (a high-floating, point-intensive task). One consequence of far cheaper ITK has been a diffusion to lower-value uses. It would be quite odd if it did not have this effect.

If that were all that lower costs achieved, one would conclude that diminishing returns were setting in. But the smaller-sized categories of computers have had their own feedback loops, with new classes of applications being invented and widely used. Most elements of IT have increasing returns to scale, from the first-copy costs of a piece of applications software to the invention costs of new kinds of storage devices. As a result, the large market size of newer categories of computing, such as the PC, is both fed by, and feeds back into, a considerable supply of new IT of various kinds. A fundamental non-linearity has been at work in the system. IT cheap enough to be used in a mass-market draws large-market complements and improvements. This makes the size of the market in IT ever larger, creating an economic return to the invention of new IT specifically shaped to that market

Diminishing returns do not quickly set in, despite the widening span of application, because the positive feedback loop is renewed when the span of application widens. Of course, sooner or later, this particular dynamic is going to run out of economic activity. Perhaps hand-held computers, or smart-cell phones, will not generate nearly as much of a positive feedback loop as PCs did. Until now, however, the reuse of fundamental IT developments in newer, cheaper categories has renewed the growth cycle.

Converting Activities from the Specific to the General

When many inventors are working on very similar problems, the possibility of exploiting scale economies in invention arises. Often the solution presents itself in the form of vertically disintegrating the common part of the invention and creating a new industry or discipline which focuses on a new 'general specialty'. The result increases the degree to which scale economies are exploited at some cost of lost specialization. This mechanism can change powerfully the pace of technical change.[14] Since much co-invention of IT applications appears to be the same inventive activity undertaken over and over again, there is a long history of efforts to split parts of it into new general specialties.

Steady progress has been made in this direction, but there appear to be limits. Within the 'technical' parts of co-invention, the history shows tremendous successes. As Friedman and Cornford (1989) document, the market-IT sector has made tremendous steps in helping IT-using firms with the technical parts of co-invention. IT products, of the types generally called 'infrastructure' and 'tools' by using firms, have taken over many of the tasks of managing hardware and managing the writing of applications software. Perhaps the most important of these developments were the invention and improvement of (a) applications-development environments and related programming tools, and (b) database management systems. But there are many other examples. The overall effect of this technical progress has been to replace duplicating efforts on the part of a large number of technical people in IT-using companies with tools that undertake the effort for them. MIS (management information strategies) departments have become, in the narrowest technical sense, considerably more productive as a result of this development.

This extension of the general taking over from the specific has, however, met important limitations. The *business* part of co-invention has resisted exploiting economies of scale and remains stubbornly local. A long series of efforts to move all business co-invention into 'general specialist' firms has largely failed. The most recent two failures are both spectacular: the 'business process re-engineering' movement and the horizontal dotcom movement. The horizontal dotcom movement hoped that all IT-using firms and industries would move into new applications areas in electronic commerce using universal ('horizontal') applications software and services. The slightly earlier BPR (Business Process Re-engineering) movement hoped that the tasks of deciding on the business logic of new applications could be turned into an 'engineering' activity that would have a new specialty, for example something that C++ language programmers could accomplish. Whilst some good came from both efforts, neither of them – nor many similar efforts – led to widespread exploitation of scale economies in the business part of co-invention. This is in contrast to successes in the technical part.

Ordering and Routinizing More and More of the Production Process

As IT has grown more capable in both hardware and software terms, and as ITK has grown cheaper, the prospect of larger and more complex applications has grown. The boundary between IT-based production in white-collar bureaucracies and other systems of production has moved steadily as a result.

The familiar example of the airline reservation system can serve to illustrate this point. It was originally invented to count something important, namely

unsold seats on aircraft. A fairly common start for regularization and routinization, indeed, is the existence of something that is obviously quantifiable and
needs counting. Once quantified, it can then support a simple operational
behaviour, such as the command: 'do not sell any seat that has already been
sold 1.48 times or more'. Operational sales decisions need to be made at a
wide number of points, including firms' own sales divisions, distribution
points (travel agents) and directly in communication with large purchasers.
That requires invention, however, in the form of IT that is able to deliver
unsold seats to various distinct 'markets'. There is also a need for technical co-
invention in the form of a system which reliably delivers information to all
groups at different sales locations and decides which of them sold seats first;
in addition co-invention is needed to decide, for example, what a large
customer can be permitted to learn about capacity and inventory from databases. In this simple narrative, we have pieced together decades of invention
involving database management systems/networks and co-invention under the
long-run goal of an integrated operational system. The point is that operations
have a tendency to become ever more tightly controlled.

The database of unsold seats becomes a database of ticket sales and capacity utilization which permits the building of analytical models which management can use to make important decisions. What kinds of routes systematically
have empty seats? That sort of information can guide allocation of aircraft to
routes and drive sales efforts to fill planes. What kinds of sales lead customers
actually to show up and fly, and what kind lead to 'no-shows'? That information can guide the joint determination of the overbooking rate (pegged at 1.48
above) and capacity. More and more complex analytical models can be built
as more and more of the production process is measured and monitored
systematically. Management functions thereby become more analytical and
systematic. Managers feed back to the tightly controlled operational system
what it is they wish to accomplish.

The database of ticket sales also becomes a marketing tool for building
complex customer relationships. Volume discounts and other mechanisms for
treating various classes of customers differently, such as frequent-flier
programmes, come into being. Learning from customer behaviour becomes
both easier (as a result of bigger databases) and more IT-intensive. Feeding
back to Marketing the information learned about customer behaviour in order
to build more complex relationships itself calls for more IT systems.
Customers, especially large ones, want to manage their side of complex relationships and this leads to more opportunities for cross-firm communication.
Because much of the production process in service industries is shared
between buyers and sellers, the marketing function may include customer-
management functions as well. These would be connected at first to measuring 'no-shows', later, in attempting to minimize the impact of 'no-shows' on

costs by means of incentives and general planning. The entire buying–selling relationship can end up being routinized and regularized, with complex contracts between buyers and sellers emerging in explicit (software based) form.

At each stage, routinization leaves behind not only databases full of facts and structures that systematically capture economic data, but also systems that increasingly rely on precise calculations using these data to support and perform decision making. The overall production process of the firm and to some degree (beginning 20 or so years ago) knowledge of customers, suppliers and distributors has grown ever more routinized and regularized.

Of course, another version of this history, adjusted for the different information economics of other kinds of firms and industries and for different kinds of commercial relations between buyers, sellers and intermediaries, has appeared in alternative contexts. In many industries the broad general themes of this section are being played out. These involve operational support, analytical decision making, internal reorganization, discrimination between customer or vendor classes and the emergence of complex contracts based upon multiple observables. At every stage, these involve not only invention but also co-invention.

Summary on the Extensive Margin

What each of the sections above shows is how the historical pattern of IT use and IT investment does not have the characteristic of falling costs which take us down a fixed demand curve. Instead of taking the economy towards diminishing returns in the first instance, IT as a general capability has found new extensive margins with which to work. Each extensive margin has set off its own cycle(s) of positive feedback. As a result, the demand curve for ITK shifts outwards, and diminishing returns do not set in.

The GPT logic of IT applies not only within each kind of application, as we saw in the second section, but also across kinds of applications, building new types of IT partly on the foundation of old kinds. This reuse of non-rivalrous IT knowledge arises from the GPT nature of IT in the large (meaning across very different kinds of applications) as well as in the small (across different applications of the same specific technologies).

Development along each new margin also has inherent limitations. Ultimately one would expect this kind of expansion to hit decreasing returns as well. For now, however, the expansion has continued with great success.

4   COMPLEMENTARITY OVER TIME

For continued costly invention and co-invention to be profitable, some force must keep the return to using ITK from falling over time. So far, we have looked at the general-purpose technology nature of IT, one powerful force which keeps the return high. A second dynamic force arises because, just as invention of IT spurs co-invention, ideas from co-invention spur new invention. This leads to continuing improvements.[15]

IT improvements over time build on the basis of earlier inventions in IT. In that sense there is a fundamental complementarity between inventions in IT at one moment in time and inventions at another. That simple remark, however, applies to all cumulative bodies of knowledge, that is to say to all science-based technologies. The particular structure of invention and co-invention described here leads to a sustained pattern of inventive opportunity for reasons that go beyond that universal force. Invention and co-invention are not only static complements; rather, their duality creates dynamic complementarities because inventions in one domain raise the economic return to inventions in the other and provide intellectual stimulus for each.

Inventions in Two Domains: Complementarity over Time

The centrepiece of the argument about knowledge creation above (see pages 118–22 and 122–5) was that a cycle of invention and co-invention creates two distinct bodies of knowledge, one about IT, the other about the applications of IT.

This feedback system is inherently dynamic because of the way that knowledge about those two areas works. It is very difficult to anticipate, even assuming a great deal of communication, how the co-development of IT and its applications should go. Typically sellers of IT announce new technical capabilities, and these either do, or do not, find a market. Sellers learn from the co-invention that actually occurs what it is that inventors of applications really want. Each new stage of learning what can be accomplished with IT-based production in using industries leads to a higher state of knowledge about broad IT generally. Thus vendor firms attack problems at a later stage using better 'technology' (in the sense of being able to make smaller and faster ITK devices) and with better knowledge of the market for new IT inventions.

Another force, growing more important over time, is the complementary relationship between existing installed ITK and BIS on the one hand, and new advances in IT and the possibility of new BIS on the other. Some of this is simple cumulativeness. After the installation of BIS facilitating operational control, analytical opportunities arise. We saw examples of this in the airline ticket discussion above. Another example is that, during the first generation of development, accounts software permits simple operational control of billing, such as getting letters out to late payers. In the next generation of development, the existence of the operational database in the AR (Accounts

Receivable) software permits analysis of what kinds of customers pay on time, and what kinds of incentives lead customers to pay on time. All of this is valuable invention that builds upon earlier valuable invention. In yet another generation, those AR systems and several other operational databases and their analytical overlays are combined into unified customer-relationship management systems. At each stage, the cumulativeness arises from the character of the investments made at earlier points: more information held explicitly in BIS lowers the costs of new BIS. This is a force that plays out at the individual IT-using firm level. It creates market opportunities for invention of new IT and for co-invention of new BIS at later times. Because of the combination of cumulativeness and new opportunity, there is a continuing positive feedback between past investments and new investment opportunities for inventors of IT and sellers of ITK.

This feedback between invention and co-invention leads to a repeated cycle of improvements in two stocks of knowledge. This process can carry buyers and sellers a long way, with improvements that are fully complementary over time. If the standards permitting different hardware and software components, including those which are written by using firms, change slowly then the process of repeated invention and co-invention leads to cumulative change. This path will be encouraged by the existing dominant firms selling IT, often with considerable success. Of course, change of that type sometimes stays on the incremental improvement path for too long a period of time, and then radical breaks with the past are required. These tend to be sponsored by entrant sellers of IT: those who come, not completely from outside the IT market, but from a different part of it.

Dynamic Complementarity between Different IT

Not all of the relationships involving complementarity happen within such narrow confines. New forms of IT are sometimes complementary to old forms. Consider the commercialization of the Internet. The Internet was used first of all in universities and governments. A series of developments, most notably the invention of the browser, brought it into widespread commercial use where it appeared as a genuinely new technology. The complementarities between this new technology and technologies already in use are striking. 'The Internet has sold a lot of PCs,' said Microsoft's CEO. Absolutely, and it has sold a lot of large computers and a lot of software, telecommunications services and equipment as well. So here we see new technical progress raising the MVP (Marginal Value Product) of capital. The complementarity also flows the other way. The prior success of the PC meant that many people could access the Internet cheaply. The prior success of BIS also meant that many business datasets could be reused or cheaply created to show, for example, the price of an item or good that was available on a web-page. New inventions of valuable applications such as e-mail, instant messaging or many forms of electronic commerce are complementary to existing IT, both as technology and as capital in place.

The complementarity between old inventions and new inventions, and the related complementarity between old investments in ITK and new ones, are heightened by the continually growing scope of BIS. Where BIS originally applied to narrow, specific tasks, such as collecting bills or scheduling a machine, they have grown to encompass, or at least affect, many of the production processes in service industries and much of the management and control of production processes in all industries. The production process includes buying inputs and selling outputs. In modern economies, many more workers are engaged in those activities than are engaged in, for example, manufacturing. Consequently BIS have grown to include many activities in which a firm interacts with its customers and suppliers, as was seen above in the airline example. The ability of BIS to cross the boundary of the firm was the next step, a path which advanced economies began to go down some 20 years ago. That is a demand-pull agenda, drawn by the value of the applications that might be generated. Substantial invention and co-invention costs remain before anything like the possibility of interorganizational computing can be realized.

Demand-pull from co-inventors creates a series of new economic opportunities for inventors. Co-inventors wish to design new applications which take advantage of the assets in existing ('legacy') applications, and which can be accessed over the (now) near-universal Internet from the (now) near-ubiquitous PC. In the first instance, this shifts out the demand curve for existing forms of ITK, as the new systems will need more capacity, newer equipment and so on. More importantly, this creates a demand for new forms of IT invention and ITK which make it easier to design and implement those new applications systems running on many different computers over a network. The trend towards networking in computer applications brings advances in telecommunications into the positive feedback loop. The economic return to making bandwidth cheaper (or more portable) rises along with the economic return to making computing cheaper (and more capable).

Convergence of Formerly Separate IT

Convergence is another powerful force preventing the onset of diminishing returns, especially for complex applications which have large potential impact. The existence of distinct clusters of IT technology gives new, complex applications a menu of supporting technologies and creates the opportunity for progress by linking those technologies together. Furthermore past investments in ITK in distinct clusters generate applications which extend beyond the boundaries of the firm and which are based on the assumption that ITK exists in other firms. This creates a very powerful complementarity between the inventions of the past and inventions of the future. Rather than crowding out the inventions that will support interorganizational computing in the future, the inventions that supported organizational and personal computing in the past raise their value.

The long-run dynamic which gives IT the power to make contributions over a long time span possesses two very distinct elements, one involving specialization, the other convergence. Very general scientific and technological knowledge underlies the basic engineering of computer hardware and software, as well as telecommunications, networking equipment and systems. That general knowledge is specialized into distinct clusters or nodes of technical progress. Within each cluster there are powerful external effects and positive feedbacks between the (specialized version of the) general-purpose technology and applications. Clusters such as telephone systems, mainframe computers and PCs have historically grown following distinct positive feedback paths. Because there is a sharing of basic technologies across these clusters, the founding of new clusters is a powerful force preventing the onset of diminishing returns.

Complementarity over All

The point of these particular examples is that diminishing returns in accumulating knowledge in specific kinds of applications and IT need not lead to diminishing returns to the aggregate use of IT. Widespread success in one applications area accumulates assets which serve as the foundation for new applications areas. The most important examples at the present time have to do with extension of applications across the boundaries of firms. Will that economic and technical opportunity be quickly exhausted? The answer is that so much employment in rich countries centres on white-collar bureaucracies which buy or sell that it seems highly likely that automation, followed by process improvement, will have a high pay-off. New ways of using old IT and combining it with new IT, as yet far from fully exploited, suggest that current processes of positive feedback and accumulation will continue.

5   INCENTIVES AND GOAL CONFLICTS

The general-purpose technology structure of IT means that there are a number of important externalities among co-inventors and between co-inventors and inventors. If all of these were internalized by contract, the economy would undertake the socially optimum rate of invention and co-invention. The modern economy is far from reaching that standard, and for important forms of co-invention and invention the social return to innovation lies above the private one. We discussed above some of the information gaps which make literal contracting a difficult task. In this section, we take up the question of why, and how, existing structures for organizing invention and co-invention do not always achieve the optimum. The existing structures which are discussed here relate to the following categories: (1) the sellers of general-purpose ITK, from computers to telecommunications switches, to operating systems, to databases and tools; (2) the sellers of packaged applications software; (3) the sellers of customized or semi-customized applications software; and (4) the using firm. Obviously considerable scale economies are achieved by having firms sell ITK to many using firms. What incentive problems remain?

The reuse externality for co-invention has already been mentioned. When the tasks of an application are reasonably well-defined and common to many users, this externality can be partly internalized by moving technical progress in applications from users (4 above) to independent applications vendors (2 or 3 above). There are some limits, as we have seen, because many applications require very extensive localization to work in particular using firms. Thus the widespread movement of applications development from the comparatively expensive (4) or (3) to (2) has been limited. The most direct accommodations involve applications software. These entail simply taking ideas from applications first invented in a clumsy or one-off way and writing a piece of software. This permits widespread use of the idea in an economical form. When firms or industries cannot easily use the same applications software (because they differ in their organizational structures or relationships to vendors, customers or products), other forms arise. Semi-customized software is used for some problems, or software is written by consultants over and over again for different firms using the same knowledge. For other problems, market IT can be altered to make writing certain kinds of applications in using firms easier, thereby lowering their costs.

There is also an important incentive problem amongst co-inventors. Suppose firm A undertakes an important new application of IT which it thinks will give it lower costs or better products than its competitors. It will not be eager to have ideas relating to new applications sold in a piece of software to competitor firm B. Neither will it be pleased to have its consultants or other semi-custom software vendors finish the application and then go over to work for firm B. Rightly firm A will think that much of the co-invented part of the application is its own invention and that having it spill out to competitors constitutes a problem. Accordingly, efforts to achieve fully the broad reuse of co-invented ideas are likely to face difficulties.[16] Only those things firms do not find strategic are quickly and widely reused by the comparatively efficient spillover mechanisms (3), instead of clumsy leakage among (4) by, for example, movements of employees to competitors and consequent labour market sales of trade secrets.

The other important externality associated with a general purpose technology lies between sellers of general products and co-inventors. In the case of IT, this externality falls between inventors of IT products and co-inventors. Each group would like to see the other experiment with a wide variety of approaches, as each group would like to have successful (co-)invention by the other group pushing out the demand curve for its products. Inventors can typically expect this behaviour from co-inventors, as there are many more of these.

There is a problem achieving adequate experimentation on the invention side in some circumstances. Certainly when an established proprietary standard is at the centre of a great deal of applications development, there is a goal conflict about competitive experimentation between sellers and buyers. This applies either to the case of adjustment cost co-invention or to the case of network effects.

The famous example from the past is experimentation with replacements for the IBM mainframe platform. Further inventions of compatible extensions to the platform by IBM provided one of the highest private rates of return investments in the economy. IBM prosecuted them with vigour, as well as with an eye to ensuring that customers remained loyal to it. Competitive alternatives were one of the lowest rates of return investments in the economy and, for a generation, as customers hoped IBM would become a bit more experimental, competitive investment and experimentation were largely lacking. Indeed the technologies which ultimately became competitors to the IBM mainframe standard were not invented as competitors, but underwent a long 'indirect entry' path, at first paid for by other uses. Only long after customers wanted them did serious alternatives appear.

Much the same story is being replayed in the Microsoft era. That particular firm has every incentive to ensure that important technical developments, such as the commercialization of the Internet, are provided in ways which keep customers loyal to *its own* particular platforms and technologies. However, given the choice to stay or not with Microsoft products, customers favour much more experimentation at the interface between the PC and the Internet. Such experiments have been blocked, however, by Microsoft's interference with the widespread distribution of products and technologies which it sees as threatening its competitive position.

As one might expect when the social return to innovation could be appropriated by any number of different firms (including existing sellers of IT, new sellers of IT, sellers of different types of IT and users of IT), contracting to internalize all the externalities is incomplete. Accordingly social returns to invention in the aggregate remain above private returns.

6   CONCLUSIONS

Much of the mechanism of IT's contribution to economic welfare follows from the socially increasing returns to scale rooted in complementarity between very different kinds of innovative activity. Within the many particular markets for IT, complementarities take the form of positive feedback between invention of new IT and co-invention of applications. Invention and co-invention are both areas with substantial innovative possibilities, so the cycle of positive feedback can be long-lived, with important inventions in one domain leading to new inventive opportunities in the other. Existing structures fail to internalize all the externalities among inventors and co-inventors, first because of limitations as to what they are able to predict about each other and, second, because existing IT-dominant firms seek to control and manage the arrival of new technology, in the process often reducing the amount of experimentation and user choice way below the feasible competitive level. These mechanisms have delayed the onset of diminishing returns for decades. Socially beneficial routinization and regularization of white-collar bureaucracies is now moving into its second half-century without signs of technological exhaustion.

The range of applications of IT has been expanding as well, this being another force that tends to offset diminishing returns. Cheaper ITK has meant that some new applications are of lower value than older ones, yet it has also set off new positive feedback cycles which have pushed out the demand for new types of IT and created new sources of value. The personal computer, for example, has not appeared merely as a cheaper form of mainframe. Rather it has served a number of new functions, most recently involving communication and information retrieval. All of this serves to increase its aggregate contribution. Here the social return once again exceeds the private one because the founding of new categories occurs by spillovers from old forms.

A final complementarity arises at an even wider scale. Over time, numerous specific IT technologies have come into widespread use. New applications today, for example, can assume widely installed bases of PCs and large organizational BIS. Thanks to recent developments, new applications currently take for granted widespread connection to the Internet. Networked applications which take advantage of those assumptions can be developed cheaply and quickly. The technical inventions of the past thus complement the technical inventions of the future by expanding the scope of applications. By means of such a mechanism, the Internet has accelerated the 20-year-old trend of applications crossing the boundary of the firm.

All of these forces will eventually be exhausted, as the contribution of any particular technology, even one as powerful and levered as IT, will ultimately hit diminishing returns. They show no near-term prospect of being exhausted, however, because although white collar bureaucracies use technology, they cannot as yet do exactly what their customers – or their managers – would like.

NOTES

1. A number of theories with very similar formal structures variously draw our attention to aggregate increasing returns (in several forms) to formalized R&D, to learning-by-doing, to product invention in 'quality ladders', to education and human capital formation and to many other things.

   Modern aggregate growth theory has not been written in a way which facilitates empirical analysis. Indeed most empirical work proceeds either by comparing growth between countries or by examining changes in growth across time in the same countries, attempting to predict them by the assets identified in the theories. These are surely two of the least promising empirical strategies ever developed in economics.

2. See Bresnahan and Trajtenberg (1995), and Helpman and Trajtenberg (1998).

3. IT vendors announce dozens of such 'paradigm shift' advances per month. The actual rate, while far lower, is well above zero.

4. A substantial management research literature, and a smaller econometric one, have characterized the invention process in organizational applications.

5. These remarks draw upon Bresnahan (2000) which contains definitions and sources. The data supporting this remark consist of surveys of expenditures on purchased technology versus technology built in-house within the corporate sector. Thus this part is literally cost accounting.

6. I emphasize the cost basis because this does not establish that buyers do more 'technical progress' than sellers do. Sellers achieve enormous economies of scale by shipping the same hardware or software design to millions of buyers (this being an important part of the equilibrium that defines the boundary in invention space between buyers and sellers) and thus may be making 'more' technical progress in whatever the appropriate physical units might be.

7. This result appears both in studies of the demand for IT, such as Bresnahan and Greenstein (1997) and Ito (1996), and in studies of firm-level returns to ITK investments, such as Brynjolfsson *et al.* (2000), Brynjolfsson and Yang (1997) and Brynjolfsson *et al.* 2000). This is not so much a cost-accounting exercise as an econometric one. Both literatures have needed to assign large business co-investment costs to ITK in order to rationalize firm behaviour.

8. Systematic statistical work on shifts in computing architectures has found substantial adjustment costs (Ito, 1996; Bresnahan and Greenstein, 1997), and the case literature on IT implementation highlights difficulties in implementing concurrent organizational changes (for example, Zuboff, 1988). Moreover, there is additional evidence that the monetary and nonmonetary costs of these adjustments is larger than the capital investments in many cases (Brynjolfsson and Hitt, 1996; Brynjolfsson and Yang, 1997; Bresnahan, 2000).

9. Because co-invention costs and successful attempts at co-invention vary between firms, there is substantial heterogeneity in the use of IT in a given cross-section of firms at any moment in time. The heterogeneity is driven, in no small degree, by differential success in co-invention and differential costs of co-invention. Cf. Bresnahan and Greenstein (1997) or Brynjolfsson *et al.* (2000). For modelling purposes, I am more interested here in this heterogeneity ex ante than in the uncertainty of co-invention which I treat as an adjustment cost to the user.

10. This is not to say that using firms do not need to undertake technical activities in order to use PCs. Indeed the costs of purchased PC hardware and software are just a down payment on the lifetime cost of ownership, which includes maintenance and support. But those are well understood as a cost of having ITK in place, not as adjustment costs or invention costs.

11. Friedman and Cornford (1989) call this 'the problem of the tenses'.

12. Links between particular IT technical progress in the late 1990s – the commercialization of

the Internet, the increase in the rate at which integrated circuits grew smaller – and the rapid rate of productivity growth in selected heavy IT-using countries at the same time, such as the USA, are very unlikely to be causal.

13.   See Bresnahan and Greenstein (1998) for an analysis of many of the major examples.
14.   See Bresnahan and Gambardella (1999) for theory in the spirit of Arora *et al.* (1998) for the way the creation of the chemical engineering discipline was centred upon making the analysis of processes routine and regular, with each new plant design or process design task building upon prior knowledge.
15.   The outcome is much like that of the 'quality ladder' models in the growth literature, for example Grossman and Helpman (1994). In those models, as here, early steps in the invention process form part of the foundation for later steps. In the models, economic agents know from the beginning which way is up the ladder, but the ladder is not instantly scaled because the incentive scheme rewards single steps as much as multiple steps. My analysis here is driven by agents discovering which of a number of apparently attractive rungs leads upwards.
16.   Ross Perot, inventor of applications software resold to many users, sensibly chose as an early body of customers the local monopoly health insurance firms in the USA in the 1960s. The semi-custom software industry he founded has had its greatest successes selling to governments and the like ever since.

BIBLIOGRAPHY

Arora, Ashish, Ralph Landau and Nathan Rosenberg (eds) (1998), *Chemicals and Long-Term Economic Growth*, New York: Wiley.

Barras, R. (1990), 'Interactive Innovation in Financial and Business Services: The Vanguard of the Service Revolution', *Research Policy*, **19**.

Bresnahan, Timothy (2000), 'The Changing Structure of Innovation in the Computer Industry', in D. Mowery (eds), *U.S. Industry in 2000: Studies in Competitive Performance*, Washington: National Academy Press.

Bresnahan, T. and A. Gambardella (1998), 'The Division of Inventive Labor and the Extent of the Market', in E. Helpman (ed.), *General Purpose Technologies and Economic Growth*, Cambridge, MA: MIT Press, 253–81.

Bresnahan, Timothy and Shane Greenstein (1997), 'Technical Progress and Co-Invention in Computing and in the Uses of Computers', *Brookings Papers on Economic Activity*, micro, 1–83.

– – (1999), 'Technological Competition and the Structure of the Computer Industry', *Journal of Industrial Economics*, **47**(1), 1–40.

Bresnahan, Timothy and Garth Saloner (1996), 'Large Firms' Demand for Computer Products and Services: Competing Market Models, Inertia, and Enabling Strategic Change', in David B. Yoffie (ed.), *Colliding Worlds: The Merging of Computers, Telecommunications, and Consumer Electronics*, Cambridge, MA: Harvard University Press.

Bresnahan, Timothy and Manuel Trajtenberg (1995), 'General Purpose Technologies: "Engines of Growth"?', *Journal of Econometrics*, Special Issue, **65**(1), 83–108.

Brynjolfsson, Erik and Lorin Hitt (1996), 'Paradox Lost? Firm-Level Evidence on the Returns to Information Systems Spending', *Management Science*, **42**(4), 541–58.

Brynjolfsson, Erik and Shinkyu Yang (1997), 'The Intangible Costs and Benefits of Computer Investments: Evidence from Financial Markets', *Proceedings of the International Conference on Information Systems*, Atlanta, GA, 14–17 December 1997.

Brynjolfsson, Erik, Timothy Bresnahan and Lorin Hitt (2000), 'Information Technology, Workplace Organization, and the Demand for Skilled Labor: Firm-level Evidence', *Quarterly Journal of Economics*, 117, February, 339–76.

Davenport, Thomas and James Short (1990), 'The New Industrial Engineering: Information Technology and Business Process Redesign', *Sloan Management Review*, **31**(4), 11–27.

David, Paul (1990), 'The Dynamo and the Computer: An Historical Perspective on the Modern Productivity Paradox', *American Economic Review*, **80**(2), 355–61.

Friedman, A. and D. Cornford (1989), *Computer Systems Development: History, Organization and Implementation*, Chichester: Wiley.

Garicano, Luis and Steven Kaplan (2000), 'The Effects of Business-to-Business E-Commerce on Transaction Costs', NBER Working Paper, W8017.

Gordon, Robert J. (2000), 'Does the "New Economy" Measure Up to the Great Inventions of the Past?', NBER Working Paper, 7833.

Greif, Avner, Paul Milgrom and Barry Weingast (1994), 'Coordination, Commitment and Enforcement: The Case of the Merchant Guild', *Journal of Political Economy*, **102**(4), 745–76.

Grossman, Gene M. and Elhanan Helpman (1994), 'Endogenous Innovation in the Theory of Growth', *Journal of Economic Perspectives*, **8**, 23–44.

Helpman, Elhanan and Manuel Trajtenberg (1998), 'A Time to Sow and a Time to Reap: Growth Based on General Purpose Technologies', in Elhanan Helpman (ed.), *General Purpose Technologies and Economic Growth, Cambridge*, MA: MIT Press.

Hubbard, Thomas N. (1998), 'Why are Process Monitoring Technologies Valuable? The Use of On-Board Information Technology in the Trucking Industry', NBER Working Paper, W6482.

Ito, Harumi (1996), 'Essays on Investment Adjustment Costs', PhD dissertation, Stanford University.

Katz, Michael and Carl Shapiro (1994), 'Systems Competition and Network Effects', *Journal of Economic Perspectives*, **8**(2), 93–115.

Litan, Robert and Alice M. Rivlin (2001), *Beyond the Dot.Coms: The Economic Promise of the Internet*, Washington, DC: Brookings Institution Press.

Malone, Thomas and Jack Rockart (1991), 'Computers, Networks and the Corporation', *Scientific American*, **265**(3), 128–36.

Milgrom, Paul and John Roberts (1992), *Economics, Organization and Management*, Englewood Cliffs, NJ: Prentice Hall.

Romer, Paul M. (1990) 'Endogenous Technological Change', *Journal of Political Economy*, **98**(5).

Saloner, Garth and W. Edward Steinmueller (1995), 'Demand for Computer Products and Services by Large European Organizations', Stanford GSB Research Paper Series, no. 1370.

Scott Morton, Michael (1991), *The Corporation of the 1990s: Information Technology and Organizational Transformation*, Oxford: Oxford University Press.

Zuboff, Shoshana (1988), *In the Age of the Smart Machine: The Future of Work and Power*, New York: Basic Books.

6. Empirical estimates of the relationship between product market competition and innovation

Philippe Aghion

1 INTRODUCTION

Both the theoretical industrial organization (IO) literature and the more recent endogenous growth literature have raised the issue of the relationship between product market competition (PMC) and innovation or productivity growth. The theoretical IO literature predicts that innovation and growth should decline with competition, because more competition reduces the monopoly rents that reward entry by new successful innovators. On the other hand, empirical work has pointed to a positive correlation between product market competition and innovative output. Several theoretical attempts have been made to reconcile the Schumpeterian paradigm with the evidence provided in these studies generating various predictions as to the shape of the relationship between PMC and productivity growth.

In particular, Aghion et al. (1997) and Aghion et al. (2001) extended the basic Schumpeterian model by allowing incumbent firms to innovate. In these models, innovation incentives depend not so much upon post-innovation rents per se, but more upon the difference between post-innovation and pre-innovation rents. (The latter were equal to zero in the basic model where all innovations were made by outsiders.) In this case, more PMC may end up fostering innovation and growth, as it may reduce a firm's pre-innovation rents more than it reduces post-innovation rents. In other words, competition may increase the incremental profits from innovating, and thereby encourage R&D investments aimed at 'escaping competition'. Hence the possibility of a positive correlation between PMC and productivity growth.

Does this mean that the Schumpeterian effect highlighted in earlier models disappears and that more competition should always enhance innovation and growth, as suggested by the empirical studies mentioned above? The model developed in this chapter, which builds upon Aghion et al. (2001), generates an inverted U-shaped relationship between the degree of product market competition, as measured by a Lerner index, and aggregate productivity growth (or the average innovation rate). The economy described in this model consists of a continuum of duopolistic industries in which, at any point in time, firms face different production costs. The firm with lower (respectively higher) unit costs is referred to as the technological leader (respectively follower) in the corresponding industry. Firms innovate in order to reduce production costs, and they do so 'step by step', in the sense that a laggard firm in any industry must first catch up with the technological leader before itself becoming a future leader. Those industries in which firms face the same (or approximately equal) production costs are referred to as 'neck-and-neck' industries. In neck-and-neck industries, competition is particularly intense and it is in those very industries that the 'escape competition' effect pointed out above is strongest. On the other hand, in non neck-and-neck, or 'unlevelled', industries, more competition may reduce innovation as the laggard's reward for catching up with the technological leader may fall (this being a 'Schumpeterian effect' of the kind emphasized in the earlier models). Finally, by increasing innovation incentives relatively more in neck-and-neck industries than in unlevelled ones, an increase in product market competition will tend to reduce the fraction of neck-and-neck industries in the economy. This 'composition factor' reinforces the Schumpeterian effect by inducing a negative correlation between PMC and aggregate productivity growth or the aggregate rate of innovations.

The contribution of this chapter is twofold. The first element is methodological. Our new data set, our indicators (in particular, measurements for product market competition, innovation output and degree of neck-and-neckness), along with more flexible econometric estimators, enable us to provide a more detailed and comprehensive empirical analysis of PMC and innovations than past literature has been able to do. A more specific contribution of this chapter is the demonstration that, with better measurement of product market competition, the Schumpeterian effect reappears in the data, and that overall the inverted U-shaped relationship predicted by the theory is obtained. Previous papers have measured product market competition using concentration indexes and/or profit shares. Market shares, however, ignore the effects of foreign firms on domestic competition, which in modern high-technology industries can be a powerful influence. Here a profit share methodology is adopted, using a Lerner index of profitability which seeks to capture the effects of competition without the need to measure domestic and foreign markets.

The empirical analysis also confirms another important prediction of the step-by-step model, namely that industry R&D is higher, and the inverted U-shaped relation between PMC and innovation steeper, in more neck-and-neck industries. These theoretical predictions are tested on a panel of British firms, using different estimation techniques (kernel, local linear and spline estimators).

The rest of the chapter is structured as follows. The second section outlines the model and formulates the main predictions concerning the relationship between PMC and innovation rates, respectively, at the firm level, industry level and economy-wide. The third section presents the data. The fourth looks at the results. The fifth provides a conclusion. There then follows an appendix which develops an extension of the model in order to allow for more than two firms in any industry.

2   THE MODEL

Consumers

Suppose that final output, y, is produced using input services, x_i, according to the following production function:

$$\ln y = \int_0^1 \ln x_i di. \tag{6.1}$$

Each sector i is assumed to be duopolistic with respect to both production and research activities, with final output generated according to

$$x_i = (x_{Ai}^{\alpha} + x_{Bi}^{\alpha})^{\frac{\gamma}{\alpha}}, \tag{6.2}$$

where a higher $\alpha \in (0,1]$ reflects a higher degree of substitutability between the two inputs in industry i.

The log preference assumption made in (6.1) implies that in equilibrium individuals spend the same amount on each basket x_i. We normalize this common amount to unity by using expenditure as the numeraire for the prices p_{Ai} and p_{Bi} at each date. Thus the representative household chooses each x_{Ai} and x_{Bi} to maximize $f(x_{Ai}, x_{Bi}) = (x_{Ai}^{\alpha} + x_{Bi}^{\alpha})^{\frac{\gamma}{\alpha}}$ subject to the budget constraint: $p_{Ai}x_{Ai} + p_{Bi}x_{Bi} = 1$, and the demand functions facing the two firms in industry i are:

$$x_{Ai} = \frac{p_{Ai}^{\frac{1}{\alpha-1}}}{p_{Ai}^{\frac{\alpha}{\alpha-1}} + p_{Bi}^{\frac{\alpha}{\alpha-1}}} \text{ and } x_{Bi} = \frac{p_{Bi}^{\frac{1}{\alpha-1}}}{p_{Ai}^{\frac{\alpha}{\alpha-1}} + p_{Bi}^{\frac{\alpha}{\alpha-1}}}.$$

Product Market Competition

Each firm produces using labour as the only input, according to a constant-returns production function, and takes the wage rate as given. Thus the unit costs of production c_A and c_B of the two firms in an industry are independent of the quantities produced. Assume that the firms compete in prices, arriving at a Bertrand equilibrium. According to the above demand functions, the elasticity of demand faced by each firm j is $\eta_j = (1 - \alpha\lambda_j)/(1 - \alpha)$, where $\lambda_j = p_j x_j$ is the firm's revenue:

$$\lambda_j = \frac{p_j^{\frac{\alpha}{\alpha-1}}}{p_A^{\frac{\alpha}{\alpha-1}} + p_B^{\frac{\alpha}{\alpha-1}}}, j = A,B. \tag{6.3}$$

Thus each firm's equilibrium price is

$$p_j = \frac{\eta_j}{\eta_j - 1} c_j = \frac{1 - \alpha\lambda_j}{\alpha(1 - \lambda_j)} c_j, j = A, B \tag{6.4}$$

and its equilibrium profit is:

$$\Pi_j = \frac{\lambda_j}{\eta_j} = \frac{\lambda_j(1 - \alpha)}{1 - \alpha\lambda_j}, j = A,B. \tag{6.5}$$

Equations (6.3)–(6.5) can be solved for unique equilibrium revenues, prices and profits. Given the degree of substitutability α, the equilibrium profit of each firm j is determined by its relative cost $z = c_j/c_{-j}$; an equiproportional reduction in both c_A and c_B would induce each firm to reduce its price in the same ratio, which, because industry demand is unit-elastic, would leave the equilibrium revenues and profits unchanged. More formally, (6.3)–(6.5) implicitly define a function $\emptyset(z,\alpha)$ such that:

$$\Pi_A = \emptyset(c_A/c_B,\alpha) \text{ and } \Pi_B = \emptyset(c_B/c_A,\alpha). \tag{6.6}$$

The substitutability parameter α is our measure of the degree of product market competition in each industry. Although α is ostensibly a taste parameter, we think of it as proxying the absence of institutional, legal and regulatory impediments to directly entering a rival firm's market by offering a similar product. Under this interpretation, α reflects in particular the influence of antitrust policy.

In this model α corresponds to standard measures of competition. It is a monotonically increasing transformation of the elasticity of substitution in demand $(\frac{1}{1-\alpha})$ between the two rivals' outputs in any industry. Given a firm's share λ of industry revenue, α is also a monotonically increasing transformation of the elasticity of demand $\frac{1-\alpha\lambda}{1-\alpha}$ faced by the firm. Furthermore, given λ, α is a monotonically decreasing function of the Lerner Index:

$$LI_i = \frac{1-\alpha}{1-\alpha\lambda_i}.$$

In our empirical analysis we use the Lerner Index itself. While in principle α is our measure of competition, given the difficulties of measuring market shares we prefer to use the cleaner Lerner Index measure directly. It needs noting that the index depends on the firm's market share λ, but it is possible to obtain estimates of α at the industry level using our data on market shares and Lerner indexes together with the above equation which we solve for α as a function of LI and λ.

The limiting case of $\alpha = 0$ defines the minimal degree of competition; the opposite limiting case of $\alpha = 1$ is the case of Bertrand competition between undifferentiated products which results in perfect competition when the two firms have the same unit cost.

A firm engages in R&D in order to decrease its relative cost. According to (6.6), the advantage of a cost reduction, and the disadvantage of a rival's cost reduction, depends on the degree of product market competition. Thus to examine the effects of competition on growth we need to characterize the profit function ϕ.

In Aghion *et al.* (2001) we demonstrate: for all $z > 0$: (a) The function $\phi(z,\alpha)$ is strictly decreasing in z for all $\alpha \in (0,1)$; (b) $\phi(z,0) = 1/2$; and (c) $\phi(z,\alpha) + \phi(1/z,\alpha) > 2\phi(1,\alpha)$ for all $\alpha \in (0,1]$ except when $z = 1$.

Part (a) states that a lower relative cost is always strictly advantageous to a firm, except perhaps in the extreme cases of zero or perfect competition ($\alpha = 0$ or 1).

Part (b) states that, when the degree of competition falls to zero, a firm's profit becomes independent of its relative cost; that is, when $\alpha = 0$ each firm faces a unit-elastic demand function, and produces an infinitesimal amount for an infinite price, yielding a revenue equal to 1/2, at negligible cost, regardless of c_j. Because of this, the incentive to innovate vanishes when $\alpha = 0$. This is the key to our anti-Schumpeterian finding below with regard to the effect that growth is enhanced, at least initially, by more competition.

Part (c) states that, when there is more than the minimal degree of competition, total industry profit is lower if firms are neck-and-neck and possess identical costs than if one firm has a relative cost advantage.

When $\alpha = 1$ we have a winner-take-all competition with profits determined by

$$\phi(z, 1) = \begin{cases} 0 & \text{if } z \geq 1 \\ 1 - z & \text{otherwise} \end{cases}. \tag{6.7}$$

Also for all $\alpha \in (0,1)$:

$$\phi(0,\alpha) = 1 \text{ and } \lim_{z \to \infty} \phi(z,\alpha) = 0, \tag{6.8}$$

$$\phi(1,\alpha) = \frac{1 - \alpha}{2 - \alpha}, \tag{6.9}$$

and

$$\frac{\partial}{\partial z} \phi(z,\alpha) \bigg|_{z=1} = -\frac{\alpha}{4 - \alpha^2}. \tag{6.10}$$

Technology Levels, R&D and Innovations

Let k denote the technology level of duopoly firm j in some industry i; that is, one unit of labour currently employed by firm j generates an output flow equal to

$$A_j = \lambda^{kj}, \quad j = A,B, \tag{6.11}$$

where $\gamma > 1$ is a parameter that measures the size of a leading-edge innovation; (equivalently, it takes γ^{-kj} units of labour for firm j to produce one unit of intermediate goods). An industry is then fully characterized by a pair of integers (l, m), where l is the leader's technology and m is the technology gap of the leader over the follower. We define π_m (respectively π_{-m}) to be the equilibrium profit flow of a firm m steps ahead of (respectively behind) its rival. For expositional simplicity, we will assume that knowledge spillovers between leader and follower are such that the maximum sustainable gap is $m = 1$. That is, if a firm is one step ahead and innovates, the follower will automatically copy the leader's previous technology and so the gap between them remains one step. Therefore, given that profitability is only dependent on the gap between leader and follower, no innovation will be undertaken by the leader.

At any point in time there will therefore be two types of intermediate sectors in the economy: levelled sectors where firms are neck-and-neck, that is $m = 0$; and unlevelled sectors where one firm is leading the other in the same industry, with $m = 1$. We denote by $\psi(n) = \frac{1}{2}\beta n^2$ the R&D cost (in units of labour) of a leader (respectively follower) firm moving one technological step ahead with a Poisson hazard rate of n (resp. $n + h$), where h is a help parameter which reflects the idea that it is easier to reinvent a technology than to discover it for the first time. Let n_m denote the research intensity put up by each firm in an industry with technological gap m, and let n_{-m} denote the R&D intensity of the follower in such an industry.

Bellman Equations

Let V_m denote the steady-state value of currently being a leader (or follower if $m < 0$) in an industry with technology gap m, and let w denote the wage rate, which we take as given assuming an infinitely elastic supply of labour. We then have the following Bellman equations:

$$rV_m = \pi_m + n_m(V_{m+1} - V_m) + (n_{-m} + h)(V_{m-1} - V_m) - w\beta(n_m)^2/2;$$
$$rV_{-m} = \pi_{-m} + n_m(V_{-(m+1)} - V_{-m}) + (n_{-m} + h)(V_{-(m-1)} - V_{-m}) - w\beta(n_{-m})^2/2;$$
$$rV_0 = \pi_0 + n_0(V_1 - V_0) + (n_0 + h)(V_{-1} - V_0) - w\beta(n_0)^2/2.$$

In words, the annuity value rV_m of currently being a technological leader in an industry with gap m at date t equals the current profit flow π_m, minus the current R&D cost $(w\beta n_m^2/2)dt$, plus the discounted expected capital gain $n_m(V_{m+1} - V_m)$ from making an innovation and thereby moving one further step ahead of the follower, minus the discounted expected capital loss $n_{-m}(V_{m-1} - V_m)$ from having the follower catch up one step with the leader. The equation for the annuity value of a follower is similarly explained. Finally, in the Bellman equation for a neck-and-neck firm, note that, if each firm only takes into account its own cost of R&D, in symmetric Nash equilibrium both R&D efforts are equal.

Now, using the fact that each firm chooses its own R&D efforts to maximize its current value, that is to maximize the RHS of the corresponding Bellman equation, we obtain the first order conditions:

$$\beta w n_m = V_{m+1} - V_m;$$
$$\beta w n_{-m} = V_{-(m-1)} - V_{-m};$$
$$\beta w n_0 = V_1 - V_0.$$

Individual R&D Intensities in Equilibrium

One can use the above equations to solve for the values V_m and V_{-m} for all $m \in N$. Using the same equations, we can also characterize the relationship between α and the individual R&D intensities n_m and n_{-m}, which are shown in Figure 6.1. There, we already see an inverted U-shaped pattern, and we also see that R&D intensities are higher and also increase more rapidly with α in the case of neck-and-neck firms.

Industry R&D

Figure 6.2 depicts the relationship between PMC and total intra-industry R&D ($n_m + n_{-m}$) for all $m \in N$. Again the relationship is inverted U-shaped, and it becomes increasingly steeper as m goes down, that is to say as the industry becomes more neck-and-neck.

Industry structure and steady-state innovation/growth rates
In the equilibrium we define μ_m to be the steady-state fraction of industries with technological gap m. We obviously have

$$\sum_m \mu_m = 1.$$

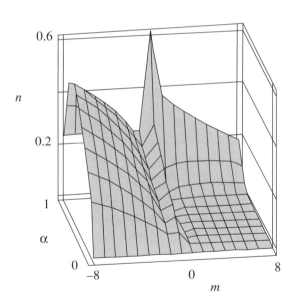

Figure 6.1   Intensity of R&D of a firm n *as a function of the technology gap* m

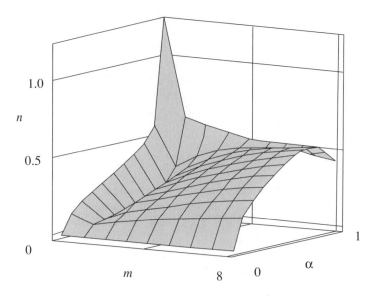

Figure 6.2   Relation between PMC (Product Market Competition) and R&D intensity at the industry level

In addition, the following equations must also hold in steady state:

$$\mu_m(n_m + n_{-m} + h) = \mu_{m-1}n_{m-1} + \mu_{m+1}(n_{-(m+1)} + h),$$

for all $m \geq 1$. The LHS of this equation represents the total flow of sectors out of technological gap (or 'state') m; the RHS represents the total flow of sectors into state m; this comprises both state $(m - 1)$ sectors in which the leader innovates and state $(m + 1)$ sectors in which the follower innovates. For $m = 0$, we simply have

$$2\mu_0 n_0 = \mu_1(n_{-1} + h).$$

In other words, a neck-and-neck sector becomes unlevelled whenever a firm in that sector innovates, and only state 1 sectors can become neck-and-neck whenever the laggard in that sector innovates. Figure 6.3 depicts μ as a function of m and α.

Now we can compute the average rate of productivity growth for the overall economy. Consider first the special case where $m \leq 1$, and where therefore only the laggard would do R&D in unlevelled sectors where $m = 1$. Each industry would follow a two-stage cycle alternating between $m = 0$ and $m = 1$,

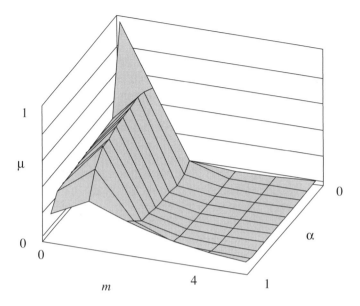

Figure 6.3   Equilibrium distribution of technological gaps m *as a function of* α

and its output x would increase by a factor equal to the innovation size γ each time a two-stage cycle is completed. The frequency at which a two-stage cycle is completed would be equal to $\mu_1 n_{-1} = 2n_0\mu_0$. Thus the steady-state rate of frontier innovations would be

$$I = 2n_0\mu_0 = \mu_1 n_{-1},$$

where, using the fact that $\mu_0 + \mu_1 = 1$,

$$\mu_1 = \frac{2n_0}{2n_0 + n_{-1}}.$$

The corresponding steady-state rate of growth is then simply equal to:

$$g = I \ln\gamma = \frac{2n_0 n_{-1}}{2n_0 + n_{-1}} \ln\gamma.$$

An increase in product market competition as measured by α, or by a decrease in the Lerner Index, leads to an increase in the incremental profit flow $\Gamma_0 = \pi_1 - \pi_0$ of a neck-and-neck firm that innovates, and therefore to an increase in the innovation rate n_0 of a neck-and-neck firm: this we refer to as the 'escape competition effect' of PMC. On the other hand, the same increase in PMC may eventually reduce the incremental profit of a laggard in an un-levelled industry that catches up with the current technological leader $\Gamma_{-1} = \pi_0 - \pi_{-1}$ and its innovation incentives n_{-1}: this captures the 'Schumpeterian effect' of PMC. This, together with the fact that the fraction of neck-and-neck sectors $\mu 0 = \frac{n-1}{2n0 + n-1}$ decreases for given n_{-1} when n_0 increases (we refer to this latter effect as a 'composition effect' of PMC), will tend to counteract the 'escape competition effect' mentioned above. The overall effect of PMC on aggregate innovation/growth in the $m \leq 1$ case, is depicted in Figure 6.4 below: *I* and *g* decrease when α is large. In this case the 'escape competition effect' is dominated by the Schumpeterian and composition effects, and they increase when α is low. In other words greater PMC will foster innovation and growth when competition is low because a large fraction of firms are in neck-and-neck industries and therefore will be trying to innovate in order to escape competition. When PMC is high, however, a large fraction of firms are in unlevelled industries where the Schumpeterian effect of PMC on (laggards') R&D and innovation is most likely to dominate. Hence the inverted U-shaped relationship between PMC and innovation/growth shown in Figure 6.4.

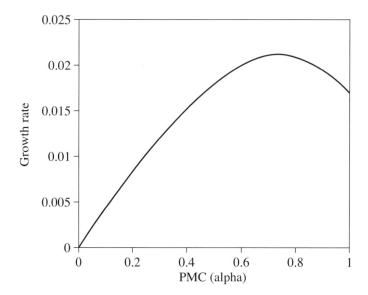

Figure 6.4   Total effect of PMC on growth when $\alpha < 1$

In the general case where the lead size m can take any integer value, one can show that the average growth rate of the overall economy denoted g is equal to

$$g = (2\mu_0 x_0 + \sum_{k \geq 1} \mu_k x_k) \ln\gamma.$$

The above equation states that the growth rate equals the product of the frequency of 'frontier innovations' (innovations by industry leaders and neck-and-neck firms which advance the industry's frontier technology) and the (log) size of innovations. Figure 6.5 depicts g as a function of α. We again obtain an inverted U-shape, with a relatively important region where the Schumpeterian and composition effects of PMC dominate.

Note that, in the appendix, we extend the model to the case where each industry comprises three firms instead of two and we show (in the case of small innovations), that (i) total R&D is highest in industries where all firms are neck-and-neck ('state a'), followed by total R&D in industries with two neck-and-neck leaders and one laggard ('state b'), followed by total R&D in industries with one leading firm and two neck-and-neck laggards ('state c'); (ii) the relationship between PMC and total industry R&D is steepest in state a, and then becomes less and less steep as we move from a to c.

3 DATA

We use two main data sources in this chapter: firm-level accounting data and administrative data from the US Patents Office. The accounting data come from Datastream. Our sample includes all firms quoted on the London Stock Exchange between 1968 and 1997. We removed firms with missing values on sales, capital or employment; deleted firms with fewer than three consecutive observations; broke the series for firms with abnormal length accounting periods; and excluded observations for firms where there was a jump greater than 150 per cent in any of the key variables (capital, labour, sales). This leaves us with a sample of around 27 000 observations affecting over 2 000 firms.

Our indicator of product market competition is one minus the Lerner Index or price cost mark-up. A value of 1 indicates perfect competition (price equals marginal cost), whilst values below 1 indicate some degree of market power. We do not observe marginal cost, however, so instead use average costs under the assumption that $AC \approx MC$. Thus our empirical Lerner Index measure is defined as

$$\frac{P \cdot Q - AC \cdot Q}{P \cdot Q} = \frac{P - AC}{P}.$$

We use accounting data to estimate this. For the numerator we use operating profits net of depreciation and provisions. In UK accounts' capital depreciation, R&D expenditure and advertising have been deducted. In theory we would like to deduct R&D depreciation (rather than expenditure), but we note that in steady-state investment in R&D, stock should equal depreciation. For growing firms, investment will be greater than depreciation, so our estimate of the Lerner Index will underestimate the true mark-up. We divided this by sales (DS137/DS104). This measure is similar to Nickell's (1996) measure of rents over value-added, the main difference being that Nickell also deduced an estimate of the cost of capital from the numerator.

This estimate of the Lerner Index has several advantages over other, more conventional, measures such as a Herfindahl or Concentration Index. In order to measure either of those, one needs to have a good idea of both the geographic and product boundaries of the market in which the firm operates. With the Lerner Index we do not need to observe such things. This is particularly important in our application as many innovating firms operate in international markets.

In accordance with our theoretical measure the Lerner Index is taken to be constant within industries. We take an average across all firms in the industry,

$$LI_{jt} = \sum_{i \in j} \left(\frac{P \cdot Q - AC \cdot Q}{P \cdot Q} \right)_{ijt}$$

where i indexes firms, j indexes industry and t indexes time.

Our industry code is measured at the three-digit SIC level in which the firm had the largest proportion of its sales in 1995. For 33 per cent of the firms this represented all of their sales. The median share of sales accounted for by the largest industry is 90 per cent. Our analysis is carried out at the two-digit level. We use the entire sample of Datastream firms to estimate the industry Lerner Index.

The firm-level patenting information from the US Patent Office dataset was matched to a subset of the firms for which accounting data were available. We have patent data for all firms with a name beginning A–L (plus all large R&D firms) listed on the London Stock Exchange between 1983 and 1985. These have been matched (by hand) to all of their subsidiaries in 1985. These data run from 1968 to 1996 and contain 461 firms, with 236 firms that patent. The patenting data are from the US Patent Office. They are a count of all patents taken out in the USA, but based on research conducted anywhere in the world. We also have information on citations to, and from, these patents. One concern that is often expressed about using patent counts involves their comparability: one patent can be significantly more valuable than another. We use these citations to weight the patents and thus provide a measure that is more indicative of the value of the patent. On average we observe patents' data for 34 per cent of the complete Datastream sample. We drop industry-year observations where we have fewer than three firms and we drop industries with no patents between 1968 and 1996.

We also need a measure of how 'neck-and-neck' firms are. We use a measure of the proportional distance a firm is from the frontier with a metric (X). Our measure is

$$NN_n = \frac{X_F - X_n}{X_F},$$

where F denotes the frontier firm (the one with the highest capital to labour ratio, or highest total factor productivity (TFP) and n denotes non-frontier. For the frontier our measure is

$$NN_F = \frac{X_F - X_{F-1}}{X_F}, \tag{6.12}$$

where $F - 1$ denotes the firm just behind the frontier.

Our measure of neck-and-neckness is based on TFP. To generate this we start by looking at the level of TFP within our sample and identifying the frontier as the firm with the highest TFP. We then use industry-level data from the OECD's ISDB database to estimate the level of TFP in other countries and use this as a proxy for the frontier where it is higher than the level of TFP in all UK firms. In order to estimate the level of TFP we assume a Cobb–Douglas production function and constant returns to scale. We can only estimate TFP in manufacturing sectors using ISDB data, but we argue that this problem is much greater in such sectors because goods are traded, unlike service sectors which are largely non-traded.

Our main interest in this chapter lies in identifying a non-linear relationship between product market competition and innovative output as predicted from the theory discussed above. Before turning to that task we want to consider the variation in our data and how well it captures the features we are interested in. In order to do this we consider a major policy event, the implementation of the European Union Single Market Programme (SMP). The main aims of the SMP were to bring down internal barriers to free movement of goods and to promote competition. Many papers have shown that these have produced an increase in competitiveness. Mayes and Hart (1994) make extra distinctions by classifying industries into three categories: (1) those where barriers were low pre-SMP, so the impact of SMP on product market competition was expected, ex ante, to be low; (2) those with intermediate levels of barriers where the SMP was expected to produce substantial reductions; and (3) those with high barriers where the SMP was expected to trigger even more substantial downward movements.

Griffith (2001) uses plant-level data in the UK to show that the impact of the SMP was to increase product market competition (bring down the Lerner Index) in those industries that were expected, ex ante, to be affected. Mark-ups in intermediate industries came down by around 5 per cent and in the industries with high barriers they came down by over 10 per cent. We find a similar result in our dataset, with greater reductions in mark-ups in those industries with highest initial barriers. This supports our use of the Lerner Index as a measure of competition, these results being discussed in more detail at the beginning of the next section.

4   RESULTS

Our main estimation strategy consists of the adoption of a semi-parametric approach. We use econometric methods which enable us to capture non-monotonicity in the relationship between product market competition and innovation predicted by the theory. It is important to use semi-parametric estimators that do not impose symmetry and allow a flexible way of recovering the turning point. Because we are dealing with count data and we want to hold constant on other characteristics, we use a Poisson Model. A kernel is not appropriate in this context, so we use quadratic splines.

Firm-level Results

We are interested in learning about the relationship between product market competition (PMC) and innovation, and particularly in establishing whether non-monotonicities exist. We seek to do this without imposing much structure. We want to estimate the following relationship

$$I_{ijt} = f(PMC_{jt}, NN_{ijt}, X_{ijt}),$$

where i indexes firms, j indexes industries, t indexes time, PMC denotes product market competition (that is, the degree of substitutability of the products in the industry), *NN* measures how close competitor firms are in cost/technology space (or whether firms are neck-and-neck) and *X* indicates other control variables. We measure an increase in product market competition as an increase in α which will be reflected in a decrease in the Lerner Index, which is monotonically decreasing in α. Hence a reduction in the Lerner Index is associated with a higher value of α, meaning greater competition.

A natural way to do this would be to use a kernel or a similar non-parametric estimator. However, our dependent variable is a count of patents which has a skewed distribution and contains many zeros. The natural estimator for this type of data is a Poisson Model.

We start by presenting unconditional estimates of the relationship between *I* and *PMC* using a kernel estimator. Figure 6.5 shows such a kernel using Gaussian-weighted results. Epanechnikov weights are favoured by some because they have a finite support lying entirely within their bandwidth unlike the Gaussian Kernel weight. We also found a similar U-shape using Epanechnikov weights (not shown).

We also use citation-weighted patents to ensure that our results are not affected by the differential value of patents. Figure 6.6 shows the same kernel using citation-weighted patents. While the mean is higher, the curve looks very similar to Figure 6.2. We use citation-weighted patents in the remainder of our analysis.

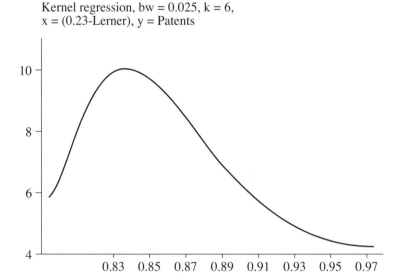

Kernel regression, bw = 0.025, k = 6,
x = (0.23-Lerner), y = Patents

Figure 6.5   Kernel using firm-level data

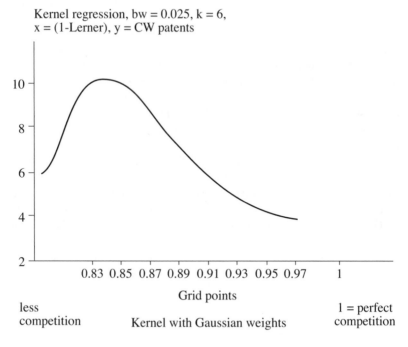

Kernel regression, bw = 0.025, k = 6,
x = (1-Lerner), y = CW patents

Grid points

less
competition

Kernel with Gaussian weights

1 = perfect
competition

Figure 6.6   Kernel using firm-level data

The local polynomial smoother runs a local polynomial estimator at every data point using a kernel weight on the local data. The advantage of this approach is that it provides a local first-order Taylor approximation to the underlying function whereas the kernel is a local zeroth-order Taylor approximation (mean only). Adding in the first-order approximation is usually the most important approximation step.

Figure 6.7 shows the local linear and we see that it looks similar to the kernel, which shows that our results are robust to bias. The bias term in Nadaraya–Watson kernels can be written as

$$(m''(x) + 2\ \frac{m'(x)f'(x)}{f(x)}\ c,$$

where $f(x)$ is the density of the Lerner Index, $m(x)$ is the underlying function and c is some constant. From Figure 6.5 we can see that our density function has the standard single-peaked shape which takes a maximum at around 0.1. The local linear regression suggests that the theoretical non-linear relationship

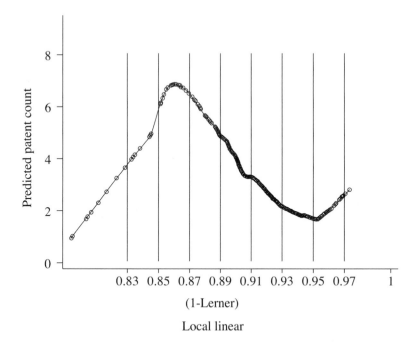

Figure 6.7   Local linear using firm-level data, citation-weighted

also has a single-peaked shape, but with a maximum at about 0.15. Hence, in the three regions we have approximately (ignoring the second order $m''(x)$) the bias term shown below:

Data region	$f'(x)$ density	$m'(x)$ of function	Bias
0<Lerner<0.1	+	+	+
0.1<Lerner<0.15	−	+	−
0.15<Lerner	−	−	+

This means that the peak of the inverted-U will be pushed to the right by the kernel bias because just to the left of the peak (at about 0.15) it is being biased down and just to the right it is being biased up. This bias will get worse with larger bandwidths. As we increase the bandwidth this peak does in fact move quite noticeably to the right (not shown). In addition, the local polynomial estimator, which does not have this bias problem, has a peak at 0.15, while the kernel has a peak at about 0.2.

The approach of the kernel and local linear to outliers is different. The

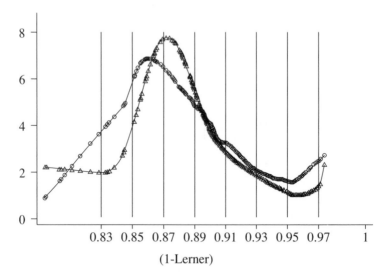

-○- Predicted patent count
-▲- Predicted patent count (citation-weighted)

(1-Lerner)

Quadratic spline in Poisson vs. Local linear

Figure 6.8   Firm-level data and citation-weighted patents

kernel minimizes absolute deviations, whilst the local linear minimizes absolute squared deviations. This means the kernel is actually more 'robust' to outliers: that is, it is less affected by distant points. This explains why the maximum value of the local linear is higher than the greatest value of the kernel: because the positive skew of patents pulls up the squared deviation minimizer more than the absolute devotion minimizer.

The kernel has problems (large mean-squared error) with endpoints both in terms of bias (as $f'(x)$ is likely to be large) and also in terms of variance (the kernel variance is proportional to $\frac{1}{f'(x)}$). The local linear is much better in this respect when the end function is approximately linear. The local linear uses internal changes as well as end values to predict the end points, which should reduce its mean squared error.

Splines are similar to the local linear regressions. The difference is that, firstly, the spline is usually a higher order polynomial rather than linear; secondly, the local region is much larger than one point and is defined as part of the spline. In Figure 6.8 we show that a quadratic spline with eight evenly-spaced knots mimics the local linear regression fairly well.

Currently we are using a quadratic spline. The main properties of splines are outlined in Table 6.1 below. Using higher order splines ensures the

Table 6.1

Spline	Basis terms	Parameters	Properties
Liner	$\sum_{i=1}^{N} (x - K_i), 1, x$	$N+2$	level equal at knots
Quadratic	$\sum_{i=1}^{N} (x - K_i)^2, 1, x, x^2$	$N+3$	level, 1st derivative equal at knots
Cubic	$\sum_{i=1}^{N} (x - K_i)^3, 1, x, x^2, x^3$	$N+4$	level, 1st, 2nd deriv. equal at knots
Quartic	$\sum_{i=1}^{N} (x - K_i)^4, 1, x, x^2, x^3, x^4$	$N+5$	level, 1st, 2nd, 3rd deriv. = at knots

Note: Knots are labelled $K_1, K_2 \ldots K_N$

derivatives are equal across knots up to a higher order at the cost of including an extra parameter.

The results from cubic and quadratic splines look almost identical (not shown). Quadratic splines were therefore chosen because of their more parsimonious parameterization.

A big advantage of using the (quadratic) spline is that we can use it within a Poisson Model. As discussed earlier, patent counts follow a highly skewed distribution, with a large number at zero (even after dropping industries with no patenting). Our patents' count process can be written as

$$p_{it} = \exp(f(LI_{jt}) + X'_{it}\beta) + e_{it}, \tag{6.14}$$

where p_{it} is the count of patents for firm i at year t, $f(LI_{jt})$ is the spline function of the Lerner Index for industry j at time t, and X denotes other conditioning variables (for example, time or industry dummies, firm size) and e_{it} is a stochastic error term. Standard errors are derived by using White's robust variance–covariance matrix which relies only on moment conditions on the mean to estimate the parameter values. In Figure 6.9 we include year dummies and in Figure 6.10 year and industry dummies. The inverted U-shape remains robust to all of these conditioning variables.

Neck-and-neck Competition

As described above, we are interested in looking not only at how innovation varies with product market competition, but also how this relationship varies with the technological distance between firms in an industry measured by differences in TFP. The general model allowing for a technological gap m between the leader and the follower in an industry suggests that a laggard

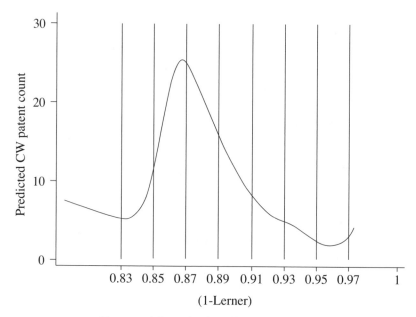

Exponential quadratic spline with year dummies

Figure 6.9   Firm-level spline estimator with citation-weighted patents

firm's R&D investment should be an inverted U-shape with respect to the Lerner Index, and that the relationship should be steeper the closer the laggard is to leading-edge technology when both frontier and non-frontier innovations occur in a step-by-step fashion.

We split the sample into quartiles by our measure of neck-and-neckness and run kernel estimators and splines on the four samples. In Figure 6.11 we show the kernels. The height of these declines as we go from the top quartile (the most neck-and-neck) to the bottom, as expected.

Productivity Growth

Patents are well-known to have a strong effect on productivity growth. This has also been demonstrated directly for our data set by Bloom and Van Reenen (2000) who find a highly significant response of productivity to both patents and patent citations. This suggests that the strong inverted U-shaped relationship which we find between competition and patenting should extend to competition and productivity growth as predicted above. We are also working on developing firm-level measures of productivity to directly estimate this relationship.

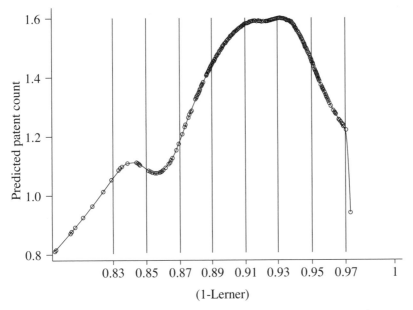

Figure 6.10   Firm-level spline estimator with citation-weighted patents

5 CONCLUSIONS

This chapter provides a first attempt at confronting theory and data on the relationship between product market competition and the rate of innovation (or the rate of productivity growth), respectively, at the firm level, industry level and across industries. Our empirical results confirm the existence of an inverted U-shaped relationship between product market competition and innovations, which in turn indicates that some kind of an 'escape competition' effect should dominate at low levels of PMC as measured by the Lerner Index. By contrast, the 'Schumpeterian effect', pointed out in earlier endogenous growth models and before those in the IO literature, should dominate at high initial levels of PMC. Our results indicate a similar inverted U-shaped relationship at the industry level and at the firm level which tends to be steeper for firms that are more neck-and-neck and/or that are closer to the leading edge in their industry.

We plan to extend our analysis in two directions. The first is to introduce wealth constraints and agency considerations between firm managers and outside investors, following up previous theoretical work by Aghion *et al.*

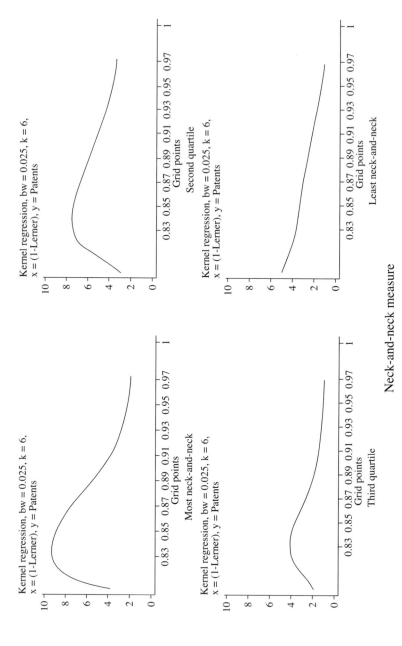

Figure 6.11   Firm-level citation-weighted patents split into quartiles by neck-and-neckness

(1999), but using the same theoretical framework as in this chapter. Preliminary work in this direction suggests that the inverted U-shaped relationship between PMC and productivity growth should be steeper for firms or industries with lower cash flow and higher debt–equity ratios.

The second extension would be to introduce entry and entry threat as alternative (or complementary) measures of competition. This again could be done using an extension of the above model with entry and exit in any industry. Preliminary simulations performed on this extended model suggest (i) an inverted U-shaped relationship between potential entry and the innovation rate; (ii) a strategic substitutability between entry threat and PMC, in the sense that the escape competition effect of PMC on the aggregate innovation/growth rate appears to be stronger the lower the entry threat and, conversely, the stimulating effect of entry on innovation appears to be stronger the lower the PMC as measured by the level of profits in neck-and-neck industries.

APPENDIX: THE THREE-FIRM INDUSTRY CASE

In this appendix we extend our basic model to allow for more than two firms in an industry. We are particularly interested in comparing the innovation incentives of neck-and-neck firms depending upon their distance from the technological frontier and/or from laggard firms in the same industry. In order to maintain the working assumption of a maximum technological gap of $m = 1$ in any industry, we assume that (i) in unlevelled industries with two neck-and-neck leaders, innovation by either leader automatically moves the current laggard one step up; (ii) in unlevelled industries where there is a single leader, innovation by the leader automatically upgrades both laggards by one step.

Restricting attention to the case of pure Bertrand competition, that is to say where $\pi_i^j = 0$ for all $(i,j) \neq (1,3)$, we will argue, analytically in the case where γ is small, and by means of simulations in the general case, that, first, if $R\&D_i$ denotes the total amount of R&D in a state i industry, then we have:

$$R\&D_1 > R\&D_2 > R\&D_3.$$

Second, a neck-and-neck firm does more R&D in state 1 than in state 2, and more in state 2 than in state 3.

Let us first express the Bellman equations corresponding to the three-firm case with a maximum technological gap of one. We have:

$$rV_0^1 = n_0^1(V_1^3 - V_0^1) + 2n_0^1(V_{-1}^3 - V_0^1) - w\beta(n_0^1)^2/2;$$
$$rV_1^2 = n_1^2(V_1^3 - V_1^2) + n_1^2(V_1^3 - V_1^2) + n_{-1}^2(V_0^1 - V_1^2) - w\beta(n_1^2)^2/2;$$
$$rV_{-1}^2 = n_{-1}^2(V_0^1 - V_{-1}^2) + 2n_{-1}^2(V_{-1}^3 - V_{-1}^2) - w\beta(n_{-1}^2)^2/2;$$
$$rV_1^3 = \pi_1^3 - 2n_{-1}^3(V_1^3 - V_1^2);$$
$$rV_{-1}^3 = n_{-1}^3(V_1^2 - V_{-1}^3) + n_{-1}^3(V_{-1}^2 - V_{-1}^3) - w\beta(n_{-1}^3)^2/2;$$

with corresponding first-order conditions:

$$w\beta n_0^1 = V_1^3 - V_0^1;$$
$$w\beta n_1^2 = V_1^3 - V_1^2;$$
$$w\beta n_{-1}^2 = V_0^1 - V_{-1}^2;$$
$$w\beta n_{-1}^3 = V_1^2 - V_{-1}^3.$$

When the size of innovations $\gamma - 1 = \varepsilon$ is small, then a similar analysis to that in section 4.1 of Aghion *et al.* (2001) implies that the profit flows π_j^i can be approximated by the asymptotic expansions:

$$\pi_1^3 = \eta\varepsilon + O(\varepsilon^2);$$
$$\pi_i^j = 0 \text{ for } (i,j) \neq (1,3),$$

where η is a positive constant. Then, substituting for the πs in the above Bellman equations, we obtain:

$$V_1^3 = \eta\varepsilon/rw\beta + O(\varepsilon^2);$$
$$V_i^j = O(\varepsilon^2), (i,j) \neq (1,3).$$

Hence, using the first-order conditions,

$$n_0^1 = n_1^2 = \eta\varepsilon/rw\beta + O(\varepsilon^2) \gg n_i^j = O(\varepsilon^2) \text{ for } (i,j) \notin \{(0,1),(1,2)\}.$$

Thus, when the size of innovations is small, one can immediately prove (i) since:

$$R\&D_1 = 3n_0^1 \approx 3\eta\varepsilon/rw\beta + O(\varepsilon^2)$$
$$> R\&D_2 = 2n_1^2 + n_{-1}^2 \approx 2\eta\varepsilon/rw\beta + O(\varepsilon^2)$$
$$> R\&D_3 \approx O(\varepsilon^2).$$

Now let us establish (ii), that is: $n_0^1 > n_1^2 > n_{-1}^3$. Using those first-order conditions and normalizing the wage at one, we can rewrite the first two Bellman equations as

$$rV_0^1 = \frac{n_0^1}{2}(V_1^3 - V_0^1) - 2n_0^1(V_0^1 - V_{-1}^3);$$

$$rV_1^2 = \frac{n_1^2}{2}(V_1^3 - V_1^2) - n_1^2(V_1^2 - V_1^3) - n_{-1}^2(V_1^2 - V_0^1).$$

The above equations imply

$$V_0^1 = f(n_0^1) - \frac{n_0^1}{r + 3n_0^1/2}(V_0^1 - V_{-1}^3);$$

$$V_1^2 = f(n_1^2) - \frac{n_{-1}^1}{r + 3n_1^2/2}(V_1^2 - V_0^1),$$

where: $f(x) = x(\frac{V_1^3}{2} + v_{-1}^3)/r + 3x/2$. Using these equations and the above first-order conditions, we have

$$V_0^1 - V_1^2 < f(n_0^1) - f(n_1^2) + \frac{n_{-1}^2}{r + 3n_1^2/2} (V_1^2 - V_0^1),$$

that is:

$$V_0^1 - V_1^2 < x(f(n_0^1) - f(n_1^2)),$$

where $x = (1 + n_{-1}^2 / r + 3n_1^2/2)^{-1} > 0$.

Now let us reason by contradiction and suppose that $V_0^1 - V_1^2 \geq 0$. Then the above inequality would imply $n_0^1 > n_1^2$ since $f'(x) > 0$. But then the first-order conditions would yield $V_0^1 - V_1^2 < 0$, a contradiction. This establishes that $n_0^1 > n_1^2$, without requiring us to make use of asymptotic approximations. On the other hand, the asymptotic expansions for n_1^2 and n_{-1}^3 show immediately that $n_1^2 > n_{-1}^3$, which in turn establishes (ii).

ACKNOWLEDGEMENTS

The following individuals made important contributions to the paper on which this chapter is based: Nicholas Bloom (Institute for Fiscal Studies and University College, London); Richard Blundell (Institute for Fiscal Studies and University College, London); Rachel Griffith (Institute for Fiscal Studies); Peter Howitt (Brown University). The author would also like to thank Wendy Carlin, amongst others, for informative feedback. Financial support was provided by the ESRC Centre for Microeconomic Analysis of Fiscal Policy at the Institute for Fiscal Studies. The data were developed with funding from the Leverhulme Trust.

BIBLIOGRAPHY

Aghion, P. and Schankerman, M. (1999), 'Competition, Entry and the Social Returns to Infrastructure in Transition Economies', *Economics of Transition*, **7**, 79–101.

Aghion, P., Harris, C. and Vickers, J. (1997), 'Competition and Growth with Step-by-Step Innovation: An Example', *European Economic Review, Papers and Proceedings*, 771–82.

Aghion, P., Harris, C., Howitt, P. and Vickers, J. (2001), 'Competition, Imitation and Growth with Step-by-Step Innovation', *Review of Economic Studies*, **68**(3), 467–92.

Aghion, P., Dewatripont, M. and Rey, P. (1999) 'Competition, Financial Discipline and Growth', *Review of Economic Studies*, **66**(4), 825–52.

Bloom, N. and Van Reenen, J. (2000), 'Real Options, Patents, Productivity and Market Value: Evidence from a Panel of British Firms', Institute for Fiscal Studies, working paper W00/21.

Blundell, R., Griffith, R. and Van Reenen, J. (1999), 'Market Share, Market Value and Innovation in a Panel of British Manufacturing Firms', *Review of Economic Studies*, **66**, 529–54.

Boone, J. (1999), 'Measuring Product Market Competition', unpublished paper, Tilburg University, the Netherlands.

Caballero, R and Jaffe, A. (1993), 'How High are the Giants' Shoulders? An Empirical Assessment of Knowledge Spillovers and Creative Destruction in a Model of Economic Growth', *NBER Macroeconomic Annual*, 15–74.

Chirinko, R., Fazzari, S. and Meyer, A. (1999), 'How Responsive is Business Capital Formation to its User Cost? An Exploration with Micro Data', *Journal of Public Economics*, **74**, 53–80.

Cleveland, W. (1979), 'Robust Locally Weighted Regression and Smoothing Scatterplots', *Journal of the American Statistical Association*, **74**, 829–36.

Dasgupta, P. and Stiglitz, J. (1980), 'Industrial Structure and the Nature of Innovative Activity', *Economic Journal*, **90**, 266–293.

Fan, J. and Gijbells, I. (1996), *Local Polynomial Modelling and Its Applications*, London: Chapman and Hall.

Geroski, P. (1995), *Market Structure, Corporate Performance and Innovative Activity*, Oxford: Oxford University Press.

Griffith, R (2001), 'Product Market Competition, Efficiency and Agency Costs: An Empirical Analysis', IFS Working Paper, WXX.

Hall, B., Jaffe, A. and Trajtenberg, M. (2001), 'Market Value and Patent Citations: A First Look', mimeo, University of California at Berkeley.

Hasset, K. and Hubbard, R. (1998), 'Are Investment Incentives Blunted by Changes in the Prices of Capital Goods', NBER Working Paper 6676.

Jacquemin, A. and Sapir, A. (1991), 'The Discipline of Imports in the European Market', in L. Winters and A. Venables (eds), *European Integration: Trade and Industry*, Cambridge: Cambridge University Press.

Levinsohn, J. (1993), 'Testing the Import-as-Market-Discipline Hypothesis', *Journal of International Economics*, 35.

Mayes, D. and Hart, P. (1994), *The Single Market Programme as a Stimulus to Change*, Cambridge: Cambridge University Press.

Nickell, S. (1996), 'Competition and Corporate Performance', *Journal of Political Economy*, **104**, 724–46.

Sleuwaegen, L. (1988), 'The Formation of the European Common Market and Changes in Market Structure and Performance', *European Economic Review*, 32.

7. Cooperation, creativity and closure in scientific research networks: modelling the dynamics of epistemic communities

Paul A. David

1 MODELLING THE WORKINGS OF OPEN SCIENCE COMMUNITIES: MOTIVATION AND BACKGROUND

The Pursuit of Knowledge and the Sources of Technological Change

Economists seeking to understand the sources of technological change have focused their attention on the dynamics of the diffusion of innovations, and the generation and distribution of knowledge underpinning the development and commercial introduction of new products or production methods. Quite rightly, their quest for clearer vision of the insides of the 'black boxes' of technology and of innovation will continue to command the major share of the analytical and empirical attention devoted to providing firmer microeconomic foundations for theories of endogenous economic growth.[1]

Compared with what has already been learned about institutional arrangements and business strategies affecting corporate R&D investments or the mechanisms enabling private appropriation of research benefits, it is surprising that very little is known about the institutional infrastructures and micromotives that influence the allocation of economic resources within the domain of non-commercial, 'academic' science. The 'science base', as the publicly funded civilian R&D sector has come to be referred to in Britain, remains a sphere of activity which economic analysis tends to discuss more in terms of *external effects* than of internal workings.[2] Research of an exploratory character, undertaken to discover new phenomena, or to explain the fundamental properties of physical systems, is cited as a source of useful innovations in instrumentation or in generic techniques valued in applied research – for example, synchrotron radiation and restriction-enzyme methods for 'gene-splicing'. Indirect cognitive contributions of a fundamental character are also seen to raise the expected marginal rate of return on investment in applied R&D by establishing 'possibilities' that may have practical application, such as the photoelectric effect described by Einstein in *Annalen der Physik* (1905), and in definitively excluding time-wasting traps which are physical 'impossibilities', as in the case of perpetual motion machines and some of the many possible configurations for the bases in the structure of the DNA molecule.[3]

Despite the cognitive significance of the activities of 'the science base', and despite its quantitative importance as the locus of employment and the training ground for expensively educated researchers, the discipline of economics is still in the early stages of systematic inquiry into ways in which the pursuit of reliable knowledge is carried on within 'the Republic of Science'.[4] Although the latter domain forms a critical part of modern 'social systems of innovation', it is one whose characteristic internal properties cannot simply be inferred by understanding the economics of industrial research and development.[5]

The Logic of Open Science as a Mode of Organizing Research

Within university-based research communities, a distinctive set of norms and conventions exist which scientists are generally disposed to support, whether or not their actual behaviours always conform to them. The norms of the 'Republic of Science' have famously been articulated by the sociologist Robert K. Merton and can be conveniently summarized under the mnemonic CUDOS. This stands for Communalism, Universalism, Disinterestedness, Originality and Scepticism.[6]

The 'communal' ethos emphasizes the cooperative character of inquiry, stressing that the accumulation of reliable knowledge is an essentially social process, however much people may strive to contribute to it as individuals. The force of the 'universalist norm' serves to open up entry into scientific work and discourse to all persons of 'competence' regardless of their personal and ascriptive attributes. A second aspect of 'openness' concerns the disposition of knowledge. Here full disclosure of findings and methods forms a key aspect of the cooperative, communal programme of inquiry. Full disclosure serves the ethos which legitimates and, indeed, prescribes, what Merton called 'organized skepticism'. It supports the expectation that all contributions to the stock of reliable knowledge will be subject to trials of replication and verification, without insult to the claimant. The 'originality' of such intellectual efforts is the touchstone for acknowledging individual scientific claims, upon which collegiate reputations as well as the material and non-pecuniary rewards attached to them are based.

By considering the logic of the organization of knowledge-producing activities, one can make a start at grasping the connection between the existence of a social system distinguished, and in some manner *regulated*, by these norms as well as the importance of non-commercially driven, exploratory science as a source of technological progress. It is possible by such means to give a completely functionalist account of the institutional complex which characterizes modern science.[7] In brief, the norm of 'openness' is 'incentive compatible' with a collegiate (reputational) reward system based upon accepted claims to priority; and it is conducive to individual strategy choices whose collective congruence reduces excessive duplication of research efforts and enlarges the domain of informational complementarities. This brings socially beneficial 'spillovers' to research programmes and abets rapid replication and swift validation of new discoveries. The advantages of treating new findings as 'public goods' in order to promote the faster growth of the stock of knowledge are thus contrasted with the requirements of secrecy for the purposes of securing a monopoly over the use of new information that may be directly, or indirectly, exploited in the private production of goods and services.

This functionalist juxtaposition suggests a logical basis for the existence and perpetuation of institutional and cultural separations between two normatively differentiated communities of research practice: the open 'Republic of Science' and the proprietary 'Realm of Technology'. These two distinctive organizational regimes serve different, yet potentially complementary, social purposes. Rather baldly stated, the former serves to enhance the growth in stocks of reliable knowledge, whereas the latter helps maximize the flow of economic rent from existing knowledge. In the long run, neither can continue to function fruitfully in isolation from the other. This being the case, the challenge for policies related to science and technology is to keep these two subsystems linked and in symbiotic balance so that the performance of social systems of innovation as a whole does not become degraded. In preparing for such a task it is important to try and redress the comparative deficiency in our understanding of the workings of open-science research communities. That is the main purpose to which this chapter is addressed.

Overview: from Local Micro-behaviours to Macro-network Dynamics

Scientific research communities may be studied as social networks within which ideas and statements circulate, acquire validity as reliable knowledge and are then recombined to generate further new ideas. Personal communications networks also form a locus for transmitting tacit knowledge and the particular skills required for interpreting and operationalizing scientific statements. This chapter builds upon an abstract, highly stylized account of the communications structure of large groupings of research scientists formed from linked, localized interpersonal networks organized around professional activities. Such an account is rooted in previous work. In David (1998), graphic-theoretic terms were used to describe the structure of social networks through which transactions in tacit knowledge were conducted. In addition, results from the application of Markov random field theory were used to extract implications of micro-level communications strategies for the collective epistemological performance of groupings.

Social networks have come to be modelled in many contexts of strategic interdependence where such structures are represented as conveying information and forging mutual trust by means of repeated transactions. This is so even if the connections between players are highly localized and brought about without the help of sophisticated technological supports. A number of lines of inquiry in game theory have converged upon local network structures as a terrain for analysing the equilibrium properties of games characterized by strategic complementaries and interactive learning on the part of players. Interest here has focused on the strategic problem that arises when it is assumed that each player interacts directly with only a subset of the entire ensemble – specifically the one in their immediate 'vicinity' – with players unable to adapt their behaviours to deal individually with each of their 'neighbours'. In such circumstances, each player must select a strategy that is common to all their neighbours.[8] Within a social network context, such a strategy choice could become generalized as a behavioural 'norm'. This has heightened interest in studying the conditions under which the dynamics of local interaction games give rise to equilibria characterized by correlated beliefs, or behaviours, in both deterministic decision frameworks and in dynamic stochastic settings. Models of the latter sort typically make use of results from Markov random field theory in order to show how local network externalities can lead to de facto standardization in choices of production methods and spontaneous formation of conventions.[9] As will be seen, the present chapter is situated in this broad category of literature.

The main goal of the analysis developed in David (1998) was to show how behaviours regarding the disclosure of knowledge and current scientific opinion by individual agents, as well as receptivity to corresponding flows of information conveyed by members of personal networks, affect the capacity of the entire ensemble to reach a collective cognitive state of 'scientific closure'. What is meant by 'closure' is simply the emergence of a preponderant 'consensus'. This condition is represented as a configuration of correlated belief orientations amongst members of a certain epistemic community, or 'scientific field', regarding the validity, or invalidity, of particular scientific propositions. The existence of a past record of matters on which informed opinion was able to reach substantial unanimity, and the prospects of an ensemble being able to achieve comparable successes in cases of new propositions, constitute collective cognitive coherence. These conditions justify the term 'invisible college' for what would otherwise merely constitute an aggregation of individual researchers.

Within the context of the model, the ability to reach 'closure' in the sense just outlined depends critically on the degree to which members of an epistemic community conform to the norms of cooperation, disclosure and universalism outlined by Merton (1973) and seen as the institutionalized basis for open, 'modern' science. This conclusion follows as a formal proposition from the close resemblance between the properties of a particular stochastic process known as the 'Voter Model', and the stylized account offered in David (1998) of the way in which researchers' interpretations of observational data are shaped (probabilistically) by the distribution of peer opinion and related tacit knowledge derived from local communication networks.

The following two sections review the structural underpinnings of the model that will be developed in this chapter. The basis for adopting the characterization of the probabilistic communication strategies of the individuals forming tacit knowledge networks is summarized in the next section. There follows, in the third section, a brief review of the main properties of the 'Voter Model', a well-studied, reversible spin system introduced by Clifford and Sudbury (1973) and by Holley and Liggett (1975).

2   MICRO-FOUNDATIONS: SOCIAL NETWORKS, TACIT KNOWLEDGE AND THE INFLUENCE OF PEER OPINION

A brief discussion should suffice to highlight key features of the social channels of knowledge communication among research scientists which are captured or, more properly 'caricatured' in the micro-level model drawn from David (1998) and described formally in the next section. Starting from recognition of the distinct, but complementary, roles of tacit and codified knowledge in the conduct of research, we consider the nature of the cognitive transactions in which members of local networks are engaged. This leads to an examination on pages 177 to 179 of the underlying incentives that reinforce cooperative exchanges of tacit knowledge within small, pre-existing networks of personal correspondents; and then to the identification on pages 179 to 182 of the special conditions under which the disclosure of provisional conclusions tending to conform to the consensus of local peer belief emerge as a rational reputation-building strategy. Extending the grounds for attributing a central importance to 'conformity effects' in the process of consensus formation, research activity is viewed on pages 182 to 185 as an iterative process of the Bayesian belief that revision of individual researchers' observations, and interpretations of their experimental results, are powerfully shaped by a priori expectations which reflect peer opinion about the subject under investigation.

Informal Knowledge Transactions inside 'Invisible Colleges'

Analysis of the economic logic of academic science's reward system comple-ments the functionalist tradition in sociology regarding the cultural ethos of modern science, doing so by laying stress upon the centrality of the norm of public disclosure of knowledge among those belonging to the Republic of Science. Thus Ziman (1984, p.58) holds that 'the fundamental social institu-tion of science is ... its system of *communication*' (italics added). Accordingly, much attention has been focused on bibliometric studies of patterns of transmission of information by means of books, journals and other archival publications in an effort to identify participants and map the respec-tive cognitive domains of the 'invisible colleges' in which these various trans-actions arise.[10] The common features of invisible colleges in science are that they remain quite fluid as to membership; are variable in size; generally do not become highly structured internally; and, in today's world of telecommunica-tions technology and cheap air travel, have become less and less localized along institutional, geographical or national lines.[11]

The existence of 'broadcast' modes of distributing codified knowledge forms an essential background to the personal, interactive transactions amongst members of modern scientific research communities. Rewards struc-tures for participants in open science are tied to publications in various media, as has been noted, and it is in this connection that rivalries within invisible colleges tend to be focused. Within these extensive communities, whose membership numbers in the hundreds, are smaller and communicatively more compact relational entities. These are referred to here as local social research networks, or simply as 'local networks'. The latter term is appropriate for the interactive, two-way communication flows among members. Characteristically, information is personally conveyed in conversations by means of telephones, faxes and e-mail messages; also by people visiting each others' laboratories, meeting for seminars or workshop presentations and circulating pre-publication drafts for private comment.

Even when more tightly clustered, such social groupings are better described as research 'cliques', than as organized 'teams', and indeed these social networks may embrace some members who belong also to other project teams. By comparison with the larger, invisible colleges formed on discipli-nary and subdisciplinary lines, the members of social networks in science tend to be rather more strongly localized in one or more dimensions of association: they may share personal histories of training, or an area of problem special-ization, or geographical and institutional proximity. Colocation is not essen-tial, but it affords more frequent opportunities for face-to-face communication and informal collaborative activity.

Circulating within the more restricted ambit of a researcher's local network will be many bits of crucial knowledge about experimental procedures, equipment functioning, data analysis algorithms and database codebooks, much of which is not revealed in published accounts of research procedures and findings. Although the development and circulation of codified knowledge traditionally was a matter of central, indeed of exclusive, interest in philosophical and sociological studies of science, the significance of non-codified, *tacit* forms of knowledge and their role in the craft practice of science has come to be more generally appreciated. Tacit knowledge, as conceptualized by Michael Polanyi (1966), refers to a common perception that we are aware of certain objects without being focused on them. Lying outside the zone of conscious attention does not make them any the less important; they form the context which makes focused perception possible, understandable and productive.

Tacit and codified knowledge should thus be viewed generally as complements, rather than substitutes, in human cognitive processes. Both as a matter of formal logic, and in practical affairs, knowledge may be either disclosed to others or kept secret, regardless of whether it exists in codified form or remains tacit.[12] The view taken here is that, in order for ideas enshrined in scientific statements to be understood and rendered operational, researchers must possess complementary tacit cognitive associations. This is because scientific inquiry draws upon sets of skills and techniques that are acquired experientially and transferred by demonstration, personal instruction and the like. Knowledge of this sort may be highly precise and intricate. That said, it is most typically conveyed as a *gestalt*, and referred to by language and signs that are idiosyncratic, rather than being reduced to constituent elements and operations denoted by standard codes from which programmes of implementation can be assembled. The importance of this kind of 'hands-on' experience in many laboratory and facility-based research disciplines makes the problem of social communication of tacit knowledge especially germane for the cognitive work of scientific fields.[13]

To simplify matters for the purpose of analysis, the model formulated by David (1998) assumes that codified knowledge can be *broadcast* effectively through a variety of public media in which the identities of authors of messages are known, but whose recipients are non-specific. On the other hand, it is assumed that messages whose cognitive content combines uncodified (or incompletely and idiosyncratically coded) information with some codified scientific statements to which craft knowledge and informal judgments relate, are emitted *locally* in the first instance. Such mixed-content messages are thus held to diffuse first within the immediate social network neighbourhoods in which they originate.

The local networks described here are not regarded as a strategic instrument whose primary functional role is one of 'capturing' and exploiting the benefits of tacit knowledge for their members. On the contrary, the benefits they provide for individual scientists *qua* research workers are those which facilitate cooperative, reciprocal transactions in a world where specialist knowledge is otherwise undisclosed. The sharing of expertise increases the chances of solving complex, multi-step problems sooner than would be the case were individuals to work in isolation. In keeping with this, it is assumed that local networks are not autarkic. By having a number of members in common with similar local social groups, they are made more or less intercommunicative. Thus complementary packets of codified and tacit knowledge, along with explicit and implied conjectures about promising lines of scientific inquiry, eventually percolate outwards from particular local networks, and so become diffused throughout the wider community of researchers who make up the 'invisible college'.

Cooperative behaviour in the form of technical knowledge sharing and the disclosure of provisional scientific judgments can emerge and be sustained within a limited social sphere without requiring the prior perfect socialization of researchers to an 'altruistic' norm of full disclosure and cooperation. This is a rather straightforward instance in which insights from the theory of repeated games are helpful in accounting, in rational terms, for patterns of reciprocated cooperative behaviour among potentially competitive researchers.[14] Small cooperative 'networks' of information sharing exist amongst researchers engaged in recurring problem-solving situations. This is because pooling of information furthers the self-interest of members in their respective races for priority *vis-à-vis* researchers situated outside the immediate 'clique'. Correspondingly, individuals who deviate persistently by withholding knowledge, or otherwise behave in opportunistic ways to the detriment of those from whom they have drawn help, risk discovery and future denial of access to pools of specialized knowledge. This in turn tends to place them at a considerable disadvantage in matters to do with problem solving.[15]

Such considerations do not imply that the normative content of Merton's communalistic standard of disclosure plays no essential role in fostering cooperation among citizens of the Republic of Science. On the contrary, networks of reciprocal information sharing are more likely to form spontaneously if potential participants expect others to cooperate, rather than to betray trust. Game theory suggests that cooperative patterns of behaviour will be sustained longer if participants have reason to encounter refusals to cooperate in retaliation for their own deviation from the norm.[16] Moreover, the detection of deviant behaviour warranting punishment, and the implementation of retribution in the form of ostracism from a particular network, will have more broadly damaging reputational consequences if norms of behaviour ('customs') are common knowledge and part of 'a shared socialization' amongst all potential members of networks. Even were the process of socialization amongst scientists to be weak and imperfect, the common 'Culture of

Science' would make it likely that the rule of priority would not tempt individuals to engage in opportunistic withholding of knowledge; rather, self-interest would prompt adherence to the norm of disclosure, at least within the restricted circles of colleagues who make up local social networks.

Two sorts of cognitive communications flows are envisaged as taking place within the local social network structures of this model. Information, in the form of codified statements, can be passed between agents by the act of one of them sending a message or 'sharing' a piece of knowledge and the other receiving, or 'reading', it. The substance of the generic message transaction comes in two parts. The first component contains (or otherwise identifies) a particular scientific statement. For example, it could be a proposition about a phenomenon in Nature, a comment about the design of a measuring instrument or a reflection about an experimental procedure. Alternatively, it could comprise a logically connected 'bundle' of all of these. The second part of the message conveys the sender's present state of belief with regard to the 'relia-bility', or 'unreliability', of the accompanying statements.

To go further and in the process resort to metaphor, one may imagine that channels of communication are multiple and that they are capable of bundling (or 'packaging') cognitively interrelated propositions so that human 'transmit-ters' and 'receivers' are able to handle a flow of numerous, more or less concurrent, messages involving distinct, cognitively independent, scientific statements. Each of these could be assigned to its own 'layer' over the network, and the resulting information-processing architecture would simulta-neously be capable of executing multiple consensus-building routines in paral-lel.[17] For ease of analytical purposes, however, the model presented here deals with only one 'layer' of discourse.

It is important to emphasize further simplifications. The nature of the messages transmitted regarding 'reliability' are not concerned with subjective probabilities as to the ultimate 'truth' of a specified hypothesis. Nor do they offer assessments of the 'degree of reliability' adhering to particular state-ments. At any moment in time the researchers (acting either as a team or as solo investigators) impose a binary classification upon whatever opinions they hold, and so mark the cognitive statements they make as having attained a level of reliability that is 'acceptable' or 'unacceptable'. These are understood to be provisional judgments, needless to say; minds remain open in the sense that at any time cause can be found to revise opinion about a statement or a set of statements.

The revision process is precisely where the cognitive content of the messages' second component (beliefs) comes into play. At least two carica-tured accounts could be given about the way scientific inquiry is conducted in the world of this model. In both, researchers revise their belief orientations with regard to the reliability, or unreliability, of propositions under discussion in ways that leave them open to being influenced, if not completely 'persuaded', by the beliefs of correspondents within their immediate social network. The following subsections sketch the two accounts offered by David (1998) in this connection, one appealing to the taste of economists looking to find rational grounds for individual behaviours, the other framed in terms of the epistemology and psychology of experimental and observational inquiry. It will be seen that the two are compatible for present purposes, so that it is not necessary to choose between them.

Conformity to Local Peer Consensus as a Reputational Strategy

Introducing further strategic considerations provides insight into the persuasive power that a prevailing consensus for, or against, a proposition can exert on an individual researcher trying to assess the validity of the proposition under consideration. Unlike the foregoing arguments from the philosophy and history of experimental science, this section is meant to be more generically 'economic' in its appeal. In the spirit of arguments suggested by Dasgupta and David (1994), we assume that a scientist working in a collegiate reward system will consider the near-term reputational consequences of current actions (including expressions of scientific opinion), as well as long-term pay-off possibilities in the form of lasting fame for 'having gotten it right'. Whether one will be found to have been 'right' in the judgment of the invisible college depends on the alignment of one's recorded (or remembered) beliefs in relation to the consensus that existed at the time amongst members of the local network to whom those beliefs were disclosed; and also on the relationship to the global consensus that emerges within the invisible college as to the 'truth' of the conjecture in question. It is possible to envisage a structure of 'expected reputational pay-offs' that makes it advantageous to have had beliefs conforming to those currently held by most of one's local network, even when the ethos of the lone scientific hero would accord maximum kudos and immortal glory to a researcher who had not conformed with local peer opinion and whose beliefs later came to be adopted by an overwhelming majority of those working within the discipline.

Consider the following example, in which c denotes conformity with the preponderance of scientific opinion in one's network, and d denotes disagreement with that consensus. For expositional convenience we will consider the case where the prevailing consensus holds a particular statement to be 'reliable/true', denoted as R. (One can treat symmetrically the case in which the consensus among the agent's reference groups holds the statement to be 'unacceptable/false', not-R or, equivalently W.) The consensus that emerges eventually in the global network, that is, the limiting configuration of beliefs among members of the invisible college, may either hold the statement to be

'Reliable Knowledge', denoted by R, or not, denoted by W ('Wrong'). But we suppose that this eventual determination cannot be known with certainty at that moment when the researcher is deciding which opinion to give on the matter. It is in this sense an unobserved 'state of (social) nature'. If the individual researcher treats the local network as the reference group whose esteem matters, we then have the following notation for possible states, to each of which there will correspond 'reputational pay-offs' for the representative researcher:

$\{c, R|R\} = b_1$: being right, with the crowd;
$\{c, R|W\} = b_2$: being wrong, with the crowd;
$\{d, R|R\} = b_3$: being in a minority and wrong;
$\{d, R|W\} = b_4$: being in a minority and right.

A suitable general pay-off structure for an epistemic community is one that assigns greater value to an individual researcher who is found to be 'right' than to an individual who embraces the 'wrong' view. But it is also plausible that being wrong in a crowd will be deemed not as bad (for subsequent reputational standing) as being found to have been wrong more or less on one's own; and being 'lonely yet right' is deemed reputationally more glorious than being correct among a crowd of one's peers. This scheme of valuation of the outcomes of the game against (social) nature corresponds to the condition $b_4 > b_1 > b_2 > b_3$.

Now let θ denote the individual's subjective probability assigned to the outcome that the global consensus eventually forms on R; that is, hold the proposition to be 'reliable'. Then the expected pay-off, B_c, to an individual whose strategy was to conform with the preponderance of peer opinion would be

$$\pi_c = \{2b_1 - (1 - \theta)b_2\},$$

whereas the corresponding expected pay-off for the strategy of dissenting is

$$\pi_d = \{\theta b_3 - (1 - \theta)b_4\}.$$

It follows that the condition $[(b_1 - b_3)/(b_4 - b_2)] > [1 - \theta/\theta]$ is sufficient for the pure strategy of 'conformity' to maximize the individual researcher's expected reputational pay-off; but when the inequality is reversed, the pure strategy of 'dissent' becomes dominant. Putting it another way, there exists a critical value θ^*, such that when $\theta \leq \theta^*$ the strategy of 'conforming' would be dominant.[18]

The intuition here is clear enough: only when the a priori probability of the proposition being true exceeded that critical value could the prospect of receiving the large pay-off $\{d, R|W\}=b_4$ for being 'right in a minority' make adopting the non-conformist strategy attractive for an expected utility-maximizing agent. Obviously, such a possibility must vanish as $(b_4-b_2) \to 0$; likewise, the pure strategy of 'conformity' would be 'locked in' at the other extreme, $(b_1-b_3) \to 0$, where being 'with the crowd' was all that mattered to one's scientific standing. But, so long as those degenerate pay-off structures did not obtain, and the critical value of θ^* was such that neither of the pure strategies could be relied upon invariably to yield the maximum expected pay-off, it would be rational for individual researchers to follow a 'mixed strategy'. That is to say, they could form a provisional opinion on the question under consideration by choosing between the available (binary) options on a probabilistic basis.

To see how a mixed strategy of that kind might be implemented, one could start by asking how the subjective estimate of probability, θ, would be formed. Although this point has not surfaced explicitly in the foregoing discussion, it is now relevant to point out that stochastic processes representing dynamic consensus formation and revision of opinions result from interactions amongst members of a finite population of agents. For some processes of that kind, the configuration of opinions in the entire ensemble will eventually become perfectly correlated on one or other of the possible binary orientations: on either 'R', or 'W' in the present example. Furthermore, as will be developed more fully later, there is one such process in which the distribution of binary opinion orientations prevailing at the start of the process constitutes the best a priori probability estimate that the limiting outcome will establish such correlation ('closure') on, say, the option R. This is the so-called 'Voter Model', a reversible spin system that is well-known in the literature on interacting particle systems.[19]

Allowing for the moment that there is sufficient warrant to work with a model focusing on the process of tacit knowledge transactions amongst members of an invisible college, the preceding discussion concerning the role of local social networks implies that the initial state of (provisional) opinions throughout the whole of the 'invisible college' would hardly be known to any of its members. The individual researchers' respective information fields on such a matter would restrict them, at best, to knowing something about the current distribution of opinion amongst members of their immediate social network. Nonetheless, the proportion among the latter who currently say 'R' when canvassed would provide the individual's estimate (θ) of the probability that the invisible college as a whole would eventually achieve 'closure' by accepting the 'R-ness' (or 'reliablity') of the proposition in question.

Postulating that the conditions hold for mixed-strategy, micro-level behaviours, it follows that the process of provisional opinion formation and revision can be described by a simple probabilistic model of cellular automata. The latter represent the 'researcher agents' who are symmetrically situated in their respective local networks and who execute the following algorithm to select a binary orientation with regard to the reliability of a pre-specified scientific proposition: at a random interval in time each agent polls the opinion messages produced by other agents belonging to the same local network. If there is unanimity amongst them (either on the reliability or the unreliability of a particular proposition), the polling agent accepts the local consensus and accordingly adapts the messages sent to neighbours concerning the validity of the proposition in question. When disagreement is found within the local network, the agent follows this quasi-Bayesian procedure: he/she probabilistically selects an opinion on the given question by a procedure that is equivalent to tossing a coin whose loading mirrors the division of opinion within the set of network neighbours. In this procedure, equal influence is implicitly accorded to the opinions of the local reference network members and, in effect, the agent selects an orientation from the binary options with probabilities that are proportional to the currently observed frequency of that orientation within the agent's local network. That procedure corresponds immediately to the mechanism postulated by the Voter Model.

Cognitive Communications: Beliefs, Bayesian Learning and Conformity to Consensus

How plausible is such an obviously artificial representation? By way of an answer which addresses at least some of the 'realistic' concerns that the foregoing discussion raises for the study of scientific communities, an alternative, 'non-strategic' account can be given. This involves the influence of information about the distribution of local peer opinion on the orientation of researchers' judgments regarding the 'reliability' of a particular cognitive proposition.

The scientists in this part of the analysis may be depicted as engaging in a bounded form of Bayesian information processing, drawing inferences from the observations generated in their own experiments, and possibly also from reports of the inferences arrived at by others whom they know to have been similarly engaged. It is assumed that they are all following a common epistemological strategy, and thus refer to the same subjective probability thresholds when declaring a particular conjecture about an underlying 'state of nature' to be either 'acceptably reliable' or 'unreliable'. Furthermore, the existence of a shared strategy would itself constitute a subject of common knowledge within the community. Indeed, it might be said to be one of the procedural rules that characterize the epistemic community in question. Consequently, every researcher views the a priori beliefs conveyed by their correspondents as having been shaped by a Bayesian revision process similar to their own, and therefore containing data worth taking into account.

Therefore the distribution of priors underlying the announced binary orientations amongst researchers with regard to the scientific proposition in question would be subject to revisions that were generated in two ways. One would be the periodic routine of Bayesian 'updating', based upon their own calculations of the likelihood of the results observed in their own experimental work and data analysis. The other would reflect the (presumed a posteriori) judgments gathered from the distribution of evaluative opinions within their own local network. These, in turn, would reflect the pooling of categorical expressions of belief communicated by members of their correspondents' networks. Inasmuch as an individual scientist's conduct of experiments and undertaking of observations are likely to occur with less frequency than the arrival of messages reporting the state of opinions held by other researchers in the network, the effects of the latter might well be expected to overwhelm those of the former. This could well be the case even were the reports from others weighted less heavily than the researcher's own findings.

That considerable weight is accorded, de facto, to peer opinion in the interpretation of observational data is suggested by the doubts that sociological, philosophical and psychological studies have raised concerning traditional views of the nature of experimental science. These critiques call into question the degree to which scientific progress actually occurs by means of the experimental refutation or 'invalidation' of conjectural propositions proposed in Popper's (1959) account of the process of scientific discovery.[20] Historians of science have contributed to the present scepticism regarding the supposedly central role played since the seventeenth century by 'crucial experiments', and the power of unalloyed 'observation' in dislodging an established consensus view. Indeed, the very occurrence of the famous Tower of Pisa experiment in which Galileo found the same rate of fall of two unequal weights dropped from the top, and in so doing undermined the authority of Aristotelian mechanics, is now considered suspect. Adler and Coulter's (1978) modern replication study revealed that the observable difference in the speeds of the objects over their 200-foot descent would have been too large to justify Galileo's reporting it as negligibly small.[21]

Similarly, through the work of Worrall (1976), revisionist history of science now informs us that the experiments of Thomas Young could not have overturned Newton's corpuscular theory of light and so established wave theory, if only because corpuscular explanations were available for both interference and diffraction.[22] There are, to be sure, striking counter-examples of instances in which experiments did prove 'crucial' in overturning a prevailing theoretical model. But, even in these cases, careful historical re-examination sometimes serves principally to expose their atypicality, and highlights the special nature of the circumstances that led to experimental results proving decisive in rapidly altering a scientific consensus.[23] More generally, close examination of the ways in which runs of results are generated in modern experimental physics (Franklin, 1986) reveals how they can sometimes appear to imply either that parameter magnitudes are conditioned by theoretical expectations, or that when initial values were obtained in contradiction of received theory, extended replications were undertaken until significant alterations caused the magnitudes to converge to the theoretical expectations.

Such considerations support the view that behaviour in conformity with peer opinion exercises powerful short-run effects in scientific consensus formation.[24] The implication of this for the toss of the (local opinion-weighted) coin procedure envisaged in the Voter Model algorithm (see the end of the previous subsection), is that this routine mimics the conduct of an inherently ambiguous experiment or observational procedure. In such a situation, the 'reading' of the results would be strongly shaped by the experimenter's (observer's) prior viewpoint with respect to the validity of the hypothesis under examination. Only when opinion in the local peer group was quite evenly balanced would the testimony of the experiment exercise much leverage on the experimenter's reported beliefs, and then the conclusions drawn from a 'face value' reading of the results would remain uncertain.

This view of individual scientists at work hardly provides a warrant for ignoring the selective element of inbuilt correction which operates in open science research processes over the longer run. Where the magnitudes in question are 'important' and widely relied upon, advances in experimental technique create opportunities for scoring scientific 'coups' by establishing new and different values from the ones previously accepted. Furthermore, as long as there is persistent acknowledged discrepancy between the theoretical expectation and the previous experimental findings, there is hope that individual researchers can achieve peer recognition and enhanced professional status by successfully reconciling the two in some new way. These aspects of science's reward structure function to set boundaries on unintended tendencies that might otherwise push the reading of empirical data towards conformity with prevailing theoretical expectations. The force of their operation imparts an evolutionary drift on the part of the dominant scientific consensus towards closer and closer agreement with, and more reliable representation of, underlying 'physical realities'.

Perhaps too optimistically, David (1998, s. 7.5.3.) suggests the possibility of arriving at a compromise between the various camps in the recent 'culture wars', based on an evolutionary epistemological synthesis. Under his proposed terms of peace, both sides would agree that a scientific community can arrive, by means of generic 'social processes', at a consensus on the acceptability of certain statements concerning the material world. Also there are rules governing the way those statements are presented and treated by members of the community which have the effect of ensuring that such a socially constructed 'truth' will remain open to revision, and even to possible rejection. There is, indeed, a long-run expectation that such social constructions will be discarded should they be found repeatedly to be difficult to square with other 'truths' – especially those which possess a higher measure of 'fit' with the logical implications and inferences drawn from an available body of empirical observations.

3   FROM STOCHASTIC SOCIAL COMMUNICATIONS TO A MODEL OF THE GLOBAL NETWORK

The strands of the preceding arguments can now be drawn together in order to examine the properties of the stochastic communications model to which they lead. For this purpose, the apparatus of graph-theoretic representation of connected local networks of research units forming an 'invisible college' is briefly introduced below. A correspondence is then asserted between the micro-level network interactions specified by the preceding sections and the Markov random field model known as the Voter Model. The latter's basic properties are reviewed on pages 185 to 187 for cases of networks that can be represented as one- or two-dimensional connected graphs. Some additional properties of the dynamics of consensus formation in variant formulations of the Voter Model are commented upon on pages 187 to 189, along with the broader significance of these, and related, theoretical results pertaining to critical properties of other stochastic structures: specifically, those deriving from the branch of probability known as *percolation theory*.

Graph-theoretic Representations of Social Networks and Random Markov Fields

For analytical and expositional simplicity we may begin with a schematic representation of the social space in which the agents constituting an invisible college of a finite and fixed size are located. This population is envisaged as being situated on a two-dimensional regular lattice. Its particular spatial configuration is described by a non-directed graph G of the kind encountered above (pp. 179–82): there is a total of N nodes in the lattice, representing the population of researchers, and there are in all $N–1$ edges, or channels, that run between pairs of nodes.

Every node has a set of four communication channels, each providing a direct connection with a single agent node. These 'correspondents' are situated respectively at the four quarters of the compass in relation to the index node. The channels, or 'edges' joining the nodes of this subgraph, can be made of equal length, l, so that a circle centred on the index agent, i, having radius l, can be drawn to pass through all of the agent nodes that are directly reachable by i's personal hub-and-spoke communication network. The five agents inscribed within the ith circle in this fashion form the local social network associated with its hub member. Alternatively, this five-agent configuration is sometimes referred to as the index agent's 'von Neuman neighbourhood'.

Another, similar five-agent von Neuman neighbourhood may be formed for hub agent j, which is one of the four nodes positioned on the perimeter of the ith circle. The ith and the jth circles therefore intersect, because their respective hub agents are located in the other's neighbourhood. By continuing to add neighbourhoods in this modular way, the entire square lattice arrangement of the invisible college may be constructed. To keep everything perfectly symmetrical and leave no nodes in boundary positions, the resulting two-dimensional lattice array can be presented in both horizontal and vertical directions, connecting the right-side edges to nodes on the left and those on the top side to the nodes on the bottom. This thereby forms a two-dimensional *torus*.

The foregoing spatial representation of an invisible college in terms of *a network of localized social networks* is an abstraction only. Choosing this particular graphical form makes the neighbourhoods, or local social networks, of each researcher symmetrical with those of all the others, and holds them fixed for the purposes of the analysis.[25] Both assumptions prove to be convenient as points of departure in the line of investigation taken here, which is perhaps the most that can be said for them. Being grounded in a static network configuration, the resulting model of local network interactions examined is enormously simplified. It is to be hoped that the gains in terms of analytical tractability compensate for inability to address phenomena that arise in ensembles formed from social networks that are neither symmetrical nor constituted of homogeneous agents.[26]

The Voter Model and its Properties

The undeniable attraction of the probabilistic routine for opinion formation set out in the preceding sections is that it corresponds directly with the well-studied linear 'Voter Model'. This is a reversible spin system that was introduced in different contexts by Clifford and Sudbury (1973) and by Holley and Liggett (1975), but is best known in the form elaborated by Harris (1978).[27] Leaving aside technicalities, this framework can be set out schematically as representing scientific communication and consensus formation in interlinked local networks. Following the notation by Kindermann and Snell (1989), we begin with the basic definitions relating to Markov random fields.

Let $G = (O,T)$ be a non-directed graph, with vertices $O = (o_1, o_2, \ldots, o_n)$ being the set of nodes representing research organizations, or simply 'researchers', and edges $T = (t_1, t_2, \ldots, t_m)$ representing the set of information transmission channels. For the moment, we restrict the discussion to connected graphs of social networks that are defined in one or two dimensions. A *configuration* x is an assignment of an element of the finite set S to each point of O. We denote this configuration by $x = (x_o)$ where x_o is the element of S assigned to vertex o. If we let $S = [u, a]$ represent assignments of the two possible opinion orientations regarding the reliability of a given scientific statement (*a* standing for 'acceptably reliable', *u* for 'unreliable'), a configuration would be an assignment of either o_u or o_a to each of the points in O. A *random field p* is a probability measure $p(x)$ assigned to the set X of all configurations, such that $p(x) > 0$ for all x. By the 'neighbours' $N(o)$ of the point o we mean the set of all points o' in O such that $(o'o)$ is an edge. A random field p is called a Markov random field if

$$p\{x_o = s | x_{O-o}\} = p\{x_o = s | x_{N(o)}\}.$$

That is, given the values at all other points of O, the value at o (either u or a in the example) can be predicted from the subset consisting only of the values assigned to the neighbours of o.

Assume now, following the 'Voter Model', that associated with each point of a graph we have a researcher or research unit, and that with every such unit there is a reference set comprised of other units; this constitutes the neighbourhood (or local social network) available for polling. At random moments in exponential time, each research unit, having polled its local network, reassesses its orientation with regard to the statement in question, u or a. At these times it will commit itself to the choice u with a probability equal to the proportion of u-oriented research units in its reference set or, correspondingly, select the other of the binary options. This procedure may be seen to be equivalent to random, equiprobable polling of the agent's neighbourhood, and the mimicking of the orientation of the selected member.[28]

The global dynamic process of migration between the alternative orientations of opinion with respect to the reliability, or unreliability, of a given scientific proposition is therefore represented as a finite state, continuous time Markov chain, with states being configurations of the form $x = (u, a, u, u, a, \ldots, u, a, u)$, where $x(i)$ is the choice of research unit i. A number of important properties of this well-studied process may now be briefly summarized.

Property 1
It is evident on even the briefest consideration that the extreme states $x^u = (u, u, u, \ldots, u, u, u)$ and $x^a = (a, a, a, \ldots, a, a)$, in which there is a perfect correlation of beliefs throughout the population, constitute absorbing states for this system. Once such a state is entered, there can be no further

change. The existence of a multiplicity (two) of absorbing states tells us plainly that *this process is essentially historical, in the sense of it being non-ergodic*: it cannot invariably shake loose from all initial configurations.

Property 2

A somewhat less obvious proposition, also true, is that for any starting state x the chain eventually will end up in either x^u or x^a. Thus, in the limit, *the process must become 'locked in' to one of its extremal solutions*. The system invariably does produce eventual 'closure' on the scientific issues submitted to it.

Property 3

There exists a limiting probability distribution over the macro-states (opinion configurations) of the system which is noncontinuous, such that, starting in x, the probability that the chain will end in x^u is equal to the proportion of u in the initial configuration x (without regard to their position in the array); and the probability that it will end up in x^a is equal to the proportion of a in the initial configuration x. Therefore, although subject to random influences, the nature of the asymptotic macro-state consensus in this system can be predicted (not with certainty, but probabilistically) from information on the initial configurations of opinions.

   The most immediately salient implication of this model is that a formal connection can be established between the social organization of science affecting the communication behaviours of micro-level agents on the one hand, and the all-important performance attribute of scientific communities in the cognitive domain on the other, that of achieving 'closure'. Another direct result is the support given to the view that 'the details of history matter' for the cognitive development of a scientific field. In this light, the propensity of scientific communities to comment on instances in which new ideas have won eventual acceptance in the face of an initial consensus against them is entirely understandable because, in the near term, such cases would constitute the rarer contingencies.

   Several technical qualifications should be noted with regard to the foregoing properties, especially as these admit of some interesting interpretations in the present context. First, the property of complete closure, in the sense of perfect unanimity, does not survive extension of the model to graphs of higher dimensionality. From simulation studies it has been established that substantial, but less than perfect, correlations in orientation emerge in the case of lattices on a three-dimensional *torus* (see Kindermann and Snell, 1980b). One may surmise, plausibly enough, that as social networks become 'less compact' by extending into still higher dimensional spaces, clusters of minority opinion are less likely to be surrounded by neighbourhoods of countervailing consensus and as a consequence tend to persist. Perhaps the recurring formation of disciplinary subspecialities in science serves as a 'social compacting process', the latent function of which is to preserve network performance in terms of the achievement of substantially strong degrees of consensus, these approaching unanimity amongst groups self-identified as 'experts'. On the other side of the coin, as was just suggested, higher dimensional social networks tend to increase the likelihood of 'heterodox' opinions surviving within small clusters of researchers who, in effect, shield each other from the conformity-inducing pressure of exposure to the preponderance of opinion within the epistemic community at large.[29]

A second point of qualification is that the properties of lock-in to closure, and the predictability of the nature of the resolution, strictly hold only in *finite* populations. If the population of a network were constantly growing at a comparatively rapid rate – at a pace sufficiently rapid for newcomers entering the field with randomly distributed beliefs about the scientific issues of the day to overwhelm the pace of the process of random polling in the local social networks – then closure would no longer be assured. Under those conditions the nature of the cognitive outcome would cease to be predictable on the basis of the system's initial configuration.[30]

This suggests a further respect in which the cognitive performance of scientific communities may be seen to depend on their organizational dimensions and dynamic attributes. Those characteristics would certainly include the rate of entry of new members in relation to the speed of informational transactions affecting the revision of scientific judgments within local social networks. Another factor requiring consideration is the 'pre-entry orientation' of new recruits, particularly in connection with the prevailing distribution of scientific opinions held by those currently constituting 'the field'. Of course, once an invisible college 'stabilizes' demographically, in the sense that its growth rate slows to the point that it is exceeded by the average rate of internal opinion polling, a substantial consensus can be expected to emerge even in the absence of strong pre-orientation as a criterion of eligibility for entry.

It is here that enhanced communications technology may prove of particular importance in supporting the rapid growth of research communities. A speed-up of the effective 'polling rate' will permit the mobilization of additional (human) resources at the research frontier to proceed more quickly, without jeopardizing the network's ability to reach closure on new questions taken up for consideration. Moreover, if improved communications technology can accelerate the pace of knowledge exchanges and opinion revision within interlinked local networks, it becomes a functional substitute for pre-orientation training of new citizens into the Republic of Science. This may serve to reduce the sort of disciplinary training that tends to curtail heterodoxy of opinion and the susceptibility of fields to radical reorientations in matters pertaining to consensus thinking.[31]

Yet another, and quite important, class of qualifications arises from closer consideration of the assumptions of the basic Voter Model with regard to the uniformity of research agents' communication behaviours. These can be highlighted more clearly by turning to a consideration of the properties of a somewhat different stochastic communications structure, one that does not assume that all actors are following the same policy of openness in their knowledge transactions with other community members.

On Imperfect Communications: Percolation Theory and Norms Supporting Openness

The population of researchers is portrayed by the basic Voter Model as being homogeneous in two distinct respects: (a) the structure of communication links between them is completely symmetrical; (b) their interactions are assumed to take a special form that is tantamount to saying that transmission of influence in dyadic transactions is deterministic, even though the identity of the dyadic pairing is probabilistic (being established by the random polling of a single member).[32] Researchers share their opinions with all who ask, as do all in the social network. Putting aside the possibility of entry, the source of randomness in the revision of beliefs within the population has to do, not with whether or not particular researchers are open to the influence of particular neighbours, but with the direction of the reorientation of beliefs that such influences bring about. The concepts and terminology of *percolation theory* provide a precise way of describing these specifications and of showing their relationship to a more general specification of the model.

The term 'percolation' refers to the dual of a diffusion process (see Grimmet, 1989). 'Diffusion', strictly speaking, refers to the random movements of particles through an ordered, nonrandom medium, as in the case of the diffusion of molecules of salt in water. By contrast, the term 'percolation' conjures up an image of droplets of water moving under the deterministic pull of gravity through a disordered, random medium such as a filtration tank filled with sand and pebbles of different sizes. When the water, entering at some source sites, eventually finds its way into enough open channels to pass through and wet the entirety of the interior surfaces, complete percolation is said to have taken place. It is from this that the mathematical statistics describing the properties of analogous processes have acquired the label 'percolation theory'.

Adapting the notation of Hammersley and Welsh (1980) to the Markov random field framework, let G be a graph in which some, none or all of the edges may be directed. Thus, as before, G consists of a set of research units (corresponding to the graph's vertices or nodes), $O = (o_1, o_2, \ldots, o_n)$. These are connected by a set of (possibly directed) edges representing channels of social communications, $T = (t_1, t_2, \ldots, t_m)$. An operative path in G from a research unit $o1$ to another research unit, o_n, is a finite sequence of this form:

$$\{t_{12}\, o_2\, t_{23}\, o_3 \cdots t_{[n-1]n}\, o_n\},$$

where t_{ij} denotes a relational line connecting o_i to o_j. The graph G is connected if, for each pair of researchers o_i and o_j, there is a path in G from o_i to o_j.

Now construct a random maze on G, as follows. Let each research node o of G be *open*, or ready with probability p_s to transmit messages that can influence any of its neighbours' opinions on the reliability of the statement at issue. Alternatively, it will be *closed* (unwilling to share its present knowledge on the question) with probability $q_s = 1 - p_s$. Similarly, each line of interpersonal or interorganizational communications t_{ij} may be thought of as potentially carrying messages that will be actually 'read' with probability p_r, or fail to be so with probability $q_r = 1-p_r$. Furthermore, we shall assume that all these events occur independently of each other. An operative path, $D = \{t_{12}\, o_2\, t_{23}\, o_3 \cdots t_{[n-1]n}\, o_n\}$ from o_1 to o_n is said to be 'open' if all its communication links are functioning and all its research nodes are ready to 'share' their knowledge conclusions. Thus the probability that the particular path D is operational in that sense is given by $(p_r\, p_s)^{n-1}$.

Let Z be some given set of 'source' research units, from which a particular 'idea' or scientific statement emerges into G. The decisions to adopt that statement as reliable (or not) can flow along any open path from a source research unit and will then similarly reorient the other units on such a path ('wetting' them, to use the metephor of natural percolation). The percolation probability $P(p_r, p_s|Z,G)$ is the probability that Z can thus reorient some infinite set of nodes in G. In the present application, it is natural to label the parameters p_r, and p_s, the mean probabilities of 'reading', and of 'sending' or 'sharing' information, respectively. In other words, in a large population, it can be expected that a proportion p_r are receptive to their neighbours' opinion on the reliability of a statement, whereas a proportion $1 - p_r$ are unreceptive. The transactional lines (edges) of G connect pairs of (nodes) research neighbours and the model supposes that a researcher already committed to disclosing a given scientific position has a chance p_s of 'infecting' a neighbour, conditional upon the latter being receptive or open to receiving that communication. Then $P(p_r, p_s|Z,G)$ is the probability that a provisional scientific opinion initially established in the 'source' research units of Z can propagate through the random maze on G and thereby become adopted universally.

Suppose that Z and G are fixed, that G is an infinite graph, and adopt the abbreviated notation: $P(p_r, p_s|Z,G) = P(p_r, p_s) = P$. Clearly, the mixed percolation probability P is a nondecreasing function of p_r and p_s, and it follows that $P(0,0) = P(1,0) = P(0,1) = 0$, while $P(1,1) = 1$. Consequently, $P_s(p) = P(p_s, 1)$

and $P_r(p) = P(1, p_r)$ will denote the node percolation and connection percolation probabilities of this system, respectively.

A fundamental mathematical property of the percolation process is that there exist some critical values of $p_r > p^*_r$ and $p_s > p^*_s$ beyond which there will be a positive probability that percolation occurs, but below which the percolation probability is zero.[33] In other words, the system undergoes a 'phase transition' when these underlying critical probabilities are attained. There are corresponding critical values at which the node percolation and edge percolation probabilities, respectively, become positive. These define the endpoints of a region above which a 'mixed percolation process' (one for which it is not certain that either all nodes or all edges of the graph are open) will have positive probability of achieving complete percolation.

What these results from percolation theory tell us in the present context is that there is a minimum level of *persistently* communicative behaviour that a finite-size scientific network needs to maintain if ideas are to percolate within it and achieve closure. Considerable significance, therefore, can be attached to this fundamental property of percolation processes. For a community of scientists to exist as a cognitively functioning entity, some critical measures of 'expected connectedness' are needed which reflect the expected communication behaviours of representative constituents. Another insight from percolation theory is that the effects on network performance of reducing the representative agent's probability of sending and receiving messages assume assymetrical forms. A given proportional reduction in the mean probability of sending messages (node openness) has a larger effect in degrading the percolation performance of the system than an equivalent reduction in the mean probability of opening a communication channel (edge openness). In view of this, the invisible college's first condition for functioning – indeed its most exacting requirement – is that the network must maintain a critical level of openness with regard to the behaviour of a 'representative node', that is the expected proportional composition of member 'types' engaged in disclosing scientific knowledge.

The representative researcher, of course, is a purely statistical construct in the percolation model framework: an average of nodes that are *permanently* open and *permanently* closed. The fraction of those which, being closed, will never 'share' (or 'write') what they have learned, therefore, must not be allowed to exceed the critical level $(1 - p_s^*)$ if the invisible college is to retain a positive probability of reaching closure on scientific questions. Thus the 'mix' of persisting behaviours is a critical matter for the system. David (1998, s. 7.7) finds considerable significance in the fact that the qualitative performance of the communication system undergoes a critical, discontinuous degradation when the mixing fraction passes a specific level, especially as the precise magnitude is not likely to be known in advance. In such circumstances it would be sensible to protect the cognitive functionality of the global network by maintaining a 'safety first' policy of selectivity with regard to the recruitment of researchers into the college; in other words, to impose some prior test of intrinsic propensity towards 'openness' with respect to what might be established in the course of research.

By the same token, the existence of strong, and universal, norms requiring cooperative behaviour on the part of researchers, especially in disclosing what they learn, together with a reward system which elicits such disclosures as the basis for establishing a collegial reputation, would serve as an important bulwark protecting the invisible college's ability to deliver a clear consensus on questions brought before it. Furthermore, inasmuch as $p_s^* > p_r^*$, designing the incentives for individual behaviour means it is reasonable that consideration of one's own 'findings' by others should take precedence over concerns about attending to other network members' messages. Publishing is more important than 'reading', in other words.

An alternative consideration is that there seems to have been a serious failure of understanding by sociological 'relativists' (amongst others) who have dismissed Merton's 'norms' as a self-serving ideology advanced by scientists in order to support their claims to special status and authority. No less mistaken is the argument that the irrelevance of the supposed ethos of open, academic science is transparent because its norms are transgressed by fallible practitioners of science who follow material self-interests or who pursue ego-driven compulsions (including the desire for fame). It is a self-evident socio-logical error to suppose that the essential features of a mode of social organization will be lost if any of its 'norms' is violated by some members at certain moments in time. Deviance is a phenomenon to be found in all institu-tionalized social relations. Any system of behavioural norms that is so rigid as to be incapable of tolerating some degree of deviant action is not likely to survive for very long. Furthermore, as can be seen from the properties of the Voter Model, some measure of intermittent (random) suspension of communi-cations on the part of individual agents is not destructive of a collective group-ing's ability to arrive at 'closure'. Still more apposite is the point underscored by the results of the percolation model. Even the presence of a small propor-tion of research workers who are persistently non-communicative does not necessarily vitiate the possibility that knowledge and provisional judgments can percolate throughout an imperfect communications system. There may be those who are transiently reticent in disclosing knowledge and provisional judgments, or are transiently non-receptive to the messages of particular colleagues; but it still remains possible for the process described in the Voter Model to result eventually in substantial 'closure'.[34]

These observations point to a formal, communications-theoretic rationale for the emphasis placed by Merton (1973) and his followers on the functional importance of the behavioural norm of openness amongst scientists, and for the corresponding tendency of relevant literature to de-emphasize the effects of particular macroinstitutional arrangements and communications capabilities on the qualitative performance of scientific communities. Still another implication of Merton's 'norms' for the conduct of non-proprietary research is brought into sharp focus by the stochastic models presented here. Disinterestedness, universality, and disclosure are crucial elements precisely because they reinforce micro-level behaviours which permit 'objectively reliable' consensuses to emerge in evolutionary fashion over the long run. They do so by enjoining members of a community to accept dissenting claims as worthy of examination without regard to the economic, social, political or national status of claimants. They do so too by insisting on disclosure as the condition for successful claims to the reputation-based rewards which go with priority of discovery. And they do so, finally, by preventing secrecy and selective disclosure of knowledge from being used as a means of stopping provisionally established consensuses from being challenged in a reasoned way.

Thus the norms characterizing open science serve to render it likely that conflicts between the constructs of social communication and the realities of the material world will be registered, and circulated, within invisible colleges. Furthermore, the ethos and reward systems of the Republic of Science encourage members to see such things as indicating opportunities for recognition and reward, rather than risks which might result in their stumbling into heresies and thence being excluded from access to the pooled knowledge of fellow scientists. As was suggested previously, an evolutionary selection process in the cognitive domain has a high chance of discarding a socially influenced consensus that is repeatedly found to fit badly with empirical observations. Moreover, as long as some substantial measure of diversity of considered opinion is preserved amongst researchers who continue to remain in open communication with each other, such 'deselections' will occur sooner. At the same time the construction of increasingly reliable bodies of knowledge pertaining to the natural and made worlds will proceed more swiftly.

KNOWLEDGE TRANSACTIONS AND GROWTH IN SCIENTIFIC COMMUNICATIONS

Structural Assumptions on the Communication System

1. The system is a connected graph with agents (at nodes) linked (by channels) to neighbouring agents.

2. Every agent has two functional modes in regard to current messages: 'writing' and 'reading'.
3. An agent in either mode can be in one of two states with regard to that mode: 'sending' or 'not sending' messages if in writing mode; 'receiving' or 'not receiving' messages if in reading mode.

Intuitions for an Elementary Dynamical System

More regularly open pathways for communications between randomly selected agents increase the expected speed of 'news' percolation.

- Faster expected arrival of 'news' makes readers monitor channels more frequently; *ceteris paribus*, this makes the network more attractive to readers.
- Larger network audiences (having more, and more attentive, readers) encourage more frequent transmissions of messages from writers; *ceteris paribus*, this makes the network more attractive to writers.
- In larger networks, *ceteris paribus*, the expected time taken for complete percolation will be greater.
- In larger networks, *ceteris paribus*, there will be a higher expected rate of emergence of novel ideas, produced by the recombination of ideas transmitted by the agents.
- A higher expected rate of arrival of 'new news' – reaching one randomly located agent from another randomly located originating agent – makes the network more attractive to join, for both readers and writers.

Remark: dynamic systems with strong positive feedbacks are potentially unstable. Small shocks can trigger growth or collapse.

Endogenous Dynamic Behaviour in the Voter Model for a Research Network

Structure of the equivalent deterministic system for the population of *N* research agents on a torus of low dimensionality
Rate of percolation, or 'closure speed':

$$S = S (N, p_s, p_r).$$

Rate of 'creativity' (generation of new ideas):

$$K = F (N, p_s).$$

Rate of arrival of new 'reliable' knowledge at a random node of the network:

$$S \cdot K = F(N, p_s, p_r).$$

Homogeneous agents' induced knowledge-sharing propensity:

$$p_s - p_s^0 = G(N, p_r).$$

Homogeneous agents' induced knowledge-monitoring and knowledge-absorbing propensity:

$$P_r - p_r^0 = H([F(N, p_s, p_r)]).$$

Equilibrium (consistent) communication propensities for a network of size N:

$$Q(p_s^*, p_r^* \mid N) = 0.$$

Endogenous network size adjustments:

$$\Delta N / [N_{t+1} - N_t] = Z(N, p_s, p_r \mid P_t, \omega_0), \text{ for } P_t = P.$$

Specifications for the Equivalent Deterministic System

Expected 'consensus' or 'closure' speed in network of size N:

$$S(N, p_r, p_s) = \frac{k p_r p_s}{N^3}, \quad k > 0. \tag{7.1}$$

Expected 'creativity' rate (generation of new ideas) in size N network:

$$K(p_s, N) = 2(\eta \, p_s N)^\mu, \quad 0 < \mu < 1, \, 0 < \eta \le 1. \tag{7.2}$$

Expected rate of arrival of new ideas at a random site in the network:

$$F(N \mid p_s, p_r) = [K(\cdot)][S(\cdot)]. \tag{7.3}$$

Determination of homogeneous probabilities of knowledge communication: (a) for 'writing and disclosing':

$$p_s = \min[(b\{p_r N\}^\beta + p_s^0), 1], \quad b > 0, \, \beta > 0; \tag{7.4a}$$

(b) for 'receiving and reading':

$$p_r = \min[(a\{F(N|p_s, p_r)\}^\alpha + p_r^0),1], a > 0, 0 < \alpha < 1. \qquad (7.4b)$$

Network Growth: Specifications of the Distributed Lag 'Stock Adjustment' Model

$$\dot{N} \approx [N_{t+1} - N_t] = (N^*_{t+1})^\lambda (N_t)^{1-\lambda} - N_t, 0 < \lambda < 1, \qquad (7.5)$$

where

$$N^*_{t+1} = \{\Omega[N_t, p_s(t), p_r(t)]P_t, \qquad (7.5a)$$

and

$$\Omega_t(\cdot) = 1/(1 + M \exp\{-\omega(t)\}), 0 < M; \qquad (7.5b)$$

and

$$\omega(t) = \{[\theta_r(p_r(t) + v\ p_s(t))] \cdot F(N_t, p_s(t), p_r(t))\} -\omega_0. \qquad (7.6)$$

For the stationary population case $p_t = P$ for all t, there is a solution set:

$$N^{**} = \Omega(N^{**}, p_r^{**}, p_s^{**})\ P,$$

which satisfies $\dot{N} = 0$.

ACKNOWLEDGEMENTS

This chapter draws on material first presented to the International Conference on Creation and Transfer of Knowledge: Institutions and Incentives, held in Castelgandolfo (Rome), 21–3 September 1995, only some portion of which was written up for publication (see David, 1998). Manuel Trajtenberg's insightful discussion, and the remarks of Adam Jaffe, Giorgio Navaretti and Jacques Thiesse, and others on that occasion, contributed substantially to my subsequent thinking about the topic. So too did the comments of Patrick Bolton, Theo van de Klundert and other participants of the Economic Theory Seminar of CentER at the University of Tilburg, and the critical discussion which was offered on the occasion of several subsequent presentations: by Olivier Favereau at the IMRI Workshop of the University of Paris-Dauphine; by Kenneth Arrow, Arie Rip and other participants in the Seminar on the Economics of Information Diffusion at All Souls College, Oxford; by Steven Durlauf and Niekke Oomes, among others, at the Santa Fe Institute; and by Fabio Pammoli and his colleagues at the University of Siena. Tom Flemming helped enormously by writing the original spreadsheet programmes that generated the simulation results for the equivalent deterministic system, and the graphics. Jean-Michel Dalle and Robin

Cowan generously shared with me their recent unpublished papers on other approaches in model-ling scientific communities at work. All those named have my enduring gratitude but cannot be held responsible for deficiencies that remain in this work.

NOTES

1. See Rosenberg (1982, 1994) on the 'black box of technology'; Aghion and Howitt (1998) and Aghion and Tirole (1998) on 'the black box of innovation'. But see, also, David (1994) on 'reopening another black box' – the economics of exploratory (academic) research.
2. This focus on the 'externalities' created by fundamental research in science derives in large part from the preoccupation of economics literature with arguments for public subsidies for such activities. See, for example, David (2001) in exemplification.
3. Crick (1988, pp.139ff) offers the case of DNA to illustrate the argument that physical science theory is of more help to biologists in establishing impossibilities than in guiding researchers to the particular solution found 'by Nature'.
4. One active part of this programme is (self-)identified with 'the new economics of science', following Dasgupta and David (1987, 1994), who took up Polanyi's (1962) conceptualiza-tion of 'the Republic of Science' in describing the domain of interest. See also, for further explorations of this territory, Arora *et al.* (1998), Arora and Gambardella (1994, 1998), Cowan, David and Foray (2000), Cowan and Jonard (2001), David (1994, 1995, 1996, 1998), David and Foray (1995), David *et al.* (1995), David *et al.* (1992), Gambardella (1994) and Trajtenberg, Henderson and Jaffee (1992). Some of the foregoing receive notice in a wider survey of the economics of science by Stephan (1996).
5. On the concept of 'social systems of innovation' see Amable *et al.* (1997). International differences in many dimensions of innovation activity, with respect both to industrial orga-nization and to performance, are finely delineated in this work. Yet, apart from noting the tendency of scientific specialization to be aligned with areas of concentration in patenting activity, very little notice is given to issues pertaining to corresponding similarities and differences in the structure and performance of 'the science base'; actually, quantitative patterns of 'scientific specialization' are inferred from those in patenting, rather than gauged from bibliometric analysis of scientific publications (see Amable *et al.*, pp.4, 249–54).
6. See Merton (1973, esp. ch. 13). On CUDOS, see Ziman (1984, p.177).
7. See, for example, Dasgupta and David (1987, 1994).
8. See, for example, Anderlini and Ianni (1995), Blume (1993), Ellison (1993) Bala and Goyal (1995), and Morris (1996).
9. See David (1988), Kirman (1993), David and Foray (1993, 1994), Dalle (1995), David *et al.* (1998), Ellison and Fudenberg (1995) and Brock and Durlauf (1997).
10. Price (1965), Narin (1976), van Raan (1988) and their followers in 'scientometrics' apply bibliometric methods to the study of cognitive structures in science, as do some proponents of the sociology of scientific knowledge (SSK). The 'translation' school of Callon and Courtial (1989) holds that social networks of research and knowledge dissemination have corresponding linkages in the cognitive domain; specifically, that they give rise there to counterpart 'connected clusters of connected nodes' in co-citation networks in papers published in the scientific literature, in patent applications and in other 'inscriptions'.
11. The same tendency has been discerned recently from bibliometric studies of formal scien-tific collaborations. See, for example, Katz (1994), Katz and Martin (1997) and Hicks and Katz (1996).
12. See David and Foray (1995) where three distinct dimensions are recognized as defining a space in which knowledge-products can be located: the codified-tacit axis, the disclosure-secrecy axis, and the public-private property axis. The implications of these dimensions are examined further in Cowan *et al.* (2000).
13. Many 'craft' aspects of scientific practice must be learned in modes of instruction akin to an 'apprenticeship' where opportunities for first-hand observation of how things are done exist,

leading to trials under the guidance and supervision of experts. Otherwise, something like the original process of acquiring mastery of such knowledge has to be repeated *ab initio*, guided and encouraged only by the belief that others have found this to be possible. A striking instance of the 'craft knowledge' deployed in science is documented by Harry Collins (1974) in his detailed and influential study of the construction of the TEA laser. See also Latour and Woolgar (1979).

14. Arguments on this proposition, which invoke *inter alia* the 'folk theorem' as applicable to the situation of researchers contemplating careers in academic science, are developed with some illustrative detail in David (1998, section 7.4). The so-called 'folk theorem' of game theory holds that (if future pay-offs are discounted by each player at a low rate) in the 'super game' obtained by repeating a finite two-person game indefinitely, any outcome that is individually rational can be implemented by a suitable choice among the multiplicity of Nash equilibria that exist.

15. Thus 'circles' or 'networks' that informally facilitate the pooling of knowledge among distinct research entities on a restricted basis can exist as exceptions to both the dominant mode of 'public knowledge' characterizing academic science and the dominant mode of 'proprietary knowledge' characterizing industrial R&D organizations. Eric von Hippel (1988) and others have described how firms tacitly sanction covert reciprocal exchanges of information (otherwise treated as proprietary and protected under the law as trade secrets) among their respective engineer employees. The existence of a 'private–professional network' upon whom engineers can call for help is, in effect, a knowledge asset of value to an employer, even though exploiting it necessitates exposing the nature of the research problems upon which the firm is working. It is significant that, for employees engaged in knowledge-trading networks, expert help from peers outside the firm can be professionally evaluated and reciprocated in kind. Someone who accepted money rather than professional assistance in repayment for help which entailed disclosed knowledge gained in the course of professional work would most probably be dismissed by an employer and prosecuted for theft of trade secrets.

16. See David (1998, p. 130) on the findings by Axelrod (1984) regarding the effectiveness of 'tit-for-tat' strategies in sustaining cooperative play in repeated Prisoners' Dilemma.

17. The condition of *independence* that qualifies the preceding formulation needs noting. It serves to eliminate the complications that can arise from inter-layer 'cognitive spillover' effects, especially those of the competitive, rather than the complementary, sort. These occur where establishing a consensus on the reliability of the statement(s) carried in layer A is likely to prompt the collapse of a previous form consensus regarding statement(s) carried by layer B. For example, the initial establishment of scientific consensus on the reliability of propositions deriving from quantum mechanical calculations about the behaviour of light could be viewed as 'unsettling' prior consensuses regarding propositions about light derived from wave mechanics.

18. The critical value is found as: $\phi^* = (b_4 - b_2)/[(b_1 + b_4) - (b_3 + b_2)]$, and from this it is evident that the restrictions $(b_4 > b_1 > b_2 > b_3)$ that are imposed in the illustrative example guarantee that $\phi^* \varepsilon\ [0,1]$.

19. Despite the anthropomorphic allusion in the name by which it is known, the 'Voter Model' discussed in the third section, as in David (1998), was originally developed in a quite different context (specifically particle physics) by Clifford and Sudbury (1973) and Holley and Liggett (1975). See Liggett (1985, ch. 5) for an overview and discussion of its relationship to the class of stochastic, reversible spin systems.

20. See David (1998, pp.134–8) for further discussion of the critiques advanced by Kuhn (1962/1970), Lakatos (1970) and Feyerabend (1975), which reinvigorated the epistemological problems posed for Popper (1959) by the writings of W.V.O. Quine (1953) and others (for example, P. Duhem). See Harding's (1976) discussion of the so-called 'Duhem–Quine problem' regarding the possibility of scientific refutation. According to Franklin's reading of the modern scepticist position (1986, pp.4, 106): whereas the theory-laden nature of experiments and 'observation' has the effect of opening the whole edifice of scientific theory to the risk of empirical refutation, particular theories or hypotheses could escape experimental falsification.

21. Franklin (1986, p.2, n.7), citing the replication study by Adler and Coulter (1978), goes on to point out that an Aristotelian could readily have modified the theory to accommodate the experimental data.

22. Moreover, the early (pre-Fresnel) wave model could not account for the rectilinear propagation of light, which was as troublesome for that theory as interference was for the corpuscular model. See Worrall (1976), discussed by Franklin (1986, p.2, n.8).

23. See, for example, Franklin (1986, ch. 1) on the experimental discovery of the non-conservation of parity in the weak interactions within the atom. This supported Lee and Yang's (1956) famous theoretical paper questioning the theory of parity conservation (mirror symmetry), which physicists had accepted as universal on the basis of its successful characterization of strong and electromagnetic interactions.

24. The implication is that the mechanism of consensus formation in science, considered as a social system, would be 'neutral' with respect to the objective truth of the proposition under discussion. This is a central proposition asserted by adherents of the so-called Edinburgh 'Strong Programme' within the field of the sociology of scientific knowledge and follows upon Bloor's (1976) seminal formulation.

25. It would appear feasible to treat the local social communication networks explicitly as coalitions, and, following the lead of Kirman *et al.* (1986), to model their endogenous formation, and possibly also their ramifying interconnections. This would involve application of concepts and analytical techniques from the branch of probability known as 'random graph theory'. See Bollobàs (1979). Although this approach has not been attempted as an extension of the consensus-formation framework employed in the Voter Model, the analysis developed beyond this paper notices the interesting use which Carayol and Dalle (2000) make of random graph theory to model the stochastic process of problem choice in science that gives rise to 'knowledge trees'.

26. Morris (1996), using mathematical tools other than those employed below, has shown that a number of the key properties of local interaction games concerning the dynamic propagation of strategies chosen in particular locations, and the existence of correlated equilibria, hold generally for a wide class of local (spatial) structures. On the other hand, the assumptions of symmetry and homogeneity are not wholly innocuous. For example, Bala and Goyal (1995) show that greater symmetry increases the speed of information diffusion in a local interactive learning game.

27. Based upon Markov random field theory, this model has lent itself to a variety of applications in the study of human and machine networks, for which a good introductory discussion is provided by Kindermann and Snell (1980). More recently, it has been extended to the analysis of the dynamics of technological competitions in economic contexts that are characterized by the existence of local network externalities. See, *inter alia*, David (1988, 1993b) and David and Foray (1993).

28. Although the intuition for this is quite transparent, David (1998, pp.140–42) may be consulted for illustrative examples of a variety of *local* network sizes and corresponding connected graphs.

29. The broader significance of this will be further remarked upon in the next subsection.

30. Kinderman and Snell (1980) report that probability theorists surmise that the dynamics of convergence to one or the other extreme (uniform consensus) configurations in a 'large' finite system would approximate those of the infinite population case. Such systems continue to migrate back and forth between the extreme states, albeit with very prolonged transit times.

31. For increases in the density and bandwidth of communication channels needed to achieve such an effect, it must be supposed that the availability of information from external correspondence constitutes the binding constraint upon the revision of beliefs. Historically, that may well have been so, and the hypothesized effects would appear to be well worth empirical investigation. But, as Herbert Simon and many others have pointed out, the superabundance of information in more recent times has made human 'attention' the scarce resource.

32. This interpretation is not the only one possible. The equivalent alternative construction of the Voter Model would admit full canvassing of the index agent's social network, but selection of an orientation (opinion) would use probability weights that reflect the observed

distribution of opinions. In this formulation the homogeneity assumptions appear in the symmetry of the connected graphs describing every agent's local networks; and also in the linear mapping derived from observed local frequencies to probability weights whereby equal influence is accorded to the opinions held by every one of the agent's 'neighbours'.

33. See Hammersley and Welsh (1980) and Grimmett (1989).
34. Trust in that capability, of course, is what has been presented (in the second section of this chapter) as underpinning the rational micro-level strategies of the agents engaged in polling their respective networks under the conditions stipulated by the basic Voter Model.

BIBLIOGRAPHY

Adler, C.G. & B. Coulter (1978), 'Galileo and the Tower of Pisa Experiment', *American Journal of Physics*, **46**, 199–201.

Aghion, P. & P. Howitt (1998), *Endogenous Growth Theory*, Cambridge, MA: MIT Press.

Aghion, P. & J. Tirole (1998), 'Opening the Black Box of Innovation', in C. Barba Navaretti, P Dasgupta, K.G. Mäler & D. Siniscalo (eds), *Creation and the Transfer of Knowledge: Institutions and Incentives*, Berlin, Heidelberg, New York: Springer-Verlag.

Alba, R. (1973), 'A Graph-Theoretic Definition of a Sociometric Clique', *Journal of Mathematical Sociology*, **1**.

Amable, B., R. Barré & R. Boyer (1997), *Les systèmes d'Innovation à l'ère de la globalisation*, Paris: Economica.

Anderlini, L. & A. Ianni (1995), 'Path Dependence and Learning from Neighbours', *Games and Economic Behaviour*, **6**.

Arora, A. & A. Gambardella (1994), 'The Changing Technology of Technological Change: General and Abstract Knowledge and the Division of Innovative Labour', *Research Policy*, **23**, 523–32.

— — (1998), 'Public Policy Towards Science: Picking Stars or Spreading the Wealth?', *Revue d'Economie Industrielle*, **79**, 1st quarter, 63–76.

Arora, A., P.A. David & A. Gambardella (1998), 'Reputation and Competence in Publicly-Funded Science: Estimating the Effects on Research Group Productivity', *Annales d'Economie et de Statistique*, no. 49/50.

Arrow, K.J. (1962), 'Economic Welfare and the Allocation of Resources for Inventions', in R.R. Nelson (ed.), *The Rate and Direction of Inventive Activity: Economic and Social Factors*, Princeton, NJ: Princeton University Press.

— — (1971), 'Political and Economic Evaluation of Social Effects and Externalities', in M. Intrilligator (ed.), *Frontiers of Quantitative Economics*, Contributions to Economic Analysis no. 71, Amsterdam: North-Holland.

Axelrod, R. (1984), *The Complexity of Cooperation: Agent-Based Models of Competition and Collaboration*, Princeton, NJ: Princeton University Press.

Bacharach, M. & D. Gambetta (1994), 'The Economics of Salience: A Research Proposal', unpublished paper, Oxford Institute of Economics and Statistics.

Bala, V. & S. Goyal (1995), 'Learning from Neighbors', Econometric Institute Report 9549, Erasmus University, Rotterdam.

Barnes, B. (1974), *Scientific Knowledge and Sociological Theory*, London: Routledge and Kegan Paul.

— — (1977), *Interests and the Growth of Knowledge*, London: Routledge and Kegan Paul.

Bloor, D. (1976), *Knowledge and Social Imagery*, London: Routledge and Kegan Paul.

Blume, L.E. (1993), 'The Statistical Mechanics of Strategic Interaction', *Games and Economic Behaviour*, **4**, 378–424.

Bollobás, M. (1979), *Graph Theory: An Introductory Course*, New York: Springer-Verlag.

Brock, W.A. & S.N. Durlauf (1997), 'A Formal Model of Theory Choice in Science', working paper, Department of Economics, Madison, Wisconsin.

Callon, M. (1995), 'Four Models for the Dynamics of Science', in S. Jasanoff, G.E. Markle, J.C. Petersen and T. Pinch (eds), *Handbook of Science and Technology Studies*, London: Sage Publications.

Callon, M. & J.-P. Courtial (1989), *Co-Word Analysis: A Tool for the Evaluation of Public Research Policy*, Paris: Ecole Nationale Supérieure des Mines.

Campbell, D.T. (1965), 'Variation and Selective Retention in Socio-Cultural Evolution', in H.R. Barringer, G.I. Blanksten & R.W. Mack (eds), *Social Change in Developing Areas, Cambridge*, MA: Schenkman Press.

— — (1974), 'Evolutionary Epistemology', in P.A. Schilpp (ed.), *The Philosophy of Karl R. Popper*, LaSalle: Open Court.

— — (1994), 'The Social Psychology of Scientific Validity: An Epistemological Perspective and a Personalized History', *The Social Psychology of Science*, New York: The Guilford Press.

Carayol, N. & J.-M. Dalle (2000), ' "Science Wells": Modelling Creativity Within Scientific Communities', paper presented at the WEHIA 2000 Conference held at CREQAM, University of Marseilles.

Caudill, Maureen & Charles Butler (1990), *Naturally Intelligent Systems*, Cambridge, MA: MIT Press.

Clifford, P. & A. Sudbury (1973), 'A Model for Spatial Conflict', *Biometrika*, **60**, 581–8.

Cole, J. & S. Cole (1973), *Social Stratification in Science*, Chicago: University of Chicago Press.

Cole, S. (1978), 'Scientific Reward Systems: A Comparative Analysis', in R.A. Jones, (ed.), *Research in Sociology of Knowledge, Sciences and Art*, Greenwich, CT: JAI Press, 167–90.

Cole, S. & Cole J. (1967), 'Scientific Output and Recognition', *American Sociological Review*, **32**, 377–90.

Collins, H.M. (1974), 'The TEA set: Tacit Knowledge and Scientific Networks', *Science Studies*, **4**, 165–86.

Cowan, R. & N. Jonard (2001), 'The Workings of Scientific Communities', MERIT – University of Maastricht working paper, paper presented at the NPRnet Project Meeting, 3–4 May, Paris.

Cowan, R., P.A. David & D. Foray (2000), 'The Explicit Economics of Knowledge Codification and Tacitness', *Industrial and Corporate Change*, **9**(2).

Cox, J.T. (1989), 'Expected Percolation Times for the Voter Model on a D-Dimensional Torus', *Annals of Probability*, **17**(4), 1333–66.

Crane, D. (1965), 'Scientists at Major and Minor Universities: A Study in Productivity and Recognition', *American Sociological Review*, **30**, 699–714.

Crick, F. (1988), *What Mad Pursuit: A Personal View of Scientific Discovery*, New York: Basic Books.

Dalle, J.-M. (1995), 'Dynamiques d'adoption, coordination et diversité: la diffusion des standards technologiques', *Revue Économique*.

Dasgupta, P. & P.A. David (1987), 'Information Disclosure and the Economics of

Science and Technology', in G. Feiwel (ed.), *Arrow and the Ascent of Modern Economic Theory*, New York: New York University Press.

—— (1988), 'Priority, Secrecy, Patents and the Economic Organization of Science and Technology', CEPR Publication no. 127, Stanford University.

—— (1994), 'Toward a New Economics of Science', *Research Policy*, **23**, 487–521.

David, P.A. (1988), 'Path-Dependence: Putting the Past Into the Future of Economics', Institute for Mathematical Studies in the Social Sciences Technical Report no. 533, Stanford University.

—— (1993a), 'Historical Economics in the Long Run: Some Implications of Path Dependence', in G.D. Snooks (ed.), *Historical Analysis in Economics*, London: Routledge.

—— (1993b), 'Path Dependence and Predictability in Dynamic Systems with Local Network Externalities: A Paradigm for Historical Economics', in D. Foray and C. Freeman (eds), *Technology and the Wealth of Nations*, London: Pinter Publishers.

—— (1994), 'Positive Feedbacks and Research Productivity in Science: Reopening Another Black Box', in O. Grandstrand (ed.), *Economics of Technology*, Amsterdam: North-Holland.

—— (1995), 'Reputation and Agency in the Historical Emergence of the Institutions of "Open Science" ', Paper presented to the National Academy of Sciences Colloquium on the Economics of Science and Technology, 20–21 October, Beckman Center, U.C. Irvine.

—— (1996), 'Science Reorganized? Post-Modern Visions of Research and the Curse of Success', *Measuring R&D Impact: Proceedings of the Second International Symposium on Research Funding*, Ottawa: NSERC of Canada.

—— (1998), 'Communication Norms and the Collective Cognitive Performance of "Invisible Colleges" ', in C. Barba Navaretti, P. Dasgupta, K.G. Mäler & D. Siniscalo (eds), *Creation and the Transfer of Knowledge: Institutions and Incentives*, Berlin, Heidelberg, New York: Springer-Verlag.

—— (2001), 'The Political Economy of Public Science', in Helen Lawton Smith (ed.), *The Regulation of Science and Technology*, London: Macmillan.

David, P.A. & D. Foray (1993), 'Percolation Structures, Markov Random Fields and the Economics of EDI Standards Diffusion', in G. Pogorel (ed.), *Global Telecommunication Strategies and Technological Change*, Amsterdam: Elsevier.

—— (1994), 'Dynamics of Competitive Technology Diffusion through Local Network Structures: The Case of EDI Document Standards', in L. Leydesdorff and P. van den Besselaar (eds), *Evolutionary Economics and Chaos Theory: New Developments in Technology Studies*, London: Pinter Publishers.

—— (1995), 'Accessing and Expanding the Knowledge-Base in Science and Technology', *STI Review – Science, Technology and Industry*, **16**, Paris: OECD.

David, P.A. & S. Greenstein (1990), 'The Economics of Compatibility Standards: An Introduction to Recent Research', *Economics of Innovation and New Technology*, **1** (1 & 2), Fall, 3–42.

David, P.A. & W.C. Sanderson (1997), 'Making Use of Treacherous Advice: Cognitive Learning, Bayesian Adaptation and the Tenacity of Unreliable Knowledge,' in J.V.C. Nye and J.N. Drobak (eds), *Frontiers of the New Institutional Economics*, San Diego, CA: Academic Press.

David, P.A., D. Foray & J.-M. Dalle (1998), 'Marshallian Externalities and the Emergence and Spatial Stability of Technological Enclaves', in A. Antonelli (ed.), *Economics of Innovation and New Technologies*, **6**(2&3), special issue on 'The Economics of Localized Technological Change', **6**(2–3), 147–182.

David, P.A., D. Foray & W.E. Steinmueller (1999), 'The Research Network and the New Economics of Science: From Metaphors to Organizational Behaviours', in Alfonso Gambardella and Franco Malerba (eds), *The Organization of Innovative Activities in Europe*, Cambridge: Cambridge University Press.

David, P.A., A. Geuna & W.E. Steinmueller (1995), 'Additionality as a Principle of European R&D Funding', Report for the STOA programme of the European Parliament, MERIT Research Memorandum 2/95/012, Maastricht.

David, P.A., D. Mowery & W.E. Steinmueller (1992), 'Analyzing the Payoffs from Basic Research', *Economics of Innovation and New Technology*, **2**(4).

Durlauf, S.N.(1997), 'Limits to Science or Limits to Epistemology?', *Complexity*, **2**, 31–7.

Ellison, G. (1993), 'Learning, Local Interaction, and Coordination', *Econometrica*, **61**, 1047–71.

Ellison, G. & D. Fudenberg (1995), 'Word-of-Mouth Communication and Social Learning', *Quarterly Journal of Economics*, **110**(1), 93–126.

Feyerabend, P. (1975), *Against Method*, London: Humanities Press.

Franklin, A. (1986), *The Neglect of Experiment*, Cambridge: Cambridge University Press.

Fuller, S. (1994), 'A Guide to the Philosophy and Sociology of Science for Social Psychology of Science', *The Social Psychology of Science*, New York: The Guilford Press.

Gambardella, A. (1994), *Science and Innovation*, Cambridge: Cambridge University Press.

Geison, G.L. (1996), 'Pasteur and the Culture Wars: An Exchange', *New York Review of Books*, **XLII**(6), April, 68–9.

Grimmett, G. (1989), *Percolation*, New York: Springer Verlag.

Hammersley, J.M. & D.J. Welsh (1980), 'Percolation Theory and its Ramification', *Contemporary Physics*, **21**(6).

Harding, S. (1976), *Can Theories Be Refuted?*, Dordrecht: D. Reidel.

Harris, T.E. (1978), 'Additive Set-Valued Markov Processes and Percolation Methods', *Annals of Probability*, **6**.

Henderson, R., A. Jaffe & M. Trajtenberg (1995a), 'Universities as Source of Commercial Technology: A Detailed Analysis of University Patenting 1965–1988', National Bureau of Economic Research working paper no. 5068.

— — (1995b), 'The Bayh–Dole Act and Trends in University Patenting 1965–1988', paper presented to the Conference on University Goals, Institutional Mechanisms and the 'Industrial Transferability' of Research, March (revised August), Stanford Center for Economic Policy Research, Stanford.

Hicks, D. & S.J. Katz (1996), 'Science Policy for a Highly Collaborative Science System', *Science and Public Policy*, **23**(1), 39–44.

Hirshleifer, J. (1971), 'The Private and Social Value of Information and the Reward for Inventive Activity', *American Economic Review*, **61**, 561–74.

Holley, R. & T. Liggett (1975), 'Ergodic Theorems for Weakly Interacting Systems and the Voter Model', *Annals of Probability*, **3**, 643–63.

Hull, D. (ed.) (1988), *Science as a Process*, Chicago: University of Chicago Press.

Imai, K. & Y. Baba (1989), 'Systemic Innovation and Cross-Border Networks', paper presented to the International Seminar on the Contributions of Science and Technology to Economic Growth, OECD Division of Science, Technology, and Industry, Paris.

Jaffe, A.B., M. Trajtenberg & R. Henderson (1993), 'Geographic Localization of

Knowledge Spillovers as Evidenced by Patent Citations', *Quarterly Journal of Economics*, **108**.

Katz, J.S. (1994), 'Geographical Proximity and Scientific Collaboration', *Scientometrics*, **31**(1), 31–43.

Katz, J.S. & B.R. Martin (1997), 'What is Research Collaboration?', *Research Policy*, **26**(1), 1–18.

Kindermann, R. & J.L. Snell (1980a), 'On the Relation between Markov Random Fields and Social Networks', *Journal of Mathematical Sociology*, **7**.

— — (1980b), 'Markov Random Fields and their Applications: Contemporary Mathematics', *American Mathematical Society*, **1**.

Kirman, A. (1993), 'Ants, Rationality and Recruitment', *Quarterly Journal of Economics*, **108**, 137–56.

Kirman, A., C. Oddou & S. Weber (1986), 'Stochastic Communication and Coalition Formation', *Econometrica*, **54**(1), 129–38.

Kitcher, P. (1993), *The Advancement of Science: Science Without Legend, Objectivity Without Illusions*, Oxford: Oxford University Press.

Knorr-Cetina, K. (1981), *The Manufacture of Knowledge: An Essay on the Constructivist and Contextual Nature of Science*, Oxford: Pergamon Press.

Kuhn, T.S. (1962/1970), *The Structure of Scientific Revolutions*, 1st/2nd edns, Chicago: University of Chicago Press.

Lakatos, I. (1970), 'Falsification and the Methodology of Scientific Research Programmes', in I. Lakatos & A. Musgrave (eds), *Criticism and the Growth of Knowledge*, Cambridge: Cambridge University Press.

Latour, B. & S. Woolgar (1979), *Laboratory Life*, Beverly Hills: Sage Publications.

Lee, T.D. & C.N. Yang (1956), 'Question of Parity Conservation in Weak Interactions', *The Physical Review*, **104**, October.

Leydesdorff, Loet (1995), *The Challenge of Scientometrics: The Development, Measurement and Self-Organization of Scientific Communities*, Leiden: DSWO Press.

Liggett, T. (1985), *Interacting Particle Systems*, New York: Springer.

Luhmann, N. (1984), *Soziale systeme. Grundrisz einer allgemeinen Theorie*, Frankfurt a.M.: Suhrkamp.

— — (1990), *Die Wissenschaft der Gesellschaft*, Frankfurt a.M.: Suhrkamp.

Marschak, J. (1971), 'The Economics of Information', in M. Intrilligator (ed.), *Frontiers of Quantitative Economics*, Contributions to Economic Analysis no. 71, Amsterdam: North-Holland.

Merton, R.K. (1973), *The Sociology of Science: Theoretical and Empirical Investigations*, N.W. Storer (ed.), Chicago: University of Chicago Press.

Molofsky, J., R. Durret & J. Dushoff (1999), 'Local Frequency Dependence and Global Coexistence', *Theoretical Population Biology*, **55**, 270–82.

Morris, S. (1996), 'Strategic Behaviour with General Local Interaction', University of Pennsylvania Department of Economics working paper.

Mulkay, M. (1979), *Science and the Sociology of Knowledge*, London: George Allen and Unwin.

Narin, F. (1976), *Evaluative Bibliometrics*, Cherry Hill, NJ: Computer Horizons.

Perutz, M.F. (1996), 'Pasteur and the Culture Wars: An Exchange', *New York Review of Books*, **XLII**(6), April, 68–9.

Polanyi, M. (1962), 'The Republic of Science: Its Political and Economic Theory', *Minerva*, **1**(1), 54–73.

— — (1966), *The Tacit Dimension*, London: Routledge and Kegan Paul.

Popper, K.R. (1959), *The Logic of Scientific Discovery*, London: Hutchinson.
— — (1963), *Conjectures and Refutations*, London: Routledge and Kegan Paul.
Price, D.J . de Solla (1965), 'Networks of Scientific Papers', *Science*, **149**, 510–15.
— — (1986), *Little Science, Big Science and Beyond*, New York: Columbia University Press.
Quine, W.V.O. (1953), 'Two Dogmas of Empiricism', *From A Logical Point of View*, Cambridge, MA: Harvard University Press.
— — (1962), 'Carnap and Logical Truth', *Logic and Language: Studies Dedicated to Professor Rudolf Carnap on the Occasion of his Seventieth Birthday*, Dordrecht: Reidel.
— — (1969), *Ontological Relativity*, New York: Columbia University Press.
Rosenberg, N. (1982), *Inside the Black Box: Technology and Economics*, London: Cambridge University Press.
— — (1994), *Exploring the Black Box: Technology, Economics and History*, London: Cambridge University Press.
Schelling, T. (1971), 'Dynamic Models of Segregation', *Journal of Mathematical Sociology*, **1**.
Shadish, W. & S. Fuller (eds) (1993), *The Social Psychology of Science*, New York: The Guilford Press.
Stephan, P. (1996), 'The Economics of Science', *Journal of Economic Literature*, **XXXIV**(3), 1199–1262.
Trajtenberg, M., R. Henderson & A.B. Jaffe (1992), 'Ivory Tower Versus Corporate Lab: An Empirical Study of Basic Research and Appropriability', National Bureau of Economic Research working paper no. 4146.
Usher, Abbott Payson (1982), *A History of Mechanical Invention*, rev. edn, New York: Dover Publications.
van Rann, A.F.J. (ed.) (1988), *Handbook of Quantitative Studies of Science and Technology*, Amsterdam: Elsevier.
von Hippel, Eric (1988), 'Trading in Trade Secrets', *Harvard Business Review*, February/March, 59–64.
— — (1994), ' "Sticky Information" and the Locus of Problem Solving: Implications for Innovation', *Management Science*, **40**(4), 429–39.
Weitzman, M.L. (1995), 'Recombinant Growth', Harvard University Economics Department working paper.
Worrall, J. (1976), 'Thomas Young and the "Refutation" of Newtonian Optics: A Case-Study in the Interaction of Philosophy of Science and History of Science', in C. Howson (ed.), *Method and Appraisal in the Physical Sciences*, Cambridge: Cambridge University Press.
Ziman, J. (1984), *An Introduction to Science Studies: The Philosophical and Social Aspects of Science and Technology*, Cambridge: Cambridge University Press.
Zuckerman, H. (1977), *The Scientific Elite: Nobel Laureates in the United States*, New York: The Free Press.
Zuckerman, H. & R.K. Merton (1971), 'Institutionalization and Patterns of Evaluation in Science', in N.W. Storer (ed.), *The Sociology of Science: Theoretical and Empirical Investigations*, Chicago: University of Chicago Press.

8. The diversity of social systems of innovation and production during the 1990s

Bruno Amable, with Pascal Petit

INTRODUCTION

The concept of an 'innovation system' (IS) refers to the various attempts that have been made to incorporate institutional elements into the economic analysis of technical change, and to study the impact these elements have had on long-term economic performance.[1] Many research projects have started out with the premise that it is necessary to get away from viewing innovation as a process of mere individual decision making undertaken independently of institutional environments.[2] Innovation necessarily implies interactions between actors (firms, researchers, universities, laboratories) and their environments. Moreover, it is wrong to think that such environments comprise nothing more than market price(s), albeit contingent. In reality, they consist of a whole set of rules, organizational forms and institutions. The differences in 'technological styles' that can be observed at the territorial level (usually a national one, although it can sometimes be a region or a wider grouping of countries), or even at the sectoral level, stem from variations in the institutional configurations that are specific to each territory. The expression 'technological style' is intentionally vague given the diversity of the characteristic features of technical change that are associated with institutional particularities: for example, the rate of change, the type of innovation (whether radical or incremental) and sectoral specialization which itself might vary as a function of the level of technological intensity or even of the long-term growth rate.

These things being so, which types of institutions need integrating into innovation systems studies? IS research derives from the economics of technical change, and a large proportion of the work that has been carried out in this field has therefore concentrated on institutions that are directly involved in scientific or technical activities.[3] These include scientific systems, research laboratories, institutions of technology and possibly universities and institutes of higher education – as well as the relationships between all such bodies and the corporate sector. However, this minimalist conception of IS is not the only one possible. Other approaches would include a wider range of institutions, encompassing a few which become involved on a more or less ad hoc basis. After all, if innovation is an accumulation of knowledge, the training system as a whole should be regarded as an important constituent of an IS. Moreover, the financial system necessarily plays a role in IS if firms are financially constrained in terms of the investments they can make in innovation. As such, innovation systems' borders, in the widest sense of the term, are moveable.

This extended concept of IS fits in with a literature which does not specifically take the economics of technical change as its starting point, but focuses instead on the varying institutional structures to be found in developed economies. The studies that have been made of the numerous 'varieties of capitalism'[4] have all followed a comparative approach when dealing with contemporary developed economies. They have looked at the way in which societies which exhibit a wide range of institutional arrangements have been able to nurture and reproduce diversity despite the growing integration of the world's economies. One aspect of this diversity is that national institutional structures cause variations in the ability of different economies to compete in a given type of production or in a given sector of activity. In a certain sense, institutional diversity leads to comparative institutional advantages.[5] Conversely, the economic (and technological or even scientific) specialization of developed economies has led people to take a closer look at the structures which characterize institutions specific to a given society.

It could be said that these other studies deal with the same topic as IS-related research projects, but without the technological determinism that is the hallmark of this latter corpus. The relationship between the two bodies of literature can be seen from two perspectives:

- ISs, in their restrictive or minimalist denotation, constitute a subgroup of the total economy. IS-related literature is therefore a sectoral application of research into the different varieties of capitalism;
- ISs, in their extended denotation, constitute another way of comprehending the differences between the various types of capitalism insofar as they attribute a specific role to innovation and to the factors that drive competitiveness and long-term growth.

A 'social systems of innovation and production' (SSIP)[6] methodology represents an attempt to transcend these two viewpoints. Along with studies which delve into the varieties of capitalism, it constitutes an all-encompassing economic approach. As such, the institutions that are deemed relevant, and which are therefore integrated into SSIP analysis, transcend the scientific and technological fields alone. Nor does SSIP postulate that scientific and technological phenomena constitute the core of the appropriate theoretical framework,

a view which one finds in extended IS approaches which define relevant institutional spheres by moving progressively outwards from a centre comprising
a minimal IS. However, an SSIP approach does attribute a specific role to
innovation and to technique, not because it has accepted that an entire country's institutions are subject to technological determinism, but because technological competitiveness (and, at a more general level, an economy's place in
the international division of labour) is a good indicator of all of the mutual
influences between institutional structures and macroeconomic trends. For the
current period at least, innovation is a useful gateway inasmuch as it can
provide access to an entire economic system. Moreover, by including institutions above and beyond those that are solely involved in scientific and technological endeavours, SSIP analysis shows that it is trying to account for, and
study, sources of innovation that may lie outside the minimalist inner circle.

The SSIP approach, as with the varieties of capitalism and the IS ones, must
cope with such issues as the potential superiority of a given economic model,
and the possibility that economies will become either more or less diverse over
time. At the same time, evolutionist arguments hold that competition will lead
to the birth of economies in which the least efficient institutional structures
will be transformed by adopting the traits of those economies showing the
greatest efficiency. The contention is nothing new, yet it has continued to crop
up from time to time. Its current version revolves around two phenomena:
globalization and the new economy.

One relatively widespread thesis is basically the following: (a) the 'new
economy' defines a new, long-term growth trajectory;[7] (b) associated with this
trajectory are various institutions that are capable of stimulating the technical
and structural changes needed to launch the technological path defined by the
new economy; (c) as would seem to be indicated on the one hand by the
United States' advance in new IT-related technologies, and on the other by its
superior macroeconomic performances during the 1990s, success requires that
countries adopt American institutional characteristics. The example of Great
Britain allegedly represents confirmation of this thesis, as well as proof that it
is possible to overcome Eurosclerosis. In sum, changes in modern capitalism
are supposedly leading developed countries towards an Anglo-American
model, replete with deregulated financial markets, 'flexible' labour markets,
technologically dynamic newly-created firms and greater competitiveness in
product markets. All in all, this constitutes a situation that is relatively different from the path followed by continental European economies since 1945.

The purpose of the present chapter is to assess SSIPs in the context of these
various factors. This requires analysing, during the first section, the theoretical foundations underlying the diversity of SSIPs. We will then study the transformations most likely to have affected the way in which various SSIPs
developed during the course of the 1990s. A third section will focus on the

comparative performances of developed economies during the past decade insofar as this relates to issues surrounding the 'new economy'. Having then observed that it is difficult to use a single model in order to account for comparative changes in various developed economies, we will use empirical analyses to delve further into the diversity of SSIPs during the 1990s. We will build upon the sorts of developments affecting SSIPs identified in Amable *et al.* (1997), and we will ask how the convergences and divergences between various types of capitalism can best be assessed. The concluding section will offer several hypotheses regarding future trends in Europe, particularly in France.

1   THE DIVERSITY AND COMPLEMENTARITY OF INSTITUTIONS

Globalization and Institutional Diversity

It has become customary to analyse contemporary transformations of economies by means of two analytical matrices that are not entirely unrelated. The first one is 'globalization' or, stated more simply, recent internationalization trends.[8] Such arguments can be rapidly summarized, as follows. We are witnessing an intensification of international economic relationships due to deregulation of commercial trade and increased competition on product markets. Because of financial liberalization, investment flows are generated which tend to generalize the principles of market-based finance worldwide. Amongst other effects, this latter trend has led to a greater need for investment liquidity; to new principles of corporate governance (in which the financial incentivization of executives plays a greater role); and to an ex post control of businesses by threat of takeover. Capital has become increasingly mobile, leading to an extension of the sphere within which private companies can act. Firms meanwhile have centred their strategies on the world market rather than national or 'regional' ones. This implies a weaker bargaining position for labour, with changes in the nature of the employment relationship leading to increased differentiation in employee status and the individualization of remuneration.[9] The main consequence of this trend is increased competition between national spaces, with competitiveness defined in terms of 'factor endowment' or infrastructure, and particularly in terms of the economic institutions present in particular territories. Also of relevance are the regulations which affect the functioning of factor markets (labour and capital), the efficiency of educational and training systems and the like.

The implications of this increased competition can be understood intuitively, some commentators arguing that countries experiencing economic difficulties should align themselves with current best practices if they wish to avoid falling behind in terms of international competitiveness. Yet how can one recognize such best practices? From an empirical point of view, they are necessarily those which have been adopted by countries that have achieved the best economic performances. Alternatively, from a theoretical point of view, best practices are those that bring markets closer to a state of perfection. Luckily, the comparative performances of developed countries over the past decade would seem to indicate the coincidence of these two criteria. The most dynamic economies are also the ones which have adopted the practices (or attitudes) that most closely approximate to the *market-based* ideal. The other economies (Japan and Europe) are supposedly suffering from overregulation, high taxes, barriers to competition and the like.

The second analytical matrix is more technological in nature, and centres on the composite notion of a 'new economy',[10] this being a concept that certain observers use to signify a relatively vast array of transformations. The effect of this intensification of technical progress has been to raise productivity gains where previously they had been stagnating (as happened in the United States). Technical progress has been concentrated in certain technologies and sectors, as suggested by neo-Schumpeterian theories concerning long-term cycles.[11] These are the ones which are involved in information and communication technologies (ICT), with innovation and technological dynamism playing a large role in the definition of competitiveness both for firms and for countries as a whole. Hence the importance of 'staying on the bandwagon' of ICT-related transformations. More than ever, technological dynamism is seen as being dependent on small innovative, or start-up, enterprises. Moreover, in order to develop, such firms need a favourable environment based upon flexible labour, ease of company creation (or disbandment) and the availability of qualified personnel and venture capital. With regard to the latter, market-based financing is viewed as more efficient than bank financing for supporting firms which aspire to exploit technological trajectories. This is not an exhaustive list,[12] but it is sufficient to highlight the major orientations of the 'new economy'.

When such analytical matrices are used to comprehend the transformations which developed economies have been experiencing, the suggestion is frequently made that, even if current orientations are not leading to the disappearance of specific national markets, they are at the very least causing a significant diminution in the diversity of modern economies. Given that such trends are being forced upon countries across the world, any delay in adapting to the new conditions leads, according to this view, to competitive handicaps. This, then, is a summary of the argument that all countries should be seeking to adapt to globalization. Even those who oppose such a point of view usually agree that the new internationalization modalities of the world's economies imply a more or less rapid convergence towards a single model, one that is based on deregulated, market-based finance; on the primacy of shareholder value; on pension funds; on the dismantling of welfare systems; on the privatization of public services; on the existence of an 'underclass'; of a digital divide, and so on. Where they differ is on whether this trend is desirable, not the diagnosis itself.

There is also a more or less homogeneous school of thought that focuses on the concept of 'diversity of capitalisms'. This diversity is not seen as something that is accidental or temporary; rather, it is the consequence of mechanisms that can be grouped under the generic title of 'institutional complementarities'.[13] In this view, countries basically diverge in terms of the institutions that characterize them, depending upon the particular aspects of the economies that are being studied at any moment in time. Thus the labour market can vary in terms of regulation, wage bargaining can take place centrally or elsewhere, and financial systems can look to banks or to financial markets. In general, education tends to be organized differently from one country to the next, with more – or fewer – ties to industry and with universities exercising varying degrees of independence. The degree of competition between private companies also varies between countries.

An initial approach would be to suppose that an optimal solution exists in each of these areas independent of the institutional configurations that are present in any of the others. The best institutional configuration for an economy is the one that is closest to the sum total of these optimal local configurations. This conception is very probably the driving force behind benchmarking efforts, and constitutes the basis of international comparisons such as those carried out by the World Economic Forum (Davos) or, more recently, by Lehman Brothers.[14] The purpose of such studies is usually to classify countries in terms of their competitiveness. To this end, a certain number of categories are defined, and countries marked for their performances in them. An overall mark is then obtained by adding up the scores from each area. The best model is the one that is closest to the profile defined as constituting the optimum local configuration. Edwards and Schanz's study is illustrative. For them, the ideal economy possesses Denmark's educational system, Sweden's technology and employment policy, the competitive environment of Finland's high-tech sector, and the fiscal system, entrepreneurial environment, economies of scale, productivity, wage flexibility and employment protection system (minimal) of the United States. It remains to be seen whether this mix of American and Scandinavian institutions would be viable. The answer is 'yes' if one believes that it is possible to play 'institutional Lego'. If one adopts a view that encompasses interinstitutional interactions, however, no such thing is certain.

Institutional complementarity does not consider institutions in isolation, but as a whole. The idea is that each institutional arrangement's existence or function within a given area is enhanced by the institutional arrangements that are in place in other areas. If certain conditions are met, negotiations between social partners in a given labour market can create the sort of stable compromises that help the workforce to receive a high level of training. In addition, physical investment is eased by the existence of close relationships between banks and firms. In such a view, the existence of durable relationships and of proximity between banks and firms enhances the implementation of long-term investment projects, and in return facilitates the establishment of stable compromises in the labour market. Conversely, a flexible labour market which fosters employee mobility is seen as complementing a financial system which facilitates the reversibility of commitments and the liquidation of investments. This means that the range of potential complementarities can be extended to cover such areas as innovation, professional training systems and the like. In conditions such as these, attempts to re-engineer institutions have no real meaning. By modifying institutions locally, one runs the risk of weakening the coherency of the institutional structure as a whole and, in the process, of diminishing economic performances instead of improving them.

An institutional complementarity approach would therefore see the survival of different models of capitalism as a reflection of interactions between institutions. It is also a complementary way of explaining institutional inertia, sometimes used as an alternative to arguments which focus on fixed costs or increasing returns. In fact, one explanation for the survival of institutions that appear to be inefficient (at a local level) draws a parallel between the increasing returns to adoption and the consequences of these increasing returns, that is to say of being forced to follow a given technological trajectory.[15] Just as increasing returns to adoption can explain why certain events lead an economy down a given technological path (one which is difficult, or even impossible, to leave), history also explains why institutions that were adopted for once good reasons survive even though these reasons may have disappeared. Consequently, institutional dependency on historical factors[16] leads to a certain amount of inertia, as well as to the survival of certain local institutions, even when they are inefficient.

With regard to institutional complementarities, certain institutions which appear to be inefficient at a local level can in fact play a crucial role in determining the overall coherency of a country's institutional structure. Employment protection policies can hamper employment as well as profitability under certain macroeconomic conditions, such as when adverse demand shock has taken place. However, they might be justified by the role they play as the guarantor of an employer's long-term commitment to an employment relationship with an employee, and by the role they exercise in providing an incentive for investments that specifically augment the value of that relationship. It is likely that the price paid in flexibility is lower than the gains that can be achieved as a result of the increased value of the employment relationship – something that only becomes visible over the long run.

Note that the existence of complementarities has been reflected in the economic policy recommendations of major international organizations such as the OECD. One focus of recent studies involves the *interaction* between competition in product markets and imperfections in labour markets.[17] This has led to policy recommendations which go far beyond advocacy of simple corrections to various market imperfections. Specifically, the anticipated benefits from correcting these imperfections are felt to be greater than would be the case if product and labour markets were assessed separately. By allowing for increased competition in product markets, the expectation might be that additional gains will be made once labour markets are deregulated. Liberalizing one market enhances the benefits to be had from liberalizing the other. As a result, the deregulation of the labour market will, in theory, be accompanied by an intensification of competition in the product market, the two types of reform being complementary.[18]

However, integrating complementarities into policy is not the same thing as moving towards institutional diversity. This is because of the ubiquity of references made to a single, optimal institutional configuration, namely the idea that increasing competition everywhere is the best way to overcome market imperfections. It remains the case that contributions to the study of the varieties of capitalism or to the existence of institutional complementarities stress diversity as the logical outcome of integrating institutional functioning (as well as influence on economic decision making) into the analytical framework.

Diverse Types of Capitalism

Numerous studies have focused on the different kinds of capitalism that exist, or on the specificity of each national model.[19] One theoretical analysis and exercise in international comparisons by Amable *et al.* (1997) highlighted four main types of 'capitalism' or SSIPs: market-based SSIPs, best represented by the United States, Great Britain, Australia and Canada; a social–democratic SSIP, best embodied by the Scandinavian countries; a meso-corporatist SSIP, seemingly tailor-made for Japan; and a 'European' SSIP best represented by France, Germany, Italy and the Netherlands. This classification process differs from other authors' approaches. Indeed, some studies tend to emphasize national specificities, considering that each country constitutes its own particular category. Others base their understanding of diversity on two polar extremes (such as the United States and Germany) and classify countries according to differences from, or similarities to, these extremes. By way of contrast, in Amable *et al.* (1997), SSIPs are seen as ideal types, not as (more or less) stylized descriptions of the main characteristics of a given country.[20] This obviates the need to come up with an exact identikit match between a given SSIP and the group of countries that best embodies it.

Identifying SSIPs involves both theoretical elements, such as the expression of the institutional complementarities that are at work in the nations comprising them, and empirical elements based on statistical indicators for these countries, the data being analysed in such a way as to identify national typologies. Devising a theoretical underpinning for the typologies derived from the empirical part of the analysis is not necessarily the same thing as 'naming' the model or the SSIP that has been discovered. It is not always possible to come up with a title or description that can correctly summarize a SSIP. Take for example the 'market-oriented' SSIP that is linked to the 'Anglo-American' bloc. The descriptor 'market-oriented' does not at first glance appear to cause any conflicts with traditional writings in the field.[21] It is an indication that the basic principle underlying the SSIP in question is a 'market' logic characterized by the significance of price-driven regulation, by competition between agents, by flexible arrangements, by speedy reactions to price signals and the like. Here the term 'basic principle' means, for example, that a market logic applies to all of the subsystems of a market-oriented SSIP by virtue of a kind of isomorphic quality.

There is more to the issue than this, however. In the logic of ideas involving institutional complementarity, notions of 'varieties of capitalism' or of SSIPs stem from complementarities between various types of institutions.[22] This can be seen by analysing the different areas where such institutions are relevant. Consider, for example, an economy with three areas (1, 2 and 3) and two possible types of institutions in each area (I and I'). The theory of institutional complementarities states that only two configurations are possible (I1, I2 and I3, on the one hand, and I'1, I'2 and I'3, on the other). This is because these configurations are stable, or perform better. This argument eliminates the six other possible types of institutional combinations, that is, mixtures of Type I and Type I' institutions. Institutional complementarities can tie the institutions to each other on a two-by-two basis, as shown in Figure 8.1 below. In this case, the two varieties of capitalism are characterized by the complementarities (C1, C2 and C3) and (C'1, C'2 and C'3). If one model is called Model M and the other model M', with M and M' having a specific meaning (a 'market' logic or a 'public' economy, for example), it appears possible to find principle M within C1, C2 and C3, and principle M' within C'1, C'2 and C'3. However, nothing indicates a priori that (C1, C2, C3) or (C'1, C'2, C'3) can be reduced to a single principle.

All of this becomes easier if complementarities can be found between a given position and all of the others. If, for example, the complementarity C1

(C'1) turns out to be indispensable to the existence of other complementarities, it can then be considered that one is in the presence of a C1 (C'1) model. Even if C1 (C'1) is not going to be found between all of the institutions in the model, it remains the case that the complementarities which derive from it are there. This institutional hierarchy provides signals as to the directions in which the model may be developing, an aspect that will be explored below.

With the exception of an institutional hierarchy that has already been clearly identified, it is generally difficult to see a model as being more than the expression of a single logic. This is especially the case when this logic has to be expressed with simplicity. Several interrelated logics are involved in determining the coherence of any given model. These logics are sometimes local inasmuch as the mechanisms involved only affect a limited number of institutions and areas. This does not necessarily imply the existence of a single unifying principle active throughout the economic model in question. However, a certain overall coherence does exist related to the behaviour of agents. The various fields may well be distinct from one another, but agents belong to several different fields, and their behaviour is determined by a system of beliefs and shared values that can help describe a particular model.

Reverting to the example of the market-based model[23] (called the Anglo-Saxon one by many authors, sometimes the 'neoliberal' or 'market-oriented' one[24]), it could be said that the logics here influence all of the institutional

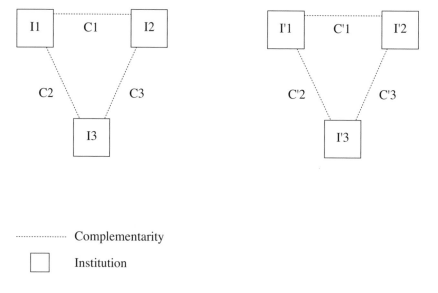

.... Complementarity

☐   Institution

Figure 8.1   Representations of institutional complementarities

arrangements found within the model. As a result, even if 'market' logic is not found within all of the subsystems of a market economy, it nevertheless conditions the localized logics. Describing one and the same model as 'Anglo-Saxon' or 'Anglo-American' might be less risky than using the term 'market-oriented'. One can always contest the pre-eminence of market mechanisms in these economies, but it is difficult to deny that Anglo-American countries possess them. The problem with the labelling, however, is that it is not very explicit about whatever it is that the countries in this model share; and it does not express any economic theory for the model. It does, however, imply a number of things, including the role played by history and culture. These implications need to be rendered explicit and justified at a theoretical level; after all, 'culture' is utilized as a last-resort argument in many comparative studies. Lastly, note that it would have been possible to describe a market-oriented SSIP as an 'Echelon', playing on the name of the information-gathering system that has been instituted at the behest, and under the direction, of the United States. This other label could open new perspectives with respect to the logic or 'coherence' of the model in question.

The fact that it may be hard to identify 'coherence' is well illustrated by the 'European' or 'Public' SSIP. In this model, there is a high chance that more than one principle is at work. Several principles may be operating and being enacted locally. It is also likely that the countries which best embody this SSIP are hybrid in nature: in certain respects Germany is close to the social-democratic SSIP, whilst the Netherlands features certain traits of the market-oriented model. The group of countries being considered here is probably the least homogeneous of all. As a consequence, this is the SSIP that is defined with the lowest degree of precision.

2   WHAT IS NEW IN THE 1990s?

Self-styled institutional complementarity approaches are sometimes criticized for being too static and for not correctly explaining the changes that affect nation states. After all, if economies are made up of complementarities that represent a combination of specific institutional forms, no single element can be modified without the system as a whole being changed. Yet, if this is so, how is it possible to explain the diffusion of new practices (such as new management principles) which constitute a readily observable empirical fact from the 1960s onwards?[25] To answer this question, the various changes need to be differentiated by category. Certain changes do not require any rethinking of institutional arrangements. To use Bruce Kogut's expression (2000), they are *institutionally neutral*. As such, they do not subvert the stability of institutional complementarities. By way of contrast, other practices can necessitate institutional changes and therefore ultimately destabilize the architecture of a given model. However, the integration of institutional complementarities into an analysis does not mean that change is impossible. Static considerations and an emphasis on coherency and stability should only be seen as instances of institutional analysis, not as a worldview.

If we want to speak of the permanence of a form of capitalism, the related institutional complementarities must be capable of being preserved in a dynamic manner. All economies undergo transformations under the influence of external factors and as a result of their own economic and institutional dynamics. Certain institutions can be modified, adapting to those transformations that have an effect on all economies at a given moment in time and without damaging the model's stability. Localized, or generalized, hybridization can take place in the absence of any radical transformation. Having said that, hybridization is not the only transformation logic that exists; institutional innovation does not merely involve recombining the same elements in a different way. The principles underlying the institutional complementarities of a given system can lead to new forms which in turn serve to preserve those principles. However, there are other types of transformations which raise questions about all of these current institutional complementarities. This is because they affect those complementarities that are most essential to a model. In sum, not all institutional complementarities have the same importance.

The aforementioned concept of institutional hierarchy allows the analysis to incorporate the possibility that major institutional changes can take place without doubts being expressed as to whether the concept of institutional complementarity constitutes a sound basis for the varieties of capitalism approach or the SSIP one. The concept of hierarchy can be understood in two different ways. The first, discussed above, concerns the manner in which institutional arrangements are conceived, with the notion of hierarchy becoming obligatory when specific institutions incorporate into their cognitive framework constraints and incentives that are associated with a different institution. For Soskice (1999), the coordination between labour and employer unions lies at the summit of the institutional hierarchy, especially in Germany (with the government and the central bank in joint second places). For Aoki (2000), it is the interrelationship between banks, firms and the employment relationship that constitutes the cornerstone of the Japanese system.

This definition of institutional hierarchy may be difficult to apply in practice if reciprocal interactions between various institutional arrangements create ambiguities with respect to the way in which various constraints imposed on each other by institutions are interpreted. The definition of complementarities and of institutional hierarchies can therefore be extended using a dynamic perspective. Dramatic change in a particular institutional complementarity (for example, the reformulation following a bout of financial deregulation, the central role played by banks in funding industry or a significant modification in forms of competition), can serve to trigger the transformation of other complementarities by raising doubts as to the structure of a given institutional configuration. This then requires changes in all of the institutions involved. It is to these types of upheavals that most analyses of modern economies refer when they discuss the influence of globalization or of the 'new economy'. By subjecting all countries to new and shared constraints, these phenomena raise questions about institutional structures. They affect certain countries more than others; and they may ultimately cause countries to adopt one and the same model. We can identify historical trends concerning homogenization, for example the Americanization of Western economies during the postwar period, Equally, we can find examples of the opposite trend.

The dynamics that have been driving capitalist economies stem from the opposition between homogenizing tendencies and the trend towards the survival of national or regional particularities. Diversity is viable if it is possible to obtain growth rates that are comparable, if not exactly the same, between countries.[26] But a configuration featuring a single model is not necessarily a stable one, if only because of implications in terms of comparative advantage. Indeed, if one believes that institutions influence the various industrial specializations of economies even more than their rates of growth, it is only possible to exploit divergences (one of the strongest foundations of international trade) if a modicum of diversity is maintained.

Which types of transformations affect all models of capitalism? At a technological level, modifications can be expected to exist upstream from the relationships that exist between the development of sciences and their applications to innovation. Techniques and processes seem to be implementing generic, moveable and decontextualized knowledge in an increasingly direct manner. Such knowledge is likely to have a multitude of applications in a wide variety of fields. At a figurative level, it is akin to reacquainting innovation with strictly scientific fields.[27] Moreover, this furthering of types of knowledge in innovation practices coincides with the transformation of sciences' own production regimes, these being influenced by the sort of industrial problems which take science away from mere academic concerns.[28] Again at a figurative level, this second trend is of much the same character as a scientific quest descending into its own fields of application. The development of this interface implies a set of relationships which lies at the heart of the modern phase of internationalization. Such a set involves academic networks, information networks and complex corporate service networks linked to companies which developed their international profile during the postwar era, first as a follow-up to overseas productive investments and later on (for more or less 20 years now) as a stand-alone initiative.

Directly tied into the interface between science and technology is a whole new dynamic involving inter-firm divisions of labour which reflect, amongst other things, the lower transaction costs which have resulted from the diffusion of new information and communications technologies. Other factors are the rise in agents' level of education and information, as well as internationalization itself, here construed as an extension of the relational and strategic fields associated with the two other structural transformations. The most noteworthy aspect of this shift relates to the development of externalization, with everything that implies in terms of a tighter coordination of subcontracting and the use of companies from different types of business for tasks whenever such companies seem the most competent. This increased competency can be viewed at two levels. Economies of scale remain an important factor, but it is principally 'economies of scope' which create the capacity for true originality. The notion of economies of scope implies that the new division of labour is a bearer of learning processes which feature an enhanced potential for innovation. This covers all sorts of considerations, including the ability to engender product innovation, to make qualitative improvements to products and processes and to formulate practical methods for overcoming those elements which constrain the principal order-giver's employment relationship. Yet the new significance of the search for economies of scope also makes it possible to transcend simple externalization processes. This can be done by encouraging the appearance of new tasks and professions characterizing companies' tertiary activities, the corporate service sector having undergone significant expansion during the last 20 years or so. Figure 8.2 tries to reproduce the various aspects of this modern, inter-firm division of labour.

This environment has encouraged a rather peculiar management of innovation activities, with small-firm start-ups being created to deal with given innovation projects. Such firms assume project launch risks by relying on new systems of venture capital funding, and by opening up their capital in the long run (assuming they are successful) to other investors using either financial, market-based funding or investments by large companies already active in the field. Hence the current interest in various forms of venture capital, which in most developed economies bears witness to the way in which countries have been able to adjust to new methods of innovation risk management, even though the proportion of total investment funded through venture capital has been very low, a mere 0.2 per cent of all investments in Europe in 1998. However, this does signify the existence of a logic wherein small firms in most European countries in both manufacturing and service sectors (those employing fewer than 50 workers) have product or process innovation rates of between 40 and 60 per cent.[29] Depending upon the particular country, such innovation-oriented, small firms have experienced varying trends. (Note that these should not be confused with small innovative firms, a standard categorization that

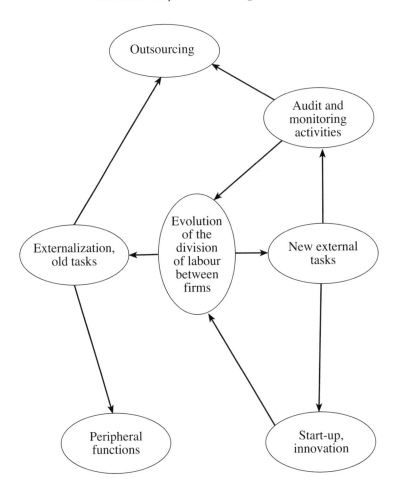

Figure 8.2   Division of work between firms

stresses the innovation capacities of 'traditional' small units.) Some of these
have succeeded in maintaining control of their paths of development, Microsoft
being a notorious example. Other innovative firms have, in the medium run,
been reintegrated into 'traditional' large companies. It is not possible to decide
which is preferable without first taking an overall view of the process.[30]

Contemporary transformations imply that a new intensive demand has
affected the way in which innovation processes are shaped. This trend is part
of a logic in which levels of competitiveness are raised on all product and
service markets, leading to greater attention to 'market demand'. However, the
usefulness of this trend stems precisely from the configuration(s) into which it

translates in terms of new arrangements and organizations, rather than just the greater attention companies pay to certain factors.

All of these elements in the inter-firm division of labour (and in the markets' functioning) have ended up modifying sources of information, along with systems used for mobilizing the types of knowledge that make up these innovation processes. This has had a profound effect on the economics of research and development. Here it is interesting to note a variation in the aforementioned adjustment of innovation processes between countries. Yet, depending upon the circumstances, there are characteristics that are relatively similar in each of the countries too. The European Community's 1996 survey of companies revealed relatively similar structures in terms of the sources of innovation-related information which firms were declaring. This similarity is a rough one at best. However, an analysis of the levels of magnitude in the various countries reveals barely any 'major structural' differences. We can view this similarity as one indicator of the universality of this current institutional transformation. Of course, this does not preclude a survival of national specificities, such as those found in information processes. Nor does it preclude the efficient utilization of information sources.

3 HOW TO EXPLAIN DIVERGENCES IN PERFORMANCE DURING THE 1990S

Before analysing the SSIPs that were identified during the 1990s, we should first establish whether the most frequent hypotheses concerning contemporary economic transformations explain differences in the recent performances of developed economies. The 1990s were characterized by large variations in economic performance: strong growth in the United States, for example, but extended recession in Japan, and recession followed by recovery in Europe. One simple explanation for these variations can be summarized as follows: the nature of technical change has been modified and, as neo-Schumpeterian economists have foreseen,[31] a new technological revolution is, in effect, driving a new phase of growth. One of the technological features of this new economy, and ostensibly a driver of productivity gains, is the new information and communication technologies (ICT). These sectors play a double role. On the one hand, they provide an arena for the highest level of technical progress, with productivity gains that are significantly above those in other sectors; they also feature a very high rate of product innovation. On the other hand, thanks to their diffusion throughout whole economies, they enable other sectors to improve their productivity and to modify what they offer in ways that stimulate innovation. Consequently, information technologies contribute both to their production and to their diffusion.

As a result, we can expect that those countries which have experienced a rapid diffusion of ICT, or which have been involved in a significant production of it, will be ahead of other countries, at least during the ascending phase of a long-term cycle. It is easier to understand this ascending phase if institutional conditions are of the sort which facilitate innovative actions – in particular, conditions relating to the flexibility of the labour market, and above all to the dynamism of money markets. Amongst these would be the availability of venture capital, the incentivization of corporate executives through the attribution of stock options and the existence of liquid financial markets. Market-based finance can be expressed by a single indicator, namely the price index of listed securities. Given such things, the dynamism of stock markets can be crystallized in terms of changes in this particular index.

Another argument is closer to traditional macroeconomics and stresses the fact that developed countries did not experience the same macroeconomic conditions during the course of the 1990s. This was because of the diversity of macroeconomic policies that were pursued ('monetary policies' in particular). The European recession of the early part of the decade was not in fact unrelated to the restrictive monetary policies carried out in light of the approaching economic and monetary union.

Is it possible to explain international variations in macroeconomic performance on the basis of the aforementioned elements? Below we test two types of equations. One explains GDP growth rates in volume terms. The other looks at standardized unemployment rates. The sample comprises the performances of ten OECD countries during the period 1991–2000. These are Canada, Denmark, Finland, France, Germany, Italy, Japan, the Netherlands, Great Britain and the United States. As previously mentioned, the explanatory variables will be ICT, the stock market and monetary policy. ICT encompasses two separate variables: the proportion of total GDP accounted for by the *ICT-producing* sectors, and the same figures for *ICT-using* sectors. Data on ICT-producing and ICT-using sectors is drawn from the ICT database of the Growth and Development Centre at the University of Groningen in the Netherlands. We have no problems in interpreting the proportion accounted for by the ICT-producing sectors as this relates to the comparative importance of activities that are directly related to ICT. The ICT-using sectors' proportion of total GDP replaces a variable that relates to the diffusion of such technologies. This is because of the well-known fact that diffusion variables for capital goods are hard to obtain for complete economies over a period of several years, and because they are not particularly reliable in any case. However, the proportion of total GDP that is accounted for by the main ICT-using sectors does not tell us anything a priori about the actual diffusion of these capital goods. The other explanatory variables are the real interest rate (which measures the restrictive nature of monetary policy) and the stock index growth rate for a particular country.

Our findings are given in the Appendix. Growth rate regressions are presented first of all. The initial model, with its fixed effects, only comes up with one single variable that is significantly associated with growth rates. This is the proportion that is accounted for by the ICT-producing sectors. The utilization of these technologies does not seem to have had any significant influence; in fact, the estimated coefficient is negative. Moreover, neither monetary policy nor stock market developments seem to have any apparent influence on growth. Note that the fixed effects are significant, indicating noticeable differences between the growth trends of various countries. This would tend to vindicate the idea that each is following a separate growth model. A random effect model presents parameters that are more interesting to interpret. The two variables that represent the importance of ICT (both production and utilization) have an obvious positive effect on growth. Note also the significantly positive effect of stock market developments, and the significantly negative impact of restrictive monetary policies. This would seem to be an ideal model for summarizing the recipe for strong growth during the 1990s: namely, technology (ICT), deregulated financial markets and an accommodative monetary policy. Unfortunately, different tests (such as those by Breusch-Pagan and Hausman) reveal a specification problem that forces us to return to a fixed-effect model whose only clear conclusion is that the countries studied were indeed following different growth models, something that the (extremely mediocre) results of the random coefficient model confirm.[32] The findings also indicate that ICT production is probably a helpful phenomenon. In general, the introduction of additional variables does not enable a satisfactory level of specification. Findings are not only unsatisfactory; they are positively fragile.

Findings from the unemployment rate test are slightly more explicit. The random effects model is satisfactory in specification-testing terms. A strong positive effect on growth rates can be observed. That is to say, once an adjustment has been made for other effects, rapid growth leads to high unemployment. The counter-intuitive possibility that growth may have a negative impact on employment finds some substantiation in theoretical literature.[33] Growth is based on innovation that possesses both creative and destructive elements. Innovation creates new jobs but destroys others, and a priori the net balance between the two is uncertain. Test findings would seem to indicate that the destructive aspect is the more significant of the two, in line with the process of *schöpferische Zerstörung* that was so characteristic of the 1990s. By itself, ICT would appear to have had a positive effect on employment. The utilization, and above all the production, of information technologies helped lower unemployment. Stock market developments did not have any significant effect and this variable is omitted from the findings presented. Monetary policy had the anticipated effect, with a 1 per cent rise in the real interest rate leading to an increase of 0.2 per cent in unemployment. The mediocre findings of the random coefficient model are only shown for information purposes. They indicate that countries are probably pursuing different models which are difficult to identify owing to the shortness of the period under study.

As the unemployment equation is more robust than the growth equation, we can pursue these estimations by integrating other variables which might account for the competitiveness of economies. The Lehman Brothers study briefly mentioned above offers a set of competitiveness indicators in the form of marks awarded to each country in areas such as education and training, technology, employment policies and the like. These variables are combined into three groups: those that concern the potential for growth, those that relate to the labour market, and those that affect prices. Technology, and the potential for growth, have already been dealt with in our estimations through the integration of ICT production and ICT utilization variables. It is therefore the two other areas that interest us. We choose one variable in each area: employment protection and competition. Each of these variables is a composite that is determined by 15 to 20 indicators.[34] Inasmuch as these are marks, the highest scores that each variable can receive correspond to the situation that, from Lehman Brothers' point of view, is the most desirable. Job protection is a bad thing (because flexibility needs to be increased) and therefore a high score for this variable corresponds to a low level of job protection. Competition is a good thing (margins can be lowered, leading to innovation), hence a high score for this variable corresponds to a high level of competition on the markets for goods and services. These variables are not available as a time-series; a single score is provided for each country.

Integrating these variables into the random effects model improves the regression. The two variables make a significant contribution to the model. As the traditional viewpoint would have it, job protection, such as it is understood in the variable devised by Lehman Brothers, contributes to an increase in unemployment. According to the estimated scores, shifting from the level of protection that is characteristic of the Eurozone to a lower level of job protection would engender, everything else being equal, a reduction of 9.75 per cent in the unemployment rate! The effect of competition is less straightforward. Greater competition increases unemployment, an effect that can be justified theoretically[35] given that greater competition renders firms fragile and forces them to make greater downward adjustments in staffing levels whenever, for example, an adverse demand shock occurs. In certain labour-market imperfection configurations (relating for example to efficiency wages), job insecurity for employees can lead to higher real salaries, which can ultimately harm employment. This would seem to be the configuration that applies to the countries in our sample. If we were to continue to use the estimations, shifting from the levels of competition characteristic of the Eurozone to ones that are prevalent in the

United States, an increase of 8.6 per cent in the unemployment rate would result.

If institutional complementarities do indeed exist, this means that it would be difficult to adopt the institutional characteristics of the United States' labour market while maintaining the product and service market competition levels of the Eurozone. The good functioning of the labour market in the United States is based on a certain type of competition in the market for goods. Returning to an argument discussed above, it is not possible to adopt only one part of a given model's institutional structure, particularly if this is the essential part. Shifting to an American model (with respect to levels of job protection and of competition, for example) would therefore only lead to a lowering of 1.15 per cent in the unemployment rate. This is not to be sneered at, but it does not necessarily represent an increase in welfare for those economic agents worried about the level of risk that would result from increased job insecurity.

The regressions presented here do not purport to account for everything. The findings are fragile, as indicated by the specification tests. They point to the models' heterogeneity, which is difficult to explain given the shortness of the time period being studied. On the other hand, the findings do seem to provide one clear indication, namely the difficulty of saying whether the key to macroeconomic success resides in pursuing an American model in the shape of 'the new economy' (deregulation and an accommodative monetary policy), or that the best model corresponds to whichever economy has the highest growth rate at any given moment in time.

4   THE IMPACT OF INTERNATIONALIZATION ON SSIP DYNAMICS

Did the main SSIP types identified in Amable *et al.* (1997) change during the course of the 1990s? More to the point, were there any modifications in the way in which the countries were grouped into four configurations or ideal types? Given the extent of the changes that took place in the general environment, one might expect internationalization to have altered the findings from previous analyses, especially in light of the apparent move towards the sort of dynamics underlying the US-driven, market-based SSIP. We have carried out new empirical analyses to study these questions, trying to ascertain whether recent changes in SSIPs have caused developed countries to remain part of the four main model categories mentioned above, or whether shifts have taken place towards the market-based SSIP.

Although these new empirical analyses are comparable to those outlined in Amable *et al.* (1997), they do diverge on certain points. They involve recent data, the latest covering the latter half of the 1990s, the oldest the year 1995.

They also cover more countries, 21 instead of 12. These are the United States, Japan, Great Britain, Canada, Australia, Italy, Spain, Portugal, Greece, France, Belgium, Denmark, Norway, Sweden, Finland, Germany, Austria, Switzerland, the Netherlands, Ireland and Korea. We have retained the earlier study's system of breaking the SSIPs down into various subsystems.

We try at first to identify country groupings by considering empirical data relating to scientific considerations, technological fields, economic structures, educational systems and labour markets. As such, this is an extended innovation system conception. However, we also start by excluding variables pertaining to fields that are directly related to internationalization, such as data on foreign trade or direct investment. We also ignore data that are related to the financial domain. Such data cover subsystems that might modify the SSIPs and require separate examination.

Findings from our initial analyses are comparable to those obtained using data from the 1980s. We first consider the general typology, doing so by integrating all of the variables. We then take a closer look at the way in which the groupings mesh with the various subsystems. To the four SSIPs found in Amable *et al.* (1997) we add countries that are similar to the initial typology. The picture now looks as follows:

- a group comprising those countries that best embody the market-based SSIP. These are former members of this SSIP (the United States, Great Britain, Canada, Australia) plus Norway;
- a group comprising those countries that embody the social–democratic SSIP. The list includes the former countries from this SSIP (Finland, Sweden, Denmark) without Norway;
- the meso-corporatist SSIP, with Korea now joining Japan;
- the 'European integration' or 'public' SSIP, made up of the countries that already belonged to this group (France, Germany, the Netherlands) minus Italy, but now including Belgium and Ireland;
- an 'alpine' variant of the preceding SSIP, comprising Austria and Switzerland;
- a 'Mediterranean' variant of the European SSIP, comprising Spain, Italy, Greece and Portugal.

Initial findings for the aforementioned variables show that some of the groupings that had been identified in the earlier study have survived. Certain groups have had to be reshuffled, with Norway drawing closer to the USA–UK bloc. But the most noteworthy result involves the differentiation of the European SSIP into three variants.

The first issue that needs addressing involves the SSIPs' putative convergence towards a market-based model. Except in the case of Norway, neither the grouping of countries, nor the economic variables that distinguish SSIPs from one another, indicate any sign of a generalized convergence towards a market-based SSIP. Globally, each SSIP maintains its own distinctive features. However, subsystem analysis shows that the SSIPs have changed and that a deeper infiltration of certain market-based mechanisms has affected most economies. This advance of market-based mechanisms is localized in a finite number of subsystems[36] and takes specific form in the progressive transformation of SSIPs (such as they are currently shaped) rather than by any radical transformation. This was one of the conclusions in Amable *et al.* (1997), and it is borne out again in this reanalysis of recent changes in SSIPs.

We should also mention traits that are common to all of the SSIPs: specifically, increased spending on R&D, on research activities in general and on economic activity in biology or IT-related sectors. This general trend in SSIPs, although varying for each of the countries concerned, reflects the advent of 'the new economy'.

European SSIP heterogeneity, as already stated in Amable *et al.* (1997), is noteworthy for its breakdown into three variants. The first is a core group at the heart of which are France and Germany. The two other variants differ from the central group in terms of their average income levels, which are higher for the 'Continental' variant and lower for the 'Mediterranean' one. This latter group is also characterized by economies possessing a lower degree of technological intensity, but even this differentiation into three subgroups does not generate particularly homogeneous groupings.

Table 8.1. below summarizes these analyses and allows comparisons between those areas where countries belonging to one and the same SSIP act more or less similarly. It also makes it possible to compare the various SSIPs with each other. The table can be read as follows: each line represents a subsystem or group of subsystems. The typologies that result from the data analysis translate into each country receiving a number that represents the group to which it belongs with respect to a particular set of data. The first row of the table represents all of the subsystems, ranging from scientific specialization to education. The typology that comes out of this analysis leads to the six aforementioned country groupings. The second row indicates the analytical findings with respect to scientific specialization. The result of this analysis is a typology comprising five country groups. The first group includes Australia and Great Britain, the second the United States, Canada, Norway and Greece.[37] This enables us to compare the finding of this subsystem analysis with the general analysis, and to identify those subsystems where countries belonging to a given SSIP are most similar to each other.

What we discover is that the market-based SSIP mainly groups countries which are similar in terms of their institutional variables: for example, labour markets, employment protection, employment structures and educational systems. The United States tends to differ from Great Britain with respect to strictly technological or scientific variables. In simple terms, the 'new economy' (in the technological sense of the expression at least) is not the only explanatory factor for the market-based SSIP.

Special attention should be paid to the factors that led Norway to join this SSIP. The country's scientific specialization is similar to Canada's and to the USA's. Its number of publications is similar to the latter country's. On the other hand, in terms of its technological innovation (as measured by patents) and industrial specialization, it is closer to Australia or Canada (two countries that are highly endowed in natural resources) than to the United States or Great Britain. Similarities can also be found on an institutional plane. The Norwegian labour market seems to share some of the 'flexibility' of the Anglo-American bloc, yet at the same time maintains features that are characteristic of the social-democratic model, particularly with regard to matters relating to employment protection.

Some interesting information can also be drawn by analysing the results for the different variants of the 'European' (or 'Public', for its continental variant at least) SSIP. The general impression from Table 8.1 is one of diversity. The reshuffled 'Public' SSIP (France, Germany, Belgium, Ireland, the Netherlands) is more or less homogeneous in terms of (1) the way in which states intervene in labour markets (except for the Netherlands); (2) employment protection (with Ireland continuing to be closer to the market-based SSIP); (3) relationships between employees and employers (except for France, which is closer to the Mediterranean variant); and (4) educational systems (Ireland again being the exception). The other areas generally feature an opposition between the country groupings that belong to this SSIP. France and Germany, for example, are close to one another in terms of their scientific specialization, but not so with regard to their technological or industrial specializations.

The alpine variant of the European SSIP collates countries that resemble one another with respect to a single subsystem, namely technological specialization. In actual fact, although data analysis situates both countries within a single group, it does not really do justice to the deeper similarities between them. In its 'Mediterranean' variant, this SSIP combines countries which possess a number of shared characteristics in fields such as the labour market and, to a certain degree, scientific specialization. However, it is difficult to distinguish any significantly shared features, with the exception of the relatively lower level of technological intensity of their production systems.

To analyse the extent to which 'internationalization' affects the stability of these SSIPs, each variable was processed separately. Whereas preceding analyses focused on the subsystems that lay at the very heart of the institutional organization of nation states, recently there has been a move towards

Table 8.1   A Comparison of Countries in Terms of SSIPs

	AUS	CAN	USA	GBR	NOR	SWE	FIN	DNK	JPN
General analysis	1	1	1	1	1	2	2	2	3
Scientific specialization	1	2	2	1	2	3	3	3	5
Number of scientific publications/GDP	1	1	5	3	5	2	1	1	4
Invented patents (specialization)	1	4	5	4	1	2	2	1	5
Controlled patents (specialization)	1*	5	4	1	5*	6	6	3	4
Industrial structure	1	1	5	5	1	2	1	2	4
Structure of GDP	1	4	4	4	6	5	6	4*	3
Labour market, active policies	1	1	2	1	1	5	4	5	2
Employment protection	1	1	1	1	4	4	4	2	3
Relation between employers & employees	1	5	5	5	1	3	3	3	5
Employment structure	1	1	1	1	1	2	5	1	3
Education	1	2	2	6	2	3	5	5	1

Note: *illustrative countries

subsystems which are more open to international influences. These influences do not only involve technology transfers that are part of the trade in goods and services (including external effects that are related to the technology in question); they also refer to the mechanisms of 'financial globalization'. This has had a big impact on national financial systems, leading in certain situations to major transformations which, a priori, have an effect on the innovation dynamics of each SSIP.

The results of these analyses are presented in Tables 8.2 and 8.3. They are presented in similar form to Table 8.1. For each table there is a general analysis covering all of the relevant subsystems, and a typology that is summarized in the first row. Table 8.2 combines findings from the different analyses of the variables that stand for trade in goods and services. Table 8.3 presents analyses of the financial systems.

The general analysis of 'internationalization' produces a country classification that divides into five groups:

- a first group that matches the market-based SSIP,
- a Mediterranean variant of the European SSIP,
- a European or Public SSIP subgroup, plus Denmark,
- Sweden and Finland, twinned together,
- Austria, Japan, Germany, Ireland, Switzerland and the Netherlands.

The typology that is drawn from the scientific, technical and industrial

KOR	GER	FRA	BEL	IRL	NLD	AUT	CZK	SPN	POR	ITA	GRE
3	4	4	4	4	4	5	5	6	6	6	6
5	5	5	3	3	3	3	5	4	4	5	2
5*	4	4	5	5	1	5	3	4	5*	5	5*
5*	3	4	5	2	2	3	3	3	3*	3	1*
4*	1	4	1	4*	4	5*	1	2	1*	2	1*
4*	4	5	5	–	4	3	–	3*	3*	3	1*
3*	2	1	1	–	2*	2	–	2*	1*	2	1*
2*	4	4	4	4	5	1	2	4	–	3	2*
2*	4	4	4*	1	4	3	2	3*	3*	3*	3*
4*	2	4	2	2	2	1	2	4	4*	4	4*
3*	3	5	5	3	1	3	1	4	4*	5	4*
1*	6	6	6	1	6	5	3	4	1*	5	4*

subsystems featured above is only partially reproduced in other analyses. Even so, certain country groupings crop up again and again and this makes it easier to interpret these SSIPs. For example, the market-based SSIP seems to be remarkably solid. Most of the countries which resemble this SSIP share certain traits in areas such as direct investment, outward-looking specializations and financial systems. These countries are similar to the overseas investment specialization model with regard to telecommunications, financial intermediation and primary goods. They import machines and metallic goods, and at least some of them specialize in aeronautics. They also possess a number of shared characteristics with respect to their highly profitable banking sectors (which play a limited role in reducing savings) and in terms of the role that institutional investors play in financing their economies and in reallocating savings.[38] Crossing variables in this way produces a representation of some of the dynamics underlying the market-based SSIP, including the specific dynamism of internationalization, a trend that relies on an extension of market-based regulations (free movement of capital, financial deregulation, the dynamism of service activities) and which seems to coincide with a certain reduction in (localized) national industrial competitiveness.

Note that the 'Mediterranean' variant of the European SSIP is also in tune with this move towards internationalization. However, given the available statistics, this result should not be accorded the same significance as the findings that relate to the market-based SSIP. We can focus on the fact that southern European SSIP countries are similar in terms of trade in services, if only

Table 8.2   A Comparison of Goods and Service Sectors in Terms of SSIPs

	USA	GBR	CAN	AUS	NOR	ITA	SPA	POR	GRE
General analysis of internationalization	1	1	1	1	1	2	2	2	2
FDI in	1	1	2	–	1	3	–	–	–
FDI out	1	1	1	–	1	1	–	–	–
Exports (specialization)	1	1	2	3	3	4	4	4	3
Imports (specialization)	1	1	1	1	4	3	2	2	3
Trade in services, Debit	2	5	1	1	3	3	1	1	1
Trade in services, Credit	5	4	3	1	2	1	1	1	1
Trade balance (specialization)	3	3	2	3	3	2	2	2	2
Contribution to trade balance	5	5	2	1	2	3	2	3	3

FDI = Foreign Direct Investment.

because of the special role that tourism plays. However, these countries also possess shared characteristics relating to their financial systems which are quite different from the market-based finance model.

That said, grouping countries by internationalization variables makes it possible to demonstrate the tensions characterizing SSIPs. These cross-SSIP groupings add a nuance to our previous conclusion, which was that the analyses presented in Table 8.1 demonstrate relative stability. The main SSIP to be affected by such considerations is the 'European' or 'Public' one, which is already very heterogeneous. The countries included in this SSIP are again combined into three different subgroupings which mesh only partially with the previously observed combinations. Most specifically, France and Germany are separated this time. A number of mechanisms help explain the 'instability' of this European SSIP. (The role played by the international trade in goods is after all relatively limited.) The differences which have been observed between the European countries are no greater than those indicated in the analyses presented in Table 8.1. Here the differences between France and Germany are not enough in and of themselves to explain the split within the Public SSIP. Even more significant are the differences which relate to trade in services. These separate France from Germany, with the former being closer to Italy, and the latter closer to countries where the manufacturing sector plays a crucial role, namely Japan and Sweden.

FRA	BEL	DNK	SWE	FIN	AUT	GER	CZK	NLD	IRL	JPN
3	3	3	4	4	5	5	5	5	5	5
3	–	–	2	2	5	4	–	5	–	2
1	–	–	2	2	3	3	–	3	–	3
1	1	1	2	2	4	1	1	1	1	5
2	3	3	–	5	4	2	3	3	5	6
3	1	–	6	6	4	6	2	6	6	6
1	4	–	3	3	4	3	4	5	3	6
3	–	3	1	1	1	4	–	3	–	4
5	4	4	4	2	4	4	4	5	4	6

Changes in the financial system have also revealed varying levels of stability among SSIPs. The market-based SSIP is remarkably coherent in terms of the ways in which national financial systems are configured, with banks playing a lesser role in corporate governance, and institutional investors (particularly pension funds) playing a greater one. There is nothing surprising about this description of the market-based SSIP. Even more significant is the absence of any real convergence of the European SSIP towards a clearly defined model. The heterogeneity of the countries which make up this latter SSIP was further emphasized during the 1990s in terms of their respective financial systems. Certain countries suffered from significant banking crises or, at the very least, from lower levels of profitability. France and Belgium are examples. Weakness on the part of the banking sector kept these countries from playing the pivotal role which financial system economic theory[39] attributes to them in terms of control over investments, industrial restructuring operations and the like.

The only real 'bank-based' financial systems are to be found in Germany and Japan,[40] those countries that seem least changed by financial deregulation.[41] This is particularly true of Germany, whose relative stability should be compared with the transformations that have hit the French financial system with respect to sources of funding and corporate control.[42]

The differences between the various financial systems become particularly

Table 8.3   A comparison of financial services in terms of SSIPs

	USA	UK	CAN	AUS	NOR	ITA	SPA	POR	GRE
General analysis	1	1	1	1	1	2	2	2	2
Banks	1	3	1	1	1	2	2	2	1
Taxes	2	5	1	1	5	3	3	5	4
Venture capital	–	2	–	–	–	3	3	3	3
Institutional investors	1	1	1	1	4	5	3	3	5

significant when we focus on venture capital. This is a special way of funding investment projects which is different both from bank funding and from market-based finance. It is similar to bank funding with respect to the specific way in which project developments are monitored, and because of the role undertaken by financial intermediaries. On the other hand it is complementary to market-based finance insofar as liquid, and highly advanced, financial markets enable projects using venture capital to place their securities with the general public. We can therefore say that the development of a particular form of venture capital funding is compatible with both bank-based and market-based financial systems.

In actual fact, analysis of the development and structure of venture capital in Europe (Amable *et al.* 1999) shows that it is over simplistic to infer that venture capital is associated with market-based financial systems alone. We should not imagine that, in order to support such a form of financing, an economy's funding systems need to be converted to Anglo-American norms. Venture capital can assume different forms and can involve funding projects featuring varying degrees of *technological* innovativeness. In general, venture capital can supplement current financial systems and develop in line with varied economic models, while leveraging the strengths and weaknesses of particular financial systems.

Possibly even more important is the fact that, for a significant amount of venture capital to materialize, a potential for innovation must exist first. From this standpoint, certain countries can offset the alleged weaknesses of their financial systems by exploiting strengths in the fields of research and technology. One can take the example of Germany, where financial markets remain underdeveloped with regard to the role they play in funding the economy and, above all, with regard to the control they exert over firms. Germany would, at first glance, appear to possess very few advantages in the race to develop venture capital, yet it is Europe's top country on this score, something that tends to prove that Anglo-American-style financial markets are not indispensable to the advance of venture capital. Even more important is a country's scientific and technological base, as well as the general adaptive capabilities of its financial system (whether bank-based or otherwise).

FRA	BEL	DAN	SWE	FIN	AUT	GER	SWI	NLD	IRL	JAP
3	3	3	4	4	5	5	5	5	5	5
5	5	2	2	5	3	3	3	3	3	4
4	3	5	3	3	4	4	2	4	5	2
1	1	4	2	5	3	3	–	5	1	–
5	5	5	5	2	4	4	2	2	–	2

5 WHICH INSTITUTIONAL ARRANGEMENTS FOR THE FRENCH/EUROPEAN SSIP?

The diversity of SSIPs is not only an academic issue. It also addresses problems relating to the definition of those structural policies that are most suited to a given situation. This aspect is especially fraught with consequences in European countries, and in France in particular. Should European policies be differentiated in order to account for the diversity of SSIPs that make up the European Union? Or should they be uniform in order to respect the principle of equality, and in order to encourage a modicum of structural harmonization?

As a geographic space, the EU encompasses five of six possible SSIPs. In actual fact, the European SSIP, which covers the EU's largest countries, is the least homogeneous of all. That being so, we can expect problems in defining 'non-differentiated' European policies in research and technology, as well as in other economic domains. A similar argument involving heterogeneity has been made with respect to the definition of a common monetary policy in a territorial space that comprises 11 (and one day 12) countries that differ greatly from each other in many respects. This argument could, *mutatis mutandis*, be extended to cover industrial or research policies. How can countries belonging to innovation systems that are governed by sometimes radically different principles be made to move in the same direction? One example is the opposition between Great Britain, which is in the market-based SSIP, and France, which is in the Public SSIP. In the former, the research system (along with the rest of the economy) is particularly responsive to measures that emphasize financial incentives, rapid decision making by economic agents and general 'flexibility'. The French system, by way of contrast, is characterized above all by the extent of coordination between various relevant parties (research centres, firms) and the stability of the relationships between them. What is clear is that the definition of an industrial or research-related policy which revolves around market-based incentives and the principle of self-organizing markets is a better match for countries belonging to the market-based SSIP than for members of the Public SSIP – in other words, for Great Britain, not France.

The European SSIP's heterogeneity poses an additional problem. The countries that comprise this model constitute some of the EEC's founding nations, notably France and Germany. These two countries are ones which provide much of the impetus for European construction in many areas. It would consequently be mutually beneficial if they were to converge ultimately towards similar policies with regard to technology and growth. Their shared proximity to one and the same SSIP is a positive factor assisting this. On the other hand the SSIP to which they belong is highly varied. Its lack of homogeneity or 'coherence' (the countries in it tending to feature as 'pairs' on many measurements) raises fears that the internationalization of the French and German economies will result in divergences, rather than commonalities. It is too simplistic to interpret the European SSIP as hostile to the principles of competitiveness and in favour of public initiatives in science and innovation. But the development of a venture capital sector in these two countries provides an illustration of differentiated adaptations. In general, changes in forms of competition are compelling all economies to develop funding modes that assume a greater proportion of innovation-related risks. The responses depend directly upon the characteristics of the SSIPs to which countries belong. The rise of such types of funding in Great Britain is no surprise. More striking for our study is the originality and success of the German approach which has been progressing with great speed and is largely based on its federal structure and its traditional mechanisms of public governance.

Current changes in SSIPs are discernible in the fields of finance and technology. The first technological dimension can be observed by reference to some of the specific changes being experienced by those countries characterized by a high level of technological intensity, for example Finland or Sweden (in the 'social–democratic' SSIP). Such countries are undergoing changes which differ from those in countries typified by a low level of technological intensity, namely those in the Mediterranean variant of the European SSIP. The two economies in the social–democratic SSIP are characterized by their production system's high level of technological intensity, by their international competitiveness, and by institutions that are very different from those found in a market-based SSIP, notwithstanding the latter model being commonly depicted as the only one capable of guiding countries into the 'new economy'. Although we should be cautious when comparing medium-sized countries such as France or Germany with small and very open economies such as Finland's or Sweden's, there is good reason to believe that the market-based SSIP path is not the only one which can promote growth based on high levels of scientific and technological intensity.

For the European SSIP to follow a high growth path, EU countries would have to increase their average technological intensity. This scientific, and above all technological, leap forward will be mainly achievable in countries possessing hi-tech activities, an extensive scientific/technical potential and a highly developed industrial sector. It is therefore important that France and Germany assume responsibility for exploring the road towards a 'new European economy'.

To follow such a trajectory, a significant increase in R&D efforts will be necessary, if only to match the relative levels of the United States, Japan or the Scandinavian countries. Given the separation of research structures between nations within the EU, we can assume that, in order to reach a given objective, they will need to run the risk of duplicating research projects, thereby incurring extra R&D expenses. Great Britain appears to be benefiting from its de facto cooperation with the American system, and this helps it to remain a member of the market-based SSIP. Although the European 'Public' SSIP does not present the same internal coherency, it appears that close cooperation adapted to the specificities of the models of the countries involved (notably those of France and Germany), will enable it to maximize benefits drawn from efforts made in the technological field.

Lastly, some predict that important financial factors such as the corporate governance issue may upset the stability of the European SSIP. As we have already seen, financial deregulation and the increased role played by financial markets have not had the same consequences everywhere. Specifically, France is the country where financial structures have undergone the greatest changes.[43] In Germany, where bank-based funding, industrial concentration and social partnerships have strengthened one another and defined an industrial model that Streeck (1991) calls 'differentiated quality production', financial deregulation has been much more limited and has not fundamentally altered the role played by banks. Nor has it raised serious doubts about the *stakeholder system* which up to now has been the mainstay of German capitalism. As such, this form of capitalism is not only based on coordination between banks and industrials, but also depends on cooperative structures between employees and firms, each group being represented by powerful collective actors. Conversely, in a country such as France which has never been characterized by stakeholder capitalism and which has therefore never had any negotiating or coordinating structures upon which such a model could be based, the deep structural changes that have affected both its financial system and its mode of corporate governance carry the potential for radical transformation of the forms which capitalism takes there.

Stakeholder capitalism not only revolves around bank-based financial systems or financial systems which encourage long-term commitments, it also requires a wide variety of other institutions to complement it. In view of the complementary relationships which exist between these institutions it should be more difficult to destabilize this model as a result of changes to any one institution. This type of complementarity is not characteristic of France, however, which has not experienced stakeholder capitalism and lacks the institutions demanded by the model, namely those which serve to reinforce negotiation and cooperation. Nor is France representative of *shareholder* capitalism, given the role played by the French state and the lesser development of the country's financial markets (until the 1990s at least). To simplify, in the French model it is the state that has been responsible for the coordination function; there are no intermediary negotiating levels such as one finds in Germany. Given the absence of public intervention, and given the framework of financial deregulation being orchestrated by the French authorities, many institutional complementarities might end up being overturned inasmuch as no stable compromise position on institutional configuration would exist between intermediary actors, unlike the situation in Germany. With changes in its financial system, France might be the only country in the European SSIP to move towards a shareholder form of capitalism. It is not at all clear, however, that such hybridization is best suited to the type of innovation that drives French competitiveness, namely coordination between public actors and firms as well as decisions made with an eye to the long term.

ACKNOWLEDGEMENTS

The drafting of this chapter was facilitated by discussions with Yann Cadiou, Ekkehard Ernst, Donatelli Gatti, Stefano Palombarini, Xavier Ragot, Bruno Théret and Jean-Philippe Touffut. The authors would like to thank the above without associating them with any deficiencies the chapter may have.

NOTES

1. On the role of institutions in economic development, see North (1990). For an analysis of the importance of institutions in innovation systems, see Amable (2000).
2. See Freeman (1995), Smith (1998).
3. See, *inter alia*, Freeman (1987).
4. See, *inter alia*, Kitschelt *et al.* (1999) and Whitley (2000) for recent contributions on this subject.
5. Soskice (1999).
6. Amable *et al.* (1997).
7. This is so whether or not this involves a new technological paradigm or a new upward phase in a long-term growth cycle.
8. There is of course a great deal of literature on globalization. For a summary of the main points, see, *inter alia*, Jacquet and Sachwald (2000).
9. See Beffa *et al.* (1999) regarding the transformations of the employment relationship.
10. See OECD (2000) and Artus (2001).
11. See Freeman and Soete (1997).
12. We could have also mentioned the disappearance of the inflation/unemployment cycle and/or trade-off, the diminished role of economic policy, and the like.
13. See Aoki (2000, 2001), Amable (2000), Amable, Ernst and Polombarini (2000), Soskice (1999), Ernst (2001), Gatti (2000), Freeman (2000) and Whitley (2000).

14. Edwards and Schanz (2001a).
15. See Arthur (1994).
16. David (1994).
17. Nicoletti *et al.* (1999).
18. On the policies' complementarity, see Coe and Snower (1997) and Orszag and Snower (1998). See Amable and Gatti (2000) concerning the incorporation of the different complementarities and for less orthodox types of recommendations.
19. Some of these studies have become renowned even outside academic circles (Albert, 1991).
20. On problems of methodology in international comparisons, see Théret (1997). Here we are following a compromise approach (ibid., pp.178–9) between increased generalization (a formalization that is based on empirical characteristics) and a diminished contextualization of universal categories (which incorporates into the indicators both contextual and universal elements). Note that Théret (1997) has also put together a country-by-country classification that is very similar to the SSIP approach, based on comparisons of levels of social protection. On this topic, also see Théret (2001).
21. The USA and the UK belong to a neoliberal market-oriented configuration, according to Soskice (1999) who contrasts them with a coordinated market-oriented economy such as Germany. This is similar to the Anglo-Saxon or American capitalism notion that had already been identified by other authors, notably by Albert (1991).
22. For more on complementarity, see Amable and Petit (1999).
23. As with all economies that are considered to be market-oriented, it may appear inaccurate to apply the term 'market-oriented' to just one SSIP. We could also speak of a 'neoliberal' model.
24. Soskice (1999)
25. See Kogut (2000) for a formulation of this type of criticism.
26. Switzerland and the United States followed the same growth trajectory between 1870 and 1990, despite clear-cut differences in their respective institutional architectures. The same could be said about France and Germany (Amable and Juillard, 1999).
27. Veltz (2000).
28. As emphasized in a study by Gibbons *et al.* (1994).
29. This is according to Eurostat data compiled by the OECD in 1999 (Table 11.4). Note in addition that France is one of the few European countries (along with Belgium, Finland and Spain) where rates are below the 40 per cent mark.
30. See Amable *et al.* (2001).
31. See Freeman and Soete (1997). We should remember that neo-Schumpeterians had been announcing the advent of an ICT-related technological revolution since the mid-1980s at least.
32. These findings are only presented for information purposes. The model is difficult to estimate given the small number of observations that were made over time.
33. See Aghion and Howitt (1998, ch. 4).
34. See Edwards and Schanz (2001b). The job protection indicator is built from indices including the notice period before dismissal, the size of the settlement, the length of the probation period, the maximum number of times fixed-term contracts can be renewed and labour union rights. The competition variable integrates elements such as sectoral concentration indices, the restrictiveness of competition-related legislation, the extent of competition from abroad and trade barriers.
35. See Amable and Gatti (2000, 2001)
36. Above all, in everything that pertains to the financial systems and, more generally, to the mobility of capital.
37. Greece is only included in this example for illustrative purposes.
38. See Paillard and Amable (2000).
39. See Allen and Gale (1999).
40. Moreover, these two countries were far from identical with respect to their financial systems.
41. A finding confirmed by more detailed analyses of financial systems in five countries (Hackethal, 2000).
42. Paillard and Amable (2000).
43. For additional proof in this respect see Goyer (2001), Hacketal (2000) or Schmidt (2001).

BIBLIOGRAPHY

Aghion, P. & P. Howitt (1998), *Growth Theory*, Cambridge, MA: MIT Press.

Albert, M. (1991), *Capitalisme contre capitalisme*, Paris: Seuil.

Allen, F. & D. Gale (1999), *Comparing Financial Systems*, Cambridge, MA: MIT Press.

Amable, B. (2000), 'Institutional Complementarity and Diversity of Social Systems of Innovation and Production', *Review of International Political Economy*, **7**(4), 645–87.

Amable, B. & D. Gatti (2000), 'The Impact of Product Market Competition on Employment and Wages', CEPREMAP-WZB, mimeo.

—— (2001), 'Product Market Competition and Employment Protection: A Case for Policy Complementarity', CEPREMAP-WZB, mimeo.

Amable, B. & M. Juillard (1999), 'The Historical Process of Convergence', unpublished manuscript.

Amable, B. & P. Petit (1999), 'Identifying the Structure of Institutions to Promote Innovation and Growth', working paper no. 9919, CEPREMAP.

Amable, B., R. Barré & R. Boyer (1997), *Les systèmes d'innovation à l'ère de la globalisation*, Paris: Economica.

Amable, B., R. Breton & X. Ragot (2001), 'Does the "New Economy" Change the Frontiers of the Large Corporation?', CEPREMAP, Paris, mimeo.

Amable, B., Y. Cadiou & P. Petit (2000), 'On the Development Paths of Innovation Systems', work package D, TSER-CDIS Project.

Amable, B., E. Ernst & S. Palombarini (2000), 'Institutional Complementarity: Labour Markets and Finance', CEPREMAP, Paris, mimeo.

Amable, B., S. Paillard & P. Petit (1999), 'Finance and Innovation: Venturing on the Risk Frontier', unpublished paper, 3–4 December.

Aoki, M. (2000), Information, *Corporate Governance, and Institutional Diversity*, Oxford: Oxford University Press.

Aoki, M. (2001), *Towards a Comparative Institutional Analysis*, Cambridge, MA: MIT Press.

Arthur, B. (1994), *Increasing Returns and Path Dependence in the Economy*, Ann Arbor: University of Michigan Press.

Artus, P. (2001), *La nouvelle économie*, Paris: La Découverte.

Beffa, J.L., R. Boyer & J.P. Touffut (1999), 'Les relations salariales en France', *Notes de la fondation Saint-Simon*, Paris.

Boyer, R. (2001), 'La diversité des institutions d'une croissance tirée par l'information ou la connaissance', *Institutions et croissance: Les chances d'un modèle économique européen*, Colloque de novembre 2000 du Centre Saint-Gobain pour la recherche en économie, Paris: Albin Michel.

Brynjolfsson, E. & B. Kahin (eds) (2000), *Understanding the Digital Economy: Data, Tools and Research*, Cambridge, MA: MIT Press.

Cadiou, Y. (2001), 'Théorie des systèmes nationaux d'innovation: une analyse comparative de la France et du Japon dans la dynamique de mondialisation', doctoral thesis, Université Paris 7.

Coe, D. & D. Snower (1997), 'Policy Complementarities: the Case for Fundamental Labour Market Reform', CEPR Discussion Paper, no.1585.

David, P. (1994), 'Why Are Institutions the Carriers of History? Notes on Path-Dependence and the Evolution of Conventions, Organizations and Institutions', *Structural Change and Economic Dynamics*, **5**, 205–20.

Edwards, J. & J. Schanz (2001a), 'Faster, Higher, Stronger. An International Comparison of Structural Policies', Structural Economics Research Papers, no. 3 Lehman Brothers.

— — (2001b), 'Lehman's Structural Database: Sources and Methods', Structural Economics Research Papers, no. 4, Lehman Brothers.

Ernst, E. (2001), 'Complémentarités institutionnelles et croissance économique à long terme', doctoral thesis, Ecole des Hautes Etudes en Sciences Sociales, Paris.

Freeman, C. (1987), *Technology, Policy, and Economic Performance: Lessons from Japan*, London and New York: Pinter Publishers.

— — (1995), 'The National System of Innovation in Historical Perspective', *Cambridge Journal of Economics*, **19**(1), 5–24.

Freeman, C. & L. Soete (1997), *The Economics of Industrial Innovation*, Cambridge, MA: MIT Press.

Freeman, R. (2000), 'Single-Peaked vs. Diversified Capitalism: the Relation Between Economic Institutions and Outcomes', NBER working paper.

Gatti, D. (2000), 'Compétences, organisations et coordination dans une économie d'innovation', doctoral thesis, Ecole des Hautes Etudes en Sciences Sociales, Paris.

Gibbons, M., C. Limoges, H. Nowotny, S. Schwartzman, P. Scott & M. Trow (eds) (1994), *The New Production of Knowledge: the Dynamics of Science and Research in Contemporary Societies*, London and Thousand Oaks, CA: Sage Publications.

Goyer, M. (2001), 'Corporate Governance and the Innovation System in France: The Development of Firms' Capabilities and Strategies, 1985–2000', *Industry and Innovation*, **8**(2), August, 135–58.

Hackethal, A. (2000), 'How Unique Are US Banks? The Role of Banks in Five Major Financial Systems', Johann Wolfgang Goethe-Universität Fachbereich Wirtschaftswissenschaften no. 60.

Jacquet, P. & F. Sachwald (2000), 'Mondialisation: la vraie rupture du XXe siècle', *Politique Etrangère*, **3–4**, 597–612.

Kitschelt, H., P. Lange, G. Marks & J.D. Stephens (1999), 'Convergence and Divergence in Advanced Capitalist Democracies', in H. Kitschelt, P. Lange, G. Marks and J.D. Stephens (eds), *Continuity and Change in Contemporary Capitalism*, Cambridge: Cambridge University Press.

Kogut, B. (2000), 'The Transatlantic Exchange of Ideas and Practices: National Institutions and Diffusion', Les notes de l'ifri, no. 26.

Nicoleeti, G., S. Scarpetta & O. Boyland (1999), 'Summary Indicators of Product Market Regulation with an Extension to Employment Protection Legislation', working paper no. 226, Economics department, OECD.

North, D. (1990), *Institutions, Institutional Change and Economic Performance*, Cambridge: Cambridge University Press.

OECD (1999), 'Tableau de bord de la science, de la technologie et de l'industrie, 1999: Mesurer les économies fondées sur le savoir', OECD, Paris.

— — (2000), 'A New Economy? The Changing Role of Innovation and Information Technology in Growth,' OECD, Paris.

Orszag, M. & D. Snower (1998), 'Anatomy of Policy Complementarities', CEPR Discussion Paper, no. 1963.

Paillard, S. & B. Amable (2000), 'Intégration européenne et systèmes financiers: y a-t-il convergence vers le modèle anglo-saxon?', CEPREMAP, Paris, mimeo.

Schmidt, R.H. (2001), 'The Future of Banking in Europe', Johann Wolfgang Goethe-Universität Fachbereich Wirtschaftswissenschaften no.72.

Smith, K. (1998), 'Innovation as a Systemic Phenomenon: Rethinking the Role of

Policy', in The Innovation Systems and European Integration (ISE) Research Project.

Soskice, D. (1999), 'Divergent Production Regimes: Coordinated and Uncoordinated Market Economies in the 1980s and 1990s', in H. Kitschelt, P. Lange, G. Marks and J.D. Stephens (eds) *Continuity and Change in Contemporary Capitalism*, Cambridge: Cambridge University Press.

Streeck, W. (1991), 'On the Institutional Conditions of Diversified Quality Productions', in E. Matzner and W. Streeck (eds), *The Socioeconomics of Production and Development*, Aldershot, UK and Brookfield, USA: Edward Elgar.

Théret, B. (1997), 'Méthodologie des comparaisons internationales, approche de l'effet sociétal et de la régulation: fondements pour une lecture structuraliste des systèmes nationaux de protection sociale', *L'Année de la régulation*, 1, 163–228.

Théret, B. (2001), 'Changes in the French Social Protection System: Path Dependencies, Timing, and International Challenges', mimeo.

Veltz, P. (2000), *Le nouveau monde industriel*, Paris: Gallimard.

Whitley, R. (2000), *Divergent Capitalisms: The Social Structuring and Change of Business Systems*, Oxford: Oxford University Press.

APPENDIX

A1   Explanation of variable: rate of real GDP growth

IT producing sectors sectors as a proportion of GDP (logs, lagged)	0.106***	0.0174***	–0.113
IT using sectors as a proportion of GDP (logs, lagged)	–0.069	0.037***	0.210
Real rate of interest	–0.000	–0.002*	0.000
Rate of growth of share index	0.014	0.019*	–0.004
Model	Fixed Effects	Random Effects	Random Coefficients
Specification test		Breusch and Pagan: 1.57 Hausman: 24.25	

Notes: Level of significance: *: 10%; **: 5%; ***: 1%.

A2 *Explanation of variable: unemployment rate*

IT producing sectors as a proportion of GDP (logs, lagged)	−3.24***	−5.29	−5.05***	−3.97***	−3.63***
IT using sectors as a proportion of GDP (logs, lagged)	−3.78*	4.19	−7.61***	−5.43***	−4.71***
Real interest rate	−0.192*	−0.079			
Competition			4.30***	3.70***	3.24***
Employment protection			−2.50***	−2.09***	−1.71***
Rate of growth of share price					
Rate of real GDP growth	23.13**	1.92	51.23***	21.67**	18.90*
Model	Random Effects	Random Coefficients	Random Effects	GLS with AR1 error term	GLS with Panel Specific AR1 error term
Specification tests	Breusch and Pagan: 109.51*** Hausman: 0.43**		Breusch and Pagan: 15.05*** Hausman: 860		

Notes: Level of significance: *: 10%; **: 5%; ***: 1%.
  GLS: Generalised Least Squares.
  AR: Aut Regressive.

9. An overview of sustainable forms of growth: the economic institutions of a European model

Jean-Philippe Touffut

Europe, Japan, the United States – and then Europe again? During the latter half of the twentieth century each of the main poles of economic development seemed at one point as if it was about to become the principal reference for economic growth. For example, the 1990s were characterized by the spectacular success of the US economy, in contrast with the sluggishness displayed by its continental European rivals. The United States' long period of expansion was supposed to go hand in hand with the emergence of a new regime of growth, one that was based (disproportionately) on the production and utilization of information technology tools. The impact of technical change raised important puzzles about the nature of economic growth, these being centred on productivity increase. In the mid-1990s, indeed, productivity in US business sectors grew at a rate close to that of the pre-1973 period. The causes of the rebound are still widely debated, although part of it is clearly due to exceptional productivity growth in the information and technology sectors.

The present text does not attempt to sort out productivity disputes. Information technologies may actually have been relatively unimportant as a source of the post-1995 productivity revival. What really matters is the transformation of economic institutions.[1] The latter play a crucial role in the types of transformations that may provide Europe with the wherewithal to benefit from information technology capital deepening. Analysing the drivers behind US expansion in the 1990s is one starting point for understanding the three possible trajectories that Europe might ultimately pursue. Whereas there is one US economy and one US polity, the EU economy is increasingly integrated yet built upon a structure of politically sovereign states. During the past decade the build-up to and adoption of the Euro, as well as strengthening trade and investment ties in Europe, have not overcome this political heterogeneity.

In the first section of this chapter, a study of US performance during seven years of uninterrupted expansion will provide a number of contrasts between America and Europe in general as well as contrasts involving nations within Europe. Specific questions will be asked concerning the controversial relationship between innovation and growth, and the conditions that have made it possible for a country to benefit from new forms of technical progress, notably the new information and communication technologies (ICT). In light of this comparison with the US economy, the question is then asked how European structures can be changed in order to sustain growth. The primary mechanisms operating at the very heart of US expansion will first be broken down. A particular focus will then be placed on the new technologies. Productivity gains may have occurred in the sectors that produce these technologies, but it would appear that their utilization has not led to any increase in the overall productivity of the other sectors that comprise the US economy. Seen as a whole, it would appear instead that this increase in productivity depends on a whole set of factors whose conjunction was the real driver during this exceptional period. Amongst these factors, the crucial ones would seem to be the organization of corporate funding, the type of research being carried out in both public and private sectors and, at a more global level, macroeconomic policy.

It is more difficult to study the situation in European countries. There is no single growth model in Europe. Far from it. Instead, we detect the main attributes of three separate configurations. The first one, which basically applies to northern European countries, corresponds to what in layman's economics is commonly called the 'knowledge economy'. It is associated with a high level of instruction and with intensive professional training. This combination involves knowledge that has been highly socialized as a result of the collective investments which have taken place. The second configuration crops up in the so-called 'deregulated' economies, systems that reserve a great deal more room for market mechanisms. These economies support a private appropriation of innovations by means of patenting mechanisms which encourage the most qualified individuals to grab innovation rents. Ireland is the best example of this configuration. The third mode of growth is an accelerated catch-up model that has been brought into being by new technological circumstances. Specifically, it is the Portuguese mode. All in all, European comparisons contradict the simplistic image of a single-faceted Europe that lags far behind the United States. In fact, certain European countries have derived even greater benefits from ICT than the United States and have created jobs at an even higher rate. This observation, in and of itself, changes the outlook for a European model. In reality, it is no longer appropriate to support European convergence towards a single model that until recently was represented by the United States. Instead, one should look to benefit from the diversity of institutions in Europe, thus promoting original trajectories towards sustainable growth.

The second section presents an analysis of the European institutions that lie at the heart of current mutations. It revolves around five basic themes. First, there are the public and private research efforts that have been taking place, and which determine the conditions in which new technologies are being created and diffused (as well as certain aspects of current corporate funding mechanisms). The second theme attempts to discern the financial system that is best for fostering the development of new companies and, at a more general level, for nurturing growth. Corporate funding structures are not the only factors to have been modified by financial internationalization. Their organization has also been changed. Thirdly, we look at the specific conception of the structuring of work in Europe. Has this system been weakened by the increase in international competition? The fourth theme focuses on the various forms of employment relationships that exist between employees and employers. Do the new forms of organization (and the atypical employment contracts that have proliferated during the late 1990s) threaten the traditional open-ended type of work contract? How can we redefine the employment relationship in such a way as to encourage both growth and an improvement in employees' living conditions? Our final theme covers changes in European systems of social protection. These have traditionally been defined on the basis of full-time, open-ended employment contracts in a society where risk involved the loss of job and income. Today, greater professional mobility and new forms of technological progress have created new and different forms of risks for employees. Is it possible to imagine a reform of the social protection system which incorporates both European specificities as well as the fundamental changes in the world of work that stem directly from technological change? The conclusion traces the outline of a European model whose constitutive principle stems from its emphasis on the diversity of European economies and on the mobilization of citizens' knowledge.

1   THE DIVERSE NATURE OF THE 1990s REGIMES OF GROWTH

American Exceptionalism

The uninterrupted expansion of the US economy starting in the early 1990s created much expectation. Talk increasingly occurred of a 'new economy' in the making. The expression was surprisingly polysemous, however, and covered a number of phenomena. Cause and effect were often confused. At least three connotations existed which need updating. The first referred to the functioning of the ICT-producing sector. This sector possesses intrinsic properties such as the nature of the production that is taking place, or the fact that its main costs stem from design and not from production. A second connotation alluded to the effect of the diffusion of new technologies on the whole of an economy. This involves, for example, the organizational changes or alterations in the rules of competition which result from the quicker circulation of information. It covers developments that effect entire economies, not merely those experienced at the sectoral level. Finally, the term 'new economy' was sometimes used to refer to changes in the nature of an economy induced by a 'dematerialization of production', with information having become the paramount resource. This final connotation was often taken to be synonymous with a 'knowledge economy'. These meanings, presented in order of increasing generality, typically reflect the views of those observers who believed that profound changes had taken place in the way modern economies functioned.

Before analysing the originality of contemporary technical changes, it would be useful to assess the notion of unprecedented US growth, a perspective which often holds that such growth stems from the stimulation and application of innovations. It is true that a recovery in investment rates is the hallmark of the recent dynamism of US companies, these firms being amongst the most competitive in the world. But their success has largely stemmed from investments in information system materials and from an increased reliance on new technologies. At the macroeconomic level, the US renewal was supposedly characterized by low inflation, very little unemployment and the disappearance of business cycles. Now an analysis of these characteristics should make it possible to distinguish between fact and fiction, and to assess the feasibility of a new era of growth in Europe. Although the chimera of novelty lessened as the US economy started to slow down, the duration of this period of growth (the longest since World War II) has been construed by many as proof that we were witnessing a new model. Which factors were crucial for US growth? Could Europe reproduce the same conditions? Should it do so? What role should be allocated to the new information and communications technologies? In the present section, US growth during the 1990s will be depicted as the result of a conjunction of factors, within which it is difficult to distinguish between that which is sufficient and that which is necessary. The following section, which involves international comparisons, specifies the preconditions for sustainable growth.

A simultaneous drop in unemployment and in inflation

US growth has been accompanied by a drop in unemployment and by low inflation. These outcomes surprised most economists. In one reading of the school of thought that currently dominates thinking, there is an ever-decreasing relationship between unemployment and inflation. The mechanism operates as follows: a drop in unemployment leads to tensions on the labour market and results in an improvement in employees' bargaining position. Less threatened by unemployment, workers make greater demands for salary increases and this leads to higher prices. This relationship between unemployment and inflation has caused certain economists to talk about a 'natural' unemployment rate, one which supposedly does not lead to an acceleration in inflation. This is called the 'NAIRU'.[2] Here it is postulated that if unemployment drops below the 'natural' rate it will trigger inflation. Yet US growth has placed this concept in doubt. The unemployment rate has, in fact, for a prolonged period dropped below all approximations of the NAIRU without triggering any rise in inflation. This finding generates concerns regarding the validity of the measurement and feeds into the current controversy regarding its usefulness. Of course, it is difficult to explain currently low inflation using traditional arguments. Two types of factors do, however, help to clarify recent price changes. Some are known effects that result from the strong dollar, such as weaker energy prices and generally lower import prices. A second group of factors refers to the internal mutations that have taken place in the US economy, such as the rapid fall in the price of computer goods.

An original macroeconomic configuration
The conjunction of a budget surplus, deficits in current and trade balance accounts, a lower savings rate and a rapid rise in stockmarket prices constitutes the second feature of US growth during the past decade. For a long time, the US situation had been characterized by 'twin' deficits: a budget deficit and a current deficit, signs of the United States' indebtedness towards the rest of the world. This situation has changed as a result of the sharp rise in government tax receipts, spurred by economic growth and, in any event, greater than anything that had been forecast. The macroeconomic impact of accelerated technological progress has probably been greater than any temporary situational factors. Indeed, we can conceive a causality that starts from the acceleration in technological progress and which explains the changes in the budget and current deficits. Technological progress creates new investment opportunities in the growth sectors. This economic dynamism leads to improvements in state finances, due to the rise in tax receipts. In addition, it leads to an increase in imports, as opposed to exports, resulting from the differential between US growth and expansion in other countries. An economy that grows more rapidly than all others tends to import more. Lastly, new investment opportunities increase demand by firms for funding and thus contribute to increased yields in US stock markets. The rise in yields has a 'knock-on' effect on household wealth, basically through the rise in people's financial holdings. Households, aware of this increase, consume more than they receive in income, leading to a drop in their savings rate. All of these causalities put together comprise a virtuous circle within the framework of the US expansion that typified the 1990s. These causalities derive from the new innovation opportunities that resulted from the acceleration of technological progress, all of which was of particular importance in the ICT sectors.

The aforementioned causal links account for the mechanisms that lie at the heart of US growth, and for the changes in the main macroeconomic aggregates (budget surplus, trade balance, household savings rates and stock market yields). Yet by themselves these mechanisms do not allow us to understand all of the phenomena that have marked US growth, the main feature of which has been the exceptional rise in total labour productivity. The period 1995–2000 was characterized by annual rises in private sector, non-farm labour productivity that were comparable to what they had been during the years 1950–72, the postwar boom years. In fact, the rates at the end of the 1990s were almost twice as high as between 1972 and 1995. It is this remarkable change in the productivity of labour that needs explaining, and specifically the role that ICT played in it.

The macroeconomic impact of innovation

To understand the influence of accelerated technological progress on growth, a precise analysis should be undertaken of the various sectors of activity in the US economy. The present section details the main empirical approaches that have led to our overriding finding, whose implications are measured and analysed in the conclusion to the present chapter. The ICT-producing sector is the one that has enjoyed exceptional productivity gains. In other sectors which also benefit from the existence of ICT, no overall gains in productivity have been observed. In other words, no increase can be seen in the US economy's overall productivity as a result of the use of computers, at least not at a macroeconomic level.

Although labour productivity has risen strongly in the United States, this is not a good indicator of technological progress. In fact, this increase may stem from a significant accumulation of capital that has taken place independently of technological change. The increase in each worker's output may, for example, arise from an increased number of machines, a situation that would not entail any technological progress. To explore this factor, the quality and quantity of machines must be determined. Similarly, the number of machines that are being used must also be established so that assessments of worker productivity incorporate a calculation of the machines' basic qualities. Simply measuring technological progress at a macroeconomic level implies simultaneously considering changes in the number of hours worked, the accumulation of capital and the use of other resources such as energy or imports. Productivity that is measured in this way is called total factor productivity (TFP). If TFP rises, this means that more is being produced using fewer inputs, specifically capital and labour. This constitutes a good macroeconomic measurement of technological progress.

This definition of total productivity allows us to fine-tune our analysis of US technological progress. The sector producing the new ICT has been experiencing an unprecedented acceleration in technological progress, leading to increases in its productivity of labour as well as in its total factor productivity. As a result of the severe competition found here, productivity gains have led to lower prices.[3] The other sectors of the economy, the ones that do not produce these technologies but which use them, have been benefiting from ICT's lower prices. Companies in these other sectors are then encouraged to replace their old machines with goods that assimilate ICT. The increased productivity in the ICT sector thus leads to an accumulation of capital in other sectors, essentially in the form of information goods and other communications materials. This increase in capital stock may explain the increased productivity of labour. But what about total factor productivity? Is a more intensive utilization of ICT enough to bring about an increase in TFP?

This question can be answered empirically. In addition, data analysis allows for a correction of cyclical phenomena incorporating improvements in the quality of the workforce. For example, we can observe that, during the period 1995–2000, TFP did not increase in those sectors that used, but did not produce, ICT. This econometric observation allows us to conclude that the main consequence of these continuing technological upheavals is the lower price of computer goods. We can also deduce that, for the moment at least, productivity gains for such factors will be restricted to the ICT-producing sector alone. This means that we have to reinterpret the impact made by these new technologies. In opposition to those macroeconomists for whom the total factor productivity growth rate indicates a new growth regime, it is possible to see ICT's main contribution as residing in the way in which it matches production to market needs. The factors affecting such matching have to do with the greater responsiveness of users, increased product differentiation and improved provision in the service sector. Consumer satisfaction can therefore rise without any increase in productivity, and it is the optimization of the profit rate that counts most. Changes in profit margin rates in the United States, which had been mostly stable throughout the 1990s, would seem to confirm this hypothesis. Many analysts, whether of a theoretical or an empirical inclination, have concluded that profit optimization does not presuppose a maximized increase in productivity. In such conditions, ICT, an instrument of rationalization in large private organizations (and even more so in large public ones), does not automatically lead to major productivity gains outside the sector where such information goods are actually produced.

Comparisons of the ICT-producing sector in the United States with the same sector in other countries shows that the former has indeed been able to derive a greater advantage from these new forms of technological progress. Until now, analysis has concentrated on the computer materials production sector. But the same observation holds, and is even reinforced, if we look at the production of goods in software, telecommunications, pharmacy and biotechnology. It remains the case that the United States' technological renewal was hardly to be expected. Just a short while ago, Japan had seemed the most 'advanced' of all countries, serving as a model in innovation and work organization matters.

However, Japanese performance (particularly in the electronics sector) did not lead to an equivalent development in the ICT sector. Historians of innovation processes have found it difficult to anticipate forms of technological progress. For example, the places where innovation takes place are not necessarily the same ones where commercial development and diffusion occur. In addition, and depending on the nature of the particular type of technological progress being assessed, the region which is recognized as being the most advanced can shift from one continent to another. The success of the Nordic countries in using ICT (especially Finland and Sweden) shows that new technologies can be driven by a whole range of institutional frameworks. Consequently, rather than simply copying the attributes of whatever country seems furthest ahead at any given moment in time, an analysis of the sources of technological success should try to define the changes that will allow each country to exploit existing technologies and anticipate new forms of innovation.

The sources of growth

Why was the United States able to derive more benefits during the past decade from informational innovations than Japan? The latter had the most innovative electronics sector, yet played a small role in the Internet's boom. The answer is that American successes were predicated on many different factors that facilitated the development of ICT. Some of these were traditional ones, but others were related to more recent and more specific changes in the US economy. Amongst the traditional sources of growth were the country's natural resources and the characteristics of its demand structure: the size of its market(s), the absence of borders and the linguistic and legislative homogeneity that make each product accessible to a large number of potential buyers.

A very different perspective holds that industrial development can be geared towards export markets and turn international trade into a substitute for the national market. For example, the German chemicals industry, which required major investments, was able to expand because of its export drives. In any event, experience shows that a certain number of key factors must all be present if growth is to occur, amongst them those relating to educational systems, financial structures and public policies.

The role of education and research   An initial component of US success is the proximity of the educational sector to the business world, particularly the link between research in universities and fundamental, or applied, research in industry. Whether private or state-funded, the reputation of US research is so great that it attracts many students from around the world. The proximity of industrial research to university research shortens the time that is required for a discovery to be exploited commercially. Just as short is the geographical distance that separates centres of fundamental research from centres of applied research and development. The cooperation on the West Coast between Stanford University and Silicon Valley is the equivalent of the suburbs of Boston close to Harvard University and to MIT where a concentration of software, information and biotechnology companies can be found.

The impact of industrial policies   Far from being a country where laissez-faire attitudes govern public policies, the United States is more than anywhere else a place where government policy is intimately tied to technological success. The antitrust laws have allowed for the development of a software sector that is independent of the counter design sector. The National Institute of Health has widely funded the biomedical research that has found its way into pharmaceuticals and contributed greatly to the many successes that have been achieved in the postwar era. The US Department of Defense's policy of supporting research actively promoted in the past advances in semiconductors, computers, software and the Internet. California, in fact, seemed to be a leading centre for defence-funded research. ICT development was therefore only partially a result of decentralizing strategies undertaken by corporations. The forms that state aid for research initiatives has assumed are, however, very different from the types of support for research that exist in Europe. In fact, such aid is allocated in US university labs on the basis of competitive application bids between researchers on projects carried out under those researchers' directions. Some monetary incentives may offer top specialists attractive financial terms and help preserve a system of meritocracy. The structure of the research itself, much less hierarchical in nature than in continental Europe, allows the most innovative initiatives to take concrete forms. In biology and instrumentation in particular, academic research could lead to start-up companies in which researchers play a major role. Although the diversity of sectoral policies precludes generalization, the United States has also been able to develop a system of aid packages on behalf of industry which cover training needs as well as relatively non-specialized research topics.

The contribution made by financial structures   Financial analysts have revisited their assessments of US market structure over the past decade. During the 1980s, American financial markets appeared to be responsible for industrial underdevelopment: investors were seen as seeking short-term profits. At the opposite end of the spectrum, banks were seen as the driving force behind the rise of the electronics sector in Japan. Retrospectively, it would appear that the configuration of US financial markets was very beneficial to the new technologies. In reality, the search for profitable and risky investments supported the development of a venture capital industry whose purpose was to bet on the most promising young firms. The successful funding of young ICT companies was actually based on a conjunction of factors which reflect the intrinsic characteristics of start-ups, as well as changes in the modes of funding available to them. By their very nature, information and communications technologies have required only small initial outlays from their producers. At the same time, legislative changes have allowed pension funds to invest in venture capital companies, leading to a proliferation of available monies. The success of this particular method of funding was due to the existence of technological 'breeding grounds' in areas such as the Internet and the software sector. Such new attitudes towards US financial markets, seen as supportive of growth, nonetheless ignored the relationship between the efficiency of financial organizations, the nature of technological progress and the level of development of firms. The US system, which enabled so many new companies to come into being, turned out to be less efficient once these firms reached other stages of development. This comment will be developed further below when we deal with issues such as the organization of European financial markets and hypotheses concerning their convergence towards a single structure.

The role of economic policy   With rare unanimity, macroeconomists agreed to attribute the longevity of growth during the 1990s to the way in which the Federal Reserve Bank managed monetary policy and, at a deeper level, to US economic policy generally. Whereas monetary policy had hardly been successful during the 1970s and 1980s, it was at the forefront of circumstance-related interventions during the 1990s. Stress was laid on the arbitrage carried out between inflationary risks and continued growth. Interest rates were managed to ensure stabilization of expectations. Investment is very responsive to such things, the research and development sector particularly so. Business activity's greater sensitivity to the dollar's exchange rate, and the ever-increasing involvement of the financial sector (especially the growing importance of bond markets) in the overall economy, induced the Federal Reserve Bank to try to fine tune the reaction of financial markets to its policy adjustments. With respect to budgetary policy, the progressive lowering of the deficit, which turned into a surplus, was made possible by sustained growth. At the same time, the battle against inflation in Europe and increased state debt in Germany following that country's reunification accentuated the contrast with the pragmatic economic policy pursued by the United States.

An end to the expansion
This outline of US growth could not lead anyone to conclude that the environment within which American companies find themselves has allowed them

to become world leaders in every sector. A number of industries (computers, microprocessors, peripherals, certain software or machine tool branches) are dominated by Asian or European companies. In the telecommunications sector, competition-enshrining legislation has not led to the imposition of US standards. Equipment and infrastructure producers such as GSM, Nokia and, until recently, Ericsson have been able to dominate the market at a global level. Even though the United States remains ahead in most software and computer manufacturing sectors, this commanding position has not brought about any increase in the total factor productivity of its other branches. At a specifically macroeconomic level, US growth could be attributable to two 'safety cushions' (cf. Alan Greenspan) that will only operate for a limited period of time. The first is lower unemployment. The second is the higher current deficit, a rise in US indebtedness towards the rest of the world. In 2001–2002, the American economy was characterized by a slowdown in production, lower profit expectations and a great number of corporate redundancy programmes, particularly in the ICT sector. In financial markets, the Internet stock bubble burst once companies began to be re-evaluated using older methods. As could be foreseen, the cyclical components of the US economy did not, de facto, disappear along with the new technologies. However, the key elements of US growth (vigorous fundamental and applied research efforts in both the university and private sectors, a dynamic labour market, appropriate risk-funding systems) do constitute benchmarks that are indispensable for understanding changes in Europe's economic institutions.

Compared with the growth that took place in the United States, European performances have been very uneven. At the same time, such diversity has confirmed the divergence between the institutions that are to be found on each side of the Atlantic. The variety of institutional configurations in Europe is briefly described in the section below, with elements of differentiation being presented in greater detail later on. Country groups can be devised according to the macroeconomic trajectory that the various countries have been following. The findings of this macroeconomic study can be summarized in two ways. The first is that technology appears to be the constituent element of the regime of growth that characterized the 1990s. The countries that experienced the fastest growth were also those which featured the best ICT-related results. The second finding pinpoints factors within these various high-growth trajectories. In particular, the Nordic countries were found to be as successful – if not more so – than the United States in terms of growth or employment, yet featured much less in terms of inequality.

Europe's Different Trajectories

The preceding section offered a complex view of US growth. Several factors interacted, one of the main ones relating to 'the new technologies'. Studying the United States by itself might give the impression that all of the elements explaining its growth are prerequisites for creating a new regime of growth. The perspective that comes from international comparisons, however, can be useful in distinguishing between circumstances that are either particular or general and between factors that are either necessary or sufficient. Such comparisons possess two virtues: they enable a more detailed understanding of the mechanisms at work in the new regime of growth and they differentiate Europe's different countries. They also provide some interesting results. It would seem that we are in the presence of three configurations that allow for a new regime of growth. Each of them depends to large extent on the new technologies.

The three institutional configurations

What are the common characteristics of those countries that recorded a sharp rise in their total factor productivity? On the basis of a study that consists of classifying economies according to whether or not they possess specific characteristics,[4] seven countries crop up in the category featuring a sharp rise in TFP. They can be organized into three configurations: a knowledge economy, a deregulated economy and a catch-up economy.

- A knowledge economy is based on a high level of general education; intensive professional training; modern teaching methods that emphasize the use of numerical skills; and close cooperation between the academic system and research centres on the one hand and firms on the other. On average, a significant proportion of output is allocated to education, software and other vehicles for the transmission of knowledge. This configuration corresponds, in a sense, to the characteristics attributed to the once-called 'new economy', insofar as a wide socialization of knowledge is organized through collective investments. Free software companies lead the dance with products that are emblematic of the knowledge economy. The market is not the dominant form of coordination. Instead, it is cooperation (in an institutionalized form) that prevails, as it were, on a national basis. The Nordic countries are the ones typifying this type of economy.
- By way of contrast, a deregulated economy tries to facilitate private appropriation of advances in knowledge. Patents and the defence of intellectual property rights are the mechanisms used by the most qualified individuals (and the firms or organizations they work for) to keep the lion's share of innovation rents. An extremely active labour market is given responsibility for assessing, at any point in time, what each individual is to be paid in light of their competencies and of current

economic circumstances. This capturing of value is moderated by the fact that product market competition tends to cause a considerable lowering in the price of information goods, with consumers ultimately benefiting from innovation-related advances. These deregulated economies, driven as they are by science and knowledge, comprise the United States, Canada, Australia and Ireland.

- A model in which national catch-up processes are accelerated as a result of new technological circumstances represents another configuration that can trigger a virtuous circle. This model exists despite (or even because of) the initial lag suffered by the particular countries in question: Portugal and Ireland in Fordist mass production. This configuration fits in with the lessons that can be drawn from economic history, just so long as it is accepted that a growth model does not necessarily entail a preordained succession of stages, and that, by seeking to catch up, certain countries can skip some of these stages. Strong job protection does not conflict with this regime, unlike the second configuration, which is typical of countries in which there is still a great deal of confidence in market mechanisms.

The lessons that can be drawn from international comparisons
This initial typology of contemporary forms of growth helps us to understand those institutions that are necessary if growth is to take place. Moreover, the findings sometimes contrast with those which could be intuitively assumed from the US example alone. Our presentation will be divided into three parts: an analysis of the US economy, reinterpreted in the light of these international comparisons; a description of an alternative mode for attaining employment-beneficial regimes of growth; and an argument in favour of our main thesis, which is that the main catalyst of growth and employment is the *utilization* of these new technologies rather than their production.

A new look at the US model   The performance of the US economy would have been less surprising if we had focused on the structural characteristics of the regime of growth rather than on its position in the international division of labour, or on the duration and form of the economic cycle that took place during the 1990s. Canada, Australia and Ireland have also become successful members of this configuration. These four economies share a confidence in the marketplace, as witnessed by their pervasive deregulation of product markets and of the institutions that govern the labour factor. The innovation system lends itself more readily to radical breakthroughs rather than simply a sort of incremental improvement.

In addition, the nature of the organization of financial markets is not really crucial. Extrapolating from US results alone could make these market reorganizations appear to be indispensable, especially in light of the way in which financial innovations have coincided with technological ones. Yet analysis reveals that venture capital and new markets such as the NASDAQ are neither necessary, nor sufficient, conditions for the growth regime that emerged during the 1990s.

The contours of the other models   The US model is often summarized by reference to several simple, but distinctive, traits: deregulated product markets, a flexible labour market and the rapid advance of market finance. The Nordic economies offer an entirely different type of structural complementarity, one that (with the exception of product market deregulation) has no common characteristics with the US model. Thus being part of a new productive paradigm can be compatible with the persistence of institutional forms that are strikingly different from the ones typifying a pure market economy. This finding, which requires additional research in order to be confirmed, highlights the existence of other configurations capable of propelling strong growth.

An international comparative analysis of changes in employment reveals that a 'more flexible' labour market is not absolutely indispensable to increasing the number of jobs available. It would appear, to the contrary, that labour market regulation is advantageous if one of the two following preconditions is present.

- A high level of education exists for the whole of the population, as well as intensive professional training. The flexibility obtained from the external mobility of an American-style workforce can in fact be replaced by a form of training that ensures a wide spectrum of aptitudes by means of polyvalence and/or through a periodic adaptation of qualifications to the imperatives of emerging productive paradigms. Austria and the Netherlands belong to this configuration. It is a variant of the knowledge economy. Here strong institutions and labour regulations will subsist even though the sum total can be adapted to the new shape of international competition and to the opportunities that the new technologies offer.
- A given level of development exists. Although unemployment policies in Spain and Portugal were different, their situations during the course of the 1990s showed that the use of labour regulations as a means of supervision did not constitute an obstacle to their 'catching up'.

Note that there is a surprising institutional complementarity between continued regulation of product markets and the significant constraints that weigh upon the labour factor. Both France and Belgium belong to such a type of configuration. Something that could be damaging in a deregulated market could prove to be beneficial if the market remains a target of public intervention. But with European integration, how much longer will this apply?

The digital effect: usage rather than production   The most optimistic authors believe that specialization in the production of microprocessors, servers and communications software leads to increasing yields that can help improve total factor productivity. They believe that the US example illustrates this phenomenon. The problem is that productivity gains will not occur if the sectors that utilize such goods do not adapt their organizations to them. Besides, international comparisons provide a new perspective on US performances, making it possible to verify whether production indeed counts for less than usage.

The degree of IT utilization seems largely dependent on the intensity of its production. What does it mean in terms of the digital sector's contribution to US growth or the hypothesis that the control of production is a prerequisite for the rapid diffusion of ICT? Boolean analysis reveals that there is no correlation between these two distinct phenomena. Similarly, it can be verified that ICT production is not a necessary precondition for being part of a new paradigm, whether of a technological or an economic kind.

With regard to the advantage of being an ICT producer, an above-average control over ICT production is not a necessary precondition for membership in a technology-driven regime of growth. Such a regime requires three conditions to be fulfilled: total factor productivity must be above average; it must be higher than during the 1980s; and firms' research and development efforts, calculated in terms of R&D spending not R&D production, must have increased. In the developed countries, it is the conjunction of a reliance on computerized capital goods and low telecommunications costs that has turned out to be the necessary precondition for membership in this regime, not ICT production per se.

Although product market deregulation is a common characteristic of the two configurations that recorded accelerated growth during the 1990s, the same did not occur in the ICT-producing sector. If this finding turns out to be a robust one, it will mean that the information and communications sector is not playing the same driving role as did public works, construction and the mass production of household durable goods during the 1960s. Countries that lack an ICT-producing sector do not appear to be penalized in terms of their growth.

The same applies to employment performances. For two of the three configurations where improvements occurred after 1990, ICT production was not the determining factor. The third institutional configuration (corresponding to those countries involved in 'catching up') is characterized by the lesser importance of the ICT sector. This finding is not surprising in light of the US example where the high-technology sector is far from being the one that managed to create the greatest number of jobs during the past decade. At the head of this list were household services, health care and new corporate services.

The triumph of the 'small' economies and the vicissitudes of the 'medium-sized' ones

Is Europe really as far behind as certain observers believe? Within the European Union, people focus readily on Germany, Italy and France, countries whose macroeconomic performances, until 1997 at least, were not very good. During the 1990s they recorded a continual deceleration in growth alongside an almost constant rise in unemployment. However, if analysis shifts to Denmark, the Netherlands, Sweden and Ireland, it appears that we are dealing with economies that were able to reconcile the preservation of a modicum of traditional European solidarity with adhesion both to new technologies and to economic and social modernity.[5]

Expanding upon these attributes, we could say that medium-sized countries seem to be cursed. At one end of the scale, continental-sized economies such as that of the United States benefit from a concentration of skilled immigrants from around the world, from the crucial role played by financial intermediation and from the existence of a large marketplace comprising extremely demanding users. The United States benefits too from the diversity built into its federal constitution, which enables a series of trials and errors to take place in line with a process similar to that highlighted in theories of economic evolutionism. At the other end of the scale, smaller economies, when faced with the uncertainties of the international economy, have long been able to develop forms of extended solidarity even as they have worked to mobilize those innovations that best suit their particular specializations and traditions. During the 1990s, these smaller countries were in a good position to reform the organization of their social protection systems completely. Hence they have developed their competencies and competitiveness in the new international environment as a response to the turnaround in the productive paradigm. The density and stability of the relationships between social partners, entrepreneurs and political leaders in these countries encourage the negotiation of mutually advantageous compromises.

By way of contrast, France, Germany and Italy have traditionally adopted different institutional configurations, ones that have been very efficient in driving a type of growth that is based on mass consumption, thanks to appropriate public interventions. Here the move towards international openness contributed to the destabilization of a mode of regulation which was overwhelmingly based on internal dynamics driven by an employment relationship which was now threatened by the emphasis on competitiveness. These countries have had to cope with the return of an earlier hierarchy of institutional forms. In this type of environment, governments have lost much of their strategic power. On the one hand, they are unable to redeploy their forces when faced with opposition from social partners who are sufficiently powerful to block the reforms they propose. On the other hand, the partners themselves are insufficiently powerful to impel a social reorganization that would no longer look to state initiatives. The *intermediate position*, between continental-sized economies and regional-sized ones, is central to Europe's difficulties in consolidating the type of growth that was evident between 1997 and 2000 in the United States. It also partially explains the tensions that have cropped up in the reform of European institutions. There is an opposition between those countries which prefer intergovernmental agreements and those which favour a Community-wide approach.

2 WHICH INSTITUTIONS ARE APPROPRIATE FOR EUROPEAN GROWTH, RESEARCH, FINANCE AND THE LABOUR MARKET?

Studying forms of growth in all their variety gives us an opportunity to again ask questions about the ways in which European institutions have been changing. The issue is no longer one of promoting convergence towards a dominant model, meaning that of the country which experiences the highest growth at any given point in time. Rather, the diversity of Europe's institutions and the differences between its various countries require orientations which take this very diversity into account. Our thinking and subsequent propositions revolve around five headings.

With respect to fundamental and applied research in Europe, it is worthwhile looking at the impact made by IT. If this factor is indeed a constituent of the new regime of growth, then European research efforts (which have been low compared with those of the United States) need to be intensified. Certain European countries lag far behind others. This raises questions about the best way of improving the production of new technologies in all European countries, as well as the ability of companies to make use of them.

The second line of thinking relates to the funding of firms. There are differences between structures pertaining to financial markets in Europe and the United States, just as there are differences between structures operating within Europe. Which of these differences is crucial? If indeed no single financial structure will be ideal for all European companies' growth needs, what is the best way of promoting diverse types of funding?

The third point concerns the role that employees play within firms. In general, can the compromise that some European countries have adopted with respect to the part workers play in these matters be generalized in such a way as to promote economic dynamism? Germany, for example, is characterized by the heavy involvement of employees in their firms' functioning. The same argument applies to a lesser extent to a number of other continental countries. Employee and union participation in company life is organized in such countries within a framework of co-management, particularly so in Germany. Co-management has been undermined by the development of financial markets and by the transformations that have affected the labour market. Is this common system of management compatible with a new regime of growth?

The fourth heading focuses on employment contracts. Current economic transformations require companies to be flexible in managing their workforces, yet at the same time to provide employees with a modicum of security, that is to say with continuity of income. The transformations mean that significant professional mobility is made possible. Our analysis starts with the surprising stability of open-ended employment contracts. Today such contracts have come under pressure from atypical forms of work contracts. These changes attest to a deep-seated change in the economic environment of companies. What are the preconditions for changing employment contracts to ensure that they incorporate the new circumstances that firms and employees face?

The fifth, and last, development relates to the systems of social protection that link to conditions of worker mobility. If employees cannot be expected to assume alone the risks stemming from a higher level of labour mobility, a unified approach to social protection will be necessary. In reality, all periods of non-employment should be covered by a system of social protection, whether these involve training, job seeking or retirement. What is the best way of strengthening training and mobility while guaranteeing that employees are protected?

Encouraging Research and Investment

The present section presents a comparison of levels of research (and of research applications) in Europe. Studies of US growth have revealed accelerated technological change in sectors such as computers, peripherals and semiconductors. These changes account for most of the acceleration in productivity gains since 1995. In practice, all of them have been concentrated in the durable goods sector. The other sectors of the economy have been scarcely affected at all. At a more disaggregated level, ICT facilitates the circulation of information and generally leads to changes in the organization of companies. It probably constitutes a key element in a new regime of growth. The present section analyses the structural differences between the United States and Europe, on the one hand, and between various European countries, on the other. These comparisons highlight the different levels of ICT diffusion in Europe. They also provide concrete illustrations of some of Europe's structural weaknesses in industrial and research matters.

Different levels of investment and research

The physical capital investment gap between Europe and the United States has tended to diminish (although the United States still operates at a higher level), but all of the indicators display the same trends with regard to investments in the knowledge economy. Spending on ICT in the United States represents 8 per cent of national wealth, as opposed to 6 per cent in Europe. The United States spends twice as much on higher education as Europe. However, it is in the area of research and development spending that the differences are most striking. Whereas during the period 1981–95 spending on fundamental and applied research followed similar trends on both sides of the Atlantic, since then, there has been an acceleration in spending in the United States and a stagnation in Europe. A more detailed analysis demonstrates that in both regions spending by the state and by the higher education sector in general evolved similarly during the years 1991–9. The divergence between the overall levels thus stems from (private) companies' spending on research and development.

This Europe-wide measurement of the gap in investment and/or in research hides very different situations. ICT provides a good illustration, with variations both in ICT utilization and in ICT production. Sweden and Finland are amongst the world's leaders in terms of the number of people connected to the Internet. The number of computers per household in Norway and Denmark is amongst the highest in the world. Lastly, Ireland and the Netherlands feature results that are well above average in certain ICT-related fields. The 'big' European countries on the other hand are less advanced.

The harmonization of European diversity

Europe's lag in investment and in research indicates that European institutions, in all likelihood, are not very good at benefiting from information technology innovations. Of course, European institutional diversity makes it difficult to coordinate research and commercialization efforts. With each country's institutions so heterogeneous, they do not converge towards a single model. This is not a problem, however. On the contrary, Europe needs to tie its policy of institutional harmonization to a policy in which diversity is viewed as a source of value. In the long run, institutional diversity is a strength because it helps to ensure the quality of researchers' innovations. More specifically, the diversity of Europe's structures and of its research organizations can help underpin the region's dynamism as well as its responsiveness.

The lack of inter-European coordination does, however, prevent the Union benefiting from the diversity of innovation systems, qualifications and specializations that exist within each country. The fragmented nature of higher education and research in Europe leads to significant extra costs, these effectively being costs pertaining to a 'non-Europe'. Europe lacks the institutional coherency that would enable it to benefit from the advantages that are possessed by each of its member states. In the United States, the role of organizations such as the National Institution of Health or the National Scientific Foundation is crucial in developing and orienting research. Nowadays, those policy incentives that are defined at a European level and which are meant to support fundamental and applied research assume varying forms in each country. Sometimes they are limited to small-sized firms, sometimes to given regions. European harmonization could clarify this situation and lead to better results.

Finally, by redefining legislation, tax regimes and norms at a European level, it might become possible for the private sector in Europe to close the investment gap with the United States. The plurality of tax systems which companies have to cope with in Europe has a greater influence on the location of new firms than on the overall level of investment or research. It would be pointless to proclaim the advantages of the diversity of European tax systems. Rather, exploiting European diversity implies a mixture of the various local actors, whether they come from universities, research organizations or firms. This opening up would be facilitated by a harmonization of legislative and incentive systems, and by the development of networks which encourage flexible forms of exchange, meaning those that do not require the creation of large structures.

Improving the Funding Mechanisms of Companies

The differences between US and European financial markets are reflected in corporate funding systems and, to a certain extent, in the orientation of economic activity. An ideal mode of funding may not exist for Europe, in which case the challenge is to coordinate and to regulate different ways of funding economic activities.

Corporate ownership structures

An initial distinction between banks and financial markets crops up in the funding systems found in the United States and Great Britain on one hand, and in the continental European countries on the other. A system that largely relies on bank funding (as in Germany or Japan) tends to encourage long-term relationships with a company's senior management. Establishments that fund a large number of firms specialize in monitoring investment projects. They can track projects as they unfold, enabling heavy investments for long periods of time. Conversely, a corporate funding system that first turns to financial markets, as in the case of Great Britain and the United States, encourages capital mobility. Through the purchase and resale of shares, funds can be rapidly reallocated to new projects. Those investment projects that have been able to demonstrate their profitability will therefore receive greater attention. But it is more difficult in a system of this sort to fund long-term projects. Shareholders demand high, and rapid, profits and shift their investments to other companies if earnings disappoint them.

In practice, the opposition between bank-based funding and financial, market-based forms is a relative one. In fact, the volume of loans to firms is not much higher in Germany than in Great Britain. Moreover, the proportion of total shares that the banks own is not very significant in terms of most countries' stock market capitalization. Comparisons between the different countries indicate that the effects of funding by banks or by non-bank shareholders are highly comparable.

The differences between the various modes of European funding are actually more striking if we look at corporate ownership structures. Shareholding in firms is clearly more concentrated in continental European countries than in Great Britain. Single shareholders hold 43.5 per cent, 34.5 per cent and 34.9 per cent, respectively, of voting rights in half of all Dutch, Spanish and Swedish companies. In Great Britain on the other hand, the median shareholder holds 9.9 per cent of voting rights, and in the United States the figure is 5 per cent. In addition, if we consider the second largest shareholders, we need to bear in mind that in continental European countries the percentage of voting rights held is much lower than is the case for the main shareholder.

Power is thus much more concentrated on the European continent, not only because of the size of each company's main shareholder, but also because of the absence of other shareholders of similar size. And there is another distinction that relates to the nature of the shareholders. On the continent, the main direct shareholders involve structures that are controlled by families or by other firms. In Great Britain, the main shareholders are financial institutions, pension funds or life insurance companies. Financial institutions manage their portfolios actively, with a great variety of holdings, each of which is relatively small in size. Family shareholders, on the other hand, maintain long-term relationships with companies and have larger shareholdings in terms of their firm's total capital.

The influence of funding systems on corporate activities

Different financial structures encourage different types of activities. A series of research projects has looked at the relationship between funding and investment, and concluded that a concentrated ownership structure promotes low-risk and long-term investment projects. By way of contrast, a less concentrated ownership structure tends to encourage more risky investment and research projects. Three different approaches were followed in these studies, entailing different conceptions of the relationship between investors and other corporate actors. These involved information, involvement and control.

1. New and risky investments such as those in ICT can lead to variations in investors' assessments of the probability of success. According to information theory, those financial markets comprising a wide range of securities holders offer a funding mode that is compatible with the sorts of investments which engender a multiplicity of yield expectations. By way of contrast, the standard forms of investment whose expected yields seem to be consensual are compatible with funding from a principal shareholder or lender committed to a long-term relationship with the entrepreneur.
2. In those theories where financial structure is seen to be a function of the involvement of investors and employees, a concentrated ownership structure is a sign of the shareholder's commitment to a firm. As a result, other corporate actors are prepared to commit themselves to their work because they are not afraid of being abandoned by the investor should some temporary difficulty arise. Conversely, a dispersed ownership structure can bring shareholders to exert pressure on a firm, inasmuch as they seek rapid returns. This pressure can sometimes lead to the adoption of innovations which other corporate actors would have refused.
3. Lastly, those theories that focus on the ability of different corporate actors to exercise control have concluded that a concentrated investment structure encourages long-term, low-risk projects, whereas a dispersed structure is more favourable to short-term, high-risk projects.

At a more applied level, we observe technological trajectories that correspond to the differences between the various financial systems analysed above. National technologies trajectories are characterized, for example, by the number of patents that are registered in each country for each sector of activity. Germany, where investors tend to be concentrated within each firm, occupies a leading role in chemicals, cars and machine tools – all sectors that require significant long-term investments. Conversely, the United States dominates patent registration in the ICT and biotechnology sectors. These branches require less significant, but riskier, investments. The dispersion of the US financial system thus encourages these types of activities.

A different type of analysis of the funding of new ICT projects explains how funding and investment can be linked both theoretically and empirically. Company financing implies the presence of various types of actors. The first mode of funding often involves the personal savings of the entrepreneur (or of persons who are close to him/her). Then comes funding from 'good fairies' or from investors who are specialists in the assumption of risk. The former will fund projects that are risky on the basis of knowing the competency of the entrepreneur. The latter will undertake a more detailed study of the project, the resources and the teams involved before deciding whether or not to invest. If the firm succeeds at each phase of the funding process, its further development will involve seeking funds on the financial markets, essentially by organizing tender bids for investment capital.

A comparison of European companies reveals the variety of outlooks firms possess concerning the role the market ought – or ought not – to play in funding their operations. German companies gaining access to the financial market for the first time are on average 50 years old. Once they have been floated on the stock market, it is rare for the majority shareholder to change. To prevent the firm's ownership structure from being altered, the new shareholder immediately becomes (by far) the majority shareholder, thus maintaining the concentration of the structure. British companies which launch rights issues for the first time are on average 12 years old. They are half the size of their German counterparts, and their ownership structure generally changes even after the initial public offering (IPO). Access to financial markets is primarily a means for Anglo-US companies (unlike German ones) to obtain resources for an acquisition-based growth, that is to say, for purchasing other firms.

The diversity of financial systems in European countries corresponds to a varied set of activities and investments. Convergence towards a single model is hardly desirable. In fact, an active and articulated management of the diversity of financial systems in Europe would appear to be the best way of encouraging investment and technological progress.

Matching a type of activity with a type of funding

No single financial structure is ideal for all. The mode of funding must be adapted to the types of activities in which a company is involved. Financial markets are efficient in nurturing new companies in a context that is marked by widely dispersed shareholdings. The development of companies might then be affected by changes in the structure, or type, of shareholders. Although the financial organization of the United States probably plays an important role in that country's creation of new and innovative companies, European systems offer advantages that can be useful for high-technology companies, particularly their later stages of development.

In describing the structural differences between the various funding systems, and in highlighting the link between structures and the activities pursued by companies, we can discover the relative institutional advantages of each. Some countries might foster the development of certain sorts of projects. That depends on the way in which the financial system is organized: types of shareholders, the role of bank lending, the concentration of companies' investments.

This observation is a plea for making the currently wide range of corporate funding mechanisms accessible at a European level. Once again, diversity in this area can be an advantage for Europe. Preferring one system of funding to another (the Anglo-US versus the continental European, for example) makes little sense insofar as corporate funding needs are specific to each company's particular level of development. Instead, funding should be organized in Europe according to a regulatory framework which enables the coexistence and stability of different methods of funding.

Such an emphasis on European diversity could have a specific impact on the Union's financial institutions. When financial institutions and banks go bankrupt, there are negative consequences which go far beyond the parties responsible for the problems. When debts go unpaid, savers and other financial institutions are also penalized. Consequently, there has to be some coordination between the emphasis placed upon preserving the funding systems' diversity (thus creating a tangible competition that will benefit entrepreneurs) and the necessary management of bankruptcy risk (which must be subjected to some sort of competitive legislation in order to keep people from taking excessive risks). Savers, and minority shareholders in particular, must be protected at the same time that a wider range of funding is offered.

The nature of corporate funding mechanisms is currently the subject of a great deal of debate. It appears to be associated with the way in which a company organizes its work rather than with the type of activity that is being pursued. Most European countries place a great deal of emphasis on employee participation in a company's life. It is in Germany that employee involvement (within the framework of co-management) is most advanced. It would be interesting to measure the economic efficiency of this employment relationship, and to see whether it has been undermined by changes in corporate funding modes, and more specifically by the increased reliance on market funding.

Defining Industrial Citizenship

Changes in the economic environment of companies, characterized notably by the opening of borders between the various financial markets and by the intensification of the trade in goods, have served to modify the objectives of firms. The opening up of financial markets has increased the proportion of Anglo-US shareholders in the ownership structures of European companies. The behaviour of shareholders and analysts has therefore moved ever closer to Anglo-US practices which emphasize shareholders' interests within firms. This raises the issue, for those firms that need to seek external funding, of the maximization of shareholders' income – and of this type of income alone. Is it possible to transcend the conflict between the interests of employees and those of employers? The present section focuses on transformations in the organization of transnational companies. Interest in these types of firms does not only stem from the fact that they produce most of the wealth in Europe and employ more than half of the working population. Big companies also provide the arena in which economic and social constraints find expression. To a large extent, it is within these firms that employee status is determined. They serve as a reference point for any legislation which seeks to introduce public interest-related elements into the work relationship. In other words, large companies, and transnational companies in particular, constitute the main backdrop to the employment relationship.

Industrial citizenship versus the world of finance

Current debate on corporate management criteria provides reminders of the specificity of continental European and Anglo-US conceptions and the widely diverging notions which exist on the subject of ownership structures (as just discussed). In the United States and Great Britain, where company ownership is split between small shareholders, the management of firms is adapted to this plurality of owners. This leaves the managers some space to free themselves from shareholders' interests. This freedom of action has been the topic of many studies which have looked at the various ways in which investors exert pressure on company management, the objective being a higher return on their investments. The hypotheses underlying these studies are that high returns encourage investment and lead to a better allocation of capital inasmuch as the most profitable investments are, in general, clearly identified.

Ownership structures in continental European companies are less dispersed. Managers co-ordinate with those shareholders with whom they can identify. The organization of European shareholding has long granted company directors a certain independence from financial markets. Cross-participations, shareholdings by banks and public ownership of capital have underpinned credit-based funding or self-financing. In a number of European countries, company managers play the role of mediators between different interest groups inside, or outside, the firm: for example, when dealing with state authorities. Despite the ways in which ownership structures and shareholder roles have changed over the course of the past decade, senior managers have continued to play such a mediating role. Employees still fulfil a special function in continental European companies. They usually give their opinion on certain management choices, thus benefiting (to use an expression developed by Wolfgang Streeck in Chapter 1) from a type of *industrial citizenship* that can be found in various versions in all continental European countries. In France, employee rights are relatively underdeveloped. But they are recognized in Germany where co-management provides a framework for relations between labour unions and employers.

Employee involvement in the decisions and the running of companies underpins an economic model that has its own specific advantages and costs. It is the opposite of a conception of the firm in which relationships are determined on a contractual basis. 'Industrial citizenship' is based on the economic gains that stem from long-term relationships within the firm. Employee involvement is manifested in cooperative behaviour and this helps to diminish staff turnover.[6] This in turn reduces the costs of looking to hire and train new workers. Cooperation leads to a reciprocal relationship of trust which encourages the circulation of information. Employees have no reason to hide information for fear it might be used against them by senior management. Cooperation also encourages employees to pursue training that is specific to their company. This enables them to envisage their work unfolding over a long period of time. Employees' aptitudes thus become more specific to the firm. This in turn tends to increase their productivity. To summarize, cooperation cuts the transaction costs that are involved in an overreliance on the market, and thus the cost of controlling hierarchical structures.

Long-term relationships and employee involvement in the firm can, however, lead to a low degree of work mobility. When new production techniques necessitate skills entailing worker training, it may be in the company's interest to turn to the labour market for solutions. Companies can, in fact, directly recruit workers who already possess the necessary qualifications. In this way, the external mobility of work can create savings in training costs and provide companies with enhanced capabilities for adapting to technological change. It is this external mobility, widely practised in the United States, that has been so beneficial to US companies.

The respective advantages of the two approaches (in terms of the work relationship that they imply) are difficult to compare in absolute terms. History has determined the evolution of corporate organization. In continental parts of Europe, firms seem to have witnessed a deeper involvement of employees in their firms. This region is more static and therefore under pressure from current changes in its environment. Although it is possible to detect the constraints that weigh upon firms, it is more difficult to evaluate their impact on forms of industrial citizenship which, depending on the specifics of a given situation, are destined either to be standardized in Europe or else to disappear.

The influence of market and financial internationalization

Two main components have an impact upon industrial citizenship. The first is the increased internationalization of national economies; the second is the restructuring and opening up of financial markets, which forces corporate managements and governments to compete in making themselves more attractive on the international stage.

The integration of the markets for goods and services has increased competitive pressures for a number of national companies which have subsequently opted for a strategy of international development. This involves reducing costs through production on a wider scale and organizing production in order to benefit from the advantages which exist in each country. However, international development necessitates large sums for investment, or else for the purchase of other firms. In most European countries, national savings are insufficient to satisfy the demand for capital. The rapid growth of international financial markets responds to this demand by increasing the proportion of Anglo-US holdings in European companies. Changing shareholder practices, part of the increased competition between financial marketplaces, puts pressure on company share prices. Low prices make a firm vulnerable to hostile takeovers, whereas high prices allow companies to use their securities as a means of exchange during merger and acquisition operations. This indirect pressure is a significant factor in changing corporate managers' attitudes towards the way in which markets assess the value of their firms.

Certain management practices are presented in such a way as to convince shareholders that theirs is a quality investment. These include developing a system that equates to US accounting practices, creating investor relations services, paying executives by means of stock options, and eliminating different types of voting rights for different types of investors (thereby guaranteeing equal rights for minority shareholders). Symbolically, companies are being held to respect accounting ratios which elevate shareholders' interests to the number one concern in management.

All in all, the integration of financial markets has led to a certain reorganization of managers' practices, which have moved closer to shareholders' objectives as a consequence. The 'company governance' theme has become increasingly central to discussions on corporate organization. Employee involvement in firms thus seems to be changing its shape, and possibly also its nature, as a result of the pressures to which industrial citizenship is being subjected in large European companies.

Differentials in labour legislation

To appreciate the magnitude of these current changes, it is necessary to distinguish between the national legislative level and the framework within which transnational companies operate. European corporate company legislation has not brought about supranational harmonization. The convergence of labour law within the European Union was probably too hard to achieve. Legally there is no such thing as a European company. Changes in European law have oriented legislation towards defining a framework which allows for coexistence of national practices. For example, the 1995 European directive on workers' councils defines constraints for transnational firms. This directive establishes a European level of negotiation for workers, a level that is superimposed on other negotiating levels yet which does not modify them. Thus national differences remain very strong.

Transnational companies arbitrate between the advantages and the disadvantages of national legislation according to the type of activity in which they are involved. Two diverging tendencies have cropped up: national systems are different from one another, with each country attempting to put forward its own strong points; yet transnational firms feature homologous structures. For the moment, firms often consider the disparities between the institutions that are responsible for supervising industrial relations to be a handicap. Nevertheless, European legislative harmonization runs up against the fact that it is almost impossible to carry out deeper transformation of national legislation. The recognition of worker rights is so different from one country to the next that in many places labour law will need to be completely remodelled. Harmonization makes it possible to avoid placing countries in competition with one other – a competition from which firms have benefited greatly, given their greater mobility compared to workers. But the history of labour law institutions is scarcely reassuring for the supporters of harmonization. There is a real risk that regulations will converge towards a minimalist legislation of the Anglo-US variety, undermining the social role that large firms play without any concurrent increase in economic efficiency. Nevertheless, convergence would make it possible to improve European corporate profitability in the short run, with other countries probably continuing to follow the same strategy. The ultimate outlook for corporate profitability would then be uncertain, and the social situation of workers unacceptable. Convergence towards deregulation implies turning one's back on the advantages European firms enjoy within a framework of industrial citizenship.

Advances in a type of labour law that recognizes employee involvement are being impeded by the differences that exist between various national accords. This heterogeneity delays the development of a common legal definition of corporate status. In addition, in an environment marked by great technological changes, a self-centred industrial *esprit de corps* could end up having the last word by granting the right of expression only to those workers who have been tightly integrated into the firm. Unemployed persons, or employees subjected to a regime of market flexibility, would not be covered. The most qualified workers would be able to benefit from a system of this nature, the recognition of their competency ensuring security of income as well as professional mobility. This new form of narrow-minded corporatism would lead to the segmentation of work relations and undermine the notion of industrial citizenship by reducing the number of workers included within its embrace.

The current trend is towards a coexistence of national legislations. Companies are happy with such a development insofar as they can benefit from different labour institutions in the same way that they have profited from the aforementioned diversity in funding modes. Nevertheless, it is a dangerous thing to place tax and social protection systems in competition with one another. It could increase pressures towards lower company taxation as well as slow the improvement of national infrastructures and employee training. Such changes in employees' living conditions and in state budgets would be deleterious over the long run.

In short, changes in the organization of European transnational companies, which have been under pressure since the opening up of markets for capital and for goods, are characterized by an ostensible convergence between some aspects of corporate workings. First of all, there are the relationships with the shareholders. The organization of firms continues, in certain cases, either to benefit from, or else to be subjected to, national legislations which diverge in terms of their definitions of 'stakeholder' statuses and the involvement such groups play in companies. These tendencies may, in the long run, undermine the notion of industrial citizenship in certain European countries, either through the fostering of competition between national systems, or else through a *minimalist* type of convergence that is driven by the desire to deregulate labour law. This convergence would be damaging insofar as it would endanger work relationships constructed on a long-term basis, while threatening the living conditions of employees and the competitiveness of companies.

Reassessing the Conditions Underlying the Employment Relationship

These deep-seated changes in the structures of corporate funding, as well as the profound reorganization of financial markets, contrast with the greater stability of the employment relationship. The impact of institutional reform on employment policies has led to major controversy. Nonetheless, at the very least a reform of the labour market should increase the likelihood of renewed productivity gains. This is because codified work relationships have been eroded in an aggressive manner, leading to increased precariousness for certain types of employee status. This has occurred notwithstanding the fact that no contractual forms have yet appeared to replace the traditional open-ended employment contract. Below we define the conditions in which a potentially rejuvenated work contract can be diffused, making it possible to raise employee autonomy and at the same time to increase work mobility for firms.

Despite the development of part-time work, most contracts remain open-ended. As determined in a 1992 international study, such contracts have been remarkably stable. They cover more than 90 per cent of all employees in OECD countries. By studying this success story, we should be able to detect those conditions that suffice in and of themselves to underpin durable contractual forms. Indeed, any new form of work contract presents itself as a mutually advantageous solution, and within the framework of decentralized negotiations between firms and employees a better solution than other contractual forms. Legislation is not a framework for action if it has been rejected by companies.

The stability of open-ended employment contracts

It is probably counter-intuitive to see the flexibility of open-ended contracts as the reason for their longevity. Yet this flexibility appears clearly in comparisons with employment relationships where workers sell their services to a firm, in much the same way that companies sell their services to other companies. The latter form of work relationship (namely self-employment) has been developing rapidly in certain countries. It now affects approximately one in ten employees in OECD countries, including a number of sole traders. It is a relationship which forces both parties to agree upon the following: an exact definition of expected outcomes; the conditions in which work outcomes will satisfy the terms of a contract; and how services will be renumerated. Conversely, the flexibility of the open-ended work contract stems from the fact that it is possible to change the nature of work even after the contract has been signed. In cases involving unforeseen circumstances, or an acceleration in technological change, the employer and the employee can agree to a redefinition of tasks or work objectives within the framework of the existing contract. To put it another way, the open-ended contract ensures that responsibility for negotiating changes in working conditions remains with the firm itself, thereby freeing it from the constraints of legal formalization. The tenor of these negotiations then depends upon such complexities as the firm's mode of organization and its methods of representing the interests of management or staff.

The conditions allowing for the diffusion of new forms of work contracts

A work contract's viability is subject to two constraints. The first is related to the existence of control frameworks that limit opportunistic behaviour by a company and/or by its employees.[7] The fact that workers and employers anticipate such behaviour on the part of the other tends from the very outset to jeopardize the prospects of genuine cooperation. This being the case, the setting up of control frameworks renders hostile actions less likely and encourages the emergence of relationships that are less prone to conflict.

The second constraint relates to the economic efficiency of the work contract in terms of employee mobility within the firm as well as training opportunities and general working conditions (including hours). These constraints depend on the firm's economic environment. An efficient work contract may turn out to be inapplicable even if, on paper, it allows for a great deal of employee autonomy and for a system of remuneration that is predicated on the results of the entire work team. The firm can ask for ways of judging the difficulty of the work involved in order to gauge the quality of the results. Employees can ask for a rigorous definition of pay systems in order to have their work assessed at a fair value. In the absence of such frameworks of negotiation, the contract may turn out to be unsuitable. The two constraints that define the current form of open-ended work contracts are thus feasibility of application and economic efficiency.

The cooperation constraint Rules must be defined so that the reciprocal obligations of workers and employers are sufficiently clear for each party to enter a contractual relationship. Two approaches to work circumscribe these obligations. The first focuses on the tasks that workers are asked to perform. This conception has been the dominant one since mass production enabled an extension of taylorist principles. The task is determined by breaking work down into its various components. It can be understood either directly on the basis of the operations that are to be carried out, or else indirectly from the tools that workers use. According to this principle, polyvalence increases as a function of the number of tasks that each worker fulfils, even though management is always responsible for prescribing the way in which work is carried out. A second conception of work, more adapted to a diversified type of production, defines tasks on the basis of the objectives that are to be reached, or the functions that are to be fulfilled. Workers, or work teams, are autonomous in determining the sequence of tasks. As explained above, this type of work relationship necessitates greater cooperation between employers and employees, implying frameworks that are adapted to the nature of the work and which therefore restrict opportunistic behaviour.

The constraint of economic efficiency In addition to the constraint of the contract's feasibility for both parties, there is also the constraint of economic efficiency. Field studies have shown that there are two ways in which efficiency constraints can be built into a work relationship. Constraints can be directly determined from production. In this case, the work is defined in terms of tasks and specific qualifications. The second way of promoting productive efficiency consists of concentrating on employees' qualifications rather than on the work itself.

Using this typology, it is easy to describe the dominant form of the work contract inherited from the era of mass production. Here work is determined within the framework of an open-ended contract and on the basis of tasks that are to be carried out. These tasks are set with an eye to production constraints. This type of work contract is probably not best shaped to the current environment of companies. Increasingly differentiated production and ever-shorter lead times stem from greater competition. The issues raised by changes in the work contract (and by changes in labour market institutions in general) relate to the way in which it is becoming possible to disseminate work relationships based on employees' qualifications and aptitudes. Within a framework comprising these sorts of relationships, the functions that are to be carried out, and the objectives that are to be reached, are determined jointly. These work relationships enable companies to gain in terms of flexibility. They imply greater cooperation within the company and, as a corollary, increased employee autonomy.

Instead of defining an abstract framework which encourages cooperation, the section below presents, in sectoral case study form, the types of organizations that enable this *modus operandi* to develop.

Rejuvenated employment relationships

In certain sectors of the economy, new types of labour contracts have started to appear. Some of them explicitly promote workforce mobility and are based on a fixed-term commitment that provides the framework for a firm's authority over its workforce. Such work relationships allow for a great deal of inter-firm employee mobility and create a situation in which the employee is not strictly associated with just one firm. In actual fact, employees have been willing to change companies rapidly, depending on the constraints of production. Firms have been leaving staff members a great deal of autonomy to carry out work as they see fit. This type of work relationship means that the tie between the firm and the worker revolves around a given project, or else around the creation of a given product or service. Once the objective has been reached and the remuneration paid, the various parties no longer consider themselves bound by reciprocal obligations.

Such employment relationships have developed particularly within communities that can be defined spatially. The most widely recognized examples are the suburbs of Los Angeles and Silicon Valley. The projects usually consist of designing a solution to a specific technical problem, for example the building of a software package or the making of a film. The issue of opportunism is resolved by means of rapid circulation of information in extremely dense professional networks which serve to mould the reputation of firms and employees, as well as the reputation of those who communicate the information itself. A firm that offers difficult working conditions could therefore be excluded from the network. In a sense, a typical service-provider relationship today, characterized by independent wage earners and highly developed relationships of trust, is reminiscent of the professional communities of earlier times. When networks ensure cooperation between wage earners and firms, they are playing much the same role as guilds did in sixteenth-century England.

The future of the traditional employment relationship

It would seem that there are two different directions in which Europe's labour contracts might ultimately develop. The first leads to a rigid variant where the interests of businesses are protected, with firms again being allowed control over the way in which employee qualifications (wherever these can be objectified), and even possibly employee interests, are defined. This leaves staff with little room for autonomy, however. The second possible direction involves a transmogrification of contracts into flexible forms oriented towards work in project-based settings. This is more in tune with the current economic environment of companies. Although the latter type of employment relationship can indeed be an efficient one, its development is restricted by the need to guarantee cooperation. Changing labour contracts thus requires the establishment of an institutional framework which constrains the opportunistic behaviour of employers, a consideration that is usually missing in debates on flexibility within the firm. We can readily imagine how social policy evaluation systems could be revised. Until now, they have been construed as a simple appendage to economic policy. If politics remains absent from the debate, the most likely outcome is that labour contracts will develop in deteriorating labour markets, that is to say wherever management – the only party to benefit from the aforementioned changes – wields power.

Reforming Social Protection Systems

Of all the factors that weigh upon negotiations between wage earners and companies, the most crucial is probably the system of social protection. Much debate has focused on the issue of the activation of employment policy. In several European countries 'flexicurity', an all-encompassing term that encapsulates the search by employees for security and the search by firms for flexibility, has become a voguish concept. Yet the direction in which European systems of social protection need to evolve does not seem to have been defined in such a way as to encourage employee mobility while also ensuring continuity of income.

The obsolescence of systems of social protection

Most European systems of social protection concentrate on protecting wage earners against lost income in times of non-employment. Implicitly, unemployment is seen as a transitional period that ultimately leads to new, full-time, open-ended contracts. This conception has been widely undermined by the erosion of the traditional work relationship, a phenomenon that has occurred as a result of two trends. The first is the rapid development of qualifications within firms themselves, generated by the diffusion of new information and communications technologies. The second is the diminished stability of production, a consequence of the ever-greater competition resulting from the internationalization of production. These factors force firms to look for increased labour mobility as well as for ways of modifying employees' individualized competencies and of structuring their qualifications. At the same time, employees themselves have new aspirations. They appear to be more interested in professional mobility, or in working schedules that better complement their private lives. Such trends are reinforced by the legitimate desires of women to receive employment oportunities and pay packages on a similar basis to men.

The relative erosion of the open-ended type of labour contract demonstrates the limitations of a traditional unemployment insurance system which merely reacts to the external risks of firms, that is to say to fluctuations in their activities. Such a system is not adapted to the new risks born of the increasingly frequent employee transitions between one job (or status) to the next, or between a period of employment to a period of training. Increased professional mobility will automatically be accompanied by a large number of transitional periods. For employees, such periods will involve, in addition to loss of income, a threatened devaluation of qualifications. Workers also face risks related to their standard of living, more as a result of the shift towards part-time work than of unemployment per se.

Redefining social protection around periods of transition

If new forms of professional mobility are to see the light of day, a fundamental change in systems of social protection is necessary. This change could be effected by transforming the current unemployment insurance into a type of employment insurance, a variant that integrates all facets of the various risks and situations stemming from the status of non-employment. In other words, transitions between employment situations need to be integrated into a single framework. Longer life expectancies and an ageing population imply that those forms which represent the transition from employment to retirement should also be incorporated into the framework. The German example demonstrates the extent to which forms of activity have changed. Some 15 years ago, transitions from unemployed to employed status represented 80 per cent of all moves away from unemployment. Nowadays, the figure is closer to 35 per cent. In other words, most workforce turnover does not occur as part of traditional core working processes, but arises between employment and other activities such as training or retirement.

Currently, transitions between various non-employed statuses occur in conditions which serve to pose problems for employees and which are usually the consequences of economic failure. Three criteria can contribute to a successful transition: increased employee autonomy and participation; the development of solidarity through a broader range of risk-sharing groups (and through the extension of this type of aid to those social groups who find it most difficult to get a job); and improved economic efficiency through increasingly decentralized decision making. As the Danish and Swedish examples demonstrate, it is possible to respect such criteria while organizing the two transitions that are the most important of all. These are the transitions from employee to trainee status and from jobs involving one status to those with another.

The relevance of employment insurance
If there is a relationship between unemployment and social protection, it involves spending money in order to combat work incapacity. The end of this particular story has not yet arrived, however. The passiveness of current employment policies (early retirement systems, social subsidizing of restructuring programmes, tax exemptions when specific categories are employed) is by no means inevitable. Improved working capabilities and, more specifically, flexible forms of work, could become the first goal of an activated employment policy. The success of the Nordic countries with regard to training systems has provided the rest of Europe with a useful model to follow. In Scandinavia, certain measures have helped institutionalize the transition between employment and training. A right to training, remunerated for example along the lines of paid holidays, enables wage earners to improve their knowledge or to acquire new qualifications within learning programmes that can be negotiated with employers. The purpose of these training stints, accessible regardless of qualification or gender, is to lend support to certain social groups. Less qualified workers, older workers or women first entering the labour market are the first to be involved. Denmark's organization can serve as a benchmark in this respect. At a practical level, it satisfies the conditions for a successful training curriculum, involving a lifelong learning programme in which qualifications and quality are clearly identified. The funding for systems of this sort can be determined by negotiations between the various social constituencies and the state.

Politics as a Catalyst for a New Model of European Employment

Many people would agree that European attempts to activate employment policies have failed. In reality, statistics demonstrate that such failures are primarily related to errors in implementation. New forms of employment insurance (yet to be defined) could comprise the very heart of activated economic policy programmes, specifically moulding the ways in which programmes are broken down and coordinated across Europe. Clearly the revitalization of Europe's social model does not require reductions in the working population. Those countries which have already succeeded in this domain did not lower the age of retirement, nor did they discourage females from seeking employment. Quite the contrary; these are the countries that have integrated many different forms of non-employment (as well as the new risks associated with them) into a unified approach to social protection. Income continuity must be guaranteed independently of workers' increasing mobility between different forms of employment or between different periods of training. This approach blurs the borders between social protection and employment policy. With respect to training, however, the building of an efficient system can interfere with certain types of employment policies. For example, the funding of non-qualified labour can bog down training programmes, thus harming the productivity of labour. Viewing employment policies solely as a source of funding for less qualified forms of work is tantamount to neglecting those current changes that call for improvements in people's working capabilities.

CONCLUSION

The forms of growth which have benefited the United States and the northern European countries during the 1990s have varied. Even so they constitute a common benchmark for prospective analyses of the dynamics currently at work. The hypothetical existence of a knowledge economy emerges from a comparison of these various forms. It also helps trace the main axes for a model of sustained growth. What characterizes these economies is the place that knowledge occupies in their production and trading systems. A knowledge economy is distinct from an information economy which essentially produces improvements in information circulation techniques. In a knowledge economy, ICT is the base product of knowledge circulation. Simply producing, or using, ICT does not necessarily imply a mobilization, or development, of knowledge. Where technological progress is limited to a codification of information, employee knowledge is not necessarily expanded. This distinction sheds some light on the current debate about the respective roles being played by the production and utilization of ICT. Growth in the United States depended both on the organization of research (the genesis of innovation) and on some state subsidies (the development and dissemination of innovation). Amongst these latter factors, the funding of innovation plays an important role in helping to launch new companies. However, the extraordinary productivity gains of the ICT-producing sector, which to a large extent accounted for US growth, have not diffused significantly through other sectors of economic activity.

On the other side of the equation, the growth of certain European economies, particularly the northern countries, has emphasized the importance of mobilizing knowledge. In Scandinavia and Finland, workforces enjoy a particularly high level of qualification, professional training structures are well developed and new technologies are widely used. These differences betweeen forms of growth in the United States and in other countries indicate that the development of a knowledge economy is driven more by the utilization of ICT, twinned with a mobilization of whatever knowledge exists in the economy, than by its production. The emergence of a knowledge economy is compatible with a diversity of configurations and European institutions if a shared framework enables better coordination, and if a consensual social model can be defined. The various analyses that have been presented in this book pave the way for discussions concerning two projects that could be used to mobilize knowledge in Europe.

The first relates to the creation, diffusion and application of knowledge. This project touches on public research, private R&D and the funding of firms. The price paid for the absence of European coordination between public and private research is particularly high because, unlike the United States, Europe reproduces identical structures in different countries and has not harmonized its incentive systems. In the United States, the federal budget contributes to the development of information technologies, coordinating the major research organizations at a national, rather than a state, level. In Europe, harmonization efforts do not mean that research efforts must be uniform. Rather, they need to emphasize the diversity of talent available in European research teams.

The creation and application of new knowledge in the productive sphere raises questions about the funding mechanisms available to firms. This issue should be dealt with differentially, depending on the stage of development of firms. Comparisons between European funding systems reveal wide variations. In all countries, the greater interconnectedness of financial markets has modified the way in which companies treat their shareholders and contributed to a transformation of shareholder structures. Moreover, funding structures still vary between the Anglo-US bloc and the continental European one. The main difference is not the opposition between bank-based and market-based funding, but structures of ownership which tend to be concentrated in the case of continental European nations and dispersed in the case of Anglo-US ones. This contrast is mirrored in the types of activity in which companies engage. A concentrated structure encourages low-risk, long-term investments, whereas a dispersed one encourages more risky investments.

Empirical and theoretical analyses indicate that corporate funding requirements vary according to the level of development and type of activity undertaken by firms. Depending on the risk involved in investment projects and on the type of employment relationships that exist, companies might prefer bank funding, concentrated shareholdings or, conversely, a broad dispersion of investors. The goal of regulating European systems should be to maintain diverse means of access by companies to credit, with financial markets and banks acting as guarantors of this access. The principal constraints remain the protection of small savers and large investors, as well as the stability of the overall financial system.

The second project deals with the nature and organization of work, particularly with respect to the development and mobilization of employees' knowledge within firms. The diverse nature of workforces and the varied work they perform are accentuated by their technical, or competitive, qualities. Depending on the situation, there is a need to organize professional mobility, or to deepen employees' involvement in firms wherever, for example, long-term relationships between firms and wage earners are mutually advantageous. The divergences observed in Europe's varying economic dynamics arise between sectors of activity that operate within one and the same country. Institutions must therefore ensure the coexistence of a variety of different employment relationships so that employee involvement remains an advantage to European firms. Long-term relationship nurture the trust and cooperation that can help develop employees' levels of training and mobilize their knowledge. Such a form of work organization cannot be achieved within the short-term mind-set that dominates the way Anglo-US firms (and some European shareholders) reason. In the latter worldview, the firm would have to adjust its staffing levels continually by using hiring and firing policies that responded to labour needs by means of external mobility. The longer the time-frame involved in cooperative and trust-based relationships (meaning employee participation in a company's life), the greater the need for harmonization at a European level of people's representations in the consultation structures of firms. Such harmonization would be particularly hampered whenever national legislative systems were engaged in short-term competition.

Employee mobility is another cornerstone of the European model. On the one hand, increased competition, pressure from financial markets and the emergence of an increasingly differentiated demand often mean that traditional forms of labour contracts are obsolete. On the other hand, some employees would like to adapt their schedules and enjoy greater mobility. The heritage of the mass production era, which used to tie a firm to its employees for a potentially unlimited period of time, has therefore been undermined. It has occurred without employee mobility having had an impact as a political issue. New legal categories are cropping up, a sign that a new worker status is in the process of being born. This new status is less dependent on people having a job than on continuity of professional activities, regardless of the jobs being filled. Economic policy must define the conditions in which there can be an emergence – as well as an acceptance by interested parties – of a largely rejuvenated employment relationship. The first condition for this change is the development, at company and employee level, of institutions which restrict opportunistic behaviour. Such institutions could be born out of the creation of networks made up of companies or employees. These would guarantee both the circulation of information and mutual surveillance.

A dynamic organization of the transitions between successive work situations should be superimposed upon a static organization of the employment relationship. This firstly involves the transitions themselves: periods of time when wage-earner status is not tied to a stable job. The activation of professional mobility also implies a redefinition of systems of social insurance. European systems of social protection were designed to assume the risks that were related specifically to the era of mass production, particularly the loss of income whenever workers moved from one job (with an open-ended employment contract) to another. However, increased professional mobility and changes in qualifications have subjected these systems of social protection to new constraints, ones for which employees are ill-prepared. It is therefore necessary to envisage a reform of social protection that directly accounts for all situations of non-employment. Periods of voluntary training should receive support from a system that compensates, at least partially, for loss of income. Transitions between jobs with different statuses should also be facilitated without substantial loss of income. This homogeneous approach to a non-employment relationship could be applied to all transitions. It would encourage greater professional mobility and a continuous change in employees' qualifications. This is something which would benefit both firms and wage earners.

Analyses of US growth, of European configurations and of certain specific institutions offer paths that Europe would be well advised to consider when looking for forms of sustained growth and economic efficiency which take into account issues relating to employment (including working conditions). Faced with an increase in indentical structures, and given the way in which companies put different countries in competition with one another, a European growth model will have to be predicated less on the harmonization of identities and more on valuing institutional diversity.

NOTES

1. The concept of an 'economic institution' covers all the formal and informal organizations and legislations that govern the way in which markets function. Moreover, the market itself can be seen as an institution, whenever private transactions become part of a network of agreements and rules. This is how Robert Solow, for example, describes the labour market.
2. The non-accelerating inflation rate of unemployment.
3. To measure price changes, the quality of the output must be taken into account. The prices given here apply to goods whose quality has remained constant, for example a computer whose processing power remains the same. Such prices are called 'hedonic'. In reality, prices do not decrease for a constant level of quality. Rather it is the quality that increases, with prices remaining more or less constant. The impact on these hedonic prices is, however, basically the same.
4. This type of 'Boolean' analysis comes from the work of the logician George Boole. For each characteristic, countries are classified according to two categories. For example, we can

distinguish between those countries that have made major investments in information goods, and the rest. The approach then consists of combining these countries and specifying their common characteristics. This method leads to a qualitative analysis of the configurations that the various countries have in common. The choice of characteristics is a key element in this approach as it determines the analytical matrix by which the various countries are to be compared.

5. In Denmark and the Netherlands, it is often argued that gains in employment were related to labour market deregulation. Institutional causes are difficult to separate from economic policy in this case.

6. Turnover is the inverse of the average time that an employee spends with one firm. The quicker the rate of hiring and resignation or firing, the greater the turnover rate.

7. The concept of 'opportunistic behaviour' refers in economic parlance to the attitude of an actor who breaks a relationship of trust in order to pursue his/her own interests.

Index